The Revolutionary Era, 1789–1850

THIRD EDITION

D1114344

THE NORTON HISTORY OF MODERN EUROPE

General Editor: DAVID CLAY LARGE, Montana State University

The Foundations of Early Modern Europe, 1460–1559
    EUGENE F. RICE, JR.
The Age of Religious Wars, 1559–1689, *2d edition*
    RICHARD S. DUNN
Kings and Philosophers, 1689–1789
    LEONARD KRIEGER
Eighteenth-Century Europe: Tradition and Progress, *1715–1789*
    ISSER WOLOCH
The Revolutionary Era, 1789–1850, *3rd edition*
    CHARLES BREUNIG and MATTHEW LEVINGER
The Age of Nationalism and Reform, *1850–1890, 2d edition*
    NORMAN RICH
The End of the European Era, 1890 to the Present, *5th edition*
    FELIX GILBERT and DAVID CLAY LARGE

The Revolutionary Era, 1789–1850

THIRD EDITION

CHARLES BREUNIG AND MATTHEW LEVINGER

W. W. NORTON & COMPANY

NEW YORK • LONDON

PRINTED IN THE UNITED STATES OF AMERICA

The text of this book is composed in Electra
Composition by Binghamton Valley Composition
Manufacturing by RRDonnelley, Harrisonburg

Library of Congress Cataloging-in-Publication Data
Breunig, Charles, 1920–
    The revolutionary era, 1789–1850 / Charles Breunig and Matthew
Levinger. — 3rd ed.
        p. cm. — (The Norton history of modern Europe)
    Rev. ed. of: The age of revolution and reaction, 1789–1850. 2nd ed.
c1977.
    Includes bibliographical references and index.
    ISBN 0-393-97860-5 (pbk.)
    1. Europe — History — 1789–1815.   2. Europe — History 1815–
1848.   3. Industrial revolution — Europe.   I. Levinger, Matthew
Bernard, 1960–   II. Breunig, Charles, 1920–   Age of revolution and
reaction, 1789–1850.   III. Title.   IV. Series.

D308 .B796 2002
940.2'7 — dc21

                                                        2001044866

W. W. Norton & Company, Inc.,
500 Fifth Avenue, New York, N.Y. 10110
www.wwnorton.com

W. W. Norton & Company Ltd., Castle House,
75/76 Wells Street, London W1T 3QT

7 8 9 0

Contents

Maps

Preface

REVISING SUCH a classic text as Charles Breunig's *The Age of Revolution and Reaction, 1789–1850* has been both a pleasurable and a daunting task. A quarter of a century after the publication of the second edition, Breunig's treatment of European political and diplomatic history remains a model of incisive and balanced historical narrative. In this edition I have sought to preserve the strengths of Breunig's account while enriching it with insights drawn from recent scholarship, particularly in the fields of cultural and social history. In some chapters, such as those on the Napoleonic era and the revolutions of 1848, few revisions have been necessary. Other parts of the book, most notably those on the French Revolution and industrialization, have required more extensive work. Since the 1970s, research on the French Revolution has dramatically altered historians' understanding of this epochal event. In place of a class-based, Marxist interpretation depicting the revolution as the triumph of an ascendant bourgeoisie over a declining aristocracy, scholars have placed renewed emphasis on the cultural and political causes of this upheaval. Over the past few decades, a rich profusion of research has also illuminated the social and cultural dimensions of the Industrial Revolution in Europe. I have incorporated some key findings of this scholarship here.

Throughout the text, I have sought to supplement the history of political events with a view to the everyday experiences of private life, for example, by examining changes in family structure and women's social roles. I have also recalibrated the geographical balance of the narrative by expanding the sections on southern and eastern Europe, as well as by exploring the impact of European political transformations on other regions of the world such as Latin America.

The new title of the book, *The Revolutionary Era*, reflects my conviction that the revolutionary forces unleashed in Europe between 1789 and 1850 far exceeded those of the "reaction." In social terms, this epoch witnessed the emergence of a far more urbanized and mobile population than had existed before, as an industrialized economy supplanted a primarily agrarian one across much of the continent. In politics, the rise of democratic, individualistic, and egalitarian ideals challenged the preeminence of Europe's monarchs and its traditional landed elites. Increasingly, even the staunchest defenders of the old order were forced to fight a rearguard action on their opponents' ideological turf. By the mid-nineteenth century, even some of the most conservative Europeans embraced—or at least acknowledged the inevitable triumph of—such principles as individual liberty, free trade, and constitutional rule. The political and economic revolutions from the late eighteenth century onward caused profound dislocations for Europeans of all social classes. Their struggles to forge new identities, and new patterns of communal life, in face of these radical changes forms the drama of our story.

M. L.
Portland, Oregon
November 2001

Introduction

Two REVOLUTIONS profoundly transformed the lives of Europeans in the years from 1789 to 1850: the great French Revolution and the Industrial Revolution. Any attempt to comprehend the history of Europe during this period requires an analysis of the subtle and complex ways in which these revolutions worked themselves out in the material existence, the institutions, and the ideas of Europeans. Some individuals and groups tried to resist or contain the revolutions; others accepted their consequences and tried to exploit them; no European was unaffected by them.

The French Revolution has traditionally been viewed as a major dividing line in modern Europe's history, an event that destroyed that complex of political, social, legal, and juridical institutions known as the "old regime" and inaugurated a new era characterized by a greater emphasis on individual rights, the spread of representative government, and the emergence of a new kind of loyalty to the nation. These generalizations about the French Revolution still retain much of their validity as long as they are qualified in some significant ways.

The break with the past was not nearly so sharp as has often been contended. Some of the traditional institutions and conceptions associated with the old regime had already been challenged earlier in the eighteenth century. A series of lesser revolts and disturbances in Europe and its colonial possessions beginning about 1760 preceded and, in some respects, contributed to the major upheaval of 1789. After 1789, many traditional institutions and ideas persisted through the revolutionary and Napoleonic eras into the age of the Restoration, from 1815 to 1848. Indeed, in most parts of Europe the Restoration was dominated by rulers who reacted against the revolutionary doctrines and who, if they could not turn the clock back to the old regime, did their best to maintain the status quo against growing pressures for reform and change.

Not surprisingly, the French Revolution had its greatest initial impact on France itself, where the revolutionaries proceeded to sweep aside the complex set of administrative institutions inherited from the old regime and to substitute for them a new, more efficient organizational structure that would at the same time be more responsive to the needs of the entire nation. This structure, further refined or altered by Napoleon, has endured substantially to the present day. In class terms, the revolution also wrought significant changes in France; the ultimate beneficiaries were the bourgeoisie, who, having eliminated the traditional privileges of the aristocracy, made certain that political power remained in the hands of the possessors of property.

Outside of France the French Revolution and the Napoleonic regime that followed had results that were both creative and destructive. During almost a quarter century of intermittent conflict among the French armies and the powers that resisted them, Europeans suffered disruption of their lives and established institutions. Old states went out of existence; new ones came into being. Territories conquered and occupied by the French underwent significant changes. In the last analysis, however, the revolutionary ideals of the French may have had more profound and lasting effects on Europe than did their armies. In the powerful revolutionary slogan "Liberty! Equality! Fraternity!"; in the fundamental political rights enunciated in the Declaration of the Rights of Man; and in the successive constitutions drawn up by the revolutionary assemblies, nineteenth-century liberals found their political programs and their source of inspiration. Even more important, France had shown during the revolution what powerful forces could be released when a people is galvanized by loyalty to a national ideal. Many of the fundamental characteristics of modern nationalism emerged for the first time during the revolution, and France provided models that were widely imitated in the century that followed.

In the long run, the Industrial Revolution undoubtedly transformed the lives of Europeans even more thoroughly than did the French Revolution, but its principal impact in the first half of the nineteenth century was restricted to Great Britain and the states lying in the northwestern tier of the European continent. Central, southern, and eastern Europe underwent similar changes only in the second half of the century. In countries affected by industrialization, long-established patterns of life were shattered as production was mechanized and moved into factories. The need to situate factories near the sources of power led to massive shifts of population and to the phenomenal growth of towns and cities. Wherever industrialization occurred, it dramatically increased the size and strength of the older bour-

geoisie and brought into existence a new social class, the industrial proletariat. That these changes in class structure would have a significant effect
upon the political life of the European states was inevitable. One of the
main themes of the period from 1789 to 1850 was the struggle of the new
manufacturing interests for political power and influence commensurate
with their rising economic status.

The revolutions of 1848 provide a striking finale to the period. In the
series of uprisings that swept across Europe in that year can be discerned
the combined effects of the French revolutionary legacy and the Industrial
Revolution. The demands of the revolutionaries still tended most often to
be couched in the political terminology of the French Revolution — constitutions, representative assemblies, and the extension of political rights — but
the movements of 1848 brought into focus underlying social discontents and
grievances that stemmed from industrialization.

The Revolutionary Era, 1789–1850

THIRD EDITION

CHAPTER 1

The French Revolution

In 1858, Alexis de Tocqueville wrote to a friend, reflecting on the political turmoil in France over the previous seventy years:

> There is . . . in this disease of the French Revolution something very strange that I can sense, though I cannot describe it properly or analyse its causes. It is a *virus* of a new and unknown kind. There have been violent Revolutions in the world before; but the immoderate, violent, radical, desperate, bold, almost crazed and yet powerful and effective character of these Revolutionaries has no precedents, it seems to me, in the great social agitations of past centuries. Where did this new race come from? What produced it? What made it so effective? What perpetuates it? [F]or the same men are still with us, even though the circumstances are different now; and they have a progeny everywhere in the civilised world.[1]

In *Democracy in America* and other books, Tocqueville had displayed an ambivalent attitude toward the political revolutions of his age. Born in 1805, he was the descendant of a family of liberal aristocrats who had initially supported the French Revolution, but several of whom had ultimately been executed during the Terror of 1793–1794. Although admiring the emancipatory impulse behind modern democratic movements, he feared their potential to plunge nations into despotism or chaos.

Tocqueville's brooding words may strike the modern observer as unduly bleak. Nonetheless, his remarks point to a phenomenon that remains a source of surprise and wonder to historians: namely, the capacity of an upheaval in eighteenth-century France to transform the stakes of political struggle throughout much of the world ever since 1789. In examining the

---

[1] Quoted in François Furet, *Interpreting the French Revolution* (Cambridge, 1981), p. 163.

history of the French Revolution, it is important to focus on two interrelated problems. First, we must account for the local conditions in France that gave birth to this great struggle. Second, we need to explore the political and cultural features that enabled the revolution to exert such a powerful and enduring influence both within France and beyond.

CRISES OF THE OLD REGIME

The eighteenth century was a period of economic expansion in France. Between 1700 and 1789, the French population grew from about 20 million to about 27 million. During the eighty years before the outbreak of the Revolution, France's artisanal and industrial production quadrupled, and its colonial trade multiplied by a factor of ten. This increase in industry and commerce resulted in the substantial growth of France's urban middle classes. The working class populace grew as well, but most workers did not share in the country's new wealth. The pressures of population growth resulted in stagnant wages and high unemployment among urban workers even in times of prosperity. During economic crises, the unemployment rate in Paris soared as high as 50 percent.

Despite this gradual transformation of the French economy over the course of the eighteenth century, much remained unchanged. In 1789, French society was still overwhelmingly rural: over 80 percent of the population worked in agriculture and lived in villages of fewer than two thousand inhabitants. Most industrial production took place in small workshops and cottages, rather than in large factories. Goods were still produced mainly by hand—the first steam engine in France went into operation only in 1785. Finally, though subsistence crises were becoming rarer, France's workers and peasants remained vulnerable to the effects of poor harvests. Rapid growth in the rural population over the eighteenth century aggravated this situation, making it difficult for peasants to support their families on the available land even in good years. Disastrous weather conditions—such as those of the years 1787–1789—could still plunge the country into famine.

The crop failures of the late 1780s compounded a severe recession that had begun in the 1770s and that lasted for over a decade. Thus, the French Revolution erupted at a moment when many merchants and entrepreneurs had suffered temporary setbacks, and when the less fortunate were facing starvation. Yet this was far from the first such crisis in French history. These economic developments in eighteenth-century France cannot alone account for the magnitude of the political upheavals of 1789–1799.

To understand the origins of the revolutionary movement in France, it is essential to examine two interlocking crises that befell the monarchical government: first, a long-term crisis of the absolutist state that had been evolving since the seventeenth century; and second, a short-term fiscal crisis, dating from the mid-eighteenth century, that provided the immediate impetus for the Revolution. Together, these crises undermined the legitimacy of the French monarchy, making possible a far more radical assault on the traditional order than had previously been imaginable.

The Paradoxical Legacies of Absolute Monarchy

The French revolutionaries distinguished themselves from all previous political insurgents by the global nature of their claims. Earlier revolutionary leaders, such as those in England during the 1640s and in Britain's American colonies during the 1770s, had fought at least partly in the name of tradition. For example, the American revolutionaries' primary grievance at the beginning of their war for independence was that the British crown had violated their "rights as Englishmen"—above all, their right not to be taxed without consent. In France, by contrast, the more radical revolutionaries believed that their mission was to destroy the existing social and political order, and to build an entirely new world on the ashes of the old.

As Tocqueville astutely noted in his classic study *The Old Regime and the French Revolution*, however, this revolutionary vision of a new beginning was in large part an illusion.[2] In important respects, the French revolutionaries completed the work that had been initiated by the absolute monarchs of the seventeenth and eighteenth centuries. Beginning during the reigns of Louis XIII (ruled 1610–1643) and Louis XIV (ruled 1643–1715), France's kings had developed a highly centralized system of administration. Disregarding the traditional governing institutions of the French provinces, they had divided France into thirty fiscal jurisdictions known as *généralités*. Each of the *généralités* was administered by a royal official, usually of humble birth, called an intendant. The *généralités*, in turn, were divided into about seven hundred smaller districts governed by officials called subdelegates, who reported to the intendants. These royal officials wielded extensive administrative and judicial powers, including the supervision of tax collection and military conscription, as well as the establishment of public works projects, police forces, and poor relief. Such was the authority of these officials that an early eighteenth-century Scottish observer remarked, "Believe it or not, the French kingdom is ruled by thirty Intendants."

By establishing an elaborate system of bureaucratic rule, France's absolute

[2] Alexis de Tocqueville, *The Old Régime and the Revolution*, edited by François Furet and Françoise Mélonio, translated by Alan Kahan, vol. 1 (Chicago, 1998), pp. 83–89, 111–24, 241–47.

monarchs undermined the long-standing governing authority of the nobility and other social elites. Until the seventeenth century, taxes had traditionally been apportioned by provincial assemblies known as the Estates. By the time of the revolution, however, the Estates had been abolished in all but a few provinces at the periphery of the realm. France's central representative assembly, the Estates General, did not convene even once between 1614 and 1789. Other traditional ruling institutions continued to exist until the end of the Old Regime, but their powers were increasingly circumscribed by royal decrees. Among these bodies were the *parlements*, the thirteen high courts of appeal, which would play an important role in sparking the initial revolutionary events.

France's Bourbon kings employed other strategies as well in seeking to undermine the political authority of the aristocracy. Louis XIV encouraged his leading nobles to live at Versailles. This stratagem allowed the king to keep a close eye on the activities of his guests, employing his powers of patronage to foil any alliances that might threaten his own supremacy. Living near the king's palace also weakened the aristocrats' ties to the land and diminished their role in governing their own communities. Likewise, over the course of the eighteenth century, the French monarchy engaged more frequently in selling titles of nobility. Between 1774 and 1789 alone, 3,389 people in France purchased offices that conferred noble status. The government adopted this practice as a means of raising money to pay the ever-expanding state debt. The sale of offices, however, had subversive effects. It created a growing privileged class whose members enjoyed substantial tax exemptions and special legal rights, but who performed no useful function in public life.

Louis XIV and his successors, in other words, enhanced French nobles' privileges while simultaneously abolishing many of their traditional political rights. The techniques of absolute monarchy thus had paradoxical effects: they created an aristocracy that was ever more splendid, yet ever less useful. The discrepancy between aristocrats' increasing social status and their diminishing public role ultimately made the French nobility—and the monarchy itself—a target for the resentments of revolutionary leaders.

A second crisis of French absolutism was cultural, as well as political, in nature. The historian R. R. Palmer has argued that the late eighteenth century must be understood as "the age of the democratic revolution" both in France and beyond. In addition to the American and French revolts, Palmer cites municipal strife in the city-state of Geneva in the 1760s and 1780s, riots in Ireland and England in 1780, and a revolutionary upheaval in the Netherlands as evidence of a general political and cultural ferment working in the period prior to 1789. By the term *democratic* he does not mean to imply that the goal of the revolutionaries was universal suffrage or some of the other features associated with twentieth-century democracy. Indeed, the alternative forms of government they favored varied greatly from country to country. All of these revolutionaries, however, challenged the continued control of government by "established, privileged, closed or self-recruiting groups." Their movements reflected a "new feeling for a kind of equality, or at least a discomfort with older forms of social stratification and formal rank."[3]

In France, the diffusion of egalitarian ideals was evident both in the realm of literature and in public life. Intellectuals of the Enlightenment, such as Voltaire, Jean-Jacques Rousseau, Denis Diderot, and the marquis de Condorcet, harshly denounced the spread of "luxury" and the social pretensions of the privileged elites. Instead, these *philosophes* emphasized the importance of "useful knowledge" that would serve to improve society as a whole. They justified their right to speak by appealing to the principle of reason, not by invoking the support of influential patrons. They argued that everyone, regardless of social status, had a right to participate in the court of "public opinion."

Jean-Jacques Rousseau (1712–1778), a watchmaker's son from Geneva, unleashed particularly vitriolic critiques of the existing social order. In his *Discourse on the Origin of Inequality* (1755), he argued that all human society was corrupt because it encouraged people to seek distinction by achieving superiority over their peers. In the most "advanced" societies, such as France of his day, he argued that the degradation of human nature through vanity and selfishness had reached an extreme. His *Social Contract* (1762) built on the logic of this earlier inquiry. Rousseau proclaimed, "Man is born free and everywhere is in chains" — words that would later be echoed by revolutionaries ranging from Thomas Paine to Karl Marx. Only a political system based on direct democracy, he argued, could avert the universal tendency toward exploitation and oppression, by encouraging citizens to devote themselves selflessly toward the common good. Though it is difficult to assess the degree of Rousseau's influence over French political thought before 1789, his logic was mirrored by key revolutionary documents such as the Declaration of the Rights of Man, as well as in the writings and speeches of leaders from Emmanuel-Joseph Sieyès to Maximilien Robespierre.

Not only did writers express increasingly egalitarian themes, but the overall prominence of literature also increased at the end of the Old Regime. The number of writers in France more than doubled between 1757 and 1784. (The Revolution itself would produce a veritable explosion of literary

---

[3] R. R. Palmer, *The Age of the Democratic Revolution: A Political History of Europe and America, 1760–1800,* vol. 1 (Princeton, 1959), p. 4.

life: Paris had four newspapers in 1788, and 184 by the end of the following year.) In practice, however, the world of literature remained sharply hierarchical during the late eighteenth century. Although a small elite of authors enjoyed fame and adoration in the Parisian salons, the majority lived a desperate hand-to-mouth existence. These struggling writers composed ruthless and crude attacks on the privileged classes, for example, pornographic satires involving Queen Marie Antoinette.

The spirit of the Enlightenment prevailed even within the government itself. Louis XVI has often been criticized as an indecisive monarch whose failures of leadership contributed to the radicalization of the revolution. Though this critique is well founded, it is important to note that the king's indecision reflected not only a personal character defect but also a wide-

The coronation of Louis XVI, 1775. The illustration emphasizes the divine right of kings: Louis receives his crown from a saint holding a cross, and cherubs stand in the background.

spread feature of French culture at the end of the Old Regime. On his ascension to the throne in 1774, Louis appointed as his first minister Anne-Robert-Jacques Turgot, an adherent of Enlightenment economic doctrines. During his brief and unsuccessful term in office, Turgot infuriated both the nobility and traditional elements of the urban bourgeoisie by arguing for the abolition of aristocratic tax exemptions and the establishment of a free-market economy. Turgot enlisted the king's support for this program, albeit only temporarily, through the curious argument that the establishment of a more egalitarian social order would reinvigorate the authority of the French monarchy, whose legitimacy had long been grounded in the principle of divinely ordained hierarchy.

During the American Revolution, not only did France lend financial and military support to the insurgency, but some nine thousand French men also went off to the colonies to fight against the British. Following their return home, a number of them became early leaders of the revolution in France. "How goes it with our darling republicans?" Marie Antoinette once asked the marquis de Lafayette. Beyond the royal family, many members of the French elite expressed similarly conflicting attitudes toward the traditional corporate social order. In both the royally chartered provincial academies and in associations such as the Freemasons, egalitarian rhetoric coexisted with the practical desire to preserve the preeminence of privileged members. Similarly, some of the largely aristocratic French *parlements*, from the 1760s onward, published broadsides against the monarchy, demanding recognition for the political rights of the "nation." Their rhetoric, which anticipated that of the revolution, was aimed at defending their own traditional political prerogatives. As events would soon reveal, all of those who sought to manipulate new egalitarian ideas in defense of old hierarchies were playing with fire.

Fiscal Crisis and Political Collapse

What brought matters to a head in the 1780s was an acute fiscal crisis stemming from lavish spending at court and the granting of widespread tax exemptions, but above all from a series of costly military engagements. The War of Austrian Succession (1740–1748), the Seven Years' War (1756–1763), and the American Revolution (1775–1781) all placed severe burdens on the French monarchy, which had been saddled with debt ever since the reign of Louis XIV. The government sought to resolve this crisis by raising taxes, which fell most heavily on the peasantry. These included direct taxes such as the *taille* (head tax) and indirect taxes such as the *gabelle*, the government monopoly on salt that kept the price of this product artificially high in much of France.

By custom, the monarchy needed to secure the approval for any new taxes from the *parlements*, which had to register the decrees in their ledgers and communicate them to the lower courts. By issuing a series of new tax edicts from the 1750s onward, the government thus thrust the magistrates of these courts into the center of French political life. Though some of the *parlements* were relatively compliant, others seized on this opportunity to demand a greater share of sovereign authority. By 1771, Louis XV had become so frustrated with the magistrates' obstructionism that he allowed his minister René de Maupeou to abolish the *parlements* altogether. This action, however, inspired such a hue and cry about the despotic tendencies of the French monarchy that Louis XVI reestablished the *parlements* on his ascension to the throne in 1774. The new king's gesture of good will permitted the magistrates to continue to rehearse their antimonarchical rhetoric while blocking royal efforts to reduce the budget deficit.

Louis XVI's other efforts at political reform also misfired. Turgot's plans to establish a free-market economy and a more equitable system of taxation foundered against the intense opposition of the aristocracy and the guilds. Aggravating matters, an economic crisis struck France in the late 1770s and worsened over the course of the following decade. This crisis, which stemmed in part from previous industrial overexpansion, was intensified by the free-trade treaty of 1786 with Britain, which hurt French manufacturing. The economic downturn meant a decline in tax revenues, so that on the eve of the revolution, over half of France's state revenues were directed toward servicing the debt.

Up until the eighteenth century, France's monarchs had employed a simple, time-honored solution to such fiscal difficulties: namely, to declare the state bankrupt and to abolish the debt altogether. The changing cultural climate of the prerevolutionary era, however, made this solution inconceivable. Louis XVI depended on the continued good will of French financiers who provided loans to the government. Equally important, state finances were no longer a matter to be discussed privately among the government and a few lenders; instead, they were now subjected to the full glare of public scrutiny. This was especially the case after 1781, when the outgoing controller general Jacques Necker published his *Compte rendu*, a report that revealed the government's serious budgetary difficulties. Over the next seven years, Necker's successors, Charles-Alexandre Calonne and Loménie de Brienne, attempted to resolve the crisis he had identified. Their strategies included sleight-of-hand with the budgetary accounts, aimed at minimizing the extent of the difficulties, as well as efforts to gain support for new tax-reform measures.

In 1786, Calonne persuaded the king to convene an Assembly of Notables, consisting of high nobles along with some prominent bourgeois financiers. Calonne asked the assembly's approval for far-reaching fiscal reforms, including the abolition of aristocratic tax exemptions. Despite the fact that the king himself had chosen the assembly's members, they refused outright to approve Calonne's plan, declaring that only the Estates General possessed the authority to enact such measures. Brienne, who took office in 1787 after Calonne's debacle with the Notables, took a variety of conflicting approaches to the fiscal crisis. First, he sought to strong-arm his opponents by exiling the Parlement of Paris to Troyes; then, a few months later, he brought them home and attempted a more conciliatory approach. When this tactic too failed to exact any significant concessions from the magistrates, Brienne finally lost patience. In May 1788, a royal edict stripped the *parlements* of their right to register laws, investing this power in a new Plenary Court created by the crown.

The public outcry that followed Brienne's action against the *parlements* signaled the culmination of what some scholars have termed the "French prerevolution." From May 1788 onward, the government effectively lost its capacity to guide events in France. In July of that year, Louis XVI gave in to the opposition by agreeing to convene the Estates General. The following month, he dismissed Brienne and recalled Necker as controller general. Unfortunately for the crown, the political turmoil coincided with an economic crisis that was exacerbating tensions both in the countryside and in the towns. Two successive bad harvests, in 1787 and 1788, were driving food prices to extreme levels, and 50 percent of the Parisian working class confronted unemployment. This widespread suffering inflamed the tensions that would explode with unprecedented force the following year.

REVOLUTIONARY POLITICS

"The Revolution is like Saturn—it eats its own children," declared the playwright Georg Büchner in *Danton's Death*. One of the most remarkable attributes of the upheaval that began in 1789 was the prolonged political instability it provoked not only in France but throughout Europe. Between 1789 and 1794 a series of increasingly radical regimes governed France. The initial revolutionary leaders during the period 1789–1792, who included progressive aristocrats and clerics as well as bourgeois activists, aimed to reconcile the nation and the king under a constitutional monarchy. The National Assembly, established in June 1789, resigned after issuing the Constitution of 1791; it was replaced by a Legislative Assembly elected under the provisions of the constitution. By autumn 1792, a republic had been proclaimed and King Louis XVI was on trial for treason. The moderate republicans known as the Girondins sought to spare the king's life, but the more radical Jacobins insisted on executing him as an enemy of the nation. The Legislative Assembly gave way to a newly elected National Convention, which officially ruled France until 1795 and produced a new instrument of government, the Constitution of 1793, which was never put into effect. During the Terror of 1793–1794, many Girondin and even Jacobin leaders perished under the blade of the guillotine, condemned for insufficient revolutionary ardor by Maximilien Robespierre and his compatriots on the Committee of Public Safety. The overthrow of Robespierre in July 1794 returned France to several years of relative stability. The Directory, established by the Constitution of 1795, assigned the executive power to five "directors" and the legislative power to a bicameral assembly. This regime, however, proved unable to defend itself against Napoleon Bonaparte's coup of 1799, which resulted in sixteen years of intensified warfare and the transmission of revolutionary ideas across the European continent.

The Revolution of the Rights of Man, 1789

The announcement of July 1788 that the king would convene the Estates General the following May ignited a firestorm of controversy. The Parlement of Paris, seeking to prevent the monarchy from manipulating the assembly in its own favor, demanded that the Estates be organized "according to the forms observed in 1614," when it had last met. Over the next few months, a torrent of political pamphlets denounced the magistrates of the *parlement* as self-serving aristocrats seeking to guard their privileges. In 1614, each of the three orders had voted in common, thus allowing the clergy (the First Estate) and the nobility (the Second Estate) two votes and the Third Estate (commoners) only one. A group of activists known as the Patriots demanded double representation for the Third Estate, so that the commoners would elect as many representatives as the other two orders combined; and for voting by head rather than by order, so that each individual vote would be counted. In this way they felt they could secure a majority for their reforms, since they could count on some defections from the clergy and on the support of a few liberal noblemen. At the end of 1788 the king accepted the first part of this plan, announcing that the Third Estate could have twice as many representatives as each of the other two estates, but he refused to determine in advance whether the voting would be by order or by head. In effect, the king's half-resolution of this problem virtually guaranteed that an explosive controversy would erupt over voting procedures when the Estates General assembled at Versailles on May 4, 1789.

Delegates to the Estates General had been named by voters who met in the chief town of each district. Members of the clergy and nobility had voted directly for their representatives, but voters from the Third Estate — that is, almost all male citizens over twenty-five — had named their delegates through an indirect system that had the effect of eliminating as candidates all but an educated elite drawn from the middle and upper bourgeoisie. Most representatives of the Third Estate were lawyers or career bureaucrats rather than peasants or wage earners. Indeed, some of the most prominent representatives of the Third Estate were maverick aristocrats or clergymen who could not have been named by their own orders. One such was Honoré Gabriel Riqueti, count of Mirabeau (1749–1791), who became one of the most prominent statesmen during the first phase of the revolution. Born of an aristocratic family in Provence, Mirabeau as a young man estranged himself from his family by his excesses, which more than once caused him to be thrown into prison. By 1789 he had achieved a reputation as a violent opponent of the privileges of his own order and was elected a representative of the Third Estate by the voters of Aix-en-Provence.

Emmanuel-Joseph Sieyès (1748–1836) was another important representative of the Third Estate drawn from a different order. During the decades before the revolution, Sieyès had hoped to rise to prominence through the ranks of the church, but his career had stagnated. In January 1789, Abbé Sieyès won national renown through the publication of a pamphlet entitled *What is the Third Estate?* Sieyès began his stinging attack on the privileges of the nobility and clergy with three questions:

1. What is the Third Estate? *Everything.*
2. What has it been until now in the political order? *Nothing.*
3. What does it want to be? *Something.*

Ostensibly, Sieyès's pamphlet was a plea for the doubling of the Third Estate and for voting by head in the Estates General, but his logic had far more radical implications. Defining the nation as a body of "useful and industrious citizens," Sieyès denounced the nobility as a parasitic "foreigner in our midst" and argued that the Third Estate alone possessed the right to form a "National Assembly." Named a delegate of the Third Estate by the electors of Paris, Sieyès played an important role in the initial stages of the revolution, participating in the drafting of the Declaration of the Rights of Man and the Constitution of 1791. Abbé Sieyès demonstrated remarkable powers of survival during the revolutionary and Napoleonic eras. Serving in successive revolutionary assemblies, he voted for the execution of the king, lived through the Reign of Terror, reemerged as an important figure in the reaction that followed, and later helped engineer the coup d'état that brought Napoleon to power in 1799.

On the momentous occasion of the assembling of the Estates General, the optimism of the commoners was tempered by the treatment they received from the king. The somber black costumes that the king required the representatives of the Third Estate to wear contrasted sharply with the rich and colorful attire of the nobility and the clergy. At a formal reception given for the delegates on May 2, Louis XVl kept the commoners waiting for hours and then received them coldly while representatives of the other two Estates looked on.

At this point, the king had still announced no decision on the crucial problem of how votes would be counted, although a speech delivered by Necker, the king's finance minister, had intimated strongly that on certain questions the vote would be by order. In protest, the representatives of the Third Estate refused to present their credentials for verification; the resulting deadlock between the king and the Third Estate lasted for five weeks and was broken only when the commoners announced that they were presenting their credentials not as delegates of the Third Estate, but as representatives of the nation. After a number of parish priests who were delegates for the clergy had joined them, the commoners issued a statement proclaiming themselves the "National Assembly" of France, representing the entire nation. This declaration, dated June 17, has been termed the first genuinely revolutionary act of 1789; it was followed three days later by the more famous

The Tennis Court Oath, by C. Monnet and I. S. Helman. Members of the Third Estate raise their arms to take the oath, June 20, 1789, as the muses of liberty ride in on clouds above.

Tennis Court Oath. On June 20, the commoners found their regular meeting place barred to them, ostensibly for repairs. They adjourned therefore to a nearby indoor tennis court and, amid great enthusiasm, swore "not to separate, and to reassemble wherever circumstances require, until the constitution of the kingdom is established and consolidated upon firm foundations." Faced with this open act of defiance, the king wavered. At first he announced his intention of maintaining the distinction among the three orders, and declared the actions of the Third Estate on June 17 and June 20 invalid. But the continued resistance of the commoners, coupled with the desertion from their own assemblies of more representatives of the clergy and a minority of the nobles, forced him to recognize a fait accompli. On June 27 he ordered the remaining delegates of the first two Estates to take their places in the National Assembly alongside the representatives of the Third Estate. The National Assembly set about its self-appointed task of giving France a new constitution.

Within two weeks, however, the deliberations of the Assembly were interrupted by popular demonstrations in Paris that gave events a more violent turn and also provided the French people with that great symbolic act which has been associated with the revolution ever since—the storming of the Bastille. The origins of these riots are obscure; apparently they were in part a reaction to what appeared to be an alarming concentration of royal troops around Paris and Versailles. The dismissal by the king on July 11 of his chief minister, Necker, who had a popular reputation as an advocate of reform and conciliation, and the appointment of several ministers of a more conservative outlook, seemed to give substance to the rumor that the king was planning a military coup d'état against the National Assembly.

Among those whipping up the enthusiasm of the crowd was Camille Desmoulins (1760–1794), a radical journalist whose pamphlets and speeches were at least partially responsible for the violence that subsequently occurred. The electors of Paris (who had earlier named delegates to the Estates General and now reconstituted themselves as an active group) were alarmed, on the one hand, by the threat of a royal attack and disturbed, on the other, by the mounting unrest of the Paris crowd; they therefore improvised a provisional municipal government and organized a militia of bourgeois volunteers, later christened the National Guard.

On July 14 a search for arms and gunpowder led these bourgeois volunteers to the Bastille, an old feudal fortress on the eastern side of Paris that had served as a prison for many years. The Bastille was a symbol of royal despotism; stories were rife about the alleged mistreatment and torture of political prisoners supposed to be confined in its deep dungeons. The approaching crowd managed to lower a drawbridge to the outer courtyard,

The storming of the Bastille, July 14, 1789. The governor of the prison, De Launay, was seized by the insurgents and was later beheaded.

provoking the prison's governor, Bernard de Launay, to give orders to fire on the crowd. When the volley was over, some ninety-eight of the besiegers lay dead and seventy-three had been wounded. Now joined by two detachments of French guards, the crowd began to fight its way into the inner courtyard and to train five cannon against the main gate. De Launay decided to surrender and ordered the main drawbridge lowered. The crowd swarmed into the prison and slaughtered six or seven of the 110 guards defending it. De Launay himself was decapitated. Ironically, the Bastille yielded only seven prisoners—five ordinary criminals and two madmen.

The fall of the Bastille, insignificant in terms of its immediate results, was an event of great symbolic importance; it marked a deepening of the revolution. Disregarding the advice of those urging him to flee the country, the king decided to attempt a reconciliation. Only a day or two after the fall of the Bastille, Louis XVI announced that the royal troops would leave Versailles and that Necker would return to his post in the ministry. He also recognized the new municipal government of Paris and the newly established citizens' militia, the National Guard. In a final gesture, he agreed during a visit to Paris to wear the tricolor cockade, which placed the white of the Bourbons between the blue and red of the city of Paris. The Paris crowd had intervened successfully, as it would on many subsequent occasions during the revolution.

Paris was not the only site of popular disturbances in the summer of 1789. At about the same time that the Bastille fell, new municipal governments were established in a number of other major cities, a development that suggests some degree of coordination in the activities of the revolutionaries. More alarming to the large landowners was the series of disturbances in the country districts, beginning before July 14 and mounting steadily through the summer. These riots, which came to be known as the Great Fear, arose in part from rumors that the feudal aristocracy, the *aristos*, as they were called by the peasantry, were sending hired brigands to attack peasants and pillage their land. There is no evidence of any large-scale brigandage or of a counterrevolutionary plot, and the origin of these rumors is uncertain. But they did create a near panic — particularly in the eastern and some of the western provinces — that ultimately resulted in violence against local lords and their stewards and in the burning of châteaux and of records of feudal obligations. Local police were helpless to stop this anarchy; the king did not dare employ regular troops for fear they might join the rebels.

As the rural violence increased, alarm spread in the National Assembly, not only among the noble deputies but also among those members of the Third Estate whose income included feudal rents from their lands. A committee appointed by the Assembly to consider the situation recommended measures of repression, but a different solution was found during the famous session of the night of August 4: first the viscount of Noailles and then the duke of Aiguillon, another liberal noble, voluntarily abandoned their feudal privileges and revenues. Then, one by one, other deputies followed suit, renouncing privileges and rights of various sorts. The clergy relinquished their tithes, the wealthy bourgeois their individual exemptions from taxation, the cities and provinces their ancient customs and privileges. Before that dramatic night was over the feudal regime in France had been abolished and all Frenchmen were, at least in principle, subject to the same laws and the same taxes and eligible for the same offices. The formal decrees that enacted these decisions, issued a week later, retreated somewhat from the ecstatic pledges of August 4. Feudal dues were not renounced outright; rather, the peasants were to compensate their landlords through a series of direct payments for the obligations from which they had supposedly been freed.

Members of the National Assembly (which was renamed the "National

Constituent Assembly" on July 7) viewed as one of their principal tasks the drafting of a constitution that would substitute a new, rational set of political institutions for the antiquated forms of the Old Regime. Before settling down to work out the details of political organization, the Assembly, following the precedent of both English and American revolutionaries, issued the Declaration of the Rights of Man and of the Citizen, a statement of the general principles on which the new order was to rest. This historic document, approved on August 27, 1789, in a sense links the eighteenth and nineteenth centuries: it is a remarkable distillation of those political ideals of the eighteenth-century Enlightenment that became, during the first half of the nineteenth century, the gospel of European liberals.

Central to the declaration, as its title suggests, is the concept that there exist certain "natural rights" that should be enjoyed equally by all citizens. The aim of every political association, the declaration maintains, must be to preserve the natural and inalienable rights of man — "liberty, property, security, and resistance to oppression." Five of its seventeen articles deal specifically with these rights, an enumeration that recalls the Bill of Rights of the American Constitution and the seventeenth-century English documents that inspired it: included are freedom from arbitrary arrest, trial by established laws, the presumption that one is innocent until proven guilty, freedom of speech and of the press, and so on. In Article 6, the declaration explicitly emphasizes the equality of all men before the law.

Popular sovereignty is the second general principle asserted in the document; or, as Article 2 puts it, "The source of all sovereignty resides essentially in the nation; no group, no individual, may exercise authority not emanating expressly therefrom." Precisely how this power was to be exercised is not specified in detail, although Article 7 contains a statement concerning the law-making powers that is strongly reminiscent of the political philosophy of Rousseau: "Law is the expression of the general will; all citizens have the right to concur personally, or through their representatives, in its formation. . . ." The declaration implies the general right to vote, or universal suffrage, but we shall see that the constitution drawn up by the Constituent Assembly interpreted the term "citizen" rather narrowly and made the right to vote dependent on property ownership.

Constitutional Monarchy, 1789–1792

In the summer of 1789, the Constituent Assembly set for itself a delicate and improbable task: to frame a constitution that would reconcile the principles of democratic and monarchical sovereignty, allowing France to be governed through harmonious cooperation between the people and their king. One moderate faction within the Assembly, led by Jean-Joseph

Mounier (1758–1806), a judge from Dauphiné in southeast France, hoped to achieve this goal by establishing a system of constitutional checks and balances. Influenced by the model of the British constitution and by the political theory of Montesquieu, whose treatise *The Spirit of the Laws* (1748) had advocated a constitution based on the balance of powers, Mounier called for the establishment of a bicameral legislative assembly and for granting the king an absolute veto over legislative proposals. This moderate group, however, quickly lost out to a more radical faction inspired by the logic of Rousseau. Figures such as Sieyès and the marquis de Lafayette (1757–1834) argued that, for the nation to express its will with a unified voice, the legislative assembly must consist of a single

FRANCE: THE GOVERNMENTS
BEFORE 1789

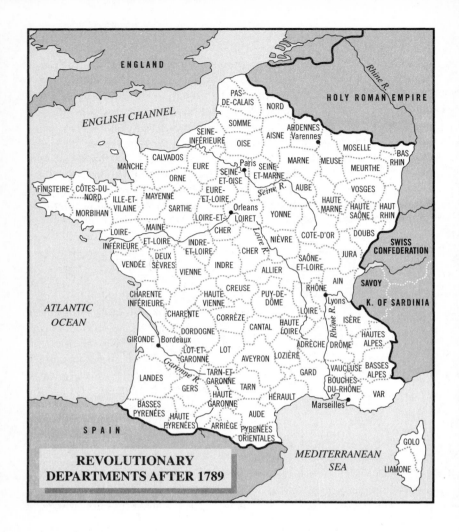

ENGLAND

ENGLISH CHANNEL

HOLY ROMAN EMPIRE

Rhine R.

PAS-DE-CALAIS

NORD

SOMME

AISNE

ARDENNES
Varennes

MOSELLE

BAS-RHIN

SEINE-INFÉRIEURE

OISE

MARNE

MEUSE

MEURTHE

CALVADOS

EURE

Paris

SEINE

SEINE-ET-MARNE

VOSGES

MANCHE

ORNE

SEINE-ET-OISE

AUBE

HAUTE-MARNE

HAUT-RHIN

FINISTEIRE

CÔTES-DU-NORD

MAYENNE

EURE-ET-LOIRE

Seine R.

Orleans

YONNE

HAUTE-SAÔNE

ILLE-ET-VILAINE

SARTHE

LOIRE-ET-LOIRET

CHER

CÔTE-D'OR

DOUBS

MORBIHAN

MAINE

LOIRE-ET-LOIRE

INDRE-ET-LOIRE

NIÈVRE

JURA

SWISS CONFEDERATION

INFÉRIEURE

DEUX-SÈVRES

CHER

Loire R.

SAÔNE-ET-LOIRE

VENDÉE

VIENNE

INDRE

ALLIER

AIN

SAVOY

CHARENTE-INFÉRIEURE

HAUTE-VIENNE

CREUSE

PUY-DE-DÔME

RHÔNE

Lyons

K. OF SARDINIA

CHARENTE

CORRÈZE

LOIRE

ISÈRE

ATLANTIC OCEAN

DORDOGNE

CANTAL

HAUTE-LOIRE

Rhône R.

HAUTES-ALPES

GIRONDE

Bordeaux

LOT-ET-GARONNE

LOT

AVEYRON

ADRÈCHE

DRÔME

LOZIÈRE

VAUCLUSE

BASSES-ALPES

LANDES

TARN-ET-GARONNE

GARD

BOUCHES-DU-RHÔNE

VAR

GERS

HAUTE-GARONNE

TARN

HÉRAULT

Marseilles

BASSES-PYRÉNÉES

HAUTE-PYRÉNÉES

ARRIÈGE

AUDE

PYRÉNÉES-ORIENTALES

GOLO

SPAIN

MEDITERRANEAN SEA

LIAMONE

**REVOLUTIONARY
DEPARTMENTS AFTER 1789**

chamber possessing the exclusive right to initiate and enact legislation, fix tax assessments, and control public expenditures, as well as the powers to declare war, ratify treaties, and supervise diplomacy. Moreover, they demanded that the king be granted only a suspensive veto over legislation, which could be overridden by the approval in three successive assemblies of the proposal in question.

The Constituent Assembly stopped well short of establishing a system of direct democracy. Though the Declaration of the Rights of Man had proclaimed that "men are born and remain free and equal in rights," the Constitution of 1791 denied this principle by dividing the population into "active" and "passive" citizens, a distinction based on the amount of direct taxes each citizen paid. Only "active" citizens — those who paid direct taxes equal in value to at least three days of labor in their particular region — had the right to vote. This arrangement denied the franchise to about a third of the adult males in France. Women and domestic servants were also excluded from "active" citizenship. To those who had taken the promises of the Assembly literally, this provision of the constitution came as a bitter disappointment. The method of election to the Assembly further emphasized the importance of property. Citizens were denied the privilege of voting directly for their representatives. Instead they met in primary assemblies to choose "electors," for whom the property qualification was considerably higher than for the voters, and these in turn named the deputies to the Assembly. The logic for limiting the franchise was twofold: first, the framers of the constitution feared the prospect of mob rule; and second, since they defined the nation as a body of "productive citizens," they held that the wealthier (and thus more "productive") citizens were entitled to a privileged political role.

Mirabeau, a dominant figure in the Constituent Assembly, proclaimed that the new constitution would unite the king and the nation in common cause against the vestiges of the Old Regime. Yet this vision of a popular monarchy proved short lived. As François Furet notes in a brilliant study of the revolution, French politics between 1789 and 1794 underwent a "rapid drift from a compromise with the principle of representation toward the unconditional triumph of rule by opinion." Like the French absolute monarchs before them, the revolutionaries held that there could be only one true expression of sovereign authority:

Legitimacy (and victory) therefore belonged to those who symbolically embodied the people's will and were able to monopolise the appeal to it. . . . Politics was a matter of establishing just *who* represented the people, or equality, or the nation: victory was in the hands of those who were capable of occupying and keeping that symbolic position.[4]

An additional factor that intensified the volatility of the revolution was the extreme degree of centralization in French politics, itself a legacy of the Old Regime. To a great extent, controlling the capital meant controlling France — which allowed the people of Paris to play a decisive role in influencing the course of the revolution at various stages. We have already noted the impact on the king of the attack on the Bastille by a Paris crowd. Popular activism again played a critical role in October 1789, when mounting unem-

[4] Furet, *Interpreting the French Revolution* (Cambridge, 1981), pp. 48, 49.

Departure of the Heroines of Paris for Versailles, October 5, 1789. The revolutionary women assembled a variety of weapons for their march on Versailles.

ployment combined with a shortage of bread had created renewed unrest among Parisians. Alarmed by the threat, the king summoned troops to Versailles, contending that he must protect the National Assembly from the Paris mob. But his action gave rise once more to rumors that he intended to use the troops against the Assembly and the revolutionary cause. In these circumstances a more or less spontaneous demonstration of Parisian women for bread on October 5 was transformed by popular agitators into a "march on Versailles." Along the twelve-mile route the women were joined by adventurers and curiosity seekers.

The climax of the October Days came early the following morning, when some of the angry crowd invaded the palace and were fired on by troops. Entering the inner rooms, they forced the queen, Marie Antoinette, to flee for her life to the king's apartments. Only by appearing on a balcony with his family was the king able to appease the crowd. Even so, he was forced to agree to leave Versailles, where he was thought to be surrounded by evil advisers, and move to Paris. Accordingly, the royal family departed the same day, in a carriage escorted by the cheering mob. The king took up residence in the Tuileries palace, in the heart of Paris, and the National Assembly followed him to the new seat of government. In effect, this move made the royal family a hostage to the people of Paris, further increasing the power of the revolutionary crowds. After the violence of the summer and fall of 1789, a calmer period ensued: for nearly three years, no serious disturbances erupted in Paris.

The National Assembly took advantage of the interlude of relative tranquility during 1790–1791 to initiate some of the most significant measures of the revolutionary era, among them the new administrative system and the confiscation of church lands and promulgation of the Civil Constitution of the Clergy. The Assembly thoroughly overhauled France's administrative system, and this revision reveals most clearly the impulse of the revolutionaries toward the kind of rationalization and systematization advocated by the philosophes. In place of the overlapping and confusing divisions, districts, and bureaus of the Old Regime, the revolutionary deputies established a new uniform administrative organization. France was divided into eighty-three *départements*, or departments; each department into *arrondissements*, or districts; each district into cantons; and each canton into communes. Each department was kept small enough so that its citizens could reach the *chef-lieu*, or capital, in no more than a day's journey by horse-drawn vehicle. Time-honored provinces such as Normandy, Brittany, and Champagne were deprived of official status. The new departments were named after rivers, mountains, and other natural features of their respective regions. Such a measure was bound to offend many Frenchmen whose attachment to their particular regions was strong, but the revolutionaries hoped precisely to eliminate differences among their countrymen, to create unity of feeling and loyalty to the new regime.

At the same time, a substantial decentralization of government was introduced. Local and regional officials were elected (again, only "active" citizens had the right to vote); at each level of government, an elected council served as both the deliberative body and the permanent executive bureau. Lacking training and experience, these officials had difficulty in carrying out all the tasks with which the royal bureaucracy had formerly been charged. The result was considerable confusion and inefficiency, particularly at the local level. Subsequently, Napoleon replaced the elected officials of the revolutionary era with a corps of appointed functionaries, carefully supervised from the capital by the minister of the interior; however, the departments and districts established in 1789–1790 survived the revolution and have persisted through numerous changes of regime to this day.

The most critical question facing the National Assembly in 1789 was how to finance the government; it was, after all, Louis XVI's failure to solve this problem that had been the immediate cause of the revolution. The easiest, and in some ways the most obvious, solution would have been to repudiate the national debt, but this option was never seriously considered by the men

Revolutionary caricature (1789). A peasant carries a cleric and an aristocrat on his back, while his crops are devoured by pigeons and rabbits (which only nobles were permitted to kill).

of property who composed the Assembly, and who in many instances were themselves creditors of the government. Other alternatives were considered and some were tried. First, the Assembly imposed direct taxes on income from land and other sources, but it failed to raise the anticipated revenue. The Assembly then instituted a "patriotic tax," a kind of voluntary capital levy, with the individual expected to give a quarter of a year's income to the government, in payments spread over three years. Since this tax was not compulsory, the results were naturally disappointing. Meanwhile the deficit in the national treasury continued to mount; the government had to find money somewhere.

The solution ultimately adopted — the confiscation of the land of the Catholic Church — was one of the most controversial decisions of the whole era, and had profound consequences for successive revolutionary governments. Among the most frequently voiced arguments used to justify the seizure of the church's land was the claim that this land was not private property in the sense implied in the Declaration of the Rights of Man.

Rather, the church was a "corporation" that existed to perform certain services and that therefore had a special status under the law. If the state assumed the obligation for guaranteeing these services, it could "take back" the land from the church. Defenders of the church challenged such reasoning, arguing that a corporation as well as an individual had certain rights and that one could no more legitimately be deprived of its property than the other. By November 1789, the decision had been reached. The Assembly voted to place the ecclesiastical land at the disposal of the state, which assumed the obligation of paying the clergy, meeting the expenses of worship, and supporting the poor.

The confiscation of church lands did not solve the financial problem of the government immediately. Land could not, after all, be used to pay the state's debts. The government planned to sell the lands; in the meantime, it issued to its creditors interest-bearing notes (known as *assignats*) that had the former church lands as security. Whoever acquired *assignats* was entitled to certain privileges in the purchase of church lands. The state was to retire the notes as the lands were sold. But not long after the *assignats* had been issued, they began to circulate as paper currency, and the government yielded to the temptation to put more and more of them into circulation. So began the inflation that formed an important part of the history of the revolution. During the later stages of the revolution, as the government

Role reversal (1789). The peasant rides on the aristocrat's back. "I knew that we would have our turn," reads the caption below. At the top of the frame is the slogan, "Long live the King, long live the Nation."

printed more and more *assignats* to meet its obligations, they lost over 99 percent of their face value. Yet the inflation of these years was not without its benefits: it enabled successive revolutionary regimes to liquidate much of the national debt by paying off their creditors in cheap money, and it spurred the growth of a class of enterprising businessmen who acquired the *assignats* at their depreciated value and used them at their face value to purchase church lands.

Perhaps more significant than the purely economic consequences of the confiscation of church lands was the new relationship established between the French state and the Catholic Church. Among the obligations the National Assembly agreed to assume were payment of the clergy and maintenance of the churches. Details of this arrangement were spelled out in the Civil Constitution of the Clergy, completed by July 1790, which not only set salary scales for the various ranks of the clergy but also reorganized the church. Old dioceses were abolished and new ones were created to coincide with the newly formed administrative departments. Parish priests were to be elected by the district assemblies and bishops were to be named by the department assemblies, the same bodies that functioned as local and departmental governments. The pope had no voice in the appointment of the clergy; he was simply to be notified of the choices.

This arrangement was unacceptable to the pope, particularly since it had been drawn up by the National Assembly without any consultation with Roman authorities. And when the Assembly decided in November 1790 to require an oath in support of the constitution and the Civil Constitution of the Clergy from all public servants, the stage was set for a bitter struggle between Pius VI, pope between 1775 and 1799, and the revolutionary government. Those priests who agreed to take the oath became a part of the new "constitutional" church; the others, a little more than half the clergy, were branded "refractory" priests by the Assembly and were subjected to intense persecution. Perhaps no single action of the revolutionary governments caused greater resentment among the French people than the policy toward the Church. Though Napoleon was later to reach a compromise with the pope that resulted in improved relations, the bitterness of many French Catholics toward the revolution and toward those who carried on the revolutionary heritage dates from this era.

The Outbreak of War and the Abolition of Monarchy, 1792

Though openly antimonarchical sentiment remained muted in France during the first years of the revolution, the king's position deteriorated rapidly in 1791–1792. Had the fate of the monarchy been left to the country's rural population, it might well have survived, but an increasingly radical minority of Parisians, acting through political organizations such as the Jacobin clubs (see below) and spreading their propaganda through popular pamphlets and newspapers, provided the impetus for the overthrow of the monarchy and the establishment of the republic. The elected assembly, including representatives from all over France, capitulated to the revolutionary Commune, a committee of Paris radicals who seized power from the legal government of the city on August 10, 1792. From this point on, the Commune played a leading role in the government of France, frequently dictating policy to the elected representatives of the nation. The weapon of the Paris radicals was force and the threat of force. Over and over again, carefully organized demonstrations staged outside the meeting place of the deputies succeeded in swaying the hesitant to a course of action desired by this or that faction of Paris radicals. In this way the will of a determined minority, sure of its goals, was imposed on the more or less passive majority of the French population.

Relations between the monarchy and the national representatives had been strained from the first months of the revolution. In June 1791, four months before the Legislative Assembly first convened (before the Constitution of 1791 went into effect), Louis XVI further alienated his subjects by attempting to flee the country and to seek the protection of the queen's brother, Emperor Leopold II. With the aid of the Swedish count Hans Axel von Fersen, an ardent admirer of Marie Antoinette, the royal family managed to escape from the heavily guarded Tuileries on the night of June 20, and the royal carriage made for a point on the border of Luxembourg. Royal troops were to ensure the safety of the king in his passage through France until he was met at the border by Austrian troops. But the plan went awry when the royal family was recognized and their carriage was halted at Varennes, near the border. There they were detained until orders came from the Assembly to seize the king and bring the royal family back to Paris. Louis XVI and his family were conducted back to the capital along roads lined by silently defiant crowds. Seeking to avoid political instability, the moderate majority in the Constituent Assembly adopted the fiction that the king had been abducted by enemies of France, and it went ahead with plans to promulgate the Constitution of 1791. But Louis himself had aggravated matters by leaving behind a declaration, which was published in newspapers around France, in which he had denounced the limitations on royal power in the new constitution and decried the humiliations to which the royal family had been subjected.

Though the king outwardly collaborated with the revolutionary government in the months that followed, he had serious reservations about the

The royal family is brought back to Paris after attempting to escape from France, June 25, 1791.

regime and his position in it. He was particularly offended by the measures taken against the church, and clearly sympathized with members of the clergy who refused to take the oath in support of the constitution. Among his advisers were many who counseled resistance to the Assembly and its decrees. And even if the king had wanted to accept his responsibilities under the constitution, such a course would have been difficult because of the activities of the *émigrés*, those who had left France in the early stages of the revolution in the hopes of stirring up a counterrevolutionary crusade to restore the Old Regime. As early as July 1789, many members of the court had fled to seek the support of the Holy Roman emperor (whose power stemmed from his rule of Austria), the king of Prussia, and other European monarchs in combating revolution and restoring the king to his rightful position. Foremost among the émigrés were the count of Provence and the count of Artois, Louis' younger brothers, who were far more uncompromising than the king in their opposition to the revolution, and whose projects Louis was forced to disavow on more than one occasion.

How long the regime would have survived in peacetime is impossible to say. The new Legislative Assembly, which met in October 1791, was torn increasingly by factionalism. Disputes between local officials and the Assembly also hampered the operation of government. Following Mirabeau's sudden death in April 1791, the moderate camp lacked effective leadership, and the king's abortive escape attempt converted many revolutionaries who had previously supported constitutional monarchy to the cause of republicanism. Between 1789 and 1792, various radical "clubs," which also came to favor a republican form of government, steadily grew in their influence. The most famous of these were the Jacobin clubs, which after the downfall of the monarchy in 1792 became the most important political group in France and provided the revolution with some of its most celebrated leaders.

The Jacobins had their origins among a group of radical deputies in the National Assembly who in 1789 formed the Society of Friends of the Constitution. This group became known as the Jacobin Club when it began to hold its meetings in the library of the former Jacobin monastery in Paris. At first it was merely a debating society, where deputies from the Assembly discussed radical policy, but it soon broadened its membership to include nondeputies as well, and established ties with similar clubs in other cities in France. Gradually, a vast network of clubs was built, with branches all over the country communicating with each other, holding district meetings, dispensing propaganda, and attempting to influence elections. The membership of the Jacobin clubs was overwhelmingly middle class, consisting primarily of professional men and educated businessmen, though a number of well-to-do artisans joined as the organization grew. With its centralized structure, its strict discipline, and its ties at the local level, the Jacobin machine possessed features later adopted by the single party of the twentieth-century totalitarian state. Mastery of the organization proved a considerable asset to radical leaders in undermining the monarchy, and it remained a valuable instrument of control after the establishment of the republic.

The major crisis that undermined the regime, however, was the outbreak of war in April 1792. These hostilities were provoked in part by the reactions (to be discussed shortly) of other European leaders to the French Revolution. In France, both the king and the group called the Girondins pressed for war, though for opposite reasons. The Girondins were members of a faction within the Legislative Assembly so named because a number of their mainstays came from Bordeaux, in the department of the Gironde. Since their most prominent spokesman at this stage was Brissot de Warville (1754–1793), they were also known to their contemporaries as the Brissotins. Brissot and some of his Girondin associates were at this time members of the Jacobin Club, but a division developed between Jacobins and Girondins in the final months of the Legislative Assembly. The two factions openly split after the National Convention was elected in September 1792.

As early as 1790, Louis XVI considered asking for the intervention of foreign powers in the hope that a military demonstration by the Austrian and Prussian leaders might strengthen his own hand and enable him to intimidate the revolutionaries. By the spring of 1792 he was convinced that his only salvation lay in a war between the revolutionary government and a coalition of European rulers, a war that—he thought—would end in defeat for the French armies. He would then act as mediator between the French people and the victorious powers. The several appeals for intervention that Louis directed to his fellow monarchs helped precipitate the conflict. Within the Legislative Assembly, the Girondins also lobbied for a declaration of war, out of the conviction that the revolutionary armies would prevail over their enemies, thus carrying the torch of liberty to oppressed peoples still living under absolute rulers. Moreover, they believed that a declaration of war would lead to the appointment of a Girondin ministry and a corresponding rise in their influence over the Assembly and the king. In the spring of 1792, both the king and the Girondins did what they could to heighten the tensions between France and its potential enemies, seeking to precipitate a conflict that they thought would serve their own purposes. Both sides fatally miscalculated: the war that began on April 20 hastened the downfall of the monarchy and strengthened the extremist elements that ultimately prevailed over the Girondins.

The initial reactions of the rulers in Europe to the revolution were complex and varied. In the light of what afterward occurred, it would be tempting to infer that all European monarchs "trembled on their thrones" at the news of the revolution and foresaw similar threats to their own positions. But this was not the case. Instead, events in France were viewed for the effect they might have on the complicated game of international politics. For the moment, France could be discounted as a major force in European diplomacy. In fact, Frederick William II, the ineffectual king of Prussia who succeeded Frederick the Great in 1786, saw the revolution at first as an opportunity for Prussia to detach France from its alliance with Austria (dating from the Seven Years' War) and to bring it into the existing alliance between Prussia, England, and the Dutch republic (Holland). Negotiations to this end proved fruitless, but they suggest that neither ideological considerations nor fear of revolution prevented the Prussian king from hoping for a tie with revolutionary France. Leopold II, the Austrian ruler, who came to the throne in 1790, sympathized with the plight of his brother-in-law and sister, the king and queen of France, but he did not undertake a crusade to rescue them from the revolutionaries. Indeed, Leopold was far more concerned at first with reestablishing order in his own Habsburg lands, which were in a state of turbulence after ten years of rule by Joseph II, his reforming predecessor. He was faced not only with demands from the Magyar nobility in Hungary for greater autonomy, and with awakening nationalist sentiment in the Bohemian part of the empire, but also with open revolt in the Austrian Netherlands (later Belgium). His principal effort, therefore, was to establish peace within the empire and to maintain peace abroad. Once he had subdued the revolt in the Netherlands, he was willing to make a gesture toward the French ruler. He joined the Prussian king, Frederick William, in the Declaration of Pillnitz (August 27, 1791), which stated that French affairs were the interest of all Europe and that the two sovereigns might intervene to protect Louis XVI if the other European powers would support them. Yet Leopold was well aware that since England would not consent to such an arrangement, he would not have to fulfill the obligation. As long as Leopold was on the Austrian throne, no war with France occurred. But his sudden death on March 1, 1792, and the succession to the throne of his less cautious young son Francis II, altered the Austrian position, bringing into prominence advisers who favored a more belligerent policy toward France.

War might still have been averted if the change in Austria had not coincided with the advent to power in France of a ministry dominated by the Girondins, who, as we have seen, were the leading advocates of a crusade of liberation. Pretexts for a conflict with Austria were not hard to find. The French government had repeatedly protested the activities of the French émigrés on Austrian soil and the leniency of the emperor toward them. France and Austria also disagreed about the claims of German princes who had been deprived of their feudal rights in the French province of Alsace by decrees passed on August 4, 1789. The princes had refused the indemnity offered by the French government, instead demanding the restoration of their rights and appealing for support to the Austrian emperor. Neither of these issues was important enough of itself to cause a rupture, but feeling had mounted so high in France that on April 20, 1792, the Assembly voted overwhelmingly to declare war on Austria. Almost immediately, the king of Prussia decided to join the Austrian ruler. Both were convinced that France, torn by factionalism and internal dissension, could be easily defeated.

Initially, their expectations proved correct. The French armies were ill prepared for the conflict. Half of the officer corps had emigrated, and many of the men had deserted; new recruits were enthusiastic but ill trained. When the French army attempted to invade the Austrian Netherlands, the French troops broke ranks and fled in disorder at their first encounter; a number of regiments even went over to the enemy. Had the Austrian and Prussian armies mounted a full-scale invasion at this point, France might have been defeated, but the German rulers were reluctant to devote all their resources to the war against France because of their concern over events in Poland, which Russian armies had entered in April 1792. Until an agreement was reached by the Austrian and Prussian rulers with Catherine the Great over the disposition of Polish territories, they hesitated to proceed against France.

The initial reverses of the war produced an internal crisis in France that culminated during the late summer of 1792 in the overthrow of the monarchy and the establishment of a republic. As news of the first defeats reached Paris, and as the military situation grew steadily worse, popular discontent over the conduct of the war mounted. French officers were charged with betraying their troops. Aristocrats and refractory priests were suspected of being enemy agents acting in collusion with the hated émigrés. Finally, many were convinced that the king himself was engaged in treasonable negotiations with the monarchs who were opposing France. To this tension and fear resulting from the war was added an economic crisis that manifested itself in higher prices, marked depreciation of the *assignats*, and a food shortage caused in part by the requisition of supplies for the armies.

All these circumstances created a new revolutionary mood in the country. But the real impetus for the "second" revolution came from a determined minority of Paris radicals—many of them members of the Jacobin clubs who were prepared to exploit the situation in order to seize power. Their first step was to secure control over the administrative districts of Paris. For purposes of administration the capital was divided into forty-eight sections, each with its own assembly of "active" citizens who ruled the district and chose representatives to the city council. Because many eligible citizens took no interest in the government of their sections, radical politicians gradually managed to gain control of the assemblies and turn them into political-action groups to be used for revolutionary purposes. These Jacobin-dominated bodies played a crucial role in the insurrection of August 10, 1792.

This uprising was triggered in part by the publication in Paris on August 3 of a manifesto that had been issued by the Prussian duke of Brunswick, commander in chief of the forces allied against France. With Prussian troops poised on the border of France, the duke declared the intention of the allies to restore Louis XVI to full sovereignty, and threatened to destroy the city of Paris if any harm should come to the royal family. The manifesto seemed to confirm popular suspicions concerning the king's treason. Representatives of the Paris sections reacted by presenting a petition to the Legislative Assembly demanding the deposition of Louis XVI. At the same time, radical leaders completed their plans for an insurrection. They abolished the distinction between "active" and "passive" citizens in the *sections* and thus secured the support of the working classes in their districts. During the night of August 9–10 the tocsin (alarm bell) was sounded, signaling the beginning of the uprising. Delegates of a majority of the *sections* succeeded in ousting the legal municipal government from the city hall and establishing a revolutionary commune as the government of Paris. Meanwhile the crowd, carefully organized by radical leaders, laid siege to the Tuileries, which was defended only by the king's Swiss Guard and a few loyal units of the National Guard. The king, losing heart, took refuge with the deputies of the Assembly in their meeting hall. As the attack on the Tuileries was intensified he gave orders to the Swiss Guard to lay down their arms, hoping that they would be spared. Instead, the crowd invaded the palace and, enraged by their own losses, butchered the Swiss Guardsmen and the royal servants as well. The king was not pursued to his place of refuge, but the Assembly, yielding to pressure from the newly formed Commune, ordered him suspended from his functions and turned him and his family over to the Commune for imprisonment.

The removal of the monarch left the nature of the regime temporarily in doubt. The Legislative Assembly was unwilling to pass judgment on the monarch, so it decided to summon a National Convention, to be elected by universal male suffrage, which would decide the fate of the king and draft a new constitution. In the meantime the Assembly named a provisional council of six ministers to hold executive power until the Convention could be named. In the weeks that followed, both the Assembly and the new ministers found their authority challenged and often usurped by the Paris Commune, which not only asserted its jurisdiction over the capital but sent delegates to the provinces to oversee and interfere with government officials. For six weeks these three bodies—the Assembly, the council of ministers, and the Commune—vied for control; more often than not, the will of the Commune prevailed.

Among the ministers named by the Assembly, the most prominent was Jacques Danton (1759–1794), a lawyer and political organizer who had risen rapidly to leadership in the Jacobin Club because of his active involvement in almost every radical plot in Paris since the beginning of the revolution. Most recently he had distinguished himself as one of the principal organizers of the insurrection of August 10. Opinions differ as to Danton's capabilities as a statesman, but he seems to have responded to the needs of the hour. He was an excellent orator, popular with the Parisians, and appeared to embody the patriotism required in the desperate situation in which France found itself. Prussian troops had continued their advance on French soil. With the enemy approaching Verdun, the last obstacle on the road to Paris, Danton called on his countrymen to defend their country: "To triumph over the enemy . . . we must be bold, still more bold, ever bold, and France is saved."

At this juncture, between the insurrection of August 10 and the assembling of the Convention on September 21, the notorious September Massacres occurred. They must be viewed against the background of military defeats that appeared to spell imminent disaster for France. The prisons of Paris were overflowing with political prisoners — refractory priests, aristocrats, and royalist sympathizers arrested after August 10. All were suspected of treason. Somehow the rumor started that the prisoners were plotting to break out and attack from the rear the armies defending France, while the Prussians attacked from the front. To forestall this rumored conspiracy, patriotic mobs fell on the prisoners, dragged them from their cells, and after summary trials, massacred them. More than a thousand were killed in this brutal fashion in a few days. Responsibility for the murders has never been determined, but the proceedings appear to have been carefully organized and no real attempt was made by the council of ministers or the Commune to halt them. Regardless of who was to blame, the September Massacres went far toward discrediting the revolution among its remaining sympathizers abroad.

Since the elections for the National Convention occurred at about the same time as the September Massacres, it is hardly surprising that royalist sympathizers stayed away from the polls; indeed, in Paris the Commune used terrorist methods to keep them from voting. Despite the provision for universal male suffrage, only seven hundred thousand out of 7 million qualified voters cast their ballots. Those whom they named to the Convention were overwhelmingly in favor of the republic. The first act of the newly assembled Convention on September 21, 1792, was the formal abolition of the monarchy in France. A supplementary decree passed the following day stated that henceforth all public documents would be dated according to a new revolutionary calendar in which September 22 became the first day of "Year I of the French Republic."

The decrees just mentioned were passed unanimously. Before long, however, the differences that had split the left in the old Assembly reappeared among the members of the Convention. On the right now were the Girondins. On the left sat the group known as the Mountain, headed by Danton and some of the other leading Jacobins. Between these two groups, each of which held about one hundred and fifty seats, lay the Plain (sometimes scornfully called the Marsh or the Belly), consisting of four hundred or more deputies who sometimes voted with the right, but usually ended by throwing their support to the Mountain.

The Triumph of the Jacobins, 1792–1793

The history of the first eight months of the Convention is the story of the struggle between the Girondins and the Mountain for control, a struggle that the Mountain had won by the summer of 1793. At first, both the Girondins and the Mountain numbered Jacobins among their members, but the leaders of the Mountain gradually forced the Girondins from the club, and eventually dominated it to such an extent that "Mountain" and "Jacobins" became almost synonymous.

Defining the essential differences between the Girondins and the Jacobins is not easy. Deputies of both factions were bourgeois, not workers, though in general the Girondins may have come from somewhat higher social strata. Both voted for the republic. Both apparently favored continuation of the war against France's enemies. It has been said that the two may have differed in temperament rather than in class or doctrine. The Girondins, who would certainly have been considered dangerous radicals in any other country in Europe at this time, now occupied the moderate position in France, convinced that the revolution had gone far enough and opposed to any further social leveling. They tended to emphasize "liberty" in their speeches, advocating — among other kinds of freedom — the exemption of trade and industry from regulation by the state. Because many prominent Girondins came from the provinces, they distrusted Paris and the interference of the Commune in national politics. Though they had done nothing to prevent the September Massacres, they subsequently condemned those who were responsible for them.

The Jacobin leaders, though by no means all alike in temperament, were more inclined to emphasize "equality" in their public declarations. They favored the elimination of all civil and political distinctions, and although they were not prepared to abandon the principle of private property, they tended to be sympathetic toward the underprivileged, and to admit the right of the government in certain circumstances to intervene in the economy for the welfare of the society as a whole. Specifically, they inaugurated a system of government regulation of prices and wages in order to control the inflation from which France was suffering, and openly advocated confiscation of the wealth of émigrés as well as of priests. Whether they favored these measures as a matter of principle or because they appeared expedient is hard to determine. Though not averse to adopting policies that would help them secure and maintain political power, the Jacobins were, it appears, genuinely convinced that they alone could save France.

Perhaps the most important reason for the victory of the Jacobins was that the Girondins had become moderates prepared to compromise or even vacillate in a situation that seemed to require bold, decisive measures. The position they took on the trial of the king is a good illustration of their weakness. The monarch and his family had remained prisoners in the tower of the Temple, a building formerly owned by the Knights Templars. The problem of what to do with the king was highly controversial. Some of the

Girondins advocated clemency; others wanted to send him into exile; still others favored a popular referendum to determine his fate. In general, the Girondins were inclined to temporize, hoping to postpone a decision indefinitely. The position of the Mountain was clear: the king was a traitor; he should be brought to trial and suffer the penalty customary for such an offense — death.

The trial of the king was hastened by the discovery in a secret cupboard in the Tuileries of a cache of documents that proved conclusively Louis' knowledge and encouragement of foreign intervention. In December 1792, therefore, the Convention constituted itself a court to try "Louis Capet" (as he was then called) for treason. After prolonged debate, in January 1793 members of the Convention were asked to vote publicly on the fate of the king. All agreed that he was guilty of treason, but there was sharp division on the nature of the penalty. The Mountain demanded Louis' death and won enough support from the Plain to carry the day. Even some Girondins at the last moment joined the majority in voting for the king's execution. The final vote was 387 to 334. Since twenty-six of the majority favored a delay in carrying out the sentence, this meant that the decision to execute

Execution of Louis XVI, January 21, 1793. The executioner holds the king's head up for the crowd to see.

the king immediately was won by a single vote. On January 21, 1793, Louis was led under a tight security guard from the Temple to the Place de la Révolution (now the Place de la Concorde), where the guillotine had been placed. Self-possessed to the end, he mounted the scaffold and, amid the rolling of drums, was beheaded.

The execution of Louis XVI marked a critical turning point in the French Revolution. By voting in favor of regicide, the Jacobin majority committed itself to an ever greater radicalization of the revolution — because these delegates knew that if a royalist regime were ever to reestablish itself in France, it might wreak vengeance on the king's assassins. Moreover, the Girondins, through their vacillation during the king's trial, discredited themselves with the minority who were shaping events in Paris. And because the Girondins were guilty of similar hesitation and disunity on other issues — the conduct of the war and the formulation of a constitution, for example — the Mountain seized the initiative and gradually consolidated its position. In June 1793, the Convention, under pressure from a carefully organized crowd, voted the arrest of a group of Girondin deputies on charges of counterrevolution, paving the way for the year-long dictatorship of the Mountain over the Convention known as the Reign of Terror.

During the winter and spring of 1793, France confronted several domestic and international crises, which the Jacobin leaders used to justify their calls for extreme measures. After the initial defeats of the spring and summer of 1792, the French armies had enjoyed a temporary change of fortune, beginning with the so-called miracle of Valmy of September 20, when French forces stopped the advancing Prussian army in northeastern France. In the fall of 1792, France defeated the Austrian armies in a series of battles, occupying Savoy, parts of the Rhineland and the city of Frankfurt, and the whole of the Austrian Netherlands. Yet these military advances, along with French challenges to existing treaties of navigation and the growing extremism of the regime, provoked other European powers to join the antirevolutionary alliances. On the execution of Louis XVI, Great Britain broke diplomatic relations with France, which led France to declare war against Britain and its ally Holland on February 1, 1793. Shortly thereafter, Spain and the Italian states of Sardinia and Naples joined the war effort against France, collaborating with Austria, Prussia, Britain, and Holland to form what is known as the First Coalition. During February and March 1793, the allies reconquered territories in the Netherlands and the Rhineland. Adding to the shock of these defeats, the commander of France's Army of the North, Charles François Dumouriez (1739–1823), who had been minister of foreign affairs in 1792, entered into treasonable negotiations with the Austrian forces in the Netherlands. He planned to lead his troops on Paris to restore the monarchy; and when his army refused to support this venture, he was forced to flee across the border and join the enemy. Dumouriez's treason sharpened the division between Girondins and Jacobins, as each charged the other with complicity in his plots.

As if the stress of defending Paris against foreign invasion were not enough, the revolutionary government was faced in March with an open rebellion in the region known as the Vendée. (This included not only the department of La Vendée but also adjoining parts of Poitou, Anjou, and Brittany.) The immediate pretext for the revolt was the government's attempt to conscript additional troops. Resentment against the revolutionary government's anti-clerical policies was intense in this strongly Catholic region. Now the peasants, generally loyal to the church and king, refused to be drafted into the republican army and exploded into revolt. They were supported in their resistance by a group of Catholic noblemen in the region whose counter-revolutionary conspiracy had recently been discovered. By May the rebels had established a Royal Catholic Grand Army, which caused serious concern to the Convention.

To the problems caused by the steady deterioration at the front and the outbreak of civil war in the Vendée was added a new economic crisis in the late winter and spring of 1793. Requisitions for the armies had depleted stocks of grain and other foodstuffs, causing riots in Paris in February. War contractors and speculators in grain profited from the situation, thus contributing to a rise in prices. The government responded by issuing a new flood of *assignats*, with the result that their value depreciated even further. When popular resentment over these hardships culminated in antigovernment riots in Paris and other major cities, members of the Mountain in the Convention realized they had to take drastic steps.

One radical faction in Paris, known as the "enraged" (*enragés*), demanded government regulation of food prices, subsidies for the poor, and a heavy, graduated tax on the wealthy to finance the war. Whereas the Jacobin leadership in the Convention was receptive to these demands, the Girondins expressed reluctance to adopt such extreme measures. In response, delegations from the Paris *sections* repeatedly petitioned for the expulsion of the Girondin deputies and hinted that the Commune was prepared to use force if the Convention failed to take action against them. In April 1793, the Convention established a new executive body, the Committee of Public Safety, which was dominated by the Jacobin leader Danton. In one of its first actions, the Committee persuaded the Convention — over the Girondins' objections — to enact a "Law of the Maximum," which limited grain prices throughout France.

Recognizing that their principal support lay outside Paris, the Girondins reacted by trying to stir up opposition to the capital among their sympathizers in the provinces. The tension reached a climax in early June. Unable to secure their demands by petitions, the Paris *sections* formed a revolutionary committee; this body, in turn, organized a mass demonstration around the Tuileries, where the Convention was meeting. Declaring that no deputy would be allowed to leave the building until the Girondin leaders had been handed over, the crowd forced the Convention vote to the arrest of twenty-nine prominent Girondin deputies. The Mountain, backed by the Commune and the Paris populace, had apparently triumphed over the Girondin opposition.

Among the arrested deputies, some refused to submit without a fight. Instead of being imprisoned, they had merely been detained in their homes, and twenty of the Girondin leaders escaped from Paris and sought to organize an insurrection against the capital. At first, it appeared that their "federalist revolt" might be successful. They were joined in their rebellion by other antigovernment groups, particularly the royalists, who were only too willing to exploit the situation. The revolt spread from the Vendée to all of Poitou, Anjou, and Brittany. Some of the major cities in France, including Lyons, Marseilles, and Toulon, fell to royalist forces. By the summer of 1793, revolts had erupted in sixty departments. Only the departments around Paris, in central France, and on the eastern frontier appeared to remain loyal to the republic. As events subsequently showed, the strength of the rebels was illusory; their forces were scattered and lacked any sort of unified command, and their various members had radically different goals.

The expulsion of the Girondin leadership from the Convention prepared the way for the dictatorship of the Mountain, which lasted from July 1793 to July 1794. Formally, the Convention, which had been elected in September 1792, remained the official sovereign assembly throughout the Terror; indeed, it remained in existence until October 1795. But the Convention had been named in part to draft a constitution that would supplant the Constitution of 1791. Though a new constitution was completed by the spring of 1793, and sent for ratification to the primary assemblies of citizens in the departments, it was never put into effect. Jacobin leaders exploited the midsummer crisis of 1793 to argue that the country could ill afford the upheaval that the dissolution of the Convention and the election of a new assembly would cause. The Constitution of 1793 was therefore suspended for the duration of the war.

The stillborn Constitution of 1793 was in its provisions the most democratic of the constitutions formulated during the revolutionary era. It provided for universal male suffrage, without property qualifications for either voters or candidates. Gone was the distinction between "active" and "passive" citizens. Representatives to the legislative body were to be named directly by all citizens who voted in primary assemblies. The legislative body was to consist of one chamber, to which an executive council would be responsible. In order to allay the fears of the provinces, the constitution provided that the departments would name the candidates for the executive council, with the legislative body selecting the twenty-four officials from these candidates.

Paradoxically, the body that adopted the most democratic constitution also supported the most dictatorial regime of the revolutionary era. The Convention continued to sit throughout the Terror, although its power was in fact vested in two executive committees which it had set up. The Committee of Public Safety, the more important of the two, was charged with general administration; it was composed at first of nine and later twelve members. The Committee of General Security was given control over the revolutionary police. Members of both of these committees were chosen from the Convention and were theoretically responsible to it, but they became practically independent in their jurisdiction. After the autumn of 1793, their membership was automatically renewed by the Convention every month. They reported to the Convention occasionally on their activities, but their

A *National Guardsman* (1793). On guard duty, the guardsman holds a gong with which to sound an alarm. He wears the simple trousers of the *sans-culottes*.

policies were never seriously challenged by that body until the summer of 1794, when the Terror ended.

All twelve members of the Committee of Public Safety were educated, middle-class radicals, members of the Mountain in the Convention. Among them were six lawyers, two army officers, two men of letters, a civil servant, and a Protestant minister. Though Danton initially played a leading role on the Committee, he was dismissed from his position by the Convention in July 1793. Thereafter, the most influential member of the Committee was Maximilien Robespierre (1758–1794), a thirty-five-year-old lawyer from Arras, in northern France. Dubbed "the Incorruptible" for the purity of his revolutionary convictions, Robespierre was unmarried, chaste, and ascetic in his manner of living. During the revolutionary era, Robespierre continued to dress meticulously in the style of the Old Regime, wearing a light blue coat and breeches and carefully powdered hair. Virtually all other patriotic Jacobin men, by contrast, abandoned the *culottes*, or fancy knee breeches, of the aristocracy in favor of the simple trousers of the workingman. (Indeed, the term *sans-culottes* was used from 1792 to 1794 to describe the active, militant members of the Paris *sections* who played so important a role during the Terror.) Robespierre exercised strong influence over the Committee of Public Safety, but his supremacy was frequently contested by the other members. Moreover, this body's power was checked to some degree by the Committee of General Security, theoretically its equal, and by the Paris Commune.

In regional and local administration the government of the Terror attempted to return to the tradition of centralization characteristic of the Old Regime. The administrative divisions established by the National Assembly — department, districts, cantons, and communes — were retained, but the Terrorist government exercised its authority through appointed officials on behalf of the Convention. In the spring of 1793, "deputies on mission" were sent out by the Convention to the various regions of France to levy troops and stimulate revolutionary enthusiasm, When these officials threatened to become too independent, they were replaced by "national agents," one in each district or commune, directly responsible to the Committee of Public Safety. At the local level the national agents collaborated in some instances with "surveillance committees" (local revolutionary police) and with the Jacobin clubs, now termed "popular societies," but the clubs played a much less significant role than might have been expected.

From Terror to Reaction, 1793–1794

Throughout the summer and fall of 1793, revolutionary crowds played a critical role in radicalizing the revolution. In July 1793, Paris erupted into chaos when the Jacobin journalist Jean-Paul Marat was stabbed to death in his bathtub by a young aristocratic woman, Charlotte Corday. In early September, when news arrived that the port of Toulon had surrendered to the English, a crowd of sans-culottes marched on the Convention to present a list of demands, including controls on food prices and the punishment of counterrevolutionaries. This action provoked the Convention to pass an expanded Law of the Maximum, which established maximum prices for basic commodities and also imposed controls on wages. In September 1793, the Convention also approved the Law of Suspects, which mandated that any "enemy of liberty" could be accused of treason. According to a definition by the General Council of the Commune of Paris, the category of "suspected persons" included not only those who actively conspired against the revolution, but also "those who received the republican constitution [of 1793] with indifference" and "those who, having done nothing against liberty, have also done nothing for it." By equating neutrality with treason, the radical Jacobins demanded the total mobilization of the French populace to defeat the enemies of the revolution at home and abroad. As the Terror escalated, they denounced the forces of counterrevolution in increasingly savage terms. "Blood is necessary to punish so many liberticidal and nationicidal crimes," wrote the William Tell Section to the Convention in a petition of November 1793. "Let the avenging blade fall upon every guilty head, let no criminal be spared. . . . Never forget the sublime words of the prophet, Marat: *Sacrifice 200,000 heads, and you will save 1,000,000.*"

The continuing military crisis also encouraged intensified efforts at popular mobilization. On August 23, 1793, the Convention, acting to meet the crisis caused by the war and the revolts in the provinces, issued a decree proclaiming a *levée en masse*, a plan for the universal conscription of French men to defend the republic:

Henceforth, until the enemies have been driven from the territory of the Republic, the French people are in permanent requisition for army service. The young men shall go to battle; the married men shall forge arms and transport provisions; the women shall make tents and clothes, and shall serve in the hospitals; the children shall turn old linens into lint; the old men shall repair to the public places, to stimulate the courage of the warriors and preach the unity of the Republic and hatred of kings.

This document, which constitutes the first appeal in modern times for the complete wartime mobilization of a people, suggests the kind of national loyalty that the revolutionary leaders hoped to inspire. They were not disappointed, for the *levée en masse* released a remarkable outburst of popular energy, characterized by Frenchmen of a later era as the "spirit of '93." Under its impetus the French armies halted the advance of the coalition forces, and by the spring of 1794 recovered territories that France had conquered in the first months of the republic and later lost. By the end of the Terror, French armies once again occupied the Austrian Netherlands and the entire left, or west, bank of the Rhine.

Part of the reason for France's military successes in 1793 lay in the nationalist spirit that infused the revolutionary armies, which differed strikingly from the attitude of the professional mercenaries who had served the Old Regime. Certain economic measures by the revolutionary government, such as price controls on foodstuffs, also aided the cause of total war by combating the continuing inflation that threatened the urban poor with starvation. Other measures included government requisitioning of supplies for military purposes at the maximum prices which had been set, the establishment of bread and meat rationing for civilians, and controls on foreign trade and exchange. Although these hastily improvised regulations proved hard to enforce, they worked well enough to fulfill some of the basic needs they were designed to meet; indeed, during the Terror the value of the *assignat* was stabilized, and even rose, and the poorest classes were able to buy their own food instead of relying on charity. The armies were successfully provisioned, and as has been noted, they were generally victorious during this period.

To achieve its second goal — the suppression of the enemies of the republic at home — the Terrorist government used both its armies and a set of special revolutionary tribunals. Most of the revolts in the provinces had collapsed by the end of the summer of 1793, but opposition continued in certain key regions, notably the Vendée and in the cities of Lyons and Toulon, both in the hands of the royalists. A concerted drive against Lyons reduced it to submission in October; Toulon, where the royalists had the help of the English, was recaptured in December. (One of the officers of the forces that took Toulon was a young artillery captain named Napoleon Bonaparte.) Bitter fighting continued in the Vendée until the end of 1793, and even after that republican troops continued to carry out bloody reprisals against the inhabitants. Responsibility for punishment of those who had participated in these revolts lay with the deputies on mission, who organized mass executions, or with special revolutionary tribunals set up for the purpose.

In the capital sat the highest court in the system of revolutionary justice, the Revolutionary Tribunal of Paris, which had been established in the spring of 1793 to deal with enemies of the revolution. At first its procedures were similar to those of a regular court of law, but as time went on its justice

The Executioner Guillotining Himself (1794). Satirical engraving attacking the government of Robespierre.

became increasingly summary. Its activities were stepped up in October 1793, when the desire for vengeance against traitors to the republic seems to have reached a peak. Among the most prominent victims at this time were the queen, Marie Antoinette (known in her trial simply as the "widow Capet"), a number of the Girondin leaders who had been arrested in June, and several former generals who had not shown sufficient enthusiasm for the republic. All met their deaths on the guillotine which stood alone on the Place de la Révolution. The Revolutionary Tribunal of Paris was alone responsible for imposing death sentences on 2,639 victims in the fifteen months of its existence.

Throughout France, about fourteen thousand executions were carried out on the orders of revolutionary tribunals; and an additional ten thousand to twelve thousand people died in prison. At least ten thousand more were executed after the defeat of counterrevolutionary revolts in the provinces. Thus, in absolute numbers, the death toll of the Terror was quite small compared with the mass violence unleashed by various twentieth-century extremist regimes, which have exterminated millions of people deemed ideologically or ethnically intolerable. Yet the logic employed by the Jacobin leadership in 1793–1794 anticipated, in important respects, the justifications invoked by subsequent perpetrators of mass political violence around the world. Robespierre and his compatriots demanded that the nation express a "single will" to advance the cause of the revolution; and they demanded the death of all "aristocratic plotters" and other "hidden internal enemies" who were hindering the formation of revolutionary virtue. This insistence on political unanimity, along with the tendency to blame any setbacks on counterrevolutionary conspirators, legitimated extreme measures against opponents of the regime.

Although the Jacobin leaders identified the privileged orders of the Old Regime as the archenemies of the revolution, only about 15 percent of those sentenced to death by revolutionary tribunals belonged to the nobility and clergy. The rest were members of the Third Estate, largely peasants and artisans. Most of the condemned were captured in regions of France that had been invaded by foreign armies, or where counterrevolutionary activity had broken out. In the Vendée, for example, the rank and file of the rebels (an estimated 90 percent) were peasants loyal to king and church, though some of their leaders were from the upper classes.

One of the reasons for the persistence of the Terrorist regime was the existence of a national emergency that appeared to demand drastic measures. With the gradual removal of the threat of foreign invasion and with the end of the civil war in the provinces, the sense of crisis abated. Just as a victorious coalition is likely to dissolve when war is over, so the victorious Jacobins began to be plagued with internal divisions and factionalism. It would be an exaggeration to refer to the several factions as political parties; rather they were loosely formed groups organized around particular individuals. The Robespierrists were the leading faction in the Committee of Public Safety by the beginning of 1794, but they were challenged by two other groups. One consisted of the Dantonists, or followers of Jacques Danton, the hero of the early days of the republic. Danton had remained one of the active leaders of the Mountain up to the fall of 1793, when he was outflanked by the more fanatic members of the Committee of Public Safety and forced into temporary retirement. But his belief that the revolution had proceeded far enough and that it was time for a return to a more moderate, conciliatory regime won him the support of a varied assortment of men — political adventurers, war profiteers, businessmen — at least some of whom hoped to benefit personally from a relaxation of the controls of the Terror. Danton's return to an active political role in the Convention early in 1794 appeared particularly menacing to Robespierrists. To the left of the Robespierrists emerged an even less coherent group around the Parisian demagogue Jacques Hébert (1755–1794); they called for an intensification of the Terror, further economic controls, a renewed attack on the church, and concentration of greater power in the radical *sections* of Paris.

Aware of the threat to his position from these groups, Robespierre proceeded vigorously against them both by playing one off against the other. The turn of the Hébertists came first, in March 1794. Capitalizing on the anti-Parisian sentiment of provincial members of the Convention, Robespierre (with Dantonist support) secured from that body the indictment of the Hébertists before the Revolutionary Tribunal; the result was death by guillotine for the Hébertist leaders. A few weeks later he turned on the Dantonists. Charging Danton and his colleagues with criminal acts committed in office, Robespierre persuaded the frightened Convention to condemn them as well.

With both opposing factions eliminated, Robespierre appeared to have the situation in control and could concentrate on creating the utopian society he called the "Republic of Virtue." But before long the dictator himself was in trouble. Many members of the Convention became fearful for their own safety after this double proscription. As if to confirm their fears, Robespierre convinced the Convention, in June 1794, to pass a law speeding up the procedures of the Revolutionary Tribunal in Paris. With these new powers the tribunal sent some thirteen hundred victims to their death in the following six weeks. With the exception of the period following the suppression of the revolt in the Vendée, no stage of the Terror witnessed a greater number of executions than occurred in June and July of 1794. The result was the rallying of Robespierre's opponents to a plot conceived by Joseph Fouché (1763–1820), a former deputy on mission who had been dismissed because of his excessive brutality toward the people of Lyons. The climax came on July 27 (9 Thermidor in the revolutionary calendar). Appearing on the floor of the Convention to deliver a speech denouncing his enemies, Robespierre found himself howled down by the deputies. His last-minute attempt to rally the support of loyal Jacobins and the Paris Commune for an uprising against the hostile Convention failed. When troops of the Convention discovered him among the insurrectionists at the Hôtel de Ville, Robespierre tried to shoot himself, but succeeded merely in shattering his lower jaw. The next day he was sent, along with more than a hundred of his associates, to the guillotine.

Robespierre's death marked the beginning of the "Thermidorean reaction" against the extremes of the Terrorist regime. This development had not been anticipated by Fouché and his fellow conspirators, who were primarily concerned with saving their own lives, but the desire of most Frenchmen for a relaxation of tensions and an end to violence was strong enough to enable the moderates to regain control. Within the next few months the Convention, under the leadership of the moderate Thermidoreans, eliminated the Paris Commune, stripped the Committee of Public Safety of its powers, closed many of the Jacobin clubs, and removed the price and wage controls imposed bv the Terrorist government.

The Thermidorean era was not without its difficulties, however. With the relaxation of economic controls, inflation and its consequent hardships for the poorer classes returned. The spring of 1795 was marked by bread riots. Working-class agitation in Paris was exploited by the survivors of the Jacobin organization, who sought to direct it against the Convention. In the end, however, the only result of these demonstrations was the elimination of the remaining Jacobin leaders, who were shipped off to exile.

Despite the success of the Thermidoreans in ending the Jacobin threat, and despite the continued victories of the French armies, which led in 1795 to the conclusion of peace with both Prussia and Spain, the Convention was not generally popular. Its lack of support was dramatically illustrated by the reception accorded the Constitution of 1795, which was completed in August. Opponents of the new constitution objected not to its specific provisions, but to the condition that two thirds of the members of the new assembly were to be drawn from the rolls of the outgoing Convention. (These members came to be called "perpetuals.") The stipulation had been

13 Vendémaire, Year IV (October 5, 1795), by I. S. Helman, based on a work by C. Monnet. The insurrection against the Convention failed. The Convention's defense was entrusted to the young and relatively unknown general Napoleon Bonaparte, whose troops dispersed the insurrectionists with a "whiff of grapeshot."

included to prevent extensive royalist victories in the forthcoming elections, but it was interpreted as merely an attempt by the members of the Convention to perpetuate their own power. Indeed, resentment against this proposal was so great that on October 5 (13 Vendémiaire) an insurrection against the Convention broke out in Paris. The uprising failed and would probably have been forgotten had it not been for the fact that the defense of the Convention was entrusted to young General Bonaparte, who dispersed the attackers with a "whiff of grapeshot." Bonaparte's success enabled the Convention to sit out its appointed term. Three weeks later the body dissolved itself, and the Directory, the last government of the revolutionary era, came into being.

The Directory, 1795–1799

In contrast to the continual radicalization of revolutionary politics between 1789 and 1794, the era of the Directory witnessed efforts to restore France to political stability. French leaders during this period were motivated above all by two concerns: on the one hand, the fear of a renewed Terror that might jeopardize their lives and liberty; and on the other, the fear of a restored monarchy, which might exact revenge against those who had collaborated with the revolution. In framing the Constitution of 1795, the Convention sought to navigate between these two dangers. Unlike the previous revolutionary constitutions, which had established a unicameral representative assembly in order to provide a single expression of the "national will," the new regime relied on a system of constitutional checks and balances to avoid political volatility. The two-chamber legislative assembly consisted of the Council of Five Hundred, which proposed legislation, and the two-hundred-fifty-member Council of the Ancients, which debated and approved it. The executive body consisted of a committee of five "directors" who were chosen by the legislative body; after the first two years the legislative body was to replace one director annually.

As in the Constitution of 1791, the suffrage was restricted, this time to those who paid a direct tax on wealth, landed or personal, and to soldiers who had fought for the republic. This provision gave the vote to fewer than 2 million adult males out of a total of 7 million; moreover, because all top officials (including representatives to the legislative councils) were elected indirectly, the real power of franchise rested with a relatively limited group of wealthy men. In addition, it turned out that on more than one occasion the directors — dissatisfied with the results of an election — simply excluded legally elected deputies and named their opponents to the vacant seats. They defended such procedures on the grounds that the regime was threatened on the right by partisans of a royalist restoration and on the left by heirs of the Jacobins anxious to establish a democratic republic. That these threats were not wholly imaginary is proved by the sizable vote that went to opposition deputies in the elections to the legislative councils in 1797 and 1799, and by the several attempts to overthrow the regime.

One of these, not very significant at the time in terms of the number of people involved or of its chances for success, was the Conspiracy of the Equals, led in 1795–1796 by François Émile Babeuf (1760–1797). Drawing his inspiration from the celebrated social reformers of the Roman republic, Babeuf called himself "Gracchus." This episode, which ended in complete failure, has been singled out for considerable attention because some people detect in the egalitarian ideas of Babeuf the germs of modern socialist doctrine. He did, in fact, go considerably beyond the Jacobins, calling for the abolition of private property and the establishment of a communal society, but he did not spell out in detail how these goals were to be achieved. He was content to proclaim as his immediate goal the restoration of the Constitution of 1793. In any event, the Conspiracy of the Equals was betrayed in advance by some of its members, and its leaders were arrested, tried, and condemned to death or exile.

Considerably more dangerous to the government was the recrudescence of the right in 1797, since the conservative camp included many who favored a restoration of the monarchy. Because the young son of Louis XVI had died in captivity in 1795, royalists regarded one of the former king's brothers—Louis Xavier Stanislas, count of Provence (1755–1824)—as the legitimate heir to the throne. The prospect of a restoration was certainly unwelcome to those former members of the Convention who had voted for the death of Louis XVI and therefore feared reprisals against themselves as regicides. When elections to the legislative councils in 1797 returned a large bloc of conservative deputies, the moment seemed opportune for a rightist coup d'état. In order to forestall such an event, the three moderates among the directors—Jean François Rewbell, Louis Marie La Révellière–Lépeaux, and the former viscount of Barras—called troops into the capital, claiming the existence of a royalist plot. Under their leadership the "loyal" members of the legislative councils nullified the elections of almost two hundred conservative deputies and condemned to deportation the two other directors, François de Barthélemy and Lazare Carnot. Barthélemy's secret royalist sympathies had been discovered, and Carnot had made the mistake of trying to heal the rift among the directors. This was the coup d'état of Fructidor (September 4, 1797); it ended, for the time being, the threat from the right.

Efforts to reestablish stability in France were hindered by ongoing domestic and international crises. The end of the Law of the Maximum, together with ongoing army requisitions and an exceptionally cold winter in 1795, resulted in massive suffering for France's common people: prices for basic staples soared by over 1,000 percent. Moreover, the government inherited an acute financial crisis from the preceding regime. By 1796 the *assignats* had depreciated to less than 1 percent of their face value. In an effort to establish the paper currency on a sounder foundation, the government stabilized the *assignats* at one thirtieth of their face value and announced that they could be exchanged on that basis for new paper money, the *mandats territoriaux*. Those who had acquired the *mandats* could use them to buy the remaining nationalized lands at a price set by the government. In this way the *assignats* were withdrawn from circulation, but the measure was ultimately unsuccessful since the *mandats*, in turn, depreciated to about 10 percent of their face value. In 1797 the Directory returned to a gold- and silver-backed currency, and although this step did not end the financial difficulties of the regime, it restored a measure of confidence among French businessmen. Other measures taken to improve the financial position of the government were the sharp curtailment of expenditures and the reorganization of the servicing of the national debt.

The latter step, though publicized as the "consolidation" of one third of the debt, constituted in fact a repudiation by the government of the other two thirds. The government thus not only temporarily undermined confidence in public credit, but also alienated many bourgeois bond holders who went unpaid. On balance, however, the financial condition of the government and the country was better in 1799 than it had been in 1795. The Directory restored a measure of order to France's finances and laid the groundwork for Napoleon's subsequent fiscal reforms.

Another major objective of the Directory was the conclusion of a general European peace, which was essential both to guarantee France's security and to reduce the domestic pressures on the regime. This goal proved elusive, however. By 1795, the Thermidorean regime had already ended the war with all of France's major enemies except Austria and Britain. In its first two years the Directory made repeated attempts to reach an agreement with Britain, but negotiations were complicated by France's determination to retain the lands that it had conquered in Belgium, Savoy, and Nice.

In 1796, the Directory launched a new assault against Austria in the Rhineland and in Italy. The twenty-seven-year-old Napoleon Bonaparte, commander of the Italian campaign, established his reputation as France's most brilliant general through a series of phenomenal successes. Advancing eastward along the Mediterranean coast, he defeated the Austrians and their Sardinian allies, ultimately gaining control of most of northern and central Italy. Then, in the spring of 1797, Bonaparte crossed the Alps and pursued the Austrian forces to within seventy-five miles of Vienna. Under the Treaty of Campoformio of October 1797, Austria recognized French domination over a new Cisalpine Republic in northern and central Italy, as well as ceding its Belgian provinces and imperial territories on the left bank of the Rhine to France.

By the end of 1797, only Britain and its ally Portugal remained at war with France; and indeed, the British ministry of William Pitt the Younger had extended cautious peace proposals. Distrustful of Pitt's initiatives, however, the Directory elected to break off negotiations and to attack Britain through its empire. Bonaparte was authorized to organize an expeditionary force of about thirty-five thousand troops for an invasion of Egypt. Supporters of this plan, including the diplomat Charles Maurice Talleyrand, argued that the acquisition of the Isthmus of Suez would allow for the construction of a canal that would give the French commercial supremacy over the British, and ultimately enable France to seize control of India through an alliance with Tipu Sahib (ruled 1782–1799), a powerful prince who had recently revolted against British rule.

In May 1798, the French expedition embarked secretly from Toulon. En route, Napoleon launched a surprise attack on the island fortress of Malta, which he took without difficulty. His forces landed at Abukir in June, captured Alexandria without firing a shot, and moved on to Cairo. Egypt, nominally a part of the Ottoman empire, was defended only by an Egyptian-born military elite, the Mamelukes. Despite their excellent cavalry they were no match for a trained European army with artillery, and went down to defeat in the battle of the Pyramids. Shortly thereafter, however, the campaign met disaster at sea. British naval forces, commanded by Admiral Horatio Nelson (1758–1805), surprised and annihilated the fleet that had transported the French expeditionary force, leaving Napoleon a virtual prisoner in Egypt. Refusing to admit defeat, he invaded Syria, another possession of the Ottoman empire, but after early successes, his army suffered from an outbreak of the plague and was forced to retreat in haste to Egypt.

Meanwhile, early in 1798, the Directory used a disturbance in Rome as a pretext for expelling the pope and establishing a Roman Republic. In the same year, the French government converted the Swiss cantons into a centralized Helvetic Republic and also imposed a regime modeled on the Directory in Holland, which France had conquered in 1795. Moreover, France attempted to send military support for an Irish rebellion against Britain, which was brutally suppressed in 1798. All of these moves alarmed France's rivals. Russia, concerned about French incursions into the Ottoman empire, allied with Britain and Austria to form the Second Coalition (1799–1802), resulting in a new period of intensified warfare.

Within France, the Directory struggled to navigate between the forces of Jacobinism and royalism. Having nullified the elections of almost two hundred conservative delegates in 1797, the directors excluded a large bloc of radical deputies the following year, when the left wing made dramatic electoral gains. In June 1799, the legislative councils retaliated by replacing four of the directors with men whose outlook was more radical. One of these was Emmanuel-Joseph Sieyès, who had served in the Convention and stayed on in the legislative body. Sieyès had nothing but contempt for the existing regime and was determined to strengthen the authority of the executive branch, by a change in the constitution if necessary. He found sympathy for his views among army leaders who were known to favor greater executive power, but feared the possibility of a restoration of the monarchy because they had served the republic.

Bonaparte, languishing in Egypt with his troops cut off from their supply lines, capitalized on the disorder in the Directory to advance his career. Abandoning his army, he slipped out of Egypt in the summer of 1799 and returned to France. Arriving unannounced on the Mediterranean coast, he established contact with the directors Sieyès and Roger-Ducos, a former Girondin, with a view to collaboration. Sieyès, who had already been contemplating a coup d'état, now determined to use Bonaparte to guarantee its success.

Having reached an agreement, the two fixed 18 Brumaire (November 9, 1799) as the date for their seizure of power. A pretext for the coup was found in an alleged Jacobin plot against the regime. The legislative councils were summoned to meet at Saint-Cloud, outside of Paris, ostensibly because they would not be subjected there to pressure from the Paris mob. Sieyès and Roger-Ducos resigned their posts in the Directory. One of the three remaining directors, Barras, was prevailed on to resign and the other two were arrested, so the government was without an executive. At this stage Napoleon appeared before the Council of Five Hundred to ask that he be given special powers to deal with the crisis confronting the country. Some of the deputies, seeing through the conspiracy, challenged him to produce evidence of a Jacobin plot. When he was unable to do so, they were on the verge of ordering his arrest. But quick action by his younger brother Lucien, who was president of the lower house, prevented the entire venture from collapsing. Lucien rallied the troops stationed outside the hall to Napoleon's cause, assuring them that he would plunge his sword through his brother's heart if Napoleon ever plotted against the liberty of the French people. Inspired by this declaration, the troops followed Napoleon's order to clear the hall of all deputies. A rump session of those sympathetic to the conspirators later voted full powers to Bonaparte, Sieyès, and Roger-Ducos, proclaiming them "temporary consuls." The coup d'état of Brumaire had succeeded; France had a military dictatorship. In this way the somewhat dreary political history of the Directory came to an end.

REVOLUTIONARY CULTURE

Although the French Revolution ended with Napoleon's coup of 18 Brumaire, the events of this volatile decade exerted an enormous influence over the subsequent history of Europe and the world. During the Napoleonic era, political movements around Europe drew on elements of the revolutionary legacy, agitating for democratic institutions, the mobilization of the "nation," and the abolition of traditional social and legal hierarchies. At home, France would experience new revolutions in 1830, 1848, and in the Paris Commune of 1870–1871, each of which adopted much of the symbolism and rhetoric first created between 1789 and 1794. (Indeed, such was the stubborn persistence of the revolutionary legacy that one prominent French historian began a polemic published nearly two centuries after 1789 by insisting, "The revolution is over."[5]) During the twentieth century, French revolutionary ideals influenced communist movements in Russia, China, and elsewhere, as well as national independence movements in Africa and Asia.

Any attempt to evaluate the significance of the French Revolution must balance the extent to which it represented a radical historical rupture against the extent to which it continued long-term developments. Throughout much of Europe during the seventeenth and eighteenth centuries, dynastic states were fielding larger armies, as well as developing more centralized and rationalized administrative apparatuses. Moreover, the fabric of feudalism had been eroding for hundreds of years before the outbreak of the revolution. In most of western Europe, the aristocracy had lost much of its traditional authority by the late eighteenth century, and social status was increasingly associated with economic class, rather than with hereditary hierarchies. In political terms, a series of revolutionary movements, including the English Revolution of the seventeenth century, the American Revolution of 1775–1783, and the Dutch revolt of the 1780s, had challenged monarchical authority elsewhere in the Atlantic world. In all these ways, the French Revolution may be seen as consolidating and reinforcing long-standing trends, rather than as changing the direction of history.

The profoundly new dimension of the French Revolution was something

[5] Furet, *Interpreting the French Revolution*, p. 1.

less tangible or quantifiable: it was rooted in the realm of political imagination. Though the world had witnessed innumerable social and political revolts before, none of these previous movements had matched the ambitions of 1789. The leaders of the French Revolution shared a political credo founded on two premises. First, they held that human society could, and should, be organized according to purely rational principles — and thus, that the authority of reason should always take precedence over that of tradition. Second, they believed that the path to this new rational order was through mass political activism — that the will of the people would lead the way to utopia. The combination of these two premises laid the foundation for a potent and volatile new form of politics that would inspire activists far beyond the borders of France.

Mobilization of the Masses

In *What is the Third Estate?* the Abbé Sieyès had defined the power of the French people in nearly mythical terms: "The nation is prior to everything. It is the source of everything. Its will is always legal; indeed it is the law itself." This bold claim marked a crucial difference between the French Revolution and previous mass political movements such as the American War of Independence. In France, popular political activism came to be interpreted through a more radical symbolic frame than had been the case with earlier movements, a development that in turn contributed to more extreme forms of political action.

The radicalization of the symbolic frame of popular politics was evident from the first months of the revolution. The storming of the Bastille in July 1789, for example, was an event of little immediate practical significance: the fall of the fortress yielded few arms and only a handful of prisoners to its conquerors. Yet the symbolic import of this event was immeasurable. Prerevolutionary journalists such as the flamboyant Simon Linguet (1736–1794) had depicted the Bastille as a dark bastion of despotism. Contemporary chroniclers thus celebrated its destruction as a triumph in the struggle for the liberation of the French people. Even more important, Louis XVI himself interpreted the fall of the Bastille as an expression of the people's will. Fearing that his soldiers might refuse his commands, he abandoned the notion of dispersing the National Assembly by force, allowing the revolution to gain momentum at a critical historical moment, and rendering future resistance against popular radicalism more difficult.

During the Great Fear of July and August 1789, the emergence of a new political symbolism likewise contributed to the radicalization of events. This wave of violence began as a relatively traditional form of rural unrest, such as had often occurred in the French countryside during times of famine.

After news spread of the fall of the Bastille, however, peasants around France suddenly turned their wrath against aristocrats whom they thought had hatched a "famine plot" to starve the people. The National Assembly's response to these events was even more extreme: on August 4 it capitulated to what the delegates viewed as the will of the people by abolishing virtually all remnants of the feudal order. In both of these early revolutionary events, the effectiveness of mass political activism stemmed partly from the fact that the government authorities, as well as the protesters, interpreted the crowds' actions as manifestations of an infallible and inexorable "national will."

By identifying the people as the sole source of legitimate political authority, Sieyès and other revolutionary leaders not merely justified but demanded the participation of the masses in political life. This activist fervor was captured most powerfully in the lyrics of "*La Marseillaise*," the anthem composed by a young army engineer in Strasbourg in April 1792, on the eve of the first battle of the revolutionary wars. "*Aux armes, citoyens!*" echoes the chorus. The nation's enemies have raised the "bloody banner" against the *enfants de la patrie* (the children of the fatherland). The citizenry must rise up and "water the fields" with the "impure blood" of tyrants in order to rescue France from its foes.

As the revolution turned increasingly radical, the desire to involve the people in politics escalated. Yet the doctrine of absolute national sovereignty posed two difficult dilemmas: first, how could a unified expression of the "national will" be found in a country of nearly 30 million people? Second, how could revolutionary leaders mobilize mass support while still controlling the course of events by preventing spontaneous challenges to their political authority from below? Throughout the period 1789–1799, popular political activism demonstrated the capacity to topple as well as to support ruling elites.

One highly visible way in which the masses were mobilized was through revolutionary festivals manifesting the patriotism and unity of the nation. Some of the first of these festivals appear to have been organized without careful orchestration from above. In November 1789, for example, twelve thousand National Guardsmen from southeast France convened on the banks of the Rhône River, swearing to uphold constitutional liberty "in the presence of Heaven, on their hearts and on their arms." Over the following months, more elaborately choreographed ceremonies were held in various provincial cities. On July 14, 1790, fifty thousand National Guardsmen and four hundred thousand spectators gathered in a torrential rainstorm on the Champs de Mars, a parade ground in Paris, to celebrate the "Festival of the Federation." The organizers of the Festival included Charles Maurice de Talleyrand, the wily former bishop of Autun, who celebrated a mass and

King Louis XVI wielding a pickaxe at the Champ de Mars, preparing the ground for the Festival of Federation (1790). Frontispiece to *Révolutions de France et de Brabant*, no. 36.

benediction, and Lafayette, who led the assembled guards in an oath of allegiance to the trinity of the nation, the law, the king.

Many of the revolutionary festivals inspired a genuine outpouring of a utopian spirit among the participants. In July 1790, thousands of Parisians of all classes joined in preparing the grounds for the Festival of the Federation: according to a contemporary illustration, even the king helped in the digging. Yet the festivals also contained an uneasy mix of symbolic elements. These spectacles were simultaneously manifestations of the revolution, physically depicting the nation as a unified communal body, and also often conservative pageants that aimed to stabilize the political order by portraying the revolution as a completed work. Moreover, the festivals' joyful celebration of national harmony coincided with a dark undercurrent of violence. The first Festival of the Federation in Paris commemorated the storming of the Bastille. Subsequent revolutionary festivals established by 1794 paid homage to other pivotal moments of revolutionary violence: the attack on the Tuileries of August 10, 1792; the execution of the king on January 21, 1793; and the insurrection of May 31, 1793, that led to the arrest of the Girondins in the Convention.

A further celebration initiated on 20 Prairial (June 8, 1794) in the Tuileries gardens was the Festival of the Supreme Being, which Robespierre intended to inaugurate a new civic religion in place of Catholicism. Robespierre's speech reflected the darkening tone of the revolution. After exalting the Supreme Being and the heroic spirit of the republic, he denounced "this monster which the spirit of kings has spewed forth over France" and declared: "Frenchmen, Republicans, it is up to you to purify the earth which they [tyrants] have defiled and to restore the justice they have banished from it. Liberty and virtue issued together from the breast of the Divinity. One cannot reside among men without the other." He then proceeded to demonstrate allegorically the triumph of Wisdom by setting fire to figures of Atheism, Vice, and Folly. From the ruins emerged a statue of Wisdom Triumphant.

Revolutionary festivals were but one means of conveying the solidarity of the French nation. In 1793 the artist Jacques-Louis David proposed to erect a gargantuan statue of Hercules on the Pont-Neuf; and throughout the Terror the image of Hercules appeared regularly in speeches by revolutionary orators, in engravings, and on the seal of the Convention. This virile giant was a male counterpart to Marianne, the female icon of lib-

The Festival of the Supreme Being, presided over by Robespierre. Drawing by Naudet. At the top of the hill stands the tree of liberty; adjacent to the hill, on a high pedestal, is a statue of Hercules.

erty, who also frequently appeared as a visual representation of the revolution.

Another revolutionary icon was the liberty tree, symbolizing the rebirth of the nation, festooned with slogans and tricolor ribbons, and topped by the red "Phrygian cap" that had been worn by slaves in the Roman empire. The liberty trees were inspired by maypoles erected by peasants in Périgord during a revolt of 1790. By May 1792, sixty thousand liberty trees had been planted in public squares and village greens around France.

Such revolutionary symbols had a profound practical impact on everyday life in France. By planting a liberty tree, the residents of a village announced their rejection of traditional authority and their loyalty to the new order. Thus, the liberty trees became a center of symbolic warfare: they were frequently uprooted or vandalized by opponents of the revolution. Clothing became another powerful marker of political allegiances. After July 5, 1792, all men in France were obligated to wear the tricolor cockade, and with the notable exception of Robespierre, virtually all patriotic Jacobin men came to wear the trousers of the sans-culottes. Many women dressed in flowing white robes like those worn by women of the Roman Republic. Both sexes rejected the wigs and powdered hair of the Old Regime in favor of simple and unaffected hairstyles. During the Thermidorean era, by contrast, men and women rapidly returned to more revealing and flamboyant clothing. Likewise, after 1794 the French once again began to indulge in the pleasures that had been banned during the Terror. Theaters, cafés, and ballrooms flourished in the freer atmosphere.

No aspect of revolutionary political mobilization had more potent or lasting significance than the military revolution exemplified by the *levée en masse*. Though the size of European armies had been increasingly steadily since the early sixteenth century, the French Revolution resulted in a massive escalation in the scale and objectives of military activity. In 1788–1789, before the outbreak of the revolution, the royal army had 150,000 soldiers. By August 1793, on the eve of the *levée en masse*, the official size of the army had climbed to 645,000 men (though many of these lacked uniforms, weapons, and training). By September 1794, the army of the Republic numbered 1,169,000 soldiers. Although probably only about 730,000 of these were in active service, this was still nearly twice as many soldiers as had been fielded by any previous European army.

Not only did the *levée en masse* increase the sheer size of the French army, it also transformed the nature of warfare. By placing all French citizens "in permanent requisition for army service," this decree inaugurated the era of total war, in which nations dedicated all of their resources to the destruction of their enemies. The army laid claim to the entire economic product of France and asserted the right to draft any adult male for military service (though initially it targeted only unmarried men between the ages of eighteen and twenty-five). Each battalion was to carry into battle a banner with the inscription: "The French people risen against tyrants." Unlike previous armies, constituted of mercenaries and unwilling conscripts, this new military force would be motivated by undying devotion to the glory of the fatherland.

The army of the Republic had mixed success in recruiting citizen soldiers. The *levée en masse* met with strong resistance in rural France, where peasants thought much more in terms of local or regional identities than in terms of allegiance to an abstract "nation." Many young men sought to evade military service; others deserted the army. Nonetheless, ideology played a profound role in intensifying the martial spirit of French soldiers and in inspiring the spectacular successes of the revolutionary and Napoleonic armies. In the words of the Prussian observer Carl von Clausewitz, the revolution gave rise to:

a force . . . that beggared all imagination. Suddenly war again became the business of the people—a people of thirty millions, all of whom considered themselves to be citizens. . . . Instead of governments and armies as heretofore, the full weight of the nation was thrown into the balance. The resources and efforts now available for use surpassed all conventional limits; nothing now impeded the vigor with which war could be waged.[6]

The Cult of Reason

For the English Whig Edmund Burke, the principal error of the French revolutionaries stemmed from their blind faith in the powers of human rationality: "When ancient opinions and rules of life are taken away, the loss cannot possibly be estimated. From that moment we have no compass to govern us; nor can we know distinctly to what port we steer." Although he had been an avid supporter of the American Revolution, Burke was an early and caustic critic of the revolution in France. In a treatise published in 1790, when many European intellectuals were still intoxicated by the glow of the revolutionaries' early triumphs, Burke anticipated a darker side to the principles articulated in the Declaration of the Rights of Man:

On this scheme of things, a king is but a man; a queen is but a woman; a woman is but an animal; and an animal not of the highest order. All homage paid to the sex in general as such, and without distinct views, is to be regarded as

---

[6] Carl von Clausewitz, *On War*, edited and translated by Michael Howard and Peter Paret (Princeton, 1976), pp. 591–92.

romance and folly. Regicide, and parricide, and sacrilege, are but fictions of superstition, corrupting jurisprudence by destroying its simplicity. The murder of a king, or a queen, or a bishop, or a father, are only common homicide; and if the people are by any chance, or in any way gainers by it, a sort of homicide much the most pardonable, and into which we ought not to make too severe a scrutiny.[7]

As Burke detected, perhaps the most potent dimension of the French revolutionaries' rhetoric was the claim that they had rendered history irrelevant. The American War of Independence had been motivated, in its initial stages, by the desire to restore the traditional "rights of Englishmen," such as the right to representation in apportioning taxes. In France, by contrast, the more radical revolutionaries argued for starting from first principles, constructing a new world on the ashes of the old. This rationalizing impulse manifested itself from the initial months of the revolution, for example, with the abolition of feudal dues and the administrative reorganization of France into *départements*. It continued throughout the 1790s: during Napoleon's Egyptian campaign, the army was accompanied by a legion of scientists who brought back to France artifacts such as the Rosetta Stone.

Some of the effects of revolutionary rationalization were long lasting. In 1790, the National Assembly commissioned the French Academy of Sciences to develop a new standardized system of weights and measures to replace the bewildering array of such systems that had existed under the Old Regime. The product of this work, carried out by Joseph-Louis Lagrange, was the metric system, which was based on a unit of length (the meter) and a unit of mass (the gram). Initially, the meter was defined as one ten millionth of the distance from the North Pole to the equator, though this definition was subsequently modified because of the practical difficulties involved in surveying this distance accurately. The gram was defined as the mass of water that would fill a cube whose sides each measured 0.01 meters. The metric system was formally established in France in December 1799, shortly after Napoleon's coup, and it has since been adopted throughout most of the industrialized world.

Other rationalizing efforts, such as the revolutionary calendar, proved more transitory. This calendar, established by the National Convention in October 1793, began the Year I with the founding of the Republic on September 22, 1792. It divided the year into twelve months of thirty days each, all of which were named after the seasons: Vendémaire (Vintage), Brumaire

[7] Edmund Burke, *Reflections on the Revolution in France*, edited by Thomas H. D. Mahoney (Indianapolis, 1955), p. 87.

(Fog), Frimaire (Frost), Nivôse (Snow), Pluviôse (Rain), Ventôse (Wind), Germinal (Buds), Floréal (Flowers), Prairial (Meadow), Messidor (Harvest), Thermidor (Heat), and Fructidor (Fruit). The remaining five days were devoted to an autumn festival celebrating the creation of the Republic. Although the revolutionary calendar remained in place until January 1806, it inspired little love from the citizens of France. Because each month consisted of three weeks, which were ten days long, the weekend was reduced to one day in ten. By eliminating Sunday, the calendar was also antithetical to Christian worship. Moreover, since the rest of western Europe already possessed a standardized calendar, the new way of measuring time created more confusion than clarity. For the same reason, other revolutionary innovations such as the decimal clock, which divided the day into ten hours of a hundred minutes of a hundred seconds, proved impractical.

This tendency to value the authority of reason over that of tradition had profound implications for the evolution of European politics. By expressing such strong faith in the possibility of ordering the world rationally, the revolutionaries established a virtually boundless vision of the capacities of political action. Their principles justified the annihilation of any system of authority that was perceived as oppressive or unreasonable. Thus, in the aftermath of 1789, the rhetoric of the French revolutionaries was adopted and transformed by numerous groups that sought to combat other forms of oppression, for example, that based on gender, race, or economic class.

The Rights of Women and Ethnic Minorities

The revolutionaries' faith in rational universal principles was tempered by their desire to prevent the breakdown of social order, which they feared might ensue if these principles were extended to their logical conclusions. This internal conflict manifested itself in debates over women's rights, the abolition of slavery, and the status of religious minorities.

Women played a central role in some of the early events of the French Revolution, such as the march on Versailles of October 1789, which brought the royal family back to Paris. During the first months of the revolution, a few political activists called for the extension of the full rights of citizenship to women as well as men. In July 1790, the marquis de Condorcet (1743–1794), one of the leading intellectuals of the Enlightenment, argued that women should be granted the right to vote. The French revolutionaries, he contended, had "violated the principle of equality of rights by quietly depriving half of mankind from the rights of citizenship." During 1790 and 1791, a small group called the Cercle Social (social circle) campaigned vocally for women's rights. A prominent figure in this movement was the Dutch woman Etta Palm D'Aelders, who compared the despotism of husbands to that of absolute monarchs. In a speech to a political club in December 1790, she declared: "The prejudices with which our sex has been surrounded . . . have changed what was for us the sweetest and the most saintly of duties, those of wife and mother, into a painful and terrible slavery."

Despite these calls for female emancipation, the National Assembly gave no serious consideration to granting women political rights in the Constitution of 1791. The delegate Talleyrand spoke for the majority of his colleagues when he declared that it was against "the wishes of nature" for women to participate in political life, and that "the common happiness" required "harmony in the division of powers" between the sexes. In this matter, as in many others, the rhetoric of the French revolutionaries reflected the influence of Jean-Jacques Rousseau. Already in the dedication to his *Discourse on the Origin of Inequality* (1755), Rousseau had contrasted the "modest graces" of the "amiable and virtuous daughters of Geneva," his idealized native city, with the "puerile" and "loose" women of other cities. Unlike these other women, who corrupted public morals and corroded liberty, the Genevan women exercised their "chaste influence" only "within the limits of conjugal union," thus ensuring political harmony and domestic tranquility. In this passage, as in his subsequent novel *La Nouvelle Héloïse* and his educational treatise *Emile*, Rousseau anticipated nineteenth-century ideals of domesticity, which drew a sharp division between the male (public) and female (private) spheres of society. During the revolution, Rousseau's ideas were invoked to vilify Marie Antoinette as a "bad mother" and unfaithful wife whose conduct damaged not only her family but also the nation as a whole.

Across the Channel in Britain, the novelist and political pamphleteer Mary Wollstonecraft took the dismissive attitude toward women's rights exhibited by Rousseau, Talleyrand, and others as a challenge. She responded with an extended treatise entitled *A Vindication of the Rights of Woman*, which was published in 1792. Wollstonecraft observed that the perpetual subjection of women to male authority had made it impossible for them to develop fully their natural talents. Because women were forced to focus their energies on pleasing men, they were unable to cultivate their own virtue and rational faculties. Women, she argued, must be educated for independence, not for dependence; their emancipation would make them more affectionate wives and mothers, and it would better enable them to raise their children as virtuous citizens.

In France, the playwright Marie Gouze, who wrote under the name Olympe de Gouges, crafted a pointed response to the revolutionary constitution's exclusion of women from active citizenship. Her Declaration of the Rights of Woman, composed in September 1791, appropriated the language of the Declaration of the Rights of Man and the Citizen. Article 1 of her Declaration began, "Woman is born free and remains equal to man in rights"; in Article 2, she declared: "The purpose of all political association is the preservation of the natural and imprescriptable rights of woman and man." Gouges not only broadened the principles of the Declaration of the Rights of Man and the Citizen to include women, but also extended the nature of these rights to the sphere of social relations: she recognized that without property rights and the right of divorce, for example, political rights for women would have little value. In 1793, France's Jacobin leaders sent her to the guillotine, both because of her "counterrevolutionary" Girondin views and because they labeled her an "unnatural" woman.

During the debates of 1793 over the new republican constitution, a few delegates to the National Convention revisited the question of whether women should be granted broader rights, but there was little support for these proposals. In October 1793, the Convention passed a decree banning women's political societies. The Jacobin delegate Jean Baptiste Amar, who introduced this proposal in the assembly, argued that women were "hardly capable of lofty conceptions and serious cogitations," and that they were "destined by nature" to perform "private functions" rather than to participate in public life. Three weeks later, when a group of women wearing red caps arrived at the Paris city hall, the radical leader Pierre Gaspard Chaumette denounced them heatedly: "It is shocking, it is contrary to all the laws of nature for a woman to want to make herself a man. . . . Since when is it permitted to renounce one's sex? Since when is it decent to see women abandon the *pious* cares of their household, the cradle of their children, to come into public places, to the galleries to hear speeches, to the bar of the senate?"[8]

In the sphere of social relations, the French Revolution also had mixed effects on women's rights. In September 1792, the Legislative Assembly legalized divorce, on the logic that an absolute prohibition of divorce represented an infringement on the liberty of French citizens. Initially the terms for divorce were defined liberally: any of seven grounds, including "incompatibility" and "mutual consent," could be invoked to justify the dissolution of a marriage. Over the subsequent decade, about thirty thousand divorces were granted in France, of which approximately 70 percent were initiated by women. This easy access to divorce—and the fact that women availed themselves of this option more frequently than men—provoked intense opposition from Catholics and political conservatives. In 1797, the legisla-

---

[8] Quoted in Lynn Hunt, editor and translator, *The French Revolution and Human Rights: A Brief Documentary History* (Boston, 1996), pp. 138–39.

ture of the Directory rewrote the divorce law to impose a six-month waiting period for divorces justified on the basis of "incompatibility." The Napoleonic Code, adopted in 1804, was more conservative yet in terms of women's legal position, severely restricting the right of divorce as well as women's rights of property ownership, and formally subordinating women to the legal authority of their husbands.

The history of revolutionary divorce law had a striking parallel in the legislation over the status of illegitimate children. In November 1793, the Convention passed a decree establishing the principle (in accordance with the revolutionary ideal of universal equality) that children born out of wedlock should have the same rights of inheritance "as those of other children." Yet this well-meaning statement of principle ultimately had disastrous effects for the law's intended beneficiaries. To begin with, the authors of the legislation felt compelled to limit the inheritance rights of children of adulterous liaisons, as compared with the children of two unwed parents (they did not even dare mention the case of offspring of incestuous relationships). By 1795, fearing the potentially corrosive effects of this legislation on the sanctity of the family, the government of the Directory severely restricted the inheritance rights of illegitimate children. For example, it denied them the ability to establish paternity unless the father freely admitted it. (Married men had already been prohibited from *voluntarily* acknowledging paternity of any illegitimate children.) Ultimately, under the Napoleonic Code, illegitimate children were assigned a legal status even more disadvantageous than had existed under the Old Regime.

On balance, the revolution had mixed effects on gender relations. On the one hand, it provided a new political language that had the potential to justify a radical reordering of the domestic sphere. The rhetoric of the "rights of man" established a framework within which women could assert claims to freedom and equality, disputing the traditional biblical authority for husbands' right to rule over their wives. On the other hand, the turmoil of the revolutionary events also provoked a powerful conservative reaction within France which sought to preserve "domestic tranquility" by returning women to the home. Many of the most ardent male revolutionary activists were highly resistant to women's participation in public life. In a sense, women paid the price for the liberation of men, as France's political leaders sought to assure the citizenry that the adoption of revolutionary principles would not produce chaos in the private sphere and the overthrow of all existing order.

The institution of slavery in the French colonies, especially on the highly lucrative sugar plantations of Saint-Domingue, created another potent dilemma for revolutionary politicians. During the early months of the revolution, an organization called the Society of the Friends of Blacks, which Condorcet had helped establish in 1788, demanded an end to the slave trade and the gradual abolition of slavery. Yet most of the revolutionary leaders initially resisted this course of action, fearing the loss of French commercial wealth and colonial power. Moreover, the colonial plantation owners exercised considerable influence over a number of delegates to the National Assembly, and they strenuously opposed any steps toward emancipation.

Between 1789 and 1791, however, the white planters of Saint-Domingue faced increasingly sharp challenges to their authority. Already in October 1789, the royal governor of the colony asserted that "the blacks all share an idea that struck them spontaneously: that the white slaves killed their masters and now free they govern themselves and regain possession of the land." Were the black slaves of Saint-Domingue to follow the example of the "white slaves" of France, he feared, the island could be awash in blood. Political tensions in the colony were heightened by its complex racial composition: alongside 465,000 black slaves, Saint-Domingue was populated by 30,000 whites and 27,000 free blacks and mulattoes. Although the majority of slave owners were white, about one quarter of the slaves in the colony were owned by free blacks. When news reached Saint-Domingue of the outbreak of the French Revolution in 1789, the white planters sent delegates to France to serve as delegates in the new National Assembly. Following the example of the whites, the free mulattoes likewise appointed delegates and demanded that they be represented too. The delegates of the white planters sought to prevent the mulattoes from being seated in the National Assembly, fearing that this would destabilize race relations in the colony. Both the whites and the mulattoes opposed the extension of rights to free blacks or slaves.

Confronted by these conflicting demands, the National Assembly initially denied political rights to free blacks and mulattoes and threatened to prosecute anyone who promoted rebellion among the slaves. Yet, in May 1791, the Assembly softened its resistance, granting political rights to all free blacks whose parents had also been free — a tiny fraction of the overall group. Three months later, in August 1791, a slave revolt erupted in Saint-Domingue; and when the National Assembly responded by revoking the rights of free blacks, they too took up arms against the island's white rulers.

The rebels' chief military strategist was Jean-François Toussaint L'Ouverture (c. 1744–1803), a self-educated slave who had obtained his freedom shortly before the outbreak of the revolt. He was dubbed L'Ouverture ("the opening") for a series of lightning campaigns he led in 1793, when he struck a brief alliance with the Spaniards on the island. Alarmed by the threat of a joint British and Spanish invasion supported by the rebel slaves, two French commissioners in Saint-Domingue decided to abolish slavery in the colony in the fall of 1793. Toussaint L'Ouverture reciprocated by leading a campaign against the British and Spanish occupying forces on the eastern part of the island. On February 4, 1794, the National Convention formally abolished slavery throughout the French colonies.

Unfortunately, the Convention's proclamation did little to resolve the racial conflicts in Saint-Domingue. Many white planters simply ignored the new law or transformed slavery into compulsory labor. The emancipation decree was also opposed by the slave owners among the free blacks and mulattoes. The turmoil on the island continued into the Napoleonic era, culminating in 1804 with the victory of the former slaves and the establishment of an independent republic which was named Haiti, a "higher place."

The principles of the French Revolution had wide-ranging implications for other groups as well. Advocates for France's Jewish population seized on these principles in order to argue against forms of discrimination such as limitations on property ownership and restrictions on the trades that Jews were permitted to practice. In September 1791, the Legislative Assembly passed a decree granting full civic equality to Jews. In other parts of Europe, such as the German states, Jewish emancipation was a gradual process over the course of the nineteenth century, involving a series of edicts abolishing various particular discriminatory practices. But in France, the boldly categorical language of the Declaration of the Rights of Man inspired a more straightforward and dramatic approach. A single sentence in length, the decree announced that Jews were entitled to active citizenship on swearing a "civic oath" and renouncing the "privileges and exceptions" that had previously been granted to members of autonomous Jewish communities, such as separate taxes. This decree by no means meant the end of anti-Semitism in France, as would be shown, for example, by the ugly Dreyfus affair of the 1890s. Nonetheless, it established a legal framework for Jewish equality that remained intact from the revolutionary era onward.

Ironically, the revolutionary demand for universal equality also had the potential to undermine the rights of subordinate groups. The Le Chapelier Law of 1791, for example, banned guilds and trade unions in France, thus rendering it illegal for workers to organize in order to demand better treatment from their employers. The logic behind this law was identical to that of the Jewish emancipation decree: namely, that any "partial association," involving only a single category of citizens, reinforced the corporate character of society, which had to be torn down in order to establish the new order. No competing allegiances must be permitted to interfere with the citizens' loyalty to the greater community of the nation.

A Bourgeois Revolution?

For much of the twentieth century, a consensus persisted among historians that the French Revolution was a natural consequence of changing socioeconomic conditions at the end of the Old Regime. Over the course of the eighteenth century, scholars argued, the French bourgeoisie was becoming steadily more prosperous and self-confident. Political power in the Old Regime, however, remained concentrated in the hands of the moribund monarchy and aristocracy. Thus, scholars interpreted the political events of 1789–1794 as a reflection of the bourgeoisie's effort to correct this imbalance by seizing political power commensurate with its newly established socioeconomic preeminence.

In recent decades, historical research has demonstrated that this social interpretation of the revolution is overly simplistic. Though a gradual expansion of commerce and industry occurred in France over the course of the eighteenth century, the majority of French economic production was agricultural even on the eve of the revolution. Most industry was centered in small shops run by craftsmen, rather than in large factories. Not until 1785 did France receive its first steam engine. Unlike in England, where the Industrial Revolution was well underway by the late eighteenth century, industrialization in France began in earnest only during the first half of the nineteenth century, several decades after the revolution.

To the extent that a new capitalist class existed in prerevolutionary France, it displayed little interest in radical political change. Many French entrepreneurs of this era were nobles, rather than bourgeois; and most prosperous members of the bourgeoisie were far more interested in joining the aristocracy by purchasing a title of nobility than in overthrowing the traditional social order. In the Estates General of 1789, few delegates of the Third Estate were merchants or industrialists; instead, a large proportion of them were lawyers and government functionaries who benefited from the economic order of the Old Regime. During the early stages of the revolution, some of the most vociferous revolutionary leaders — Mirabeau, Talleyrand, Lafayette, Condorcet, among others — were themselves aristocrats.

Not only did French capitalists play a relatively limited role in leading the revolution, but it is also unclear whether they derived much immediate benefit from it. Indeed, some revisionist scholars have argued that the revolutionary events actually retarded France's economic development during the late eighteenth and early nineteenth centuries by reasserting the authority of traditional bourgeois social groups against the new entrepreneurial classes.[9]

---

[9] For example, Alfred Cobban, *The Social Interpretation of the French Revolution*, 2nd ed. (Cambridge, 1999).

Moreover, the revolutionary wars, along with the attendant military requisitions, inflicted heavy damage on certain sectors of the economy. France's Atlantic and Mediterranean ports, such as Marseilles, were devastated by the wars, and textile towns in the north and east, among them Lyons, also suffered heavily. In the words of Simon Schama, "The 'bourgeoisie' which Marxist history long believed to be the essential beneficiaries of the Revolution was, in fact, its principal victim."[10]

Although this revisionist scholarship has convincingly refuted many conventional assumptions about the French Revolution, the events of 1789–1799 may still be considered a "bourgeois revolution" in a more limited sense. Some scholars have argued that, despite the absence of an industrial revolution in eighteenth-century France, a growing consumer culture contributed to the rise of a democratic political sociability. This interpretation focuses on the transformation not of modes of production, but of patterns of consumption among the French middle classes. "By 1789," writes Colin Jones, "the nation . . . was used to making choices. . . . In the revolution, we might hypothesize, citizen-voters were presented with a series of political consumer choices and were called on to evaluate the quality and the utility of the political commodities offered."[11]

Other historians have drawn a distinction between the revolution's causes and its consequences. They observe that the revolution, even though it was not led by the capitalist bourgeoisie, furthered the establishment of an egalitarian society and an industrialized economy in France. According to this view, the revolution was motivated primarily by political rather than by economic concerns: the revolutionaries' main goal was to establish a free and politically united nation, and they attacked the social fabric of the Old Regime as an essential step toward this end. Thus, the creation of a free-market regime may be seen more as a by-product of the revolutionaries' political aims than as the central goal of their program.

This interpretation of the revolution's character is persuasive. It is difficult to assess the revolution's short-term impact on the French economy, primarily because it unleashed twenty-three years of nearly uninterrupted warfare from 1792 to 1815, which had complex and contradictory economic effects. But over the long run, by clearing away the tangled web of privileges and regulations that constituted the Old Regime, the revolution eliminated

---

[10] Simon Schama, *Citizens: A Chronicle of the French Revolution* (New York, 1989), p. 787.

[11] Colin Jones, "The Great Chain of Buying: Medical Advertisement, the Bourgeois Public Sphere, and the Origins of the French Revolution," *American Historical Review* 101 (1996), p. 39.

many of the impediments to France's industrialization. For example, in 1789, over twenty-five hundred internal customs posts existed within France, all of which were abolished by the revolution. Likewise, by selling off the lands of the Catholic Church, the revolutionaries increased the fluidity of land ownership, a useful factor in economic development. The abolition of trade guilds and the ban on labor associations made it easier for capitalists to start new enterprises and to control their workers. Finally, by eliminating titles of nobility, the revolution channeled the social ambitions of the populace into new directions. Rather than seeking to distinguish themselves by acquiring titles, citizens of France focused their energies increasingly on the acquisition of wealth. Thus, the desire for social distinction became a factor contributing to economic growth.

Though the revolution had important effects on France's economic development, its cultural consequences were even more profound. To a great extent, the events of 1789–1799 provided a script that has inspired subsequent revolutionary movements around the world. It set the precedent for mobilizing the populace at large, both for political action and for waging war, to a greater extent than ever before. Perhaps most important of all, it established rhetorical conventions for framing protests and demands for equality that could be utilized and modified by disenfranchised groups of every stripe: women, slaves, industrial workers, religious minorities, and the subjugated peoples of the colonial world. Over the past two centuries, around the world, various constituencies have drawn on this rhetoric in order to demand political and social rights. In this sense, it is hardly an exaggeration to say that all of modern history may be understood partly as an attempt to come to terms with the challenge of the French Revolution.

CHAPTER 2

The Napoleonic Era

WHATEVER VIEW one takes of the character of Napoleon Bonaparte, whatever aspect of his achievement is emphasized, whether one admires him as a superb military leader or condemns him as the forerunner of twentieth-century dictators, one cannot deny that he dominated his age. He barely qualified as a native Frenchman, for he was born in Corsica into a family of impoverished nobles in 1769, just a year after the island had been taken over by France from Genoa. As a youth, he secured a state scholarship and studied in military schools in France. Partly because he considered himself an alien in a foreign country, he was forced to rely on his own resources and worked assiduously. He became a conscientious student of history and geography as well as of military strategy and tactics. In 1785, when he was only sixteen years old, he was appointed a second lieutenant in the artillery, but because of his foreign extraction his chances for promotion in the royal army were not particularly good. The advent of the revolution suddenly opened up new prospects for him. He returned to Corsica and devoted his energies for the next three or four years to the movement for Corsican independence, which had been his dream since childhood. This phase of his career ended when he broke with Pasquale di Paoli (1725–1807), the leading Corsican patriot, and his entire family was banished from the island. Abandoning his earlier plans, he now became an ardent French patriot and Jacobin.

His role in recapturing the port of Toulon from the royalists and the English in the winter of 1793 earned him a promotion from captain to brigadier general and attracted the notice of the influential politician Barras, who later proved of assistance to him. The fall of Robespierre brought Bonaparte a temporary reversal of fortune. He was arrested as a Terrorist, deprived of his commission, and briefly imprisoned. Subsequently, however, Barras had him put in charge of the defense of the Convention when it was threatened by the uprising of October 1795, and his success in this enterprise led to his appointment as commander in chief of the Army of the Interior. At this point he met Josephine de Beauharnais (1763–1814), the attractive widow of an aristocratic general who had died on the guillotine during the Terror. She was six years his senior, had two children, and was without a fortune, but the young Napoleon fell violently in love with her and married her on March 9, 1796.

Two days before his marriage he was appointed to command the army in Italy, where he first demonstrated his qualities as a military genius; brilliant in offensive warfare, he put emphasis on great speed and mobility and on surprise attacks to disconcert the enemy. He emerged from the Italian campaign a national hero. The failure of the Egyptian expedition of 1798–1799 did not dim his reputation, partly because the full story of its failure was not known until later.

What manner of man was Napoleon at the time of his accession to power in 1799? From the mountains of conflicting testimony written by his contemporaries, almost invariably biased, it is nearly impossible to arrive at a composite picture. Count André François Miot de Melito (1762–1841), a French councillor of state, who met Napoleon for the first time during his Italian campaign in 1796, recorded his impressions in his memoirs:

I was quite astonished at his appearance. Nothing could be more unlike the idea my imagination had formed of him. . . . I saw a man below the middle height and of an extremely spare figure. His powdered hair, oddly cut and falling squarely below the ears, reached down to his shoulders. He was dressed in a straight coat, buttoned up to the chin, and edged with very narrow gold embroidery, and he wore a tricolored feather in his hat. At first sight he did not strike me as handsome; but his strongly-marked features, his quick and piercing eyes, his brusque and animated gestures revealed an ardent spirit, while his wide and thoughtful brow was that of a profound thinker. He made me sit near him and we talked of Italy. He spoke in short sentences and, at that time of his life, very incorrectly.

Most of his contemporaries agreed that he had a remarkable intelligence and an unusual capacity for sustained effort and intense concentration. The following comment by Jean Chaptal (1750–1832), his minister of the interior, who knew him perhaps as well as anyone, discusses his performance as First Consul immediately after the coup d'état of 18 Brumaire (November 9, 1799):

We met in the First Consul's rooms almost every evening, and deliberated from 10 till 4 or 5 A.M. It was in these conferences that I came to know the great man to whom we had just entrusted the reins of government. Though still young,

Bonaparte, the Consul (1798). A famous unfinished portrait of Napoleon in his prime by David.

and with little experience of administrative detail, he brought to our discussions an astonishing clarity, exactness, power of argument, and width view. An untiring worker, and full of resource, he collected and co-ordinated facts and opinions relating to every part of a huge system of administration with unrivalled sagacity. ... Though he worked as much as twenty hours out the twenty-four, he never showed signs of mental or physical fatigue.[1]

He manifested some of these same qualities as a military commander, his decisions being based on careful planning and detailed knowledge rather than intuition. What seemed to be sudden flashes of insight were actually the fruit of painstaking rational analysis. "Every operation must be done according to a system," he said, "because chance cannot bring about success."[2] This reliance on reason led many to view Napoleon as a good son of the Enlightenment, but another side of his character made him one of the great heroes of the romantic era. Although he adhered to no established religion, he still felt that his life was guided by what be called his "star," and he referred frequently to the workings of "destiny." And although he might

---

[1] Quoted in James M. Thompson, *Napoleon Bonaparte: His Rise and Fall* (Oxford, 1952), p. 150.
[2] Quoted in Georges Lefebvre, *Napoléon*, 4th ed. (Paris, 1953), p. 67.

employ careful calculation to achieve specific goals, his ultimate aims seem to have been limitless and undefined. He admired Alexander the Great, Caesar, and Charlemagne not so much for their specific achievements as for their visions of universal empire, which fired his own imagination and inspired his actions. Georges Lefebvre, suggesting the romantic dimension in Napoleon's personality, says, "[The realist] determines his goal, taking into account the possible, and if his imagination and the desire for glory drive him on, he knows where to stop."[3] Napoleon quite clearly was not a realist in this sense, for he recognized no limits to his ambition. This, in the long run, proved his undoing.

One of the questions most often raised in discussions of Napoleon's domestic policies is whether his regime carried on and—as he said—"crowned" the revolution, or whether it constituted a reversal or denial of the revolution. The answer depends in part, of course, on our definition of the revolution: on whether we are thinking primarily of the accomplishments of the National Assembly and the Legislative Assembly during the moderate phase between 1789 and 1792, or viewing it as the whole succession of regimes between 1789 and 1799, including the Terrorist government and the Directory. Apologists for the view that Napoleon was a true "son of the Revolution" argue that the constructive achievements of the initial period were cut short or interrupted during the rule of the Convention and the Directory, and that with his accession to power as First Consul, Bonaparte undertook to complete the work of the revolution. Opponents of this view grant that many measures completed during the Consulate and the empire stem from reforms initiated under the constitutional monarchy, but they argue that the character of Napoleon's political institutions, the way in which he dealt with the opposition, the strict control of opinion during his regime, and indeed the entire spirit of his administration were in direct contrast with the ideals of 1789. Some contend further that Bonaparte really had far more in common with the enlightened despots of the eighteenth century than with the revolutionaries. According to this view, he displayed the same passion for rationalization and systematization that characterized Frederick the Great and Joseph II of Austria, and whatever reforms he instituted were enacted on his initiative within the framework of a despotic government that permitted no criticism. He was, it is argued, the ruler who carried the principles of enlightened despotism to their logical extreme. In the sections that follow, we shall weigh the evidence in support of these opposing interpretations.

---

[3] Ibid., p. 68.

THE CONSULATE, 1799–1804

The government that emerged from the coup d'état of 18 Brumaire was merely a provisional regime. It was up to the three victors who had been named "consuls" — Bonaparte, Sieyès, and Ducos — to provide France with a new constitution and a stable government. After a decade of revolution, civil disorders, and foreign wars, most Frenchmen were willing to sacrifice what appeared to them the illusory benefits of liberty for a regime that could ensure internal tranquility and peace. On the day following the coup d'état, the consuls swore to end the civil conflict that had continued sporadically in the west, stabilize finances, codify the laws, and terminate the foreign war with an honorable peace. Most of the energies of the First Consul and his government during the next five years were devoted to the fulfillment of these promises.

The Constitution of the Year VIII (1799), drafted by Sieyès with Bonaparte's collaboration, provided a set of institutions that appeared to preserve republican forms but at the same time gave considerably increased powers to the executive. Although the constitution stipulated that the three consuls who held the executive power were to be elected to ten-year terms by the Senate, it specifically designated as the first incumbents of these offices Bonaparte and the two men he had chosen as his colleagues — Jean Jacques Régis de Cambacérès (1753–1824) and Charles François Lebrun (1739–1824). Instead of two chambers, the national legislature now had three — the Senate, the Tribunate, and the Legislative Body. But their activities were circumscribed and the ways in which their members were chosen made them relatively ineffective. The Senate consisted of eighty men named for life. Initially, a majority of them were to be appointed by the outgoing second and third consuls, who became senators themselves. This group, in turn, was to select the remaining senators from lists presented to them by the Legislative Body, the Tribunate, and the First Consul. What in fact happened was that both the original list of senators and the remainder were selected, with Bonaparte's approval, by Sieyès, one of the outgoing consuls. He, too, named the members of the first Legislative Body and Tribunate.

The Senate had no direct legislative powers unless the constitutionality of a measure was at issue, but it had the power to name the members of the other two chambers from a list of "notables." The notables were chosen through universal suffrage — the only feature of the constitution that was ostensibly democratic — but the privilege of voting was now even less meaningful than it had been under the Constitution of 1791 or the Directory. The voters could elect only a group of notables in their own commune, who then elected one tenth of their number to serve as notables of the department. These, in turn, elected one tenth of their number to become the notables of France, from whom the Senate chose the members of the Tribunate and the Legislative Body. The Tribunate, consisting of a hundred men, had the power to discuss measures submitted to it by the First Consul or his advisers, but did not have the power to vote on them. The Legislative Body, three hundred men, had the power to accept or reject measures, but could not discuss them. Since membership in all three bodies was appointive rather than elective, the consuls had little to fear in the way of opposition.

Despite this elaborate set of legislative institutions, the actual work of drafting laws fell to the Council of State, a group of experts appointed by the First Consul and directly dependent on him.

If there were objections to the authoritarian character of this constitution, they were hardly expressed, for the popular vote registered 3,011,007 in favor and only 1,562 opposed. There is little question that the regime was popular with a great majority of Frenchmen. The new First Consul considered the plebiscite an overwhelming vote of confidence, since his name had appeared in the constitution.

NAPOLEON'S ADMINISTRATION

Napoleon revised his initial constitution in 1802, when he had himself proclaimed consul for life, and in 1804, when he became emperor. In each case he sought approval for the increase of his powers through plebiscites which returned him overwhelming majorities. As First Consul, and later as emperor, he carried out an impressive series of administrative, financial, educational, and legal reforms.

Those who view Napoleon as a son of the revolution point out that he completed the administrative system whose main lines had been laid down by the National Assembly. It is true that he retained the basic geographical divisions established in 1789, but in many other respects, his contributions in this sphere marked a reversal of the basic principles of administration that had guided the revolutionaries. For example, in place of the elected officials and local self-government of the years 1789 to 1792, he substituted the centrally appointed bureaucrats who have been at the heart of France's administrative system ever since — prefects for the departments, subprefects for the districts, and mayors for the communes. Though local councils still functioned to assist the appointed officials, they too were named from Paris rather than elected. The French have apparently come to prefer such a centralized bureaucracy to the kind of federal structure found in the United States and to the decentralized institutions characteristic of Britain, but such a preference is not in harmony with the intentions of the pioneers of the revolution.

The same emphasis on centralization can be seen in Napoleon's approach to financial problems. The Directory had attempted to restore fiscal stability to France by withdrawing the inflated paper currency that had plagued preceding revolutionary governments and by repudiating two thirds of the national debt. Despite these measures no way had been found to augment revenues, and the credit of the government had been seriously impaired. Napoleon realized that an effective method of assessing and collecting taxes was essential. Therefore, instead of leaving with municipal officials the power to draw up the tax rolls and collect taxes levied by the central government, he turned this responsibility over to representatives of the central government—a general director at Paris, deputy directors for each department, and inspectors and assessors in each commune. In this way the entire machinery of taxation was tightened up, receipts were increased, and the government could predict its expected revenues more precisely. Although the French have proved remarkably ingenious in devising means of evading taxes, the basic system established by Napoleon has persisted to this day.

Another means by which Napoleon succeeded in raising revenues to meet his enormous expenditures was through the revival of indirect taxes on consumer articles such as liquors, tobacco, and salt. In addition, he could draw on what was termed the *domaine extraordinaire*, a fund supplied by contributions, subsidies, and confiscations from conquered countries. In 1800 Napoleon decreed the creation of the Bank of France, which was intended to ease the problem of government borrowing, stabilize the currency, and facilitate the payment of annuities. In 1803 it was given the exclusive right to issue bank notes in Paris; not until 1848 could it do this for the entire country. Technically a private institution, it acquired a special status because its shareholders included the First Consul, members of his family, and leading state officials.

In economic matters Napoleon was essentially a mercantilist—that is, he wanted to strengthen France economically and was prepared to do this through regulation of the economy and direct state intervention wherever it appeared necessary. The needs of war and the supplying of his armies were, of course, of primary importance to him, but he was also preoccupied with ensuring a regular food supply, particularly to Paris, where shortages or high prices might result in discontent or disorders. The suppliers of food, the peasants, generally flourished under the Consulate and the empire, especially those who were called on to produce substitutes (such as sugar beets) for foodstuffs that could no longer be imported from overseas.

Napoleon vigorously supported the expansion of French industry, but his measures toward this end were not an unqualified success. Under the leadership of Jean Chaptal, his minister of the interior, a society for the encouragement of national industry was established and efforts were made to enlist the support of French scientists and engineers in developing new manufacturing techniques. The results were particularly striking in the textile industry, where the copying or adaptation of English machines led to dramatic progress in the manufacture of cotton. The government claimed, probably with some exaggeration, that output of French cotton mills quadrupled in the four-year period from 1806 to 1810.

The development of the mining and metallurgical industries was less impressive. Despite the need for armaments, much of France's iron needs continued to be supplied by small, inefficient hand foundries that produced low-grade work. Many manufacturers prospered under the Napoleonic regime, but they complained of the regulation and petty restrictions on their operations. Perhaps the group least satisfied with Napoleon's economic policies were merchants, who saw their overseas trade dwindle as France succumbed to British control of the seas. Attempts were made to find new sources of supply and new markets on the Continent, but the volume of foreign trade never achieved the total under Napoleonic rule that it had attained under the Old Regime.

Napoleon is often given credit for continuing and elaborating on the system of public education inaugurated during the revolution. The principle of free, elementary education for all children had been first proclaimed in the Constitution of 1791 and was reaffirmed by the Convention, but little progress was made during the revolutionary years in the establishment of primary schools. Nor was the Napoleonic government much more successful in expanding the system of primary public education. It has been estimated that only one out of every eight children of school age could be accommodated in primary schools existing in 1813. At the secondary level the Convention provided for the establishment of state-supported "central schools," one for each department and five to be located in Paris. Although some difficulties were encountered in getting these into operation, the quality of the teaching in the central schools was high and they were flourishing during the early years of the Consulate. However, in 1802 Napoleon abolished the central schools and substituted for them *lycées* under more direct government supervision. He also permitted the existence of a limited number of private secondary schools. The lycées were intended quite frankly as "nurseries of patriotism." The Napoleonic regime prescribed the curriculum and the teaching schedules, appointed the teachers, and set up a system of inspectors to enforce the regulations. Discipline in the schools was on military lines: students wore uniforms, classes began and ended with drum rolls, and students received military instruction from retired officers. In 1808, Napoleon further centralized education by establishing the *Université* — not a university in the usual sense of the term, but a single system incorporating the whole range of public schools from the elementary level up through institutions of higher learning. Again, the purpose was to ensure greater control over education and promote loyalty to the regime. Private and church schools continued to exist under limited supervision by the state even after 1808, but the Université embodied the principle recognized during the revolution that education, controlled and supported by the state, should be available to all male citizens. Though girls were eligible to attend primary schools, they were denied admission to the lycées and the Université. Napoleon argued that the best approach was for girls to be educated at home by their mothers in sewing and other "female occupations."

In Napoleon's own opinion, and in the opinion of subsequent generations, one of the most significant achievements of his administration was the compilation of a series of five law codes, begun when he was First Consul, although not entirely completed until after the establishment of the empire. Of these, the Civil Code — referred to simply as the Code Napoléon — was the most important. The revolution had prepared the way for the First Consul by sweeping away most of the statutes and legal privileges of the Old Regime, but the various revolutionary assemblies had made relatively little progress in the drafting of new legal codes. With his passion for order and speed, in August 1800 Napoleon appointed a committee of several of France's most prominent lawyers to draft a Civil Code, and he made sure that it was completed within six months. Keenly interested in the enterprise, the First Consul presided over about half the sessions of the Council of State in which provisions of the draft were discussed in detail. The promulgation of the code was delayed until early in 1804, however, because of opposition to certain articles by the Tribunate and the Legislative Body — one of the few instances in which these chambers delayed proposed legislation.

The finished product has been termed a compromise between some of the most important ideals of the revolution and the needs of the authoritarian Napoleonic regime. One of the fundamental principles of the revolution was retained: the equality of all (male) citizens before the law. The code provided a uniform system of law for the entire country, guaranteed religious liberty and the supremacy of the secular state, and asserted the right of the individual to choose his own profession. In some of its other provisions the code showed the influence of Napoleon's authoritarian outlook. For example, the sections relating to family life reinforced the authority of the father over his children and mandated the subordination of the wife, whose property was legally placed at the disposal of her husband. Revolutionary legislation had required the equal division of property among heirs, but the code permitted greater freedom to the head of the family in disposing of his estate.

The right of divorce by mutual consent was recognized but was restricted in the interests of family unity. In practice, divorce was far more difficult to obtain for women than for men. Whereas a husband could divorce his wife for a single incident of adultery, a wife could not do so unless her husband were to have a mistress live in their home. Women had no standing to bring or defend lawsuits; instead they had the same legal status as minors.

Some of the later codes — for example, the Code of Civil Procedure promulgated in 1806 — bore a close resemblance to laws under the Old Regime. Both the Code of Criminal Procedure and the Penal Code, begun under the Consulate but not completed until 1810, reflected the increasing despotism of the Napoleonic regime in that they prescribed strict penalties for political offenses as well as for crimes against persons and property. Whereas revolutionary legislation had changed criminal procedure so that the defendant was presumed innocent until proved guilty, the code reversed this change, restoring the presumption of the defendant's guilt. A Commercial Code, drawn up in 1807, was much less complete than the other codes and merely retained many of the ordinances of the monarchy.

Criticisms have been leveled against the Napoleonic codes, but as a whole they were a remarkable achievement. For brevity and clarity of expression the Civil Code was unmatched; any citizen could look up any point with a minimum of difficulty in a volume so small that it fitted into his pocket. Although the lawmakers assumed that their codes conformed to nature and were therefore universally applicable — just as the philosophes and the revolutionaries had supposed that the principles they set forth were "natural laws" — the codes were in fact strongly national in their origin. They drew on earlier distillations of Roman law that had prevailed in the south of France and on the Teutonic customary law common to the northern provinces. These were combined and blended with the laws promulgated during the revolution, which had so drastically undermined the hierarchical structure of French society and altered the status of the individual. The resulting amalgam was a set of legal codes adapted to the bourgeois-oriented society that came into being with the revolution, a society which stressed the equality of all citizens before the law but at the same time preserved the principle of private property. This adaptation explains, in part, why the French codes were borrowed or imitated so widely during the nineteenth century. They were, of course, applied directly by the French to many of their conquered territories, including the Austrian Netherlands, Holland, Switzerland, Luxembourg, and a number of the German states. But the influence of the codes spread farther, to the New World where it affected the laws of Canada, Louisiana, and parts of Central and South America, and even as far as Japan.

The Suppression of Dissent

Critics of Napoleon generally acknowledge his achievements with respect to the administrative system, education, and law, but they emphasize aspects of the Napoleonic regime that seemed directly to reverse the intentions of the original revolutionaries. To begin with, the political system established in 1799—the Consulate—constituted a denial of the doctrine of popular sovereignty which was at the heart of the Declaration of the Rights of Man and the Citizen.

Although French citizens were given the right to vote, their vote was essentially meaningless since members of the Napoleonic assemblies were appointed rather than elected. Moreover, the legislative bodies themselves, restricted in their functions by Napoleon's first constitution, were progressively shorn of their limited powers in the ensuing years. Bonaparte could argue that his mandate from the people came in the form of periodic plebiscites, but these plebiscites were inevitably invoked to ratify decisions already made. In contrast, the initial constitution of the revolution (the Constitution of 1791), though it too fell short of the ideal of popular sovereignty because of its restrictions on the franchise, did provide for an assembly that had genuine legislative powers and truly shared sovereignty with the king. Napoleonic parliamentary institutions were from the beginning little more than window dressing for what was essentially a dictatorship.

The Napoleonic regime was marked, too, by drastic curbs on freedom of expression. Article 11 of the Declaration of the Rights of Man and the Citizen had proclaimed: "Free communication of ideas and opinions is one of the most precious rights of man. Consequently, every citizen may speak, write, and print freely, subject to responsibility for the abuse of such liberty in the cases determined by law." No principle was violated more consistently by the Bonapartist government. A few months after Napoleon came to power the number of Paris newspapers was reduced from seventy-three to thirteen. Eventually, the remaining papers in Paris and the provinces became little more than government organs printing official news dispatches and suppressing any information considered detrimental to the regime. The government was also on guard against literary works that might prove politically harmful. Particular attention was paid to the theater, which was placed under the general supervision of agents who subjected all plays, old and new, to rigorous censorship.

In order to enforce such regulations, a large and elaborately organized police force was necessary. Supervision of the police was entrusted to the notorious Joseph Fouché, who had been dismissed from his post as a deputy on mission under the Terror because of his excessive brutality. Fouché created what the Empress Josephine termed "a vile system of espionage" for the surveillance of the personal lives of thousands of individuals suspected of harboring subversive sentiments. The constitutional prohibition of the arbitrary detention of individuals was—in practice—consistently violated. Some political opponents of the regime were kept under close watch in assigned residences; others were detained in insane asylums. After 1810 they were held in "state prisons," where the number of political prisoners rose by 1814 to an estimated twenty-five hundred. The resulting atmosphere—reminiscent of Paris under the Terror—was certainly at odds with the principles of individual liberty and freedom of speech proclaimed in 1789.

Because he was first and foremost a soldier, Napoleon reserved a special place in French society for the military. Indeed, his top-ranking officers were showered with favors and came to form an elite that staffed his court and enjoyed special privileges in the empire. Appointment as a marshal of France was the highest honor Napoleon could confer, and it was granted to relatively few. Some were given this title as a reward for personal loyalty or to pacify a particular army clique, but the most outstanding marshals were brilliant generals such as Louis Nicolas Davout (1770–1823), a superb tactician who never lost a battle; André Masséna (1758–1817), who distinguished himself in a number of battles, and particularly at Wagram (1809); and Michel Ney (1769–1815), termed by Napoleon "the bravest of the brave" for his exploits as a general in numerous campaigns of the revolutionary and Napoleonic eras. Although many marshals had begun their lives as sons of peasants or members of the petty bourgeoisie, they were created dukes or princes, with titles recalling their victories or the provinces they had conquered. Holders of such titles were also rewarded with generous pensions, large bequests, and grants of "fiefs" in Germany or Italy. Some even became kings. Thus Joachim Murat (c. 1757–1815), husband of Napoleon's sister Carolina and one of Napoleon's most flamboyant marshals, was named king of Naples in 1808. Napoleon's ideal of the "career open to talent" was strikingly realized in the lives of many of his marshals.

Peace with the Church: The Concordat

After his accession to power, Bonaparte made no immediate public statement about the status of the Roman Catholic Church in France. But he was convinced that the religious issue had to be settled, if possible by a concordat with the pope. The French clergy remained divided into two groups: the constitutional clergy, who had taken an oath to the revolutionary government, and the legitimate—or refractory—clergy, who were either in hiding or in exile, but who retained the sympathy of many French Catholics. Napoleon realized that to win the support of the refractory clergy he would need the aid of the pope. He was further led to seek a settlement with the

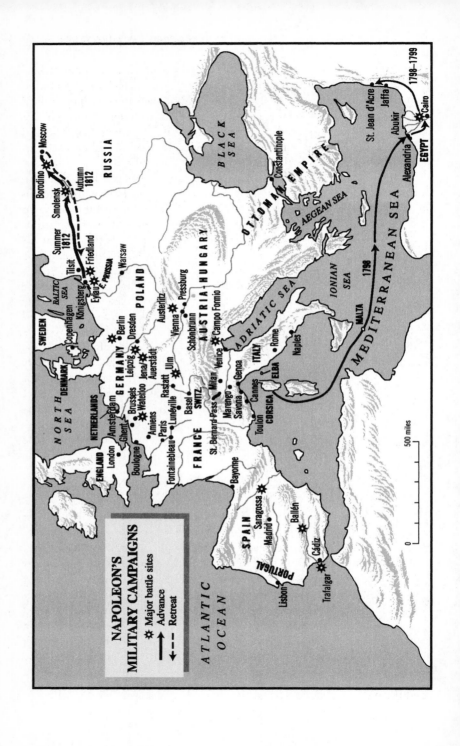

NAPOLEON'S
MILITARY CAMPAIGNS

✵ Major battle sites
→ Advance
- - → Retreat

church by concern for those Frenchmen who had acquired nationalized church lands during the revolution and were anxious to have the church formally renounce its title to these lands. Although Napoleon had no firm religious convictions—he was the first to admit his own opportunism in this respect—he was convinced that France was fundamentally Catholic and that the support of the authority of a revealed religion would be useful in securing the submission of French citizens to law and order.

In 1800, after a successful military campaign in northern Italy had reinforced Napoleon's domination there, he opened negotiations with representatives of Pius VII, pope between 1800 and 1823. The threat of military force and the possibility of a further reduction of the papal territories loomed in the background of the discussions. Nevertheless, the pope's diplomats engaged in delaying tactics and the Concordat underwent some twenty-one drafts before it was acceptable to both Rome and the French state. Though the Concordat of 1801 was something of a compromise, the Napoleonic state was the principal gainer. Catholicism was recognized not as the state religion, but as the religion of "the great majority of French citizens" and of the three consuls of the republic. The semiprivileged status given the Catholic faith sufficed to reconcile the papacy and the refractory clergy. Priests were permitted the free exercise of Catholic worship "in conformity with the police regulations which the government shall deem necessary for the public tranquility." The pope agreed to recognize as valid the titles of all those who had bought church lands confiscated by the revolutionary government. Since the relinquishment of these lands, together with the abolition of the tithe, left the church with much reduced revenues, the state agreed, as it had under the Civil Constitution of the Clergy, to pay the salaries of bishops and priests, who were required, before assuming their functions, to take an oath of fidelity to the government. French bishops and archbishops were to be nominated by the government and canonically instituted by the pope; they, in turn, had the right to name members of the lower clergy.

In the Concordat, Napoleon achieved his principal goals. The agreement ended the division within the French church, reconciled the refractory clergy to the republic, and gave the necessary security to owners of former church lands. The principal gain for the church, in addition to state salaries for the clergy, was the assurance that the Catholic religion could be practiced freely once again in France. Yet the reservation to this right—the agreement concerning police regulation—left an opening by which the government could (and did) control the church in France. One other concession to the church was French recognition of the Papal States; however, the pope did not regain the territories of Ferrara, Bologna, and the Romagna, which had been incorporated into the Cisalpine Republic in 1797. The Concordat was not universally popular in France, but it had the enthusiastic support of well over half the nation, and the reconciliation of France and the papacy was celebrated on Easter Sunday in 1802 by a Te Deum at Notre Dame in Paris.

As a corollary to the settlement with the Catholic Church, Napoleon established a working arrangement with the Protestant churches in France, which were organized into consistories (one for every six thousand of the faithful); like the Catholic clergy, Protestant ministers received salaries from the state. Toward Jews, of whom there had been an estimated forty thousand in France in 1789, Napoleon pursued a somewhat more complex policy because he regarded them more as a people than as a religious group and hoped ultimately for their assimilation. By decrees passed between 1806 and 1808 they, too, were grouped into local consistories that were supervised by a Central Consistory in Paris, headed by the emperor. During the revolution, Jews had attained civil status and the right to enter all offices and types of business, but many had continued to serve as livestock traders and money-lenders. Because of complaints against high interest rates charged by Jews in certain parts of France, the Napoleonic government subjected them in all but a few regions to special legislation relating to loans as well as to certain other restrictions. Jews resented these decrees as discriminatory, but the purpose of the emperor seems to have been, in part, to reduce hostility toward the Jews and thereby to promote their assimilation into the community.

INTERNATIONAL DEVELOPMENTS

After his accession to power as First Consul, Napoleon made offers of peace to Austria and Great Britain, the two remaining members of the Second Coalition. When these offers were spurned he decided on a major campaign against Austria, in which he won a decisive string of victories that resulted in favorable peace treaties for France with both Austria and Britain.

The End of the Second Coalition:
Peace with Austria and Britain

Napoleon's campaign of 1800 against Austria added to the legend of his military heroism. With his armies striking again through both Germany and Italy, Napoleon took personal command of a French force of forty thousand in a dramatic march across Great St. Bernard Pass into Italy. There he fell on the Austrian flank and took the city of Milan. He encountered the main body of the Austrian army in the battle of Marengo (June 1800), where only the timely arrival of a relief force under General Louis Desaix (1768–1800) enabled him to turn what appeared to be a catastrophe for France into

Napoleon crossing the Great Saint Bernard Pass (1800–1801). This romantic painting by David associates Napoleon with the ancient Carthaginian general Hannibal, whose name is inscribed in stone along with Napoleon's at the bottom left. The reality was more prosaic: Napoleon crossed the pass riding on a mule.

victory. When Napoleon followed up his defeat of the Austrian armies in Italy by pressing the invasion of Austria through Germany, the Austrian emperor was ready to sue for peace. The treaty concluded at Lunéville in February 1801 reaffirmed the cessions Austria had made in the Treaty of Campoformio and forced Austria to abandon its remaining possessions in the Italian peninsula (with the exception of Venice and the surrounding region) and to recognize the independence of the Batavian (Dutch), Helvetic, and Ligurian republics. Gone was the earlier promise of French support for Austria's claims to Bavarian territory, and France now asserted the exclusive right to settle the question of indemnification of the German princes who had lost territories along the left bank of the Rhine.

Once again Britain was the sole member of the coalition to hold out. Although the British had reconquered the island of Malta from Napoleon, had expelled the French from Egypt, and had taken a number of former Dutch and Spanish colonies, their sentiment for peace was strong, for British merchants hoped to regain access to continental markets. Napoleon, too, was anxious to secure an honorable peace that would leave him free to consolidate his position in France and in Europe. In the ensuing negotiations, the British were at a disadvantage because Pitt had resigned as prime minister in the spring of 1801. His successor, Henry Addington (1757–1844), was a much inferior statesman whose representatives were no match for the

French. The Treaty of Amiens (March 1802) was greeted with dismay in Great Britain; it seemed that the British had conceded everything and the French nothing. Among the more important provisions were the following: Great Britain returned to France or to its allies—i.e., to Spain and the Batavian Republic (Holland)—all the colonial territories it had won since the beginning of the war with the exception of Trinidad (taken from Spain) and Ceylon (ceded by the Batavian Republic).

The French agreed to evacuate the kingdom of Naples and the Papal States and recognized the return of the island of Malta, captured by Napoleon and later retaken by the British, to the Order of the Knights of Malta. France also recognized the independence of the Ionian Islands. These seven islands lying in the Ionian Sea off the western coast of Greece had been occupied by the French in 1797. But the Russian fleet seized them in 1799 and established them as the Septinsular ("seven islands") Republic, under Turkish protection and Russian guarantee. The Russians, in fact, occupied them until 1807. From the British point of view, the treaty's omissions were more significant than its provisions. No mention was made of France's many conquests on the Continent. France was left in control of Holland, Belgium, the left bank of the Rhine, Switzerland, and most of the Italian peninsula. The independence of the various republics which had been set up under French authority was not guaranteed; they were clearly nothing more than satellites of the French state. Most important, France was left a free hand in reshaping Germany. Nor did British negotiators secure any agreement from the French concerning the restoration of commerce with the Continent, although most continental ports were now in French hands. British merchants who had looked forward to the revival of trade with the Continent were among the treaty's bitterest critics.

In attempting to understand why the British government accepted the terms of the Treaty of Amiens, we must recall both Britain's overwhelming desire for peace after nine years of war and the relative weakness of the new ministry. Furthermore, the treaty did leave intact Britain's strongest weapon, its navy. Britain's mastery of the seas was unaffected; in fact, the war had heightened its superiority in this respect. Whereas the French had lost close to half of their fleet, the British had almost doubled the strength of their navy. Therefore, they were now in a position to renew hostilities against the French whenever it seemed desirable to do so. Meanwhile, they could wait to see whether Napoleon would be satisfied with his conquests or whether he was ambitious for further expansion.

The Reorganization of Germany, 1803

Napoleon profited from the brief interlude of peace afforded by the Treaty of Amiens to reshape drastically the map of Germany. His power to do this stemmed from the Treaty of Basel (concluded by France with Prussia in 1795) and from France's treaties with Austria—Campoformio in 1797 and Lunéville in 1801. Through these treaties France had acquired all the German territories lying along the left bank of the Rhine, an important step in the fulfillment of its long-standing goal of expanding to its "natural frontiers." As far as Germany was concerned, the central problem created by these treaties was how to compensate or indemnify those princes who had lost territories to France. The treaties themselves had suggested a solution by proposing the secularization of at least some of the old ecclesiastical principalities of Germany—which had been ruled for centuries by archbishops or bishops with temporal as well as spiritual powers—and their annexation to states which had been promised compensation.

Prussia and many of the lesser states favored the proposed secularization. Even Austria, despite ancient ties with the Roman Catholic Church, cast covetous eyes on the archbishopric of Salzburg and some of the smaller ecclesiastical territories. An imperial congress summoned in 1797 at Rastatt in accordance with the provisions of the Treaty of Campoformio failed to produce agreement among the German states on the problem of indemnification. To end the deadlock, the imperial Diet agreed to turn the problem over to an imperial deputation (*Reichsdeputation*) consisting of eight members. Before this body could meet, however, Napoleon proceeded to make his own arrangements for Germany. Talleyrand, his foreign minister, having accepted bribes and gifts from German rulers who hoped to acquire this or that piece of territory, drew up the terms of the settlement. After concluding separate treaties with Prussia and some of the states of secondary rank, Napoleon imposed the entire arrangement on the imperial deputation and eventually on the Austrian emperor.

The final terms were embodied in a document known as the Imperial Recess of 1803. In accordance with its provisions, 112 states of the Holy Roman Empire went out of existence, their territories being incorporated into neighboring states. Of the ecclesiastical states, all but one, Mainz, were destroyed—and even the archbishop of Mainz lost some of his territory. Of approximately fifty free cities, only six remained: Frankfurt, Augsburg, and Nuremberg, and the three Hanseatic cities—Lübeck, Hamburg, and Bremen. The principal beneficiaries of the settlement in Germany were Prussia and Bavaria, each of which gained about five times as much territory as it had lost on the left bank of the Rhine, and the southwestern German states of Baden and Württemberg. Although Austria gained territory in the south to compensate for the loss of imperial possessions in the west, the overall settlement further undermined the Austrian position with respect to Germany by eliminating the ecclesiastical states that had traditionally supported the Habsburgs and by strengthening Prussia and some of the secondary states. Certainly part of Napoleon's intention in intervening in Germany had been to decrease both Austrian and Prussian influence by attracting to France's orbit a group of secondary states indebted to France for territories they had acquired and willing to accept French leadership in the hope of further favors. In this he was successful, since Bavaria, Baden, and Württemberg tended to look to France for leadership during the following decade.

Haitian Independence

During the lull in military activity in Europe in 1802–1803, Napoleon also initiated a campaign to establish French dominance in the New World. His intention was to consolidate French control over the rich sugar-producing colony of Saint-Domingue and to expand French influence from there into North and South America. The fierce resistance of the colony's former slaves and free people of color, however, inflicted a crushing defeat on the French expeditionary forces, compelling Napoleon to abandon his ambitions for a new American empire.

The principal obstacle to his designs was the former slave Toussaint L'Ouverture, who had established his control over the island in the 1790s. Named commander in chief of the island by the French Convention in 1797, Toussaint remained formally bound to France, but he had made significant moves toward establishing Haiti's independence. In 1798 he had expelled all French officials from the island and persuaded the British to withdraw their forces as well. He had also reorganized the plantation economy to rely on free workers, rather than slaves. Initially Napoleon supported Toussaint, dubbing him a "black Washington" who had saved "for France a great and important colony." Ultimately, however, Napoleon resolved to reestablish French supremacy over the island. In January 1802, a military force led by General Charles Leclerc landed in Haiti; four months later, in May, Napoleon issued a decree restoring slavery throughout France's Caribbean colonies.

Five months of heavy battlefield losses persuaded Toussaint to seek a settlement with the French. When he appeared for the peace negotiations, however, the French seized him and transported him back to France, where he died in the dungeon of Fort-de-Joux, in the French Jura. Toussaint's betrayal, along with the news of the restoration of slavery, motivated the former slaves to take up arms again. An epidemic of yellow fever among the French soldiers completed the decimation of the military force. By October 1802, twenty-four thousand of the thirty-four thousand French soldiers dispatched to Haiti had died; eight thousand were hospitalized; and only two thousand remained healthy. Faced with this catastrophe, Napoleon abandoned his plans for a western colonial empire. "Damn sugar, damn coffee, damn colonies!" he declared on hearing the news of General Leclerc's death from fever. Napoleon cut his losses by withdrawing from Haiti and selling the Louisiana Territory to the United States in 1803. On January 1, 1804, the Haitian general Jean-Jacques Dessalines proclaimed himself ruler of the newly independent nation.

Unfortunately, the independence of Haiti was achieved at great cost to the people of the new nation. In October 1804, Dessalines had himself crowned emperor. A few months later, he initiated a campaign of revenge against the white French planters who remained on the island. His soldiers laid siege to the town of Santo Domingo for twenty-two days, until a French squadron arrived in the harbor. Fearing a renewed occupation of the island, Dessalines ordered a massacre of all of the French whites on the island — though he spared all British and American whites, as well as priests and skilled workmen. Dessalines was not the first to practice racial warfare in Haiti: General Leclerc had ordered the methodical drowning of more than a thousand blacks in Le Cap harbor shortly after his arrival on the island. Nonetheless, the massacre of the white planters resulted in long-lasting economic and political isolation for Haiti, impoverishing the island's inhabitants for generations to come.

THE EMPIRE, 1804–1814

In 1802 the French had reason to be grateful to Napoleon, for in less than three years he had brought about the apparent pacification not only of his own country but of Europe as well. The ratification of the Treaty of Amiens, concluding peace with France's last remaining enemy, was followed in a few days by the celebration of the Concordat with the papacy. Many of the former opponents of the regime had become reconciled to it as success followed success during the first years of the Consulate. Others — principally die-hard Jacobins and republicans who accused Bonaparte of having betrayed the revolution — had been exiled or imprisoned. Toward monarchists and émigré nobles Napoleon's policy was much more lenient. After the victory of Marengo in 1800, Napoleon removed the names of some fifty thousand from the list of émigrés drawn up during the revolution. (This list included some nobles who had not actually left the country but were nevertheless classified as émigrés.) In the spring of 1802, after the conclusion of peace, he extended full amnesty to another fifty thousand on condition that they return to the country by September 1802 and take an oath of loyalty to the constitution. To those whose estates had been seized but not sold he promised full restoration of their property. Only a thousand intransigent nobles were excluded from this amnesty. These measures served to eliminate practically all organized opposition within the country. Bonaparte was now ready to take the first steps toward the establishment of the empire.

The Proclamation of the Empire, 1804

As early as 1800 Napoleon's brother Lucien had tried to determine the popular reaction to the establishment of hereditary rule for the Bonapartes, and had concluded that such a move would be premature. In 1802 circumstances seemed more auspicious, and the Tribunate was prompted to declare that the nation owed "a signal pledge of gratitude" to the First Consul for his work of pacification. The Senate responded to the suggestion, but instead of offering to retain Napoleon as First Consul for life, merely proposed to extend his term by ten years. Keenly disappointed, Bonaparte seized the initiative and referred the decision to the people in a plebiscite. The question, as finally formulated by the all-powerful Council of State, was simply this: "Is Napoleon Bonaparte to be made Consul for life?" The French people responded with an overwhelming affirmative (3,568,885 in favor, 8,374 opposed), and the Life Consulate was proclaimed in August 1802. To accompany this change the Senate approved alterations in the constitution that increased the powers of the First Consul and strengthened the Senate (now clearly under Bonaparte's control) at the expense of the Tribunate and the Legislative Body. Although two other consuls remained in office, ostensibly sharing power with the First Consul, the Consulate was now a monarchy in all but name.

However, Napoleon felt that further preparations were essential before be could assume a royal title. He had to be made to appear as the indispensable ruler of the nation, the one bulwark between France and a state of anarchy. This impression, he decided, would be created by the discovery of a conspiracy, a plot to restore the Bourbon dynasty, which would appear to threaten the very existence of the regime. Many émigrés still in exile did indeed favor such a restoration. In due course, secret agents of the Napoleonic government, posing in England as monarchist sympathizers and supplied with funds from the treasury to finance the project, approached the leaders of a planned coup who were also receiving a subsidy from the British government, anxious to encourage any plot for the removal of the First Consul. With the conspirators now on French soil, the so-called Cadoudal conspiracy was suddenly exposed; at the proper moment early in 1804, government agents swooped down and arrested Georges Cadoudal (1771–1804), a royalist from Brittany; General Charles Pichegru (1761–1804), one of the former revolutionary generals; and General Jean Victor Moreau (1763–1813), Napoleon's chief rival as a military commander, whom the first two secretly in Paris had attempted to persuade to join the conspiracy. All three were imprisoned, and the details of the plot were bared in the newspapers. Pichegru was subsequently found strangled in his cell. Cadoudal and several other conspirators were tried and executed. General Moreau, who in point of fact refused to participate in the plan, was found guilty but permitted to go into exile in America. Even after the leaders of the plot had been exposed, no specific representative of the Bourbon family could be found implicated. The only clues that were picked up seemed to lead to the duke of Enghien (1772–1804), a Bourbon prince of the collateral line of Condé, who had been living in the German state of Baden and had allegedly come to Strasbourg to communicate with English agents. On the flimsiest of evidence Napoleon ordered a contingent of troops to invade Baden, a neutral territory, arrest the duke of Enghien, and bring him to Paris. He had firmly decided on condemning the duke to death. Although he discovered even before Enghien reached the capital that the charges against him were false, he went ahead with the summary military trial and had him executed within twenty-four hours of his arrival. The speed and brutality with which this action was taken caused a temporary revulsion against Napoleon in some quarters, but most Frenchmen were relieved that the plot had been discovered and the apparent threat to the regime overcome. All who had a stake in the maintenance of the status quo — peasants who had acquired nationalized lands during the revolution, merchants and businessmen who benefited from the prosperity and order achieved under the Consulate, bureaucrats and military men whose fortunes were tied to those of Bonaparte — were willing to approve when the Tribunate proposed that Napoleon be proclaimed emperor and that the imperial dignity should be hereditary in the Bonaparte family. A plebiscite once again approved overwhelmingly what was, in fact, a fait accompli.

In the newly revised constitution (sometimes referred to as the Constitution of the Year XII), the first article began, "The government of the republic is entrusted to an emperor," and the document went on to specify the method to be followed in determining the succession within the Bonaparte family. This curious amalgamation of political forms appeared also on the coinage, which subsequently bore on one side the words République Française and on the other, Napoléon Empereur. Napoleon's reasons for choosing to be "emperor" are not hard to determine. He could hardly call himself king; the Bourbon pretender had not abandoned his claims to the throne, and in any event that title would have been inconsistent with the revolutionary origins of Napoleon's government. Besides, "emperor" carried more grandiose overtones, recalling both the rulers of Rome and Charlemagne, who had been emperor as well as "king of the Franks." Certainly the title

The crucial moment of the coronation. Napoleon abruptly turns his back to the pope (right) who was to crown him, faces the audience, and with a theatrical gesture, places the crown on his own head. Sketch by David for his celebrated painting now in the Louvre.

suggested that his dominion would extend far beyond the borders which had circumscribed the France of the monarchy.

Napoleon's ambitions also led him to seek a legitimization of his title greater than could be conferred by the French Senate. Accordingly, he succeeded in persuading Pope Pius VII to come to Paris to lend the papal presence to his coronation in December 1804. Such an act required the pope to abandon certain scruples since a legitimate Catholic prince still claimed the throne of France, but the good will of the most powerful ruler in Europe was not to be dismissed lightly. Besides, Pius was assured by Napoleon's representatives that he would both anoint and crown the emperor. But a few hours before the coronation, the pope was informed that the procedure had been changed. In the climax of the impressive ceremony, in Notre Dame, Napoleon took the crown from the pope, turned his back on him, and facing the audience, placed the crown upon his own head. In this manner he proclaimed to the pope and to all others present his independence of any earthly authority.

War with Britain and the Third Coalition

Historians have speculated on what would have happened to the Napoleonic empire if it had enjoyed a decade of peace. The French people were, on the whole, satisfied with the ruler who had ended the insecurity of the revolutionary era and provided them with a stable regime and relative prosperity. But could Napoleon Bonaparte have survived a decade of peace? His reputation had been built initially on his military victories. And despite his active program of domestic reforms in the years after 1799, his power essentially rested on his command of the army and on the military glory surrounding his name. Moreover, the romantic element in his character made it impossible for him to limit his ambitions. Could a man who in a few short years had achieved mastery over the French nation and had successively defeated the other major powers of Europe have settled down to the relatively prosaic tasks of government and administration? Napoleon was impelled by an almost compulsive drive toward further military exploits and the expansion of his newly founded empire.

Responsibility for the renewal of war between France and Britain in May 1803 lay almost entirely with France. The rest of Europe may well have been ready to settle down to an era of peace after the decade of wars that had ravaged the Continent. The territories that France had annexed by 1803 could largely be regarded as lying within France's "natural frontiers." True, French influence extended to the so-called sister republics in Holland, Switzerland, and Italy, but the peoples of these regions still had a degree of autonomy, and at least some of them benefited from the introduction of French institutions into their territories. The other major European powers had apparently acquiesced in the extension of French influence into these regions; at least, they had signed treaties with France that did not specifically withhold approval of French acquisitions. Addington, the British prime minister, certainly regarded the Treaty of Amiens as more than a temporary truce, but the same cannot be said for Napoleon. For a number of reasons Napoleon regarded a resumption of the war with Britain as inevitable, or rather, he took certain steps which made it inevitable. In the first place, he revealed fairly soon that he had no intention of maintaining the status quo on the Continent. Even before the peace with Britain had been formally signed, he imposed a new constitution on the Cisalpine Republic (henceforth called the Italian Republic) and had himself appointed its president. A few months later France formally annexed the neighboring state of Piedmont. Dissension between centralists and federalists in the Helvetic Republic gave him a pretext for intervening there, mediating the dispute, and establishing a new state, the Swiss Confederation, which became a close military ally of France. His drastic reorganization of Germany has already been discussed.

Second, and even more alarming to the British, there was evidence of renewed French designs in the eastern Mediterranean. Napoleon sent one of his officers, Colonel Horace Sébastiani (1772–1851), to that region as a military observer, and saw to it that a report of his findings was published (January 30, 1803) in the official government newspaper, the *Moniteur*. Sébastiani's most provocative conclusion was that Egypt, because of its weakened military condition, could easily be recaptured by the French.

A third cause for continued antagonism between France and Great Britain was Napoleon's stubborn refusal to accept British commercial and colonial supremacy. He regarded his own hopes for the economic domination of the Continent as doomed to frustration as long as Britain retained this superiority. How to destroy it was a problem that occupied Napoleon for the remainder of his career. Napoleon first tried to challenge Britain's colonial dominance by building his own empire in the Western Hemisphere. In the wake of the debacle in Haiti in 1802, however, Napoleon decided to concentrate instead on undermining Britain's commercial supremacy. Having been brought up in the mercantilist tradition, he was convinced that continental markets lost to British manufacturers would go to the French and provide a further stimulus to French industry and commerce. In effect he was merely continuing policies dating from the Anglo-French commercial and colonial rivalry of the seventeenth and eighteenth centuries. His principal innovation, as we shall see, was his attempt to apply to the entire continent of Europe a policy which had hitherto been restricted to France and, during the 1790s, to those regions immediately dependent on France. Now France would become the senior partner in a Europe-wide economic system. But the success of such an enterprise depended on French domination of the entire Continent, and on France's ability to enforce the restrictions imposed on trade with the British. Not until 1806 did Napoleon control enough of Europe to inaugurate his famous Continental System, whose purpose was the destruction of British trade and the achievement of economic mastery of the European continent. His policy in 1802 foreshadowed the Continental System, for he refused to supplement the Treaty of Amiens with any sort of commercial agreement that would have permitted British merchants to trade with France, and he tried to extend this ban to France's allies. Probably no other action by Napoleon did more to consolidate British opinion in support of a renewal of the war with France.

Tensions between Britain and France culminated in the outbreak of war in May 1803. Napoleon used as a pretext for renewing the conflict Britain's refusal to evacuate the island of Malta. This was a technical violation of the terms of the Treaty of Amiens, but the expansion of his own domination over Italy and his designs elsewhere on the Continent certainly provided the British with adequate grounds for retaining control over this island outpost in the Mediterranean. The war that began in 1803 dragged on indecisively for two years. Napoleon found himself unable to achieve a quick victory, partly because the French fleet was bottled up in its own ports by superior British squadrons, but also because Britain was soon joined by other nations, forming the Third Coalition.

At first, Napoleon seriously entertained the idea of invading England. In the fall of 1803 he concentrated a force of one hundred and fifty thousand men on the coast at Boulogne and ordered the construction of a flotilla of twelve hundred flatboats to transport the troops across the Channel. Subsequently, he decided that the invasion forces required support and devised a plan for several French squadrons to escape from the blockaded ports, lure units of the British fleet to the high seas, evade them, and return to the Channel to join the invasion forces. In March 1805, he was finally able to put this plan into operation. A French squadron under the command of Admiral Pierre Villeneuve (1763–1806) slipped out of Toulon and joined a Spanish squadron (Spain, too, had become involved in the war against Britain), and the combined fleet made for the West Indies. As Napoleon had hoped, the British took the bait. Admiral Horatio Nelson set out in pursuit with a British fleet. But when Villeneuve attempted to evade Nelson and return to Europe to support the projected invasion, the plan began to go awry. Nelson ascertained the direction of the French fleet and managed to warn the British admiralty, which promptly stationed ships off the northwest coast of Spain to intercept Villeneuve's squadron. Villeneuve took refuge in the port of Cádiz, where he was promptly blockaded again by British units.

Although Villeneuve was blamed for the failure of the project, Napoleon had decided to abandon the invasion even before he got word of his admiral's retreat. Publicly he claimed that French troops stationed at Boulogne were needed on the Rhine to counteract the mobilization of Austrian armies, but probably the decisive factor was the return of Nelson's fleet, for he knew that the Franco-Spanish fleet would be no match for it.

Napoleon's fears were dramatically confirmed later that year. Admiral Villeneuve, contemptuously ordered by the emperor to make for a Mediterranean port, sailed out of Cádiz. Admiral Nelson intercepted Villeneuve's signals and prepared to meet him at the strait of Gibraltar. On October 21, 1805, off Cape Trafalgar, Nelson's ships overwhelmingly defeated the enemy fleet in six hours of ship-to-ship fighting. At the end of the battle only eleven of the thirty-three French and Spanish ships managed to regain their harbor. The British lost no ships, but they did lose their admiral; Nelson was fatally wounded in the first hour of fighting. The Battle of Trafalgar was unquestionably one of the decisive battles of the Napoleonic wars, for it ended definitively all French hopes of challenging Britain's mastery of the seas.

By one of those ironic twists of history, France's defeat at Trafalgar coincided almost to the day with the surrender of twenty thousand Austrian troops to Napoleon at Ulm, in Bavaria. Napoleon had lost no time in moving his Grand Army (as he now called the forces hitherto intended for the invasion of England) to the Rhine and invading German territory. His goal was now the defeat of the Third Coalition, which had been formed against France during 1804–1805.

Among the leaders of this coalition was Tsar Alexander I of Russia, whom the British government had approached in 1804 with a view to forming an alliance against France. Alexander, one of the most colorful individuals of this era, had ascended the throne only three years earlier, at twenty-three. His role as ruler of Russia from 1801 to 1825 will be examined in detail in a later chapter; here it is important to note that his actions as a military leader and diplomat, like his polices at home, were frequently marked by unpredictability and inconsistency. Son of the unstable autocrat Paul I, Alexander had been brought up by his grandmother, Catherine the Great, who saw to it that he was given a liberal and humanist education by his Swiss tutor, Frédéric César de La Harpe. The principles inculcated in Alexander by this training were at odds with the respect for the army and the pride in himself as a soldier that he had derived from his father. His instability (some have diagnosed his condition as schizophrenia) was further heightened by the sense of guilt he felt over his father's violent death. Although he played no direct role in Paul's assassination, he is known to have been aware of the plot to depose him and to have done nothing to stop it. On his accession, he surrounded himself with liberal advisers and even talked of granting Russia a constitution, but little came of his promises except for some administrative and legal reforms. As he grew older and as Russia became involved in wars against France, Alexander turned more and more conservative. Ultimately he regarded himself as a divinely appointed savior of Europe destined to defeat Napoleon, the Antichrist.

In 1804 he was receptive to Britain's proposals for an alliance for two reasons. First, he felt the French emperor was violating certain accepted standards of conduct in international relations — in his abduction of the duke of Enghien from the independent state of Baden, for example. Second, he was convinced that Napoleon posed a threat to Russia's interests in the Ionian islands, in the Balkans, and in central Europe, where Alexander looked forward to becoming an arbiter. The alliance formally concluded between Britain and Russia in 1805 reiterated some of the aims of the Second Coalition — an independent Holland that would include the Belgian provinces and constitute a barrier against France in the north, and to serve the same function in the south, an independent kingdom of Sardinia, controlling Savoy, Piedmont, and the former Republic of Genoa. Other goals, less carefully defined, included the elimination of French influence in both

Germany and Italy and the strengthening of Prussia on the Rhine. Alexander also expressed his intention of establishing a reconstituted Polish state, and proposed that some sort of international body be set up after the war to enforce the peace settlement.

Francis II of Austria was understandably hesitant about renewing the war against France, having lost so much territory in the wars of the First and Second coalitions. Nevertheless, steps taken by Napoleon to consolidate French control over northern Italy led Austria in November 1804 to conclude a defensive treaty with Russia which provided for joint resistance against any further French aggression in Italy or Germany. When Napoleon decided in 1805 to transform the Italian Republic into a kingdom of Italy, with himself as king, Austria prepared to join the coalition with Britain and Russia. As we have seen, Austria's mobilization of its armies gave Napoleon the excuse he needed for transferring his troops from the Channel coast to the Rhine border.

General Mack (Baron Karl Mack von Leiberich, 1752–1828), commander of the Austrian forces in Germany, played from the start into Napoleon's hands by penetrating far ahead of his reinforcements; thus the French were able to outflank and encircle his troops at Ulm. From Ulm, Napoleon moved on without hindrance to the Austrian capital of Vienna. There he heard the news of the defeat at Trafalgar and became aware that his enemies of the Third Coalition — Russia, Austria, and Britain — might be joined by another ally, Prussia. The king of Prussia had preserved his neutrality for a little more than a decade, but the expansion of Napoleon's influence in the German states and the violation of Prussian territory by French forces under General Jean Baptiste Bernadotte (c. 1763–1844) during Napoleon's campaign against Austria drove the Prussians to threaten support of the coalition. Before these plans could materialize, however, Napoleon met the main armies of the Russians, supported by the Austrians, near the little Moravian village of Austerlitz, and on December 2, 1805, the first anniversary of his coronation as emperor, achieved one of his most brilliant victories. Weakening the right wing of his own forces in order to provoke a Russian attack on it, he concentrated the full strength of his own attack on the Russian center. His strategy worked perfectly, for having destroyed the center, he was able to turn and annihilate the Russian forces that had advanced on his right. The defeat at Austerlitz cost the allied forces between twenty-five thousand and thirty thousand casualties; Napoleon lost fewer than nine thousand, including dead and wounded.

The stunning victory at Austerlitz brought about the collapse of the Third Coalition when the Russians pulled back their troops and informed the Austrians they could count on no more Russian support. Austria saw no alternative but to sue for peace. Prussia hastily dropped its plan for opposing France, and instead, entered into negotiations with Napoleon that resulted in an alliance and the cession to France of minor territories in return for Prussian annexation of Hanover. The terms imposed on Austria were contained in the humiliating Treaty of Pressburg (December 26, 1805), which deprived Austria of virtually all its remaining possessions in Italy and awarded its imperial territories in western Germany to Bavaria, Württemberg, and Baden as rewards for their support of Napoleon in the war just ended.

Defeat of Prussia and Russia: The Treaties of Tilsit, 1807

The victory at Austerlitz at the end of 1805 and the formation of a Franco-Prussian alliance in February 1806 brought little more than a brief respite for the Napoleonic armies. Within a few months Napoleon was at war with Prussia, the one power that had managed to remain at peace with France for over a decade.

One explanation for the change in Prussian policy lies in the personality of its monarch, Frederick William III, who had come to the throne in 1797. Though a man of good intentions, he was characterized by weakness of will and vacillation, traits that are particularly unfortunate in an absolute ruler. Frederick William preserved the governmental institutions that had been shaped by his great-uncle, Frederick the Great, among them a cabinet of councillors. Whereas under a strong monarch these officials had executed the will of the ruler, under Frederick William they exerted their own influence on the king. Unfortunately for the Prussian state, these officials were divided in their counsel, some favoring a policy of conciliation and compromise with Napoleon, others urging an alliance with Austria or Russia and resistance to the French. Prussian policy was consequently erratic during the first years of Frederick William's reign, though the group advocating compromise with Napoleon generally held the upper hand. By the summer of 1806, however, those favoring resistance to France could point to developments that made war with Napoleon appear the only possible course of action.

Prussia's resentment arose in part from the domination that Napoleon now exercised over all parts of Germany that lay outside the boundaries of Prussia and Austria. For it was at this time (July 1806) that Napoleon established the Confederation of the Rhine, a union of fifteen German states, including Bavaria, Württemberg, Baden, Hesse-Darmstadt, and Berg. The rulers of the Confederation states had little choice but to submit to French control since the probable alternative would have been direct absorption into the French empire. With Napoleon as its protector, the union was later expanded to include practically every state in Germany except Austria and

Prussia. One consequence followed less than a month after the establishment of the Confederation, when Napoleon finally announced the end of the thousand-year-old Holy Roman Empire. When the rulers of states belonging to the Confederation declared that they no longer recognized the empire, Francis II was forced to abandon his traditional title; he retained only the new title that he had assumed two years before: Francis I, emperor of Austria.

Another source of trouble between France and Prussia was to be found in the alliance itself. The treaty had awarded the state of Hanover to Prussia in return for territories on the right (eastern) bank of the Rhine, which Prussia turned over to France and its allies. When, in the course of the next few months, the Prussian king heard that Napoleon had offered to restore Hanover to Great Britain in exchange for the withdrawal of British protective forces from the island of Sicily, he naturally viewed this proposed bargain as a betrayal of the worst sort. The fact that the Anglo-French negotiations broke down did not diminish Frederick William's resentment over Napoleon's duplicity.

In response to these and other provocations the Prussian king concluded a secret agreement with Tsar Alexander that assured Prussia of Russian support in the event of an attack by France. Even before Russia had ratified the treaty, Prussia mobilized its army against the French. The final blow to Franco-Prussian relations was Napoleon's ruthless execution of Johann Philipp Palm, a Nuremberg bookseller who had circulated a pamphlet entitled *Germany in Her Deepest Humiliation*; the tract had called on Saxony and Prussia to save Germany from destruction at the hands of the French emperor. The disparity between the relative insignificance of the crime and the severity of the punishment offended almost all Germans and helped to arouse Prussian sentiment against France. The war began in October 1806.

Frederick William's decision to mobilize his troops before he had been assured of adequate Russian support was a mistake. Prussian troops were outnumbered two to one, and they turned out to be no match for the well-trained armies of Napoleon. On October 14, 1806, before the Russians could arrive to support them, the Prussians were defeated simultaneously at Jena and at Auerstedt. After this decisive victory the French pursued the Prussian armies through their own country until they had captured Berlin. The king was forced to take refuge in East Prussia.

Having extended his domination to northern as well as central Germany, Napoleon now stood face to face with Tsar Alexander's Russian armies. His inclination was to engage the Russians immediately and put an end to the war, but the terrain and general conditions were much less favorable than they had been in the Prussian campaign. Winter was approaching, and he feared the losses that would be involved in fighting on the muddy reaches of East Prussia. When he nevertheless took the chance, at Eylau in February 1807, he lost fifteen thousand men in a battle that settled nothing. The Russians suffered even heavier casualties, and both sides were forced to fall back and wait until spring to renew the conflict.

As was so often the case, Napoleon profited more from the delay than did his enemy. While the Russians and Prussians waited for subsidies from the British and tried vainly to persuade the Austrians to join them, Napoleon called up some eighty thousand new recruits from France and Italy and thus gained the numerical superiority that helped him to win a decisive victory at the battle of Friedland in June 1807.

Despite his heavy losses, Tsar Alexander could have continued the war against the French, but he decided instead to sue for peace. He had been disappointed by the reluctance of Austria and Britain to support him more actively, and feared that continued fighting might provoke an uprising by the Poles. In addition, a pro-French faction of advisers that was gaining strength in his entourage was encouraging him to reach an understanding with Bonaparte. Napoleon was receptive to the tsar's peace overtures partly because of the heavy losses his armies had suffered in the year just past, but also because he hoped that an agreement with Russia would permit him to close Baltic ports to British shipping and goods.

The negotiations between Napoleon and Tsar Alexander constituted one of the most dramatic episodes of the Napoleonic era. On a raft moored in the middle of the Niemen River, the two young emperors met for a series of conferences in which they appeared to contemporaries to be dividing up the European world. And as if to heighten the drama, the hapless Frederick William of Prussia was left on one of the river banks, riding up and down the shore, waiting for the outcome of conversations that would determine the fate of his country. For several days the two rulers matched wits, and in the end, each felt he had triumphed over his opponent.

Two treaties — the treaties of Tilsit (July 1807) — resulted from the discussions: one concerned France and Prussia; the other settled issues between France and Russia. In the former, Napoleon carried out his intention of humiliating the ex-ally who had dared to oppose him. The king was allowed to retain his throne, but Prussia lost some of its most valuable territories and half its population. Prussian lands to the west of the Elbe were ceded to France; these, with some adjacent areas, formed the new kingdom of Westphalia, which was given to Napoleon's brother Jerome. In the east, Prussia lost the Polish provinces that it had secured in the eighteenth-century partitions of Poland; they were established as the duchy of Warsaw and assigned to the king of Saxony. A separate military convention reduced the Prussian army to a minimum force and provided that French troops would occupy key Prussian fortresses until an indemnity, or war contribution, had been paid to France.

In the treaty with Russia, the tsar formally accepted the Napoleonic conquests in central and western Europe by recognizing the Confederation of the Rhine and the claims of Napoleon's brothers to the thrones of Holland, Naples, and Westphalia. Napoleon led the Russian emperor to believe that in return for this recognition of the French hegemony in Germany and Italy, he was acknowledging Russia's claim to an eastern European empire. Specifically, the treaty provided that Napoleon would offer his good offices as a mediator in the conflict between Russia and Turkey that had broken out in 1806, a war he had himself helped to provoke by encouraging the sultan. A secret clause stipulated that if mediation failed, Napoleon would make common cause with Russia in a war against the Ottoman empire and that France would agree to the cession of the Turkish European provinces of Moldavia and Walachia to Russia. Meanwhile, Russia agreed to withdraw its fleet from the Mediterranean and to yield control over the Ionian islands to the French. Finally, the tsar offered to mediate between France and Britain. But if the British refused to restore all conquests they had made since 1805 and to respect the freedom of the seas, Russia would declare war on Britain, close the Baltic ports to British products, and call on the Baltic states, Austria, and Portugal to join in the struggle. Since there was little likelihood of Britain's accepting the suggested conditions, Napoleon thought he could count on Russian support of his efforts to eliminate British trade with the Continent. The question of who benefited most from the treaty turns less on the actual terms than on the subsequent interpretations made of the agreement by the two rulers. We shall discover that neither Napoleon nor Alexander lived up to the promises made at Tilsit, and each rapidly became disappointed with his new ally. How much faith either ruler put in the alliance is difficult to say. Perhaps neither had too many illusions about its permanence. By 1810, both were coming to the conclusion that a renewal of the war between them was inevitable.

Napoleon's Grand Empire

After the battle of Austerlitz in 1805, Napoleon began to speak openly of the Grand Empire which he was constructing in Europe to replace the practically defunct Holy Roman Empire. Indeed, as we know, Francis of Austria, the Holy Roman emperor, had seen the handwriting on the wall as early as 1804, when Napoleon crowned himself emperor of France. Francis had taken the precaution of naming himself hereditary emperor of Austria as well.

Napoleon's Grand Empire included, first of all, the French empire proper: metropolitan France and the areas formally annexed to France, such as a sizable strip of Italian territory extending down the western coast to a point halfway between Rome and Naples. In 1810 Holland was eliminated as a satellite state and directly incorporated into the empire. This nucleus was administered directly from Paris; as new territories were added, they were simply divided into departments ruled by prefects, just like the original eighty-three departments. Beyond the borders of the French state, Napoleon established a series of dependent, or satellite, states; their relationships with France were not uniform, but their rulers were all appointed by Napoleon (indeed, many were members of his own family) and owed allegiance to him. Among these states were some of the "republics" created during the revolutionary era. A third category of states, later added to the Grand Empire, included those which retained their independent status but became "allies" of France, forced to submit to its economic and military directives and to join in the wars against its enemies. For a time both Prussia and Austria fell into this category.

The process of assigning rulers to the dependent states began in 1805, on

The Salon Frascati in 1807, favored meeting place of the wealthy. Note the dress and decor, typical of the Empire era.

the Italian peninsula. Once Napoleon had taken the title of emperor he could hardly remain merely "president" of the Italian Republic. He therefore decided to convert this republic into the kingdom of Italy, and after pretending to offer the throne first to his older brother Joseph and later to his stepson Eugène de Beauharnais, announced that because of their refusals he would assume the title himself. He added that his kingship was only provisional: ultimately the new kingdom would go to his chief heir, who would abandon his rights to the French empire as a condition of becoming king of Italy. Eugène de Beauharnais, for the time being, was named viceroy of Italy.

At the end of 1805, after the battle of Austerlitz, Napoleon added a second state to the Grand Empire, the kingdom of Naples. Angry with the Bourbon ruler of Naples for having violated his promise of neutrality by inviting British and Russian forces into Neapolitan ports, Napoleon declared that "the dynasty of Naples has ceased to reign." In March 1806, within a month after a French detachment had taken over the kingdom, Napoleon proclaimed his brother Joseph king of Naples and Sicily. In 1808, Joseph moved on to Spain, and Joachim Murat, Napoleon's brother-in-law, received the crown of Naples.

The pattern established in Italy was also followed elsewhere on the Continent. In 1806 Napoleon dissolved the eleven-year-old Batavian Republic and named his younger brother Louis to the throne of the short-lived kingdom of Holland. To his brother-in-law Murat went, in 1806, the newly created duchy of Berg, in the Rhineland, which was later expanded at the expense of Prussia. To his brother Jerome he assigned the kingdom of Westphalia, created after Tilsit in 1807. These royal relatives of the emperor were of course bound to him by personal ties, although they were nominally independent of France.

To what extent did the establishment of this sprawling empire spread French institutions to the rest of Europe? Did the dependent states of Germany and Italy, forced to contribute men and money to the support of Napoleon's armies, derive some compensating advantages from French rule? The extent to which French reforms and legislation were introduced varied as greatly from one part of the empire to another as did the characters of the individual administrators and rulers named to govern the several territories. In regions directly annexed to France institutions were established that were, in theory, the same as those existing in metropolitan France itself, though some adjustments were inevitably made to language and local circumstances. In the newly created departments — and in the dependent states as well — the emperor or his vassal rulers attempted to introduce the Napoleonic codes, the French administrative and financial system, and forms of political representation comparable to those existing at home. It was the general policy also to abolish serfdom, eliminate feudal dues, and prohibit the inheritance of large estates. With respect to the church, Napoleon hoped to apply throughout the empire the policies that had been developed in France: the insistence on the supremacy of the lay state over the church, the abolition of monastic institutions, the establishment of a system of public instruction, and so on. Resistance to the secular control of education was, as one might expect, particularly strong in parts of Italy. Often the rulers of the dependent states, in closer touch than the emperor with the problems of their particular regions, proved more flexible in the matter of imposing French institutions. When Louis Bonaparte, the ruler of Holland, protested to Napoleon that several provisions of the Code Napoléon should be dropped in Holland because they ran counter to Dutch prejudices, his advice was refused with the words, "If you revise the Code Napoléon it will no longer be the Code Napoléon. . . . The Romans gave their laws to their allies; why should not France have hers adopted in Holland?"

Many peoples of the Grand Empire benefited from the introduction of more efficient administrative institutions, more equitable laws, a more just distribution of the burdens of taxation, and other improvements brought by French rule. The changes were particularly advantageous to those who had been living under the antiquated hierarchical institutions of some of the petty states of Germany or in a state such as the kingdom of Naples. At the same time, the attempt to impose from above institutions that affected established prejudices, personal relationships, and daily routines met with a mixed reception even from those who might have gained most from such changes. It is one thing for a people to achieve reforms as the result of its own efforts; another, to have those reforms mandated by a conqueror.

In the last analysis, Napoleon came to be viewed more as a conqueror than as a liberator. Membership in the Grand Empire brought disadvantages as well as rewards. As the Napoleonic wars progressed, the vassal states were required to contribute more and more heavily to their support, providing not only financial subsidies but recruits to supplement the imperial armies. (Of the six hundred thousand men in the forces which invaded Russia in 1812, only a third were native Frenchmen; the rest were of twenty different nationalities.) Regions that did not suffer directly the ravages of warfare were often required to support armies of occupation. Most annoying to the business and trading classes were the galling economic restrictions that formed a part of Napoleon's Continental System, and the hordes of French agents and inspectors required to enforce those restrictions.

In later years, after his defeat and exile, Napoleon tried to create the impression that during his reign he had championed the nationalist aspirations of Germans, Italians, Poles, and other scattered peoples. He could thus contrast himself with the restored rulers of Europe who, after his downfall, held these peoples in subjection or thwarted their hopes for unity. To what extent was this claim justified? Can Napoleon, as some have contended, be viewed as the architect of German and Italian unity, the defender of Polish nationalism?

In two respects he did stimulate the nationalist sentiments of certain European peoples, though perhaps not in the ways he later suggested. By decreasing the number of states in Germany and Italy, his rearrangement of the map of Europe may have contributed to a greater sense of unity among both peoples. At the end of the eighteenth century, Germany consisted of nearly eighteen hundred states, principalities, free cities, and lesser semi-autonomous political entities. Yet the conquests of the revolutionary and Napoleonic armies left only the truncated states of Prussia and Austria, the Confederation of the Rhine (fifteen states at the outset), and a few lesser territories. In addition, Napoleon's decree of 1806 put an end to the anachronistic Holy Roman Empire. He thus cleared the way, unintentionally, for those who subsequently espoused the cause of a united Germany. In the Italian peninsula, the political organization established by the French was destroyed in 1815, but the fact remained that Italians could look back to a time under Napoleon's rule when the numerous states had been combined into only three separate parts: the regions directly incorporated into the French empire, the kingdom of Italy, and the kingdom of Naples and Sicily. Italy had not known so great a measure of unity since the era of the Roman Empire. Also, by establishing the duchy of Warsaw in 1807 and adding western Galicia to it in 1809, Napoleon revived the hopes of the Polish people for an independent state.

A second, and more important, way in which Bonaparte contributed to the growth of nationalist sentiments among Europeans was by arousing patriotic resentment among the peoples subjected to French domination. How strong such feelings were among the rank and file is difficult to determine. The soldier who served in an army pitted against the French probably fought because he had to rather than out of any sense of loyalty to his nation. The peasant doubtless resented the requisition of his crops or the physical damage to his property caused by warfare, but this reaction did not necessarily result in a new allegiance to his ruler or a new sense of unity with his compatriots. However, among a minority of intellectuals during this era can be detected a new patriotic spirit. The philosopher Johann Gottlieb Fichte (1762–1814), for example, sought to inspire German national sentiment through his Addresses to the German Nation, delivered in Berlin in 1807 and 1808. Ernst Moritz Arndt, a poet and historian, toward the end of the Napoleonic era published a series of poems calling on Prussia to liberate all Germany from the yoke of the French tyrant. In Italy, the Carbonari ("charcoal burners"), a conspiratorial organization later devoted to the cause of Italian unity, began as a group devoted to resistance to the French occupation. None of these individuals or groups attracted a mass following before 1815, but the seeds sown during the Napoleonic era bore fruit in the nationalist movements of the nineteenth century.

As for Napoleon's own feelings toward these various national groups, his actions during his years of rule speak louder than any later words. His ruthless subjugation of the peoples of the Grand Empire to French national aims and aspirations, his imposition of French rulers and French institutions on the dependent states, suggest no profound understanding of national differences or sympathy with nationalist goals. When he destroyed traditional institutions and upset the dynasties of petty rulers in central Europe, he did so not in order to encourage German or Italian national aspirations, but rather to rule the peoples of these territories more effectively and to exploit their resources for his own military or economic advantage. If Bonaparte was motivated in his conquests by any transcendent ideal, it was the ideal not of a federation of equal nations, but rather of a universal empire, like the Roman Empire or that of Charlemagne.

The Continental System, 1806

The Continental System did not emerge suddenly, but was the culmination of a policy of restrictions on trade with Britain adopted by France during the revolution and continued by Napoleon after his accession to power. Only at the end of 1806 did Napoleon feel secure enough in his control over Europe to undertake an all-out effort to destroy British trade with the Continent. Having acquired the kingdom of Naples in that year, he was able to close one of the major remaining points of access for the British, the Neapolitan ports. Even more important was the French defeat of Prussia, which gave Napoleon control of the north German ports, the principal entrepôts for British goods going to the Continent. With the famous Berlin Decree of November 1806, he formally inaugurated the Continental System, banning all commerce with the British. Hereafter, British subjects on the Continent were subject to arrest; all goods belonging to Great Britain or coming from its factories or its colonies were subject to confiscation. Any vessel, regardless of nationality, coming directly from the ports of Britain or its colonies was forbidden access to continental ports. Since the decree was binding on all of France's dependent states and allies, Napoleon was, in effect, trying to establish a barrier extending from the north German ports to the tip of the Italian peninsula. Because of the condition of the

French fleet, Napoleon could not hope to enforce a blockade of British ports; the principal intention of the decree was to prevent all vessels (neutral as well as British) from bringing British or colonial goods into continental ports. The emperor's aim was to secure for continental — preferably French — manufacturers and merchants those markets that had formerly been controlled by the British.

Even before the Berlin Decree, the British had instituted a blockade of their own on goods flowing in and out of continental ports on the North Sea and the English Channel. After the decree, Britain retaliated by announcing that all neutral ships plying between coastal ports from which English ships were excluded would be considered liable to capture and condemnation as lawful prizes. The economic struggle between the French and British lasted until about 1812, but the principal goal of the Continental System — the destruction of British trade — was never achieved. Napoleon's plan was basically sound: if he had really succeeded in excluding British commerce from Europe, British credit would have collapsed. But British commerce never was excluded from Europe; British goods continued to flow in by a variety of means. Smuggling operations were carried out on a large scale, particularly through Holland and northwestern Germany. In many instances, customs officials were bribed to allow prohibited goods to enter. By 1810 the British were selling a great many "licenses of trade" that guaranteed neutral ships immunity from capture by British vessels and thus permitted them to carry British goods safely to the Continent. Such ships could be provided with false papers that certified their departure from a non-British port and the non-British origin of their cargo.

In the last analysis, Napoleon simply did not have the navy or the vast corps of loyal civil servants and customs inspectors required to make the system work throughout the entire continent. Frenchmen might respond to his patriotic appeals to defeat the British by adhering to the restrictions imposed by the Continental System, but the natives of the dependent and allied states had much less reason to heed such regulations. Merchants who saw their volume of business reduced and consumers who were deprived of products they desired were only too willing to find loopholes by which they could evade the restrictions. Most discouraging to the emperor was the fact that instead of increasing, French trade and business activity declined. For the British blockade achieved its principal purpose, which was not to prevent imports from reaching the Continent, but to weaken the enemy by destroying his commerce and shipping. Numerous French shippers and merchants went out of business as their vessels languished in continental ports blockaded by the British navy.

By 1810, the Continental System was working so badly that Napoleon decided to take advantage of its weaknesses and exploit them to the profit of France. What he did, in effect, was to become a smuggler himself: he authorized the auction of prize cargoes (including goods formally prohibited from entry) if the purchaser paid a duty of 40 percent. Then he instructed his customs agents to admit prohibited goods on condition that they had been falsely labeled by their sellers as prize cargoes. In this way he increased the revenue from duties and permitted the entry of those goods which were particularly in demand. However, this step constituted the abandonment of the purpose of the Continental System and obviously undermined the entire operation. Thus at a time when Napoleon was still enjoying political and military victories, he had already suffered a major economic defeat.

The Peninsular War, 1808–1813

In 1807, with peace temporarily assured in central and eastern Europe, Napoleon became involved in warfare in an entirely different quarter of the Continent. He had long resented the loyalty the ruler of Portugal showed his British ally and was determined to crush the Iberian kingdom and make it conform to the Continental System. To fight Portugal, Napoleon had to secure passage for French troops through Spain. This he did by vaguely promising its senile Bourbon monarch, Charles IV (ruled 1788–1808), that he would divide Portugal between France and Spain. But as we shall see, once French troops had secured a foothold in Spain, Napoleon found a pretext for overthrowing the Spanish monarchy as well. The invasion of Portugal was merely the prelude to the subjugation of the entire Iberian peninsula.

The Peninsular War is important in the context of Napoleon's whole career, for many historians have viewed the beginning of this war as the turning point in the emperor's military fortunes. For the first time he seems seriously to have underestimated the degree of resistance he would arouse and the difficult nature of the warfare he would encounter, the result, in this instance, of the mountainous terrain. Some of the initial French defeats can be ascribed to the ineptitude of the military commanders; when Napoleon took personal command, he was more successful. But the Spanish campaign proved a steady drain on his resources and dragged on indecisively until the final ejection of the French in 1813.

Although the Portuguese royal family fled to Brazil in the face of the invasion, resistance to the French continued, and the Portuguese soon had the support of a British army under the command of Sir Arthur Wellesley (1769–1852), later duke of Wellington, who defeated the French in his initial encounter with them. Meanwhile, a force of one hundred thousand French troops had crossed the Spanish border, ostensibly to protect the

Spanish coasts against the British. In March 1808, an opportune rebellion against King Charles IV stemmed from the unpopularity of the queen's favorite, Manuel de Godoy (1767–1851). Charles abdicated in favor of his son Ferdinand VII. Profiting from the unsettled situation and from antagonisms within the royal family, Napoleon refused to recognize Ferdinand and succeeded in getting him, as well as his father and Godoy, across the Franco-Spanish border, presumably to settle the dispute among them. The outcome of this maneuver was the forced abdication of the son, which left the throne vacant. Napoleon thereupon arranged for a petition to be drawn up by a number of responsible Spanish officials requesting that the throne be given to Joseph Bonaparte. Only too happy to comply with this request, the emperor agreed, and Joseph abandoned his rights to the kingdom of Naples to become king of Spain.

What Napoleon failed to recognize was that the antipathy shown by the Spaniards toward their ruler did not necessarily imply a corresponding enthusiasm for rule by the French, for the deposition of the Bourbons was greeted by a general uprising which drove the French from Madrid. After a number of reverses during the summer of 1808, Napoleon decided to take personal command of the forces in Spain and succeeded in recapturing the capital. But failing again to understand the motivations of the Spanish people, he undertook a series of reforms—including measures against the Catholic Church, such as ending the Inquisition and decreasing the number of monastic establishments—which merely alienated the populace further. Despite a number of victories against the Spanish and the British, who had come to their aid, Napoleon was unable to bring the war to an end. Many of the inhabitants took to the hills to engage in guerilla fighting; because the country was decentralized and disorganized, opposition was particularly difficult to overcome. Indeed, the city of Cádiz, in southwestern Spain, never submitted to French control, and it was here that a national assembly was elected in 1810 to draw up a new constitution for Spain.

The Short War with Austria, 1809

The unexpectedly strong resistance to Napoleon's armies in the Iberian peninsula, and the difficulties he encountered there, served to encourage his enemies elsewhere on the Continent. When, in 1808, Napoleon was forced to withdraw large contingents of the Grand Army from Germany for use in the Spanish campaign, the war party in the Austrian court urged Emperor Francis to seize the opportunity to embarrass his traditional enemy. After Austria's defeat at Austerlitz, Francis' younger brother, Archduke Charles Louis, had undertaken a partial reorganization of the army; this step had been matched by corresponding administrative reforms designed to strengthen the country in a future conflict with Napoleon. Francis himself was reluctant to renew the conflict with the French without allies, and he rightly guessed that no significant support would be forthcoming. Tsar Alexander was still formally allied with France; indeed, the agreements of Tilsit had been reaffirmed at a meeting between the two at Erfurt in September 1808. Prussia, its territory still occupied by French troops, was engaged in a series of drastic reforms and was in no position to rise up against the French. Despite these misgivings, Francis was persuaded to take the risk. It was pointed out to him that France had half of its forces tied up in Spain in a war that was increasingly unpopular at home, and that the German peoples could not fail to respond to an appeal to liberate their territories from French domination.

Throwing caution to the winds, Austria began the war in April 1809 by invading Bavaria. Napoleon was aware of the danger of his position. When it became clear that no support would be forthcoming from Russia, he hastily called up fresh recruits and ordered two divisions from Spain rushed to the east. Despite the improvised character of these forces, Napoleon's first moves showed that he had lost none of his skill as a military leader. Within a matter of days he had counterattacked and halted the Austrian advance. He followed up his advantage by marching his armies down the Danube to Vienna at a pace of twenty miles a day. Meanwhile, Archduke Charles Louis was regrouping his troops on the left bank of the Danube. When Napoleon crossed the river and attacked, he met with vicious resistance from the Austrian forces; after two days of fighting, he was forced to recross the Danube, having lost some twenty thousand men. The Austrians also suffered heavy casualties, but they took satisfaction from the battle because they had beaten back an army commanded personally by Napoleon. After this encounter both armies remained at a standstill for seven weeks while reinforcements were brought up. When Napoleon attacked again, his was the superior force, and he carried the day with a victory at Wagram. The battle was not nearly so decisive as Austerlitz had been, but the archduke saw no purpose in continuing the war and a week later he asked for an armistice.

Austria had challenged the conqueror and had been met defeat for the fourth time. By the Treaty of Schönbrunn (October 1809) it lost an additional thirty-two thousand square miles of territory, with some 3.5 million inhabitants. A good part of the ceded area went to Bavaria, and the duchy of Warsaw was strengthened by the annexation of western Galicia. To the south, Napoleon combined formerly Austrian territories with the Ionian islands to constitute a new state, the Illyrian Provinces. A final provision of the treaty forced Austria to adhere to the Continental System and to break off all ties with Great Britain.

The Empire in 1810

In terms of square miles of territory under French control, the year 1810 marked the apogee of the Napoleonic empire. The defeat of Austria at Wagram in 1809 extended the domination of the French southward and eastward down the Adriatic coast. Because his brother Louis had shown himself as king of Holland more sympathetic to Dutch than to French interests and had consistently violated the Continental System by allowing British goods to be smuggled in through Holland, Napoleon deprived him of his throne in 1810 and incorporated the Dutch kingdom directly into the French empire. With other areas along the North Sea coast also added to it, the French empire proper now consisted of 130 departments (instead of the original 83) and extended in a great arc from the Baltic Sea at the base of the Danish peninsula to a point on the Italian coast south of Rome. The Grand Empire stretched from the southwest coast of Spain to the limits of the duchy of Warsaw, on the border of the Russian empire.

Napoleon appeared to be at the height of his power, virtually unchallenged throughout Europe. Except for the continuing war in the Spanish peninsula and the economic struggle with Great Britain, the period from 1810 to 1812 was relatively peaceful for the empire. By this time he had also taken steps toward the solution of a problem that had been plaguing him for years — the absence of a son to inherit his vast domain. His marriage with Josephine, contracted in 1796, had failed to produce an heir. More than once since becoming emperor he had considered the possibility of securing a divorce; neither partner to the marriage had remained faithful to the other. Yet Napoleon seems to have been reluctant to separate himself definitively from the woman who had inspired in him his greatest passion.

Nevertheless, marriage with the younger sister of Alexander of Russia was discussed at Tilsit in 1807 and again in 1809; the offer was finally refused by the tsar, ostensibly because the girl was too young. After the defeat of Austria in 1809, the emperor's representatives entered into negotiations with the Austrian court to arrange his marriage to the eighteen-year-old Austrian princess Marie Louise (1791–1847). Prince Metternich, Austria's foreign minister, immediately took up the proposal, seeing in it a chance for Austria to achieve at least temporary security in its relations with France. For Napoleon the marriage offered not only the hope of a male heir but also the prestige of affiliation with the oldest royal house on the Continent. Unable to obtain the consent of Pope Pius VII to the annulment of his marriage with Josephine, he secured the annulment from a subservient ecclesiastical body in Paris, retired Josephine to her château at Malmaison, and married Marie Louise in April 1810. Within a year she had borne him a son, who was given the title of king of Rome. The dynasty now appeared secure.

Beneath the apparent stability of the empire in the years 1810–1812 lay a number of signs of weakness and deterioration. We have spoken of the resentment aroused in the dependent states by the Continental System and the enforced levies of men and money to support Napoleon's wars. Even in France there were signs of growing discontent. A business recession in 1810–1811 diminished the regime's standing with the bourgeoisie, hitherto Napoleon's strongest supporters. The war in Spain was never popular with the French and aroused considerable opposition to the emperor. The burden of conscription in France reached down to younger and younger men during the Spanish campaign and the Austrian war of 1809, and by 1810 there were disturbing rumors of an impending war with Russia. Finally, devout Catholics, who had regarded Napoleon at the time of the Concordat as the restorer of the faith in France, were shocked by his dealings with the papacy in the years following the proclamation of the Empire. Relations between the pope and the emperor deteriorated steadily after 1805 because of difficulties in the administration of the Concordat and the high-handed action of Napoleon with respect to papal territories in Italy. Gradually, what had been left of the church lands after the establishment of Napoleon's kingdom of Italy was either absorbed into that kingdom or occupied and administered by the French. In May 1809, when Napoleon proposed formally to incorporate the remaining Papal States into the French empire, the pope threatened him with excommunication. Napoleon's response was to have Pius VII arrested and taken to Savona, near Genoa, where he was held prisoner. From there he was transferred in 1812 to Fontainebleau. Such an act, culminating the entire series of aggressive moves against the church, earned Napoleon the bitter emnity of devout Catholics throughout Europe.

As early as 1809 a number of individuals saw the handwriting on the wall and began to lay the groundwork for the regime that would succeed Bonaparte's. Among those most active in such plotting was the consummate opportunist Charles Maurice de Talleyrand, who managed to serve and to survive most of the governments that succeeded each other between 1789 and his death in 1838. Born to an aristocratic family in 1754, Talleyrand began his career as a liberal priest and was awarded the bishopric of Autun on the eve of the revolution. As a member of the Estates General he sided with the Third Estate; in the National Assembly he supported the confiscation of church lands and the Civil Constitution of the Clergy. In 1791, having been placed under the ban of the church by the pope, Talleyrand entered the diplomatic service. On the execution of Louis XVI, he sought refuge in the United States, returning to France only after the establishment of the Directory in 1795. After serving for two years as minister of foreign affairs for the Directory, he resigned in 1799, in time to help Bonaparte to

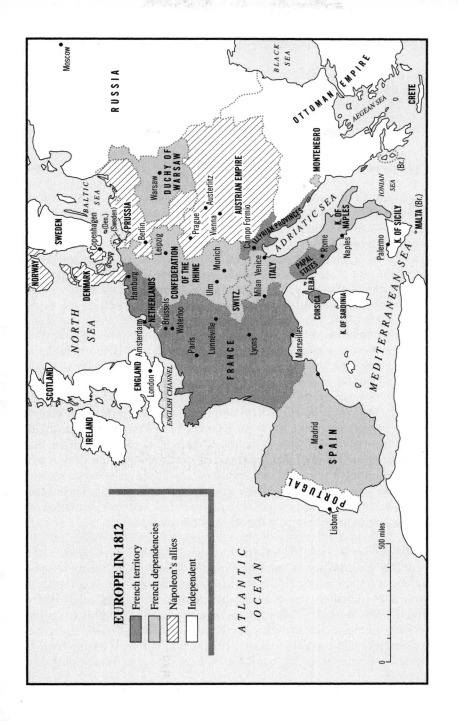

EUROPE IN 1812

- ■ French territory
- ▨ French dependencies
- ▨ Napoleon's allies
- □ Independent

500 miles

ATLANTIC OCEAN

NORTH SEA

BALTIC SEA

ENGLISH CHANNEL

MEDITERRANEAN SEA

ADRIATIC SEA

IONIAN SEA

AEGEAN SEA

BLACK SEA

Moscow

RUSSIA

SWEDEN

NORWAY

DENMARK

Copenhagen ○(Den.)

○(Sweden)

PRUSSIA

Berlin

DUCHY OF WARSAW

Warsaw

SCOTLAND

IRELAND

ENGLAND

London

Amsterdam

NETHERLANDS

Brussels

Waterloo

Hamburg

Leipzig

CONFEDERATION OF THE RHINE

Munich

Ulm

Prague

Vienna

Austerlitz

AUSTRIAN EMPIRE

Campo Formio

ILLYRIAN PROVINCES

SWITZ.

Lunéville

Paris

Lyons

FRANCE

Marseilles

Milan

Venice

ITALY

Rome

PAPAL STATES

ELBA

CORSICA

K. OF SARDINIA

Palermo

K. OF NAPLES

Naples

K. OF SICILY

MALTA (Br.)

MONTENEGRO

OTTOMAN EMPIRE

CRETE (Br.)

SPAIN

Madrid

PORTUGAL

Lisbon

power in the coup d'état of Brumaire. As Napoleon's minister of foreign affairs from 1799 to 1807 he helped ensure French supremacy in Europe, and in 1806 was rewarded by the emperor with the title prince of Benevento. In 1807 he resigned his post as foreign minister and in 1809 established contact with the Austrian diplomat Metternich, with a view to providing for future contingencies. He was to play an active role, as we shall discover later, in persuading the victorious allies to accept the restoration of the Bourbon dynasty in 1814, served again as foreign minister — this time for the Bourbon king Louis XVIII — and represented France at the Congress of Vienna in 1814 and 1815. Before his death he assisted one more French ruler — Louis Philippe — to the throne, in 1830; he ended his career as French ambassador to Britain in the 1830s.

Talleyrand's reputation has suffered at the hands of historians who view him as the prototype of the Machiavellian statesman and faithless diplomat. They charge that his primary concern was enriching himself and ensuring his survival in power in the bewildering succession of French governments from 1789 to 1830. Even his defenders concede his egotism and attribute his survival to the facility with which he adapted his utterances, public and private, to the ideology prevailing at a particular moment. This was perhaps easy for him since, in the last analysis, he adhered to no abstract ideals or principles. But his apologists have also contended that one consistent thread underlay his actions throughout his long career: his concern for France and his loyalty to its interests. His skills as a diplomat and a negotiator were always directed toward improving his country's international position. He deserted Napoleon, it is argued, when he found himself unable to restrain the emperor's insatiable ambition and realized it would ultimately destroy his country. Cutting his ties with the emperor, he laid the groundwork for the restoration of the Bourbon dynasty; in the peace settlement following the Napoleonic wars he was remarkably successful in restoring his defeated country almost immediately to the ranks of the great powers.

The Invasion of Russia, 1812

Despite the evidence of mounting dissatisfaction with his regime, Napoleon began preparations in the spring of 1812 for the campaign against Russia that ultimately was to prove disastrous for him. Like Adolf Hitler almost 130 years later, Napoleon saw two powers blocking his plans for complete European domination — Great Britain and Russia. Like Hitler, he tried unsuccessfully to subdue Great Britain, and when his attempt failed, turned eastward, convinced that if Russia were defeated, Britain must also succumb.

We have seen that the relationship between the two emperors, Napoleon and Alexander, was an uneasy one from the start. The ink was hardly dry on the agreements made at Tilsit in 1807 when Napoleon annexed the newly created duchy of Warsaw to the Confederation of the Rhine and sent thirty thousand troops into the region, a move that appeared very threatening to the Russian empire. His interest in consolidating his control over the Poles was further revealed when, after the defeat of Austria in 1809, he incorporated western Galicia into the duchy of Warsaw, leading Alexander to suspect his designs on territories taken by Russia from Poland in the eighteenth-century partitions. It also became clear to Alexander that Napoleon was far from willing to concede to Russia the free hand in the dismemberment of Turkey that the tsar thought he had obtained at Tilsit. As Russia's war with Turkey dragged on, Alexander realized that even if he were victorious, Napoleon would probably block his plans for expansion into Turkey's provinces in southeastern Europe. The nature of Napoleon's own designs in the Balkans is not entirely clear, but there can be no doubt that he was determined to prevent Russia from taking Constantinople. Finally, Alexander viewed with misgivings Napoleon's marriage to Marie Louise in 1810 and his consequent alliance with Austria.

Napoleon's principal grievance against the tsar was Alexander's failure to enforce the Continental System in his own ports. True to the agreement made at Tilsit, Russia declared war on Great Britain, but Alexander never pursued the war actively, and his administration of the regulations against British trade left much to be desired. When Napoleon asked Russia in 1810 to confiscate all neutral ships in its ports on the ground that they were carrying British goods, Alexander refused. Instead, he issued a decree later in the year that specifically encouraged the entry of neutral ships into Russian harbors. It was clear to Napoleon that the alliance was nearing its end. Late in 1810, Russia formally withdrew from the Continental System.

Anticipating conflict, both rulers sought allies. Each hoped for the support of Austria and Prussia, but the presence of the Napoleonic armies in Germany and the recent defeats that both Prussia and Austria had suffered at Napoleon's hands left them little choice but to submit to his demands. Accordingly, in 1812 Prussia pledged to contribute twenty thousand men, and Austria thirty thousand, to Napoleon's Grand Army. Unable to win support in Germany, Russia formed an alliance with Sweden. According to its terms, Sweden agreed to join Russia in the war against Napoleon in return for a promise of Russian assistance in annexing Norway, then in Denmark's possession, at the end of the war. Denmark was to be compensated with other territory. Ironically, Sweden's decision to join Russia was made by Crown Prince Bernadotte, once one of Napoleon's generals, who in 1810 had been named heir to the throne by the Swedish Estates. During this period also, Russia ended the wars against Turkey and Great Britain, and concluded an alliance with Great Britain against France.

In preparation for the invasion, Napoleon assembled his Grand Army in eastern Europe. Its strength at the time of the invasion in June 1812 was approximately four hundred and fifty thousand; by the time reinforcements were brought up, it numbered about six hundred thousand — and was probably the largest military force that had ever been brought together. In its ranks were not only French soldiers but contingents of Italians, Poles, Swiss, Dutch, and Germans (from the Confederation of the Rhine, Austria, and Prussia). Napoleon planned to have the predominantly French contingents of the army advance in the center, supported by an Austrian army to the south and a Prussian army to the north. Crossing the Niemen River in June, he hoped to drive a wedge between the two main Russian armies, surround them, and defeat them separately. His objective for the campaign of 1812 was Smolensk, where he hoped to impose terms on the tsar. If Alexander refused to submit, Napoleon would winter at Smolensk and renew the war in the spring of 1813 with a drive on Moscow.

He proceeded according to this plan. What disrupted his calculations was his failure to engage the main body of the Russian armies before he was deep into Russia. The Russian generals, fearing the numerical superiority of the enemy, repeatedly avoided giving battle. Advancing relentlessly across the Russian plains under a blazing July sun, Napoleon lost thousands of men through the ravages of heat, disease, and hunger, and through desertion. When his troops finally reached Smolensk in mid-August, the Russians fought only a rearguard action and then left the city to the invader. According to his original plan Napoleon was to halt here, and he was urged to do so by some of his subordinates. Instead, he made the fatal decision to press on to Moscow. General Mikhail Kutuzov (1745–1813) had been given orders to halt the advance on Moscow at Borodino, and there, on September 7, Napoleon met the main Russian force. The two armies fought bitterly, in a battle that left some seventy thousand dead and wounded. In the end, both sides claimed victory, but it was the Russians who retreated, leaving the path to Moscow open. When the French finally reached Moscow on September 14, they found it practically deserted; within a few hours, fires broke out in the city, set presumably by those who had stayed behind for this purpose by order of the retreating military governor. Because most Moscow dwellings were built of wood, the fires spread swiftly, and within a week almost three quarters of the city had burned to the ground. For five weeks Napoleon remained in the empty, devastated city, as the morale of his troops rapidly deteriorated. His offer of a truce having been rejected by Alexander, he waited in vain for the tsar to come to terms. Finally, unable to supply his troops so far from their bases, frustrated in his hope of achieving a decisive victory, and fearing the onset of the Russian winter, on October 19 he began his catastrophic retreat from Moscow. His troops were harassed by attacks by Kutuzov's army and prevented from following a shorter southern route to Smolensk. At the beginning of November, cold weather set in and caused additional suffering for the hungry, beleaguered French forces. By the time they reached Smolensk, only half of the troops who had left Moscow remained. The climax of the catastrophe came in late November when the retreating forces, attempting to recross the Berezina River, were subjected to murderous fire by Russians both behind and ahead of them. From this point on, the retreat became a rout as the army lost all semblance of organization and disintegrated. On December 18, the last remnants of the Grand Army straggled across the Niemen River, from which they had set out in June. Of six hundred thousand men, no more than thirty thousand remained. The rest, apart from deserters, had been killed or captured.

Napoleon had left the army early in December, before it reached the Niemen, and had hastened back to Paris. The full extent of the disaster was not known in France immediately, but rumors were trickling back and Napoleon wished to be present personally to quiet misgivings in the capital.

The Last Remnants of the Grand Army en route to Smolensk, by Faber du Faur. At the beginning of November 1812, cold weather set in, exacerbating the suffering of the hungry, beleaguered French forces.

The rout of Napoleon's army at the Berezina River, November 26, 1812.

His main reason for returning, however, was to organize a new army. Far from being shattered by the defeat he had just suffered, he was more determined than ever to renew the war against his two enemies, Russia and Great Britain. Three weeks after he got back to Paris he demanded from the Senate a draft calling up three hundred and fifty thousand new recruits.

The War of Liberation, 1813–1814

Fifteen months elapsed between the end of the disastrous Russian campaign and the triumphal entry of the allied armies into Paris on March 31, 1814. What is perhaps surprising is that the French managed to hold off their enemies for so long. That Napoleon succeeded in raising a force of a quarter of a million men by the spring of 1813 was a miracle, but of course the men in this army were not the seasoned troops he had used at Austerlitz and Jena. Moreover, the final campaigns of the emperor were seriously handicapped by shortages of arms, ammunition, and equipment. Indeed, some military historians argue that France's defeat was caused as much by the lack of matériel as by the lack of men. A final reason for the defeat of Napoleon was that his enemies, after almost two decades of intermittent wars against France, succeeded in temporarily setting aside their differences and uniting to achieve victory.

The cornerstone of the coalition that defeated Napoleon was laid in March 1813, when Prussia and Russia formed an alliance and called on Austria and Great Britain to join them. The response was not immediate, but the potentialities of the coalition were augmented by an agreement at about the same time between Great Britain and Crown Prince Bernadotte of Sweden. In return for a large subsidy from the British, Bernadotte promised to furnish thirty thousand Swedish troops to be used against the French. The war between the allies and Napoleon's reconstituted army began in the spring of 1813. Despite two nominal victories in May, Napoleon's losses were heavy, and he willingly agreed in June to an armistice, which lasted most of the summer. This pause turned out to be of greater advantage to his opponents than to himself. When the fighting began again in August, Metternich had decided to take Austria into the war on the side of the coalition, and Great Britain had signed a treaty providing the allies with heavy subsidies. Metternich reached his decision after Napoleon refused to accept an agreement calling for the abandonment by France of most of its conquests in the interest of a balance-of-power settlement for the Continent. For the first time in his career Napoleon found himself confronted by the united forces of four major powers. Besides his French troops, he had only contingents from the Confederation of the Rhine supporting him. Nevertheless the emperor attacked, and within two weeks, had inflicted a defeat on one of the allied armies at Dresden (August 1813), in his last major victory on German soil. From that time on, however, the campaign went badly for the emperor, as his subordinate commanders met with a series of reverses. Early in October, Bavaria withdrew from the Confederation of the Rhine and joined the alliance against the French. The climax of the fall campaign came in a series of decisive battles around Leipzig in mid-October, when all the allied armies converged on the French in what came to be known as the Battle of the Nations. After several days of preliminary fighting, the allies, in a single nine-hour engagement, drove the French armies back to the gates of Leipzig, winning a shattering victory. Deserted by his remaining German allies, Napoleon was forced to retreat across the Rhine; the Confederation of the Rhine had come to an end.

What made the debacle in Germany even more serious was a series of setbacks in other parts of the empire. A revolt in the Dutch provinces, followed by an allied invasion there, resulted in the restoration of the prince of Orange as ruler in Holland. An army raised by Eugène de Beauharnais in northern Italy at Napoleon's instigation met with defeat by the Austrians. Finally, the year 1813 saw one reverse after another in Spain, as the duke of Wellington advanced against a French army weakened by the transfer of important contingents to the German front. By the middle of the year,

Joseph Bonaparte had fled to France, and the French were retreating from region after region. In November, Wellington crossed the Spanish frontier into France and laid siege to the city of Bayonne.

Before the allies invaded France from the east, they made an offer of peace to Napoleon that would have left France with its "natural frontiers" of the Alps and the Rhine. Metternich later admitted in his memoirs that the allies had no intention of keeping this promise, that it was made in the belief that Napoleon would refuse, thereby assuming responsibility for continuing the war. Metternich's assumption proved correct. Napoleon did not reject the offer outright, but stalled in such a way that the allies could withdraw it and still blame him for the prolongation of the conflict.

In the beginning of 1814 the allied armies, two hundred thousand strong, crossed the Rhine. Napoleon, left with only ninety thousand soldiers, many of them mere youths, fought a brilliant defensive campaign in these desperate circumstances. Shifting his troops swiftly in order to attack the divided allied forces piecemeal, he managed still to win isolated victories against the Prussian general Gerhard von Blücher (1742–1819) and the Austrian prince Karl Philipp zu Schwarzenberg (1771–1820). But the rawness of his troops, their numerical inferiority, and the lack of equipment finally decided the issue. While he made a desperate attempt to throw himself on the rear of the allied forces in Lorraine, the leading contingents of the invaders pressed on toward Paris. With the final storming of Montmartre by the allies, the French were forced to capitulate. On March 31 Tsar Alexander and King Frederick William made their triumphal entry into the capital. Napoleon had meanwhile hastened back to Paris, hoping to make a last-ditch stand, but he arrived too late and retired to Fontainebleau. Even at this stage he urged his marshals to join him in an assault on the city, but they refused. Prince Talleyrand, who had remained in Paris, now used his position as vice grand elector to summon the Senate, and influenced that body to declare that Napoleon and his family had forfeited the throne of France. Hoping to

His Monument. A Janus-faced Napoleon looks to the past and the future at the beginning of the year 1814, shortly after France's defeat at the battle of Leipzig.

salvage something, Napoleon thereupon announced his abdication in favor of his son. But the allies would have none of it, and forced him to make his abdication unconditional. Within a month he had departed for the tiny island of Elba, off the Italian coast, where the allies, with a certain degree of irony, granted him sovereign control.

The Bourbon Restoration and the Hundred Days

Although during the final stages of the war, there had been differences among the allied leaders about the selection of a successor to Napoleon, these had been largely resolved by the time of his defeat. Partly because of the skillful machinations of Talleyrand, who was the spokesman of a royalist minority in Paris, the allies settled on the count of Provence, a younger brother of the beheaded Louis XVI, to rule as Louis XVIII. (The title of Louis XVII was reserved for the second son of Louis XVI, who had died in captivity during the French Revolution.) The news that a Bourbon would occupy the throne was not greeted with particular enthusiasm by the French people, but the king's initial pledge that he would not discriminate against individuals because of their past opinions and that he intended to grant a liberal constitution to France helped reconcile those who feared the consequences of a royalist restoration.

The relatively lenient treatment given France by the allies in the Treaty of Paris (May 30, 1814) was expressly designed to facilitate the resumption of power by the Bourbons. Hoping to establish a balance of power, the statesmen who drew up this treaty saw that reducing France to second- or third-rate status would serve no useful purpose and would undermine the prestige of the restored Bourbon dynasty. The new king had not, after all, been responsible for the aggressive conquests of France in the wars just ended; his government should not be required to pay the penalty. Accordingly, France was allowed to retain the territories that it had held on November 1, 1792; these included parts of Savoy, of Germany, and of the Austrian Netherlands, as well as a few enclaves such as Avignon. But France was forced to recognize the independence of the remainder of the Austrian Netherlands, Holland, the German states, the Italian states, and Switzerland. All of France's colonies, with the exception of Trinidad, Tobago, St. Lucia, and Mauritius (Île de France) in the Indian Ocean, were returned to her by Great Britain. Britain also retained the island of Malta. Perhaps most surprising is the fact that France was not required to pay an indemnity to the victorious powers, or even to give back the art treasures that Napoleon had pirated from foreign cities during the wars.

Despite these advantages, the regime encountered difficulties from the start. The way in which the new constitution, the Charter of 1814, was presented irritated popular sensibilities, for the king expressly stated that the Charter was a "gift" to the French people granted by the king "in the nineteenth year of our reign." By this move, Louis XVIII appeared not only to be denying the principle of popular sovereignty but also to be ignoring the fact that the revolution and the Napoleonic interlude had even existed. The provisions of the Charter itself belied this view, for the document incorporated many features of the Declaration of the Rights of Man and the Citizen and the Constitution of 1791 and maintained the administrative institutions of the empire. But the uneasiness of the more liberal elements in France was enhanced by the growing influence in court circles of the king's younger brother Charles Philippe, count of Artois (1757–1836), who was far more conservative than the king and was the unofficial leader of the faction known as the Ultraroyalists, or Ultras. This group openly regarded the Charter as a mere stopgap and called for the establishment of an absolutist regime and the restoration of the Roman Catholic Church to its former privileges. Finally, certain measures taken by the new government alienated specific groups of Frenchmen. Army officers and soldiers suffered from the conversion of the army to a peacetime footing, with a consequent reduction of pay; manufacturers resented the sudden tariff reductions, which subjected them to foreign competition; peasants looked on uneasily as the government returned large tracts of unsold national land to the original owners.

Many of the ills from which the French people suffered in 1814–1815 were attributable to the transition from a wartime to a peacetime economy, but the new government received the blame for them. Napoleon Bonaparte, who had become increasingly restive under the restraints imposed on him at Elba, was kept well informed of the mood of his former subjects and had decided by the midwinter of 1815 that the moment had come for his return to power. Taking advantage of the British commissioner's absence from the island, he commandeered several vessels and embarked for France. He landed at Cannes on March 1, 1815, and made his way northward through the mountain passes of Dauphiné, encountering practically no resistance. Indeed, most of his former soldiers rallied to his standard. Most prominent among them was Michel Ney, the duke of Elchingen, one of Napoleon's most distinguished generals. Named a marshal of the empire in 1804, Ney had helped persuade Napoleon to abdicate in May 1814, and he had become a peer of France on Louis XVIII's restoration. Ney initially denounced Napoleon's escape from Elba, but when he was dispatched at the head of an army to intercept Napoleon in southern France, he impulsively rejoined his old commander. The cities that lay on Napoleon's route opened their gates to welcome the former emperor. By the time he reached Paris on March 20, Louis XVIII and his entourage had fled across the border to Ghent, and the empire was once again proclaimed. In this way began the period known as the Hundred Days; it lasted until Napoleon's defeat at Waterloo in June.

In an effort to win the support of those groups that had formerly opposed his regime, Napoleon adopted during this period the liberal pose which he was to elaborate further during his final years in exile. Claiming that he had been prevented from offering reforms earlier by the need to defend France against European kings and aristocrats, he provided in his new constitution for an extension of the suffrage, the institution of a responsible ministry, and the elimination of press censorship. The announcement of these changes was greeted with a certain amount of skepticism, and Napoleon was aware that, in the last analysis, what he needed to ensure his position was a military victory.

News of Napoleon's escape from Elba struck the capitals of Europe with the force of a bombshell. March found many of Europe's leaders in Vienna, where they had assembled at a congress in the fall of 1814 to deliberate on the disposition of Napoleon's former empire. Within an hour after the reception of the news, Metternich had secured agreement from the monarchs of Austria, Russia, and Prussia to renew the war against Napoleon. Great Britain subsequently branded Napoleon an "outlaw" and joined the three eastern powers in a new alliance directed against him.

Napoleon realized that his situation was precarious. Against the combined allied forces, which were estimated at seven hundred thousand, he was able to marshal an army of only two hundred thousand, of whom more than a third had to police the interior and defend his frontiers. Nevertheless he determined once more to strike boldly. On June 15 he crossed the Belgian border, seeking to make contact with the armies of Blücher, commanding the Prussians, and the duke of Wellington, commanding a combined force of Belgian, Dutch, German, and British troops. He hoped to split the two armies and defeat them individually. An initial victory against Blücher caused the Prussians to retreat, and Napoleon, having dispatched thirty thousand of his own troops to pursue them, turned to support Marshal Ney against the forces of the duke of Wellington. But the emperor had miscalculated the direction of Blücher's retreat. The Prussian troops evaded the pursuing French forces, and Blücher succeeded in regrouping them in a position from which he could lend support to Wellington. Thinking that the Prussians were no longer in the area and also handicapped by the absence of thirty thousand of his own troops, Napoleon launched an attack on Wellington at Waterloo. Wellington had the numerical advantage, and because he was fighting from the shelter of a ridge, was able to conceal the strength of the forces massed at his rear. What for a time appeared to be a deadlock between the two armies was turned into an allied victory by the return of Blücher's divisions, which were thrown on the French right. By the end of the day, there remained only half of the forces Napoleon had taken into battle at noon, and these fled in undisciplined panic. This was a defeat that even Napoleon could not survive. Four days later he abdicated once again, and frustrated in an attempt to escape to America, he surrendered to the captain of a British warship off La Rochelle. To the British fell the responsibility for serving as Napoleon's jailers; this time he was shipped off to the lonely island of St. Helena in the South Atlantic.

THE ACHIEVEMENT AND THE LEGACY OF NAPOLEON

During the six years that remained to Napoleon, he had little to do beyond reliving and reviewing his epic career. An individual of lesser stature might have engaged in sterile regrets over mistakes made, opportunities lost, and betrayals by trusted individuals, and indeed Napoleon's memoirs are not altogether free of regrets of this sort. But he was more concerned with arranging and ordering his version of the events of his career so as to impose an appearance of unity and coherence on his achievements. The fruits of this effort are to be seen in his memoirs, sometimes referred to as "the gospel according to St. Helena," which often bear scant resemblance to events that actually took place and are particularly distorted when they deal with the emperor's intentions and motives. But they are nonetheless important, since the account of the emperor's life constructed at St. Helena forms the basis for the Napoleonic legend that emerged after his death and was embellished by successive biographers and admirers.

The essence of the myth that the dethroned emperor attempted to construct was that he had been a liberal and a son of the revolution, aiming to carry on and complete the reforms begun during the revolutionary era and to bring these benefits to the peoples of Europe still living under the antiquated institutions and reactionary rulers of the Old Regime. Writing during an era that witnessed the restoration of many of these very rulers and institutions, he sensed that this image would have a particular appeal.

We have already seen that a number of Napoleon's measures under the consulate and the early empire—the Code Napoléon, the overhaul of administrative structures, and the stabilization of finances—can be interpreted as bringing to completion reforms initiated during the revolutionary years. In these respects, Napoleon could pose legitimately as the consolidator of the achievements of the revolution. Furthermore, the attempt to introduce many of these changes into the vassal states as well as all of the French empire seems to justify his claim that he was the standard bearer of the revolution throughout Europe.

On the other hand, these reforms were made within the context of a political system that denied individual citizens any real voice in their government and consistently stifled the free expression of opinions through censorship and surveillance of those suspected of opposition to the regime. Such an atmosphere certainly constituted a betrayal of principles embodied in the Declaration of the Rights of Man and the Citizen, and its existence seems to weaken Napoleon's argument that he was a true son of the revolution.

In assessing Napoleon's long-range impact on Europe as a whole, it is difficult to separate his policies and their influence from those of the revolutionary governments that preceded him, but there is no question that the Europe of 1815 was very different from that of 1789 and that the Napoleonic regime was responsible for many of the changes. Particularly in those regions that had been directly incorporated into the French empire, many Napoleonic institutions lasted after 1815. Mention has already been made of the persistence of the Napoleonic codes in the Low Countries, in Rhineland Prussia, in the kingdom of Naples, and in various smaller German principalities. Even where the codes were suppressed, they exercised an influence on laws which replaced them. Although the administrative division of the empire into departments, districts, and communes was abandoned after 1815 by most regions that no longer formed part of France, Napoleon's highly organized bureaucracy with its appointed officials following the orders of the central government was admired and imitated by rulers seeking greater control and efficiency in their states. Other Napoleonic institutions that survived or were imitated elsewhere include his police system, his tax-collection organization, his Concordat with the Catholic church, and, of course, the Napoleonic army and system of military education.

As far as social changes were concerned, the abolition of serfdom and of other features of the feudal regime (decreed in some cases by the revolutionary governments, in others by the Napoleonic regime) helped to transform the old order in the Low Countries, the Rhineland, and in a number of German and Italian states. We have seen that the defeat of Prussia by the French armies stimulated the Prussian king to order a series of reforms, including the abolition of serfdom, in 1807. All these changes, combined with the impact of the Napoleonic codes, with their emphasis on equality before the law, freedom of land ownership, and the safeguarding of private property, worked ultimately to the advantage of the bourgeoisie and even of the peasantry. In other words, the pattern of social life in western Europe and in parts of central Europe had been significantly altered. Attempts might be made after 1815 to restore the political systems that had existed prior to the revolution, but the social changes were, for the most part, irreversible.

Napoleon had initially been welcomed, at least in some quarters, as a liberator intent on freeing the nonnoble classes from traditional obligations and restrictions. In the long run, however, enthusiasm turned to resentment as it became clear that the member states of the Grand Empire were merely satellites of France, their chief function being to supply the emperor with men, money, and supplies for his further conquests. Napoleon's new order, if considerably less brutal than Hitler's in the following century, was hardly more appealing to contemporaries. Certainly few Europeans outside of France lamented his downfall in 1814.

Perhaps the greatest long-term impact of Napoleon was felt beyond the boundaries of Europe. Even before his coup of 1799, Napoleon's Egyptian campaign had spread the ideals of the French Revolution to the Middle East, encouraging efforts at political modernization by rulers such as Muhammad Ali, viceroy of Egypt from 1805 to 1849.[4] The Peninsular Campaign of 1808–1813 destabilized the Latin American empires of Spain and Portugal, resulting in their complete dissolution by the 1820s. The new generation of Latin American independence fighters, led by charismatic figures such as Simon Bolívar (1783–1830) and Antonio José de Sucre (1795–1830) embraced the language of the French Revolution while imitating the methods of Bonaparte. Indirectly, Napoleon's legacy reverberated long after his death, influencing the political tactics of subsequent revolutionary leaders in Asia, Africa, and elsewhere. Thus, Napoleon played an instrumental role in transforming the revolution into a truly global phenomenon.

Though "the gospel according to St. Helena" was never universally accepted, time transformed Bonaparte's reputation both in France and beyond. Napoleon did not come to be viewed as the apostle of liberal and nationalist causes. What captured the popular imagination of succeeding generations instead was the vision of Napoleon as a man of the people who made his way to the top, or as the daring general, the brilliant strategist, who commanded hundreds of thousands of men and succeeded in mastering for a time an entire continent. In the relatively prosaic age that followed his downfall, an era of prolonged peace, the exploits of Napoleon the soldier, the limitless quality of his ambition, made him a romantic hero more glamorous than any creation of fiction.

---

[4] See for example the articles by Elbaki Hermassi and Nikki Keddie in *The Global Ramifications of the French Revolution*, edited by Joseph Klaits and Michael H. Haltzel (Cambridge, 1994).

CHAPTER 3

The Industrial Revolution and the Remaking of European Society

THE CATACLYSMIC events beginning with the French Revolution of 1789 permanently transformed the landscape of European politics. Despite the best efforts of conservative leaders to contain the spread of revolutionary principles, only a partial "Restoration" proved possible after Napoleon's demise in 1815. Throughout Europe, nineteenth-century monarchs had to contend with democratic and nationalist movements that challenged their sovereignty, and old social elites struggled against the tide of individualistic and egalitarian ideals.

Yet the beginnings of industrialization caused even more profound changes in the lives of Europeans than the political upheavals of this era. The Industrial Revolution involved a complex series of developments that occurred first in eighteenth- and nineteenth-century England but that were repeated, with variations, in the northwestern tier of states of the European continent in the first half of the nineteenth century, in parts of Germany and in northern Italy after 1850, and reached eastern and parts of southern Europe only at the end of the nineteenth century or the beginning of the twentieth century. Indeed, some of the developments associated with the Industrial Revolution are continuing today in Asia, Africa, and Latin America under the label "economic development" or "economic modernization."

Despite important differences among the societies in which industrialization has occurred, it is possible to find some common denominators in the process—particularly in those European countries first affected. Initially the Industrial Revolution in England and on the Continent involved the substitution of machines driven by water power or steam for simple tools operated by hand or foot. This, in turn, resulted in significant changes in the organization of production. For example, the shift in textile manufacturing from spinning and weaving by individual laborers in their homes to production of cloth by machinery required workers to be concentrated in factories whose location was determined by proximity to the sources of power. This transformation also necessitated the use of new raw materials: whereas domestic textile producers had worked mainly with wool, the new factories relied primarily on cotton grown by slave labor in the American South. Such a change yielded tremendous increases in productivity, but it was fraught with important material and psychological consequences for the laborers. For it required mass migrations of population, led to the emergence of new cities and the expansion of old ones, and wrought major changes in the worker's mode of life.

Besides textile manufacturing, two other industries were particularly important in the Industrial Revolution in Britain and generally played a key role in industrialization on the Continent: coal mining and the manufacturing of metals. Innovations in these industries stimulated and were stimulated by changes taking place in the production of textiles. The development of an effective steam engine by the 1770s and its introduction in textile mills required improved exploitation of Britain's coal resources as a source of fuel. Iron was the raw material essential for the construction of machinery and engines used in the mills and mines. This first wave of industrialization, lasting through the mid-nineteenth century, was followed by a "second industrial revolution" after 1850, which was marked by the development of new sources of energy, notably petroleum and electricity, and new materials such as steel and aluminum. A "third industrial revolution," driven by the development of microelectronics since World War II, is currently underway, exercising effects of a similar magnitude on the world economy.

Together with the French Revolution, the Industrial Revolution laid the foundation for the modern age, creating distinctive challenges for nineteenth-century Europeans. Growing urbanization and disparities of wealth, along with increasing physical and social mobility, resulted in powerful tensions within European society. The early stages of industrialization coincided with the breakdown of older, stable agrarian communities, and contributed to an increasingly individualistic, but also an increasingly polarized economy. The inhabitants of Europe's cities had to negotiate their lives in a new world of machines.

ORIGINS OF THE INDUSTRIAL REVOLUTION

Some historians have questioned whether the economic transformation of Europe beginning in the late eighteenth century can rightly be termed a "revolution." Unlike the political revolutions of this era, industrialization occurred only gradually. Already in the seventeenth century, a process sometimes called "protoindustrialization" had begun in much of western Europe, with the production of yarn, dyes, and cloth in small rural cottage industries. The increasing wealth of the urban middle classes in the Netherlands, Britain, and France also stimulated the demand for luxury consumer goods, resulting in a growing number of workshops producing items such as furniture, china, glassware, and fine clothing. Historians have sometimes referred to this growth in economic demand as a "consumer revolution" that paved the way for mass production by creating new markets. Not only did industrialization have its roots in these earlier events, but even at the end of the nineteenth century, the triumph of the factory system remained incomplete: the great majority of productive activity remained centered in small workshops and in agriculture throughout most of Europe.

However incremental in pace, the developments in Europe between 1750 and 1850 represented the greatest economic transformation in all of human history up to that time. In 1750, overland travel in Europe was frequently no faster than during the era of the Roman Empire. By the 1860s, the trip from London to Rome took sixty hours, and it was possible to circumnavigate the globe in less time than had been required for a round-trip between London and Naples in 1750. During the 1820s, the first steam locomotives were demonstrated in Britain. By 1850, Europe had 14,500 miles of railroad track; by 1880, the amount had exploded to 102,000 miles. During the ten year period 1700–1709, a total of 22 patents were issued in England. A century and a half later, during the decade 1840–1849, the number was 4,581. As these statistics illustrate, this period witnessed not only far-reaching changes in the material conditions of life, but also the rise of the expectation that economic and technological change would continue indefinitely at an ever accelerating pace.

Conditions for "Industrial Takeoff"

No single cause accounts for the quickening of economic activity after the mid-eighteenth century, which is sometimes described as Europe's "industrial takeoff." Rather, these changes stemmed from the combination of a variety of factors, including population growth, advances in methods of agriculture, the expansion of overseas trade and banking institutions, improvements in transportation networks, political liberalization, and technological innovation.

Even before the Industrial Revolution wrought a transformation of European society, a dramatic increase in population began to disrupt Europe's traditional way of life. Beginning in the eighteenth century, particularly after 1750, the population of most European countries began to grow rapidly. During that century the Habsburg empire expanded from 20 to 27 million, Spain grew from 5 to 10 million, and Prussia from 3 to 6 million. France's population increased somewhat less rapidly, from 20 to 28 million, and Britain's from 9 to 16 million. This growth continued through the nineteenth century but at significantly different rates. Britain and the states that joined to form the German Empire in 1871 continued to grow very rapidly, each trebling its population during the nineteenth century, whereas the growth of France's population slowed down markedly. Some of the states of southern and eastern Europe had to wait until after 1870 for their major growth. For Europe as a whole, the population doubled between 1800 and 1900. The cumulative effect of this population explosion after 1750 was tremendous, particularly when we consider that the rate of population growth in Europe as a whole had been only 3 percent during the century 1650–1750. Even without industrialization European society would have been subjected to unprecedented stresses.

In the absence of detailed population statistics for the eighteenth century, demographers differ in their explanations for this sudden population increase. Some have noted in its initial stages an increase in the birthrate, at least in some countries, but most have laid greater stress on a significant drop in the death rate after 1750. More children survived infancy, and more adults lived to an older age. For this a number of reasons have been offered. Improved hygiene and advances in medicine spared Europeans from some of the worst endemic diseases and plagues. An increase of the food supply limited the famines that had periodically plagued Europe and provided somewhat better diets. In this connection, the introduction of potato cultivation was one of the most important agricultural innovations in western and central Europe, since it enabled people to survive even though they might be living in great poverty. In some regions, the opening up of land not previously under cultivation also contributed to higher food production and provided an inducement to peasants to increase the size of their families. Finally, improvements in the maintenance of public order and security meant that life was not so hazardous as it had been in an era of greater brigandage and violence; nor were there so many civil and religious wars as there had been in the seventeenth century.

Europe's dramatic population increase had dynamic consequences for

European society and institutions. Increased numbers of people inevitably place pressures on available resources and stimulate competition for those resources. For example, although new land was opened up for cultivation, the growth of the rural population ultimately outstripped the supply of land available and forced many peasants or children of peasants to seek their livelihood elsewhere. Population growth, in its early stages, resulted in a higher percentage of youth in society; this may have added vitality but it also contributed to greater social turbulence. In the long run, changing patterns of population growth affected traditional family structure as parents were called on to support larger families or see the unity of the family disrupted by the departure of those seeking a living beyond their traditional home or village. A longer life span meant greater numbers of old people to be cared for.

The demographic transformation of Europe after 1750 thus had mixed economic effects. On the one hand, it stimulated industrialization by establishing a large, mobile populace available to work in new urban factories, as well as by creating a greater demand for mass-produced goods such as clothing. On the other hand, it also sometimes limited the availability of investment capital because of the need to devote more resources toward the subsistence needs of a country's inhabitants. Certain regions that experienced rapid population expansion during the late eighteenth century, such as Russia and some other parts of eastern Europe, had low per capita incomes and low rates of economic growth.

In England, the Industrial Revolution was closely related to the changes in methods of farming and stock breeding during the eighteenth century that had constituted an agricultural revolution. These came about when the large landowners, politically secure after their victory over the crown during the revolutions of the seventeenth century, sought to exploit their dominant position and to increase their money incomes. Their efforts to cultivate the land more efficiently and to introduce improved methods of stockbreeding were hampered by the system of open fields, common lands, and semicollective methods of farming inherited from an earlier era. For success, their experiments needed large enclosed fields, so the landowners tried to speed up the process of "enclosing," or fencing in, their land by having the so-called acts of enclosure passed. As a result of these acts, which were unopposed in Parliament, vast areas were brought under more efficient cultivation and the landlords did achieve greater productivity—at the expense of thousands of small farmers who were forcibly ejected from their homes and from lands their families had cultivated for centuries. The enclosures brought about a marked increase in food production; British farms could now support a larger population with the work of fewer individuals. Some of those displaced from their farms ultimately sought employment in the new manufacturing centers and thus provided some of the surplus labor without which no industrial revolution can gain momentum.

Another source of new wealth was the growing volume of colonial trade. For the European countries bordering the Atlantic Ocean—notably Britain, the Netherlands, France, Spain, and Portugal—this trade meant not only profits for merchants, but also access to raw materials and markets for manufactured goods. The American colonies sent products such as sugar, rum, tobacco, silver, timber, and furs to their home countries in return for finished consumer items. Because the colonies depended heavily on slave labor, many European merchants engaged in a three-way "triangle trade": they shipped manufactured goods to West Africa to be exchanged for slaves; on arrival in the Americas, the slaves were traded for colonial products that were shipped back to Europe. During the eighteenth century, British, French, and Dutch merchants, along with Americans, all played an important role in this commerce. In the early nineteenth century, Europeans increasingly shipped mass-produced cotton cloth to both Africa and the Americas. Thus, the industrialization of Europe was achieved partly through the enslavement of Africans.

Economic prosperity was a necessary but not a sufficient condition for the expansion of industry in eighteenth-century Europe. Britain had a better developed banking system and credit facilities than those on the Continent, which made it easier for wealth from agriculture and colonial trade to be directed toward financing new industrial enterprises. The London Stock Exchange, founded at the end of the seventeenth century, enabled companies to raise investment capital by selling shares in their enterprises. In continental Europe, by contrast, most enterprises had to finance themselves. Britain also led the Continent in the establishment of insurance and liberal incorporation laws, both of which contributed to the rise of entrepreneurialism.

Well-developed transportation networks, facilitating the movement of goods between producers and markets, were another important prerequisite for economic growth. Britain and some other states of northwestern Europe, such as France and the Low Countries, enjoyed an important head start in this regard. The French absolute monarchs of the seventeenth and eighteenth centuries, for example, had embarked on an ambitious program of road building and canal building. The improvement of transportation systems accelerated after 1820, with the advent of steam-powered ships and railroad locomotives. These developments, as well, initially affected the states of northern and western Europe disproportionately. Spain's industrialization was inhibited by the country's lack of navigable rivers, as well as by the absence of railways until after 1850. In the sparsely populated German states, a multitude of tolls and customs barriers complicated domestic trade until 1834, when the establishment of the Zollverein, or customs union, led to the abolition of internal tariffs within most German territory.

The relationship between political liberalization and industrialization is a subject of debate among historians. Many scholars once believed that laissez faire economic policies, under which the government avoided interfering with the free market, were a critical factor explaining Britain's early economic leadership. More recent research has clouded this picture to some degree. During the eighteenth century, the British government imposed tariffs and other policies influencing trade, stemming from the Navigation Act of 1651; later, it regulated various industries such as railways and banks, as well as enacting legislation concerning working conditions, public health, poor relief, and other issues. Scholars have concluded that not only did the British government frequently intervene in the marketplace, but that government regulation elsewhere in Europe sometimes proved beneficial for economic development. This was especially true for countries that industrialized later in the nineteenth century, such as the German states: in these regions, protective tariffs and government subsidies often helped shield indigenous enterprises from rapacious foreign competition.[1]

In *The National System of Political Economy*, published in 1841, the German political economist Friedrich List (1789–1846) made a powerful case for the selective use of protective tariffs, which influenced subsequent policy makers in much of central Europe. List was a liberal who had lived in exile in the United States for six years from 1825 to 1831. With his years of experience on two continents, he argued that untrammeled free trade often had the effect of consolidating the preeminence of dominant economies — such as Britain's — over less developed ones such as those of Germany and the United States. Tariffs, he concluded, were often necessary to encourage the development of fledgling national industries, provided that such measures were regarded as "a first step on the road that eventually leads to universal free trade."

Although markets were rarely entirely free during the nineteenth century, certain liberal social and economic policies served as important catalysts for industrialization. Britain, unlike most of continental Europe, possessed a large domestic market (including all of England and Scotland) unfettered

---

[1] See for example A. J. Taylor, *Laissez-faire and State Intervention in Nineteenth-Century Britain* (1972); David S. Landes, *The Unbound Prometheus: Technological Change and Industrial Development in Western Europe from 1750 to the Present* (Cambridge, 1969), pp. 124–230.

by internal tariffs and tolls. The abolition of hereditary serfdom and of restrictions on the freedom of movement made possible the formation of a mobile, urbanized labor force. Serfdom had been eliminated in Britain long before 1800, but it remained in force in Prussia and some other German states until the Napoleonic era. In Russia, serfdom was abolished only in 1861; not coincidentally, Russia's industrialization began in earnest only at the end of the nineteenth century. Likewise, by eliminating the economic monopolies of urban craft guilds, the governments of France, Prussia, and other states encouraged competition in manufacturing, which ultimately stimulated growth. One additional development that may have contributed to the emergence of a mobile workforce in England was the adoption of a new system of poor relief in the eighteenth century. These poor laws, which provided an early form of social insurance, may have given rural inhabitants confidence that they could move away from their homes without risking starvation.[2]

A final indispensable factor enabling the establishment of large industrial enterprises was technological innovation. The machines that powered the new factories would have been impossible without the advance of scientific and engineering knowledge in Europe over the preceding centuries. Technological improvements, however, were not primarily motivated by advances in the realm of pure science. Rather, new production techniques evolved in response to specific economic demands — as is illustrated by the history of textile manufacturing in eighteenth-century Britain.

Beginnings of the Industrial Revolution in Great Britain

Many of the factors that made possible Britain's transition to an industrial economy during the late eighteenth century were present in other European countries as well. Populations were growing throughout Europe during this era; and scientific knowledge was shared across the Continent. Several countries, including the Netherlands and France, were as prosperous as Britain, and had highly developed transportation networks along with substantial agricultural surpluses. Why then did the Industrial Revolution begin in Great Britain? While no simple answer suffices, the explanation appears to lie in the unique confluence of social and economic conditions in Britain, including the displacement of rural populations by enclosures, the availability of raw materials and investment capital as a result of burgeoning trade, and the existence of colonial markets for textiles and other finished goods.

That some of the key inventions that revolutionized the textile industry

[2] Peter M. Solar, "Poor Relief and English Economic Development Before the Industrial Revolution," *Economic History Review* 48 (1995), pp. 1–22.

were British achievements owed not so much to the native genius of the people as to the demand for greater quantities of goods produced more efficiently and cheaply. British hand labor could not compete successfully with Asian labor in the production of cotton cloth. But if cotton could be spun and woven by machines, British manufacturers could clearly capture the market. This was the stimulus that led to improved spinning devices and more efficient looms.

It was to be expected, therefore, that in the early years of the Industrial Revolution the innovations would be most obvious and the results most striking in the manufacture of textiles, particularly cotton cloth. Of special interest is the way in which improvements in one part of the manufacturing process stimulated advances in another part. The first notable invention, a hand loom which halved the time required for weaving, came in 1733. This loom stimulated the demand for yarn, and thus for a spinning process that could produce yarn in great quantities; the need was filled by James Hargreaves (d. 1778), who developed the spinning jenny, a simple hand device by which six or seven threads could be spun simultaneously. About 1770 Richard Arkwright (1732–1792), a Lancashire barber, further accelerated the spinning process by inventing the water frame, which used water power to spin many threads at a time. The introduction of the cumbersome water frame and the later substitution of steam for water power required that the spinning process be moved into a mill or factory. Arkwright's first water-driven factory, established in 1771, gave employment to almost six hundred workers. The revolutionary developments in spinning soon caused the production of yarn to outstrip the weaving capacity of the hand looms and thus stimulated the development of a power loom. Within a half century both spinning and weaving had been mechanized. But it took some time for these inventions to be put into general use and for textile production as a whole

Hargreaves's spinning jenny. The spinning jenny was one of the key innovations in the revolutionizing of textile manufacturing.

to be brought within factory walls. Even as late as the 1830s some cloth was still being produced in cottages.

The new technology also found early expression in Britain in two other key industries: coal mining and metallurgy. Coal was a source of fuel for the new engines, and iron was the raw material essential for building the machines themselves. Clearly, advances in textile manufacturing depended on improvements in both coal production and iron manufacturing. The rich coal deposits of the British Isles had been largely untapped as long as wood was available as fuel. In the early eighteenth century the near exhaustion of the forests meant that wood was too precious to be used for fuel and charcoal too scarce to be used in smelting iron; a new source of fuel and a new process for smelting iron were required, and coal filled both of these needs. By 1700 the first coal-mining shafts had been sunk, but their depth was limited by the presence of underground water. Until a successful method for removing this water could be found, coal production was restricted. A steam-driven pump, invented in 1712 by Thomas Newcomen (1663–1729), and improved on in the two succeeding decades, made possible the working of seams in and below the watery layers and thus increased the output of the mines. Because of its limitations, Newcomen's invention was used solely for pump-

The Newcomen engine, invented in 1712. The first steam engine, used to pump water from mineshafts.

The Rocket. George Stephenson's steam locomotive, 1829.

ing water from the mines. In the 1770s the Scotsman James Watt (1736–1819), with the financial backing of Matthew Boulton (1728–1809), perfected a much more versatile steam engine that was to serve as a new source of power for a great variety of industries.

Britain had adequate resources of iron ore, but until a method of smelting iron without reliance on charcoal (and hence wood) could be found, these supplies could not be exploited. The pioneer in developing a new smelting process for iron was Abraham Darby (1678–1717) of Coalbrookdale. In 1709 he succeeded in smelting quality pig iron with coke instead of charcoal. The consequences of his discovery did not immediately transform the industry, however, because Darby's iron was suitable only for castings and was not thought to be pure enough to serve as material for forges. Only in 1783–1784 did Henry Cort (1740–1800) develop puddling, or rolling, a process in which he used coke to burn away the impurities in pig iron, making it suitable for use in forges. Cort's discovery freed the forgemasters from reliance on charcoal-produced iron and thus led to a remarkable expansion of the iron industry.

By 1800, then, all of the elements essential for a technological revolution were present. Fuel, in the form of coal, was plentiful; high-quality iron was available for machines and other uses; and the steam engine provided abundant and dependable power. Perhaps the greatest single remaining need was for speedier and more efficient methods of transportation to bring together the various elements involved in production. Between 1760 and 1830 the building of an extensive system of canals greatly facilitated the movement of goods from one part of England to another and drastically reduced the cost of transporting such heavy commodities as coal, iron, timber, stone, and clay. But it was the advent of the railroad in the 1830s and 1840s that made possible the rapid distribution of raw materials and finished products so characteristic of modern industrial societies. Coal had been transported by horse-drawn vehicles on rails for several decades, but not until the 1820s, when a practicable steam locomotive was constructed, could the possibilities of the railway be realized. The successful run in 1829 of George Stephenson's *Rocket* at a speed ranging up to sixteen miles an hour on the newly constructed Liverpool and Manchester Railway marked the real beginning of the railroad age in Great Britain. Within two short decades after 1830 some sixty-five hundred miles of rails were laid, and the impact of the railroad began to be felt in almost every phase of British life.

Industrialization in Continental Europe

At the conclusion of the Napoleonic wars in 1815, Great Britain had emerged as the world's foremost industrial power. Steam engines, which were still curiosities on the European Continent, were in widespread use in British textile factories and in mines. Britain produced as much as four fifths of the world's coal and half of the world's iron, and the country's industries were processing over twenty times as much raw cotton as they had fifty years earlier. Yet, over the course of the nineteenth century, other nations came to challenge Britain's economic supremacy. Germany, which industrialized rapidly during the late nineteenth century, surpassed Britain in its total economic output by 1910 (although it still lagged behind on a per capita basis). In the United States, a country whose industrialization also occurred primarily after 1850, per capita production exceeded Britain's by 40 percent on the eve of World War I.

Because many countries that were among Europe's poorest at the beginning of the nineteenth century—particularly in eastern and southern Europe—were also the slowest to industrialize, the inequalities of wealth within Europe increased dramatically during this period. In 1800, the three "richest" European countries had an average gross domestic product (GDP) per capita about 45 percent higher than that of the three "poorest." By 1860, the differential had increased to about 160 percent; and by 1913, it was 240 percent.

By modern standards, economic growth proceeded slowly and irregularly in nineteenth-century Europe. Between 1830 and 1910, the total GDP of European countries increased by an average of 1.7 percent per year, and only 0.9 percent on a per capita basis. Today, a growth rate of 1 or even 2 percent per year is often interpreted as a sign of economic stagnation. Yet, during the three centuries preceding the Industrial Revolution, 1500–1800, per capita income had increased by no more than 0.2 to 0.3 percent annually. According to this measure, the nineteenth century witnessed a veritable explosion of economic activity. The growth of GDP in various European countries and the United States is summarized below:

Approximate Per Capita Gross Domestic Product, 1820–1913
(in 1990 U.S. dollars)

	1820	1850	1870	1890	1913
Austria	1,528	1,661	1,875	2,460	3,488
Belgium	1,291	1,808	2,640	3,355	4,130
Denmark	1,225	1,700	1,927	2,427	3,764
France	1,218	1,669	1,858	2,354	3,452
Germany	1,112	1,476	1,913	2,539	3,833
Hungary	—	—	1,269	1,682	2,098
Ireland	954	—	1,773	2,225	2,733
Italy	1,092	—	1,467	1,631	2,507
Netherlands	1,561	1,888	2,640	3,113	3,950
Portugal	—	1,100	1,085	1,227	1,354
Russian empire	751	—	1,023	925	1,488
Spain	1,063	1,147	1,376	1,847	2,255
Switzerland	—	—	2,172	—	4,207
United Kingdom	1,756	2,362	3,263	4,099	5,032
United States	1,287	1,819	2,457	3,396	5,307
Western Europe	1,292	—	2,110	—	3,704
Southern Europe	804	—	1,108	—	1,572
Eastern Europe	772	—	1,085	—	1,690

Source: Angus Maddison, *Monitoring the World Economy, 1820–1992* (Paris, 1995), pp. 194–200, 244. See also Paul Bairoch, "Europe's Gross National Product: 1800–1975," *Journal of European Economic History* 5 (1976), pp. 276–277, 285–286.

Although economic growth during the first half of the nineteenth century was generally strongest in the northwestern tier of European states, there were exceptions to this pattern. Belgium, for example, was the first continental country to industrialize, developing substantial textile and iron production by the 1830s. By 1860, Belgium had the densest network of railroads of any European country. Holland, by contrast, industrialized relatively slowly, despite its advantageous economic position during the eighteenth century: the Dutch benefited from commercial prosperity far greater than Britain's, relative to population, along with efficient agricultural methods, a highly developed network of water transportation, and a flexible social structure. Several factors explain Belgium's lead in economic development. Unlike the Netherlands, Belgium possessed abundant deposits of coal and iron ore; and its strategic position between Britain and northern Germany encouraged railroad building for freight transportation, which in turn stimulated further economic growth. Moreover, the Belgian government adopted various policies that supported industrialization, investing heavily in transportation improvements, as well as initially enacting protective tariffs to shield nascent enterprises from foreign competition.

France industrialized more slowly than Britain, despite its commercial wealth and other economic advantages. It had a slower rate of population growth during the nineteenth century than most of Europe, and agricultural policies favorable to small peasant holdings meant that fewer rural workers were displaced from the land. Thus, France lacked a mobile, urban workforce on the scale of Britain's. The French focused more on luxury goods than on cheap mass production, and small workshops remained more important than large factories throughout much of the century. Nevertheless, many large machine-powered industries developed in France during this era. Throughout the period 1815–1870, France was the largest producer of pig iron on the Continent; and by 1850, French companies had nearly 4.5 million mechanized cotton spindles — about the same as the rest of the Continent combined.

The political upheavals in France between 1789 and 1815 had mixed effects on the nation's long-term economic development. On the one hand, the instability of governing regimes, along with ongoing warfare against the other European powers, had cut France off from trade with Britain and inhibited economic growth. Some aspects of the Napoleonic legal system also had a chilling effect on new investment, for example, its harshly punitive bankruptcy laws and its restrictions on the formation of corporations. On the other hand, by abolishing the whole fabric of guilds, internal tolls, and other traditional forms of economic regulation, the revolution had cleared away many obstacles to the development of a capitalist economy. Moreover, the prohibition of strikes under the Le Chapelier Law of 1791, which remained in force until 1864, placed businesses in a more dominant bargaining position with their workers than was the case in Britain.

Among the German states, Switzerland had achieved the greatest degree of industrialization by 1850, with a well-developed textile industry. From the 1830s onward, mechanized textile production had also begun in the Rhineland in western Germany, as well as in Saxony and Silesia to the east. To some extent, however, the German states skipped over the "first industrial revolution," which centered around the production of textiles, coal, and iron. During the latter half of the nineteenth century, Germany became a leader in the "second industrial revolution," developing new techniques for manufacturing high-quality steel, which in turn made possible new machines such as petroleum-powered turbine engines. By 1900, Germany was also an important producer of chemicals, precision machinery, and electrical equipment.

The Scandinavian countries, especially Denmark and Sweden, also experienced rapid economic growth during the late nineteenth century. Part of this expansion resulted from an increase in iron and steel production, as well as from a boom in railroad building. Much of the Scandinavian economy, however, continued to center around agriculture and extractive industries: for example, Denmark was a large exporter of dairy products and pork; Sweden produced substantial amounts of timber.

The countries of southern Europe industrialized only slowly over the course of the nineteenth century, as a result of handicaps such as poorly developed transportation networks, lack of access to raw materials and energy sources, and legal conditions that were inhospitable to investment. The decline of this region relative to northern Europe was especially striking in Portugal and Spain, which had dominated the Continent economically during the sixteenth and seventeenth centuries. In 1800, Portugal still ranked among the five richest countries in Europe; a hundred years later, it was among the three or four poorest. On the Italian peninsula, an economic divide emerged between northern states such as Piedmont and Lombardy, which developed manufacturing centers, and southern states including Naples and Sicily, whose economies remained relatively untouched by industrialization. This sharp north-south division, which still persists today, inhibited the formation of a strong unified nation-state, even after Italian unity was formally proclaimed in 1860.

In most of eastern Europe, certain prerequisites for economic growth were largely absent: for example, transportation networks were generally poorly developed, and these regions lacked both investment capital and large urban centers that might serve as centers for industry and trade. Moreover, the persistence of serfdom and a rigid aristocratic order in parts of eastern Europe, including Russia, obstructed the emergence both of a mobile workforce and of an entrepreneurial middle class. Within the Austrian Habsburg empire, some industrialization occurred over the course of the century, notably in the region surrounding Vienna and in the Bohemian territories near Prague. Elsewhere, however, the development of a capitalist economy proceeded extremely gradually until the final decades before the outbreak of World War I.

THE SOCIAL IMPACT OF
INDUSTRIALIZATION

The revolution in technology and in the organization of production inevitably had a tremendous impact on the societies in which it occurred. Some reference has already been made to changes in class structure caused by the Industrial Revolution: the rapid expansion of the bourgeoisie and the emergence of a new urban proletariat. But it is important to look more closely at the effect of these changes on the lives of individuals, particularly those whose destiny it was to spend their lives digging coal or operating the machines in the factories. Perhaps never before in human history had so radical a transformation occurred in humans' occupations or in their physical environment. In one country after another an increasing proportion of the working people spent their lives not cultivating the fields and living in small, isolated villages, but toiling in factories or mines and living in large, crowded cities.

It is easy to exaggerate the speed of this transformation even in Great Britain, where it appeared to occur most rapidly. British people did not simply move from farm to city overnight. Although the enclosure of common lands accelerated in the last decades of the eighteenth century, many small farmers stayed on as landless agricultural laborers or tried to eke out a living by spinning or weaving in their cottages. Only gradually did they start drifting to the mills, which were at first located near the streams that supplied the water power. Initially, cotton manufacturers in the north had so much difficulty attracting laborers that they resorted to the employment as "apprentices" of groups of pauper children from London and the south. But with the general application of steam power to the cotton industry after 1800, factories tended to be located in towns and cities near the sources of

Manchester, from the entrance to the London and North-Western Railway.

coal, and there a labor supply was more readily available. The phenomenal growth of certain key industrial cities occurred in the first half of the nineteenth century. Between 1801 and 1850, for example, the population of Manchester rose from 77,000 to 303,000; that of Liverpool, from 82,000 to 397,000; and that of Birmingham, from 71,000 to 242,000. Some cities expanded as much as 40 percent in a single decade. As one might expect, the most rapid growth occurred in factory cities, but port cities expanded with an increase in overseas trade and older administrative centers grew as governments assumed more responsibilities and centralized their functions. Paris and London owed their growth in the nineteenth century not so much to new industrial enterprises as to rising trade, growth of banking facilities for administration of vast amounts of capital, and to the multiplication of administrative personnel needed for governing their respective countries. Also, artisans and shopkeepers who had formerly lived in provincial towns gravitated to larger cities where opportunities appeared to be greater. Some older towns and cities, untouched by new industrial enterprises or bypassed by railroads, saw their population dwindle. In short, countries affected by industrialization and population growth underwent vast internal migrations.

The Condition of the Working Classes

Much has been written about material conditions in the new factory cities but less attention has been paid to the quality of life and the psychological responses of urban immigrants.[3] For those who came directly from the country-side, life in the cities marked a real break with the past and required considerable adjustment. The monotonous routine of factory labor, the crowding, and the newness of the environment must have imposed serious strains on the formecountry dweller. Charles Dickens (1812–1870) caught the atmosphere of these depressing industrial cities in his celebrated novel *Hard Times* (1854). Here is his description of "Coketown," a fictitional representation (some would say a caricature) of one of the industrial towns of Lancashire:

It was a town of red brick, or of brick that would have been red if the smoke and ashes had allowed it; but as matters stood it was a town of unnatural red and black like the painted face of a savage. It was a town of machinery and tall chimneys, out of which interminable serpents of smoke trailed themselves for ever and ever and never got uncoiled. It had a black canal in it, and a river that

---

[3] One of the best contemporary documents on this subject is Friedrich Engels's *The Condition of the Working Class in England* (originally published in German in 1845; first published in England in 1887). For a stimulating analysis of Engels's work and its background, see Steven Marcus, *Engels, Manchester, and the Working Class* (London, 1974).

ran purple with ill-smelling dye, and vast piles of buildings full of windows where there was a rattling and a trembling all day long, and where the piston of the steam-engine worked monotonously up and down like the head of an elephant in a state of melancholy madness. It contained several large streets all very like one another, inhabited by people equally like one another, who all went in and out at the same hours, with the same sound upon the same pavements, to do the same work, and to whom every day was the same as yesterday and to-morrow, and every year the counterpart of the last and the next.[4]

It is not difficult to imagine the disorientation and loneliness of an individual thrust suddenly into an environment such as this. Moreover, the experience of the British laborer was to be duplicated on the Continent during the course of the nineteenth century as vast numbers of country dwellers gravitated to the new industrial cities.

The impact of the city on individuals and families shows up in statistical information. Rates of suicide, insanity, and crimes against property were notably higher in cities than in rural districts. The divorce rate was three or four times higher in the cities, and there were twice as many illegitimate births. The relative youthfulness of urban immigrants made for a certain dynamism in the city environment, but it also may explain the higher incidence of agitation and riots. Among the first generation of those who moved to the cities, many seem to have remained attached to their rural roots and returned to their villages at harvest time or whenever the opportunity presented itself. With the passage of time, however, the boundaries between urban and rural identities hardened. In one country after another affected by the Industrial Revolution, the ratio between city dwellers and country dwellers shifted. By 1850 the British population was over half urban; Germany passed this point only in 1900 and France, not until 1930.

Living conditions in industrial cities were frequently deplorable. Some British cities which had made progress earlier in paving their streets and covering their sewers were unable to handle the massive influx of new inhabitants, and a deterioration of conditions occurred. In newer urban centers streets were often no better than rutted paths. Municipal governments were unable to meet the need for an adequate water supply and for sewage disposal. Many sewers remained open, and rivers were polluted by waste materials. The following is an excerpt from a famous Report on the Sanitary Condition of the Labouring Population drawn up in 1842 by Edwin Chadwick, a reformer who was responsible for some of the early public-health legislation passed in Great Britain. This passage describes conditions in Leeds, a factory city located in Yorkshire:

---

[4] Charles Dickens, *Hard Times* (New York, 1966), p. 17.

[N]umbers of streets have been formed and houses erected without surface drainage — without sewers — or if under drainage can be called sewers, then with such as, becoming choked in a few months, are even worse than if they were altogether without. The surface of these streets is considerably elevated by accumulated ashes and filth, untouched by any scavenger; they form nuclei of disease exhaled from a thousand sources. Here and there stagnant water, and channels so offensive that they have been declared to be unbearable, lie under the doorways of the uncomplaining poor; and privies so laden with ashes and excrementitious matter as to be unuseable prevail, till the streets themselves become offensive from deposits of this description; in short, there is generally pervading in these localities a want of the common conveniences of life.[5]

Where housing already existed buildings were divided and redivided to the point where the poorest families had only one room or shared a room with another family. Newer housing was no less cramped and was often jerry built and flimsy. Not surprisingly, disease and epidemics flourished in the new industrial cities, and the mortality rate was high.

Among students of the Industrial Revolution one of the most disputed questions has concerned the material and psychological condition of the factory hands employed in the burgeoning industrial cities. Some writers have contended that workers in the new industries were little better than slaves at the mercy of their capitalist employers, suffering physical and psychological privations of the worst sort. Adherents of this view dwell on the long working hours, the low wages, and the poor living conditions of the workers. They stress the evils of child labor and the alienation of workers from their employers. There is no question that workers in the early stages of the Industrial Revolution were badly off compared with their modern counterparts. But critics of this interpretation argue that the workers' condition should be viewed not in terms of later standards but in a contemporary context. Was the condition of early factory workers really worse than that of agricultural laborers in the same period or the period just preceding? How did industrial workers view their own situation? That evils existed, particularly in the early phases of the Industrial Revolution in England and on the Continent, no historian denies. But more recent interpretations point out that significant benefits resulted from industrialization even for the workers and have challenged or qualified many of the charges brought against the Industrial Revolution by the traditional school.

First and foremost, the Industrial Revolution brought about a tremendous increase in productivity and, with it, a substantial rise in per capita income.

[5] Quoted in J. F. C. Harrison, *Society and Politics in England, 1780–1960: A Selection of Readings and Comments* (New York, 1965), p. 155.

Moreover, as David Landes has pointed out, this rapid growth was self-sustaining:

> Where previously, an amelioration of the conditions of existence, hence of survival, and an increase in economic opportunity had always been followed by a rise in population that eventually consumed the gains achieved, now for the first time in history, both the economy and knowledge were growing fast enough to generate a continuing flow of investment and technological innovation, a flow that lifted beyond visible limits the ceiling of Malthus's positive checks. The Industrial Revolution thereby opened a new age of promise.[6]

On balance, the evidence concerning the impact of industrialization on workers is mixed. Various studies have detected substantial increases in the average wages of British workers from the 1820s onward.[7] Many factory workers appear to have earned higher wages than were offered in the countryside, allowing them to afford better food and clothing than were available to their rural counterparts — though unskilled workers often struggled for subsistence. Critics of the "pessimistic" school point out that such writers arrive at their conclusions partly from evidence with a built-in bias — that is, the reports of Parliamentary commissions set up in the early nineteenth century by reformers whose purpose was to expose the worst abuses of the system. Moreover, the hardships of the working classes in Britain cannot be blamed exclusively on industrialization. Such factors as rapid population growth and the postwar depression following the Napoleonic wars also contributed to widespread destitution.

Most of the material benefits of the Industrial Revolution, however, were felt by workers only after the mid-nineteenth century. The early generations of factory hands had to cope with extreme fluctuations in their wages and the prospect of sudden unemployment, along with a growing gap between their incomes and those of the urban middle classes. Furthermore, the "optimistic" analyses of wages generally fail to take into account certain deleterious effects on the workers' living conditions, such as the lengthening and intensification of the workday. They also ignore the declining ability of workers to supplement their income through domestic work such as gardening and baking, as well as through participation in the barter economy. Rates of

---

[6] David S. Landes, *The Unbound Prometheus: Technological Change and Industrial Development in Western Europe from 1750 to the Present* (Cambridge, 1970), p. 41.

[7] For example, Peter H. Lindert and Jeffrey G. Williamson, "English Workers' Living Standards during the Industrial Revolution: A New Look," *Economic History Review* 36 (1983), 1–25; N. F. R. Crafts, *British Economic Growth during the Industrial Revolution* (Oxford, 1985), Ch. 5.

infant and child mortality among the working classes of the new industrial cities were often shockingly high. In Mulhouse, a French textile town, between 1823 and 1834, 56 percent of children born to spinners died before age two. In Manchester in 1837, the average age of death for "mechanics, labourers, and their families" was only seventeen years, compared with thirty-eight years for families of professionals and gentry.[8]

Even relatively well-paid laborers could find themselves suddenly laid off owing to an industrial slump. Because all of their income had gone in normal times to pay for the necessities of life, they had nothing to fall back on during periods of unemployment or illness. Although charitable organizations or workers' mutual-aid societies might provide temporary assistance, such institutions could not support large numbers of unemployed for prolonged periods. In such circumstances workers might become desperate and resort to violence. It is significant, for example, that the Revolution of 1848 in France was preceded by a serious industrial as well as agricultural depression that left many workers unemployed and hungry.

Certain intangibles must also be considered in a comparison of the lot of the industrial worker with that of the agricultural laborer. Farmers or farm hands may have worked just as many hours as factory hands, their living conditions were undoubtedly crude and primitive, and they were probably subject to just as great a variety of diseases. But they worked out of doors, their daily tasks were probably more varied, and their opportunities for recreation were undoubtedly greater. It was in part to the discipline of the mill and the sheer monotony of their routine that the early factory hands objected. Also, the crowding together of human beings into ugly, hastily built cities tended to sharpen their discontent. Finally, the extensive employment of children in the textile mills and in the mines was a scandalous feature of industrialization that weighed on the consciences of some industrialists as well as on those of humanitarians and reformers. The revelation that child apprentices, some as young as seven, were forced to work up to twelve and fifteen hours a day, six days a week, in the cotton mills of the north, came as a shock to many Britons and inspired legislation to restrict child labor as early as 1802. Yet because of inadequate enforcement of the laws, the exploitation of children continued at least until 1833, when the first effective Factory Act forbade the employment in textile mills of children under nine years of age and restricted the labor of those between nine and thirteen to forty-eight hours a week. Though we cannot contest the long-

---

[8] The "pessimistic" case is eloquently restated by Wally Seccombe in *Weathering the Storm: Working-Class Families from the Industrial Revolution to the Fertility Decline* (London, 1993), pp. 71–80.

Children sent to work in the cotton factories, 1840.

range benefits accruing from the Industrial Revolution, we must recognize that the price paid in human suffering during its early stages was great.

Expansion of the Middle Classes

The nineteenth century has sometimes been described as the "century of the middle class," reflecting the growing power and prestige of the bourgeoisie in Europe during that epoch. It is perhaps more accurate, however, to refer to this group as the "middle classes," because the bourgeoisie was highly diverse in its social composition. Vast differences in wealth and style of life characterized the various categories of the middle classes. Long before the nineteenth century, affluent merchants and bankers constituted an elite within the bourgeoisie whose style of life rivaled or surpassed that of many aristocrats. This group tended to look down on the new industrialists and entrepreneurs who emerged with the Industrial Revolution, though mutual economic interests ultimately narrowed the gap between them. Professionals such as lawyers, doctors, government officials, and writers made up another important element of the middle classes whose political influence increased out of proportion to its numbers during the nineteenth century. To the lower middle class belonged the shopkeepers whose income was far below that of the merchant princes but who had a clear sense of their status as property owners and prided themselves on their avoidance of manual labor. The fortunes of this group varied greatly during the nineteenth century; some of them expanded their enterprises and prospered in the growing cities, whereas others tended to stagnate or to lose out in competition with larger businesses.

The French Revolution enhanced the status of the middle classes in ways that have been described earlier — by eliminating traditional privileges of the aristocracy and the clergy, by establishing institutions of government that gave greater representation to the middle classes, by removing many of the legal barriers to bourgeois advancement, and by proclaiming fundamental rights that in theory belonged to every human being regardless of birth. The spread of French ideals and institutions to other peoples during the revolution and afterward provided a rationale for similar advancement of non-privileged classes elsewhere in Europe.

But the Industrial Revolution, by stimulating the growth in wealth and in numbers of the middle class, undoubtedly had an even greater impact on its conquest of power and prestige. Even before industrialization, the expansion of trade and commerce had led to a significant growth in the economic power of this class throughout Europe, but the bourgeoisie during the century of industrialization from 1750 to 1850 "created," in the words of Karl Marx, "more massive and more colossal productive forces" than had been produced by "all generations put together." The wealth generated by these new productive forces thrust the bourgeoisie into a commanding position and enabled its leaders to assert their power in a decisive way. Of course, this result was achieved at different times in different parts of Europe depending on the progress of industrialization and the degree of resistance of traditionally established classes and institutions. In Britain, France, and the Low Countries, where its economic strength was the greatest, the middle class succeeded by the 1830s or 1840s in gaining control of the machinery of government. In central Europe, where industrialization lagged behind, the bourgeoisie emerged later as a political force; lacking unity and a coherent set of goals, the middle class made a bid for power in the revolutions of 1848 but encountered stubborn resistance from the monarchs and older privileged groups. In the long run, however, wherever industrialization occurred, the middle-class drive for power was irresistible. All the European rulers had to come to terms with the bourgeoisie, whether by granting them political representation, by enacting legislation favorable to their economic interests, or both.

Though the bourgeois elites, including industrialists, merchants, and professionals, became more powerful over the course of the century, many craftsmen and artisans confronted increasing economic insecurity. Artisans, who were an important part of nineteenth-century society, do not fit neatly into any of the broader social classes or categories: some social historians rank them in the lower middle class, some classify them as workers; still others view them as a separate social group with their own peculiar attributes and attitudes. Artisans were those who possessed a specific traditional economic skill such as tailors, printers, butchers, and blacksmiths. Into this same category fell construction workers of various sorts (carpenters, masons, painters) as well as cabinetmakers. Most of these had traditionally been concentrated in towns or cities and were normally organized into guilds, though guild organization had declined in some countries during the seventeenth and eighteenth centuries. Artisans tended to pride themselves on their skill, which resulted from a long apprenticeship and enforcement by the guild of high standards of workmanship. Working independently or with a few other craftsmen, artisans normally carried their productive operation through by themselves. It is obvious that their attitude toward their work and the pride they took in their product might differ radically from that of factory workers or coal miners whose operations were more routine and who frequently contributed only one step toward the completion of the final product.

Many activities of the artisans survived the Industrial Revolution and were relatively unaffected by it. As late as 1850, for example, there were still as many artisans as factory workers in Great Britain. Particularly in France, where an aversion to mass-produced manufactures long persisted, artisans remained an important social group throughout the century. In some instances, however, the process of industrialization threw artisans and craftsmen into direct competition with the newer industries and resulted in their eventual displacement. The fate of the hand loom weaver and of others engaged in home manufacture of textiles is perhaps the most obvious example. Within a matter of a few decades the revolution in textile manufacturing described earlier led to the ruin of those who adhered to traditional methods. Unable to compete with cheaper, more efficient mechanized production, some tried to hang on by working even longer hours at home; others gave up and went to work in the factories. Occasionally, artisans also resorted to violent protest. A closer examination of some of the riots and revolutions that occurred during the first half of the nineteenth century in France and in central Europe has shown that in many cases revolutionaries who have been labeled "workers" were in fact artisans or even proprietors of small shops.

The Mechanization of Everyday Life

In Britain by the mid-nineteenth century, only 20 percent of the population was employed in agriculture — a dramatic decline from the 80 to 90 percent that was typical of the preindustrial era. In other European countries, industry displaced agriculture more slowly, but these regions too experienced a steady shift of population from the countryside to the cities. This increasing urbanization, along with the mechanization of production, changed the rhythms of life for nineteenth-century Europeans of various classes. Work schedules, previously governed by the sun and the seasons, came to be ruled by the clock. In the new industrial enterprises, employers resorted to strict time-keeping as a means of controlling their workers and maximizing the efficiency of production. Members of the middles classes carried pocket watches to help them follow increasingly regimented schedules. The advent of the electric telegraph during the mid-nineteenth century permitted instantaneous communication across great distances. Indeed, time itself became standardized. The adoption of Greenwich Mean Time in Britain predated the industrial age: it had been established in order to synchronize stagecoach schedules around the country. But the increasing volume of rail travel from the 1830s onward meant that a greater proportion of the population had a need for the precise measurement of time. In 1884, Greenwich Mean Time was adopted as a universal base zone for the entire globe.

Europeans approached the railway age with awe and trepidation. Some authors speculated about the medical risks posed by travel at the previously unheard of speeds of fifteen or twenty miles per hour. King Frederick William III of Prussia worried about the potentially "democratic" effects of rapid intercity rail travel. Nonetheless, during the late 1830s, after seeing the train passing his carriage as he traveled between his palaces in Berlin and Potsdam, he began riding this line himself. The 1844 painting *Rain, Steam, and Speed: The Great Western Railroad*, by J. M. W. Turner, captures the mix of exhilaration and terror inspired by the Industrial Revolution. In this picture, a train with its illuminated carriages rushes toward the viewer across the trestle of a high bridge. A glint of yellow light shines off the front of the locomotive, symbolizing the spark of human intelligence and power. The painting is a blur of blue, gold, and black: the details of landscape and sky are obliterated by the rapid pace of the oncoming machine.

Despite the harsh conditions of nineteenth-century urban life, industrialization resulted in astonishing new creations. The 1851 Great Exhibition in London, held in the huge iron and glass Crystal Palace, celebrated Britain's technological and economic accomplishments. The Crystal Palace covered nineteen acres and reached a height of 108 feet at its peak. Over a six-month period, fourteen thousand exhibitors displayed one hundred thou-

Rain, Steam, and Speed—The Great Western Railway (1844), by J. M. W. Turner.

sand objects from Britain, its empire, and other nations around the world. Six million visitors of all classes attended the exhibition from around Britain and elsewhere in Europe, many of them traveling by means of the new network of railroads.

By facilitating the rapid transport of people and goods, industrialization also helped mitigate certain age-old causes of human suffering. Throughout the preindustrial age, societies around Europe suffered from periodic famines due to crop failures, the last of which erupted during the mid-nineteenth century. As late as 1847 in Prussia and other parts of Germany, poor harvests resulted in widespread malnutrition and increased mortality. A far more serious and protracted famine occurred in Ireland between 1845 and 1851, where a potato blight caused about a million deaths from starvation and forced nearly 2 million people to emigrate to Britain and the United States. These famines had multiple causes. For example, the crisis in Ireland was aggravated by the abject poverty of the Irish Catholic tenant farmers, most of whom paid high rents to British Protestant landlords. An additional problem was the lack of a well-developed transportation infrastructure, which stymied efforts to deliver effective food relief to the afflicted regions.

Since the 1850s, Europe has been largely spared from widespread subsistence crises caused by bad harvests, which were a recurring feature of premodern life. (Famines caused by wars or political upheavals, such as Stalin's Soviet collectivization program during the 1930s, have unfortunately not been eradicated.) In part, this improvement in nutrition reflects the generally favorable climactic conditions that have blessed European agriculture over the past one hundred fifty years. To a great extent, however, this phenomenon is the consequence of two factors directly related to industrialization: first, the increasing level of overall prosperity, which has enabled Europeans to import foodstuffs from abroad; and second, the improvement of transportation networks, which has made it possible to move perishable items quickly to remote destinations. The capacity of most Europeans to feed themselves generously, even in periods of rapid population growth, is testimony to the long-term material benefits of the Industrial Revolution.

The Crystal Palace, 1850–1851, engraving by Joseph Nash. An interior view of transept, looking north.

THE QUEST FOR NEW COMMUNITIES

The Industrial Revolution was a deeply disorienting social transformation for members of all classes. In Europe's new industrial cities, the early generations of factory hands often faced social isolation in an anonymous urban environment: as the historian E. P. Thompson has noted, industrialization broke down the paternalistic "moral economy" of traditional English life.[9] Aristocrats and clerics found their authority undermined, not only by the legal reforms enacted during the era of the French Revolution and Napoleon, but also by increasing urbanization and the rise of the capitalist economy. For the bourgeoisie, industrialization also fundamentally altered the rhythms of life, for example, by sharpening the divide between workplace and home, as well as between the economic roles of men and women.

This rupture in the older social fabric stimulated efforts to seek new forms of community, or to reinvent existing ones. Political ideologies such as conservatism and nationalism, which will be discussed in the next chapter, sought to provide fixed bearings in a rapidly changing world by rooting individuals within greater historical communities. In everyday life, communities took shape through the reorganization of urban spaces, the transformation of bourgeois family life, and the creation of new institutions for working class solidarity. In all of these ways, nineteenth-century Europeans sought to make themselves at home in a radically transformed world.

City and Suburb

The early nineteenth century witnessed the rapid growth of cities across western and central Europe. Between 1800 and 1850, the population of greater London expanded from 1,117,000 to 2,685,000, Paris from 581,000 to 1,053,000, Vienna from 247,000 to 444,000, Berlin from 173,000 to 419,000, and Madrid from 160,000 to 281,000. The rising number of inhabitants frequently resulted in elevated property values in the central cities, forcing workers to move to substandard urban housing or to less expensive areas on the fringe of town. For members of the middle classes, the noise, pollution, and congestion of the new industrial cities provided further incentives for moving out of the urban centers.

During the premodern period, the richer and more prestigious elements of the urban population had generally lived in the heart of the cities, while the outlying areas had been reserved for the poor. Up through the early eighteenth century, according to the *Oxford English Dictionary*, the term

---

[9] E. P. Thompson, *The Making of the English Working Class* (New York, 1966).

"suburbe" had indicated a "place of inferior, debased, and especially licentious habits of life." This division of neighborhoods, however, had never been absolute. Paradoxically, because social distances between rich and poor were so starkly defined, the members of the urban bourgeoisie felt little need to segregate themselves geographically from the working classes; thus the home of a rich merchant might be surrounded by dwellings of the poor.

In much of continental Europe, the central cities remained the preserve of the bourgeoisie throughout the nineteenth century and beyond. Massive urban redevelopment schemes, such as the rebuilding of Paris under Baron Eugène-Georges Haussmann beginning in the 1850s, created boulevards and open spaces for the enjoyment of wealthier residents, while displacing workers to housing projects on the edge of the city. In Britain, however, the nineteenth century witnessed the abandonment of the central cities by the middle classes, along with the emergence of a new ideal of suburban life.

Already in the mid-eighteenth century, rich English financiers and merchants had begun to construct weekend villas in the countryside, allowing them to enjoy a genteel rural existence while still preserving their workaday ties to the city. Toward the end of the century, certain wealthy bourgeois families took up permanent residence in communities such as Clapham, five miles outside of London, overlooking the Thames. By the 1830s, the phenomenon had spread from the wealthy to the solidly middle class, with the building of cottages and semidetached villas in developments with picturesque names such as Park Village, Park Crescent, and Victoria Park. The pastoral overtones of the word "park" made this a favorite label, whether or not there was any actual park in the vicinity.

The movement of the bourgeoisie to the suburbs had momentous consequences for social relations in Britain. By separating the home from the workplace, it sharpened the division of gender roles, with wives remaining at home with their children while husbands traveled into the city to work. Moreover, it intensified the gap between workers and their employers, thus reinforcing consciousness of class differences. An 1857 visitor's guide to Manchester contrasted the "encircling . . . outskirts or suburbs" consisting of "long vistas of enchanting villas," and resembling "so many Edens," with the factory zone adjacent to the commercial core; here dwelled "the mass of the laboring, sweltering, spinners and weavers of Manchester" in "crowded alleys of two-story houses, which run in innumerable labyrinths." As the Reverend R. Parkinson remarked of Manchester in 1839: "There is no town in the world where the distance between the rich and the poor is so great, or the barrier between them is so difficult to be crossed. . . . There is far less *personal* communication between the master cotton-spinner and his workmen . . . than there is between the Duke of Wellington and the

Park Village East, Regents Park, designed by John Nash during the 1820s.

humblest laborer on his estate." The urban historian Robert Fishman states the point more bluntly: "Where an aristocracy had surrounded themselves with the lower orders as a sign of their privilege and status, the keynote of the bourgeois city was to be separation and willful blindness. Suburbia accomplished both."[10]

Family Life

In a lecture series delivered in Manchester in 1864, the art critic and essayist John Ruskin defined the home as a "sacred place, a vestal temple." Though "the man, in his rough work in the open world, must encounter all peril and trial . . . he guards the woman from all this," so that the house might become "the place of Peace; the shelter, not only from all injury, but from all terror, doubt and division." Ruskin's vision of the home resonated with that of other Victorian authors such as Coventry Patmore, who portrayed the true wife as the "angel in the house," and Charles Dickens, whose novels were populated by heroines acting as agents of redemption. Historians sometimes refer to this ideal as the "cult of domesticity" in nineteenth-century Europe.

Before the advent of the industrial age, no clear boundary had existed between the workplace and the home. In agrarian communities, every mem-

---

[10] Robert Fishman, *Bourgeois Utopias: The Rise and Fall of Suburbia* (New York, 1987), p. 84.

ber of the household had played a role in raising crops and tending livestock; likewise, market-oriented activities such as spinning yarn had been often by carried out by women working at home. In urban middle-class households, there had been a similar blurring of domestic and economic life. Such houses had been residences not only for husbands, wives, children, and members of the extended family, but also for apprentices, laborers, and servants. Bourgeois men usually had conducted their businesses out of their homes, and though the male head of the household had held primary responsibility for the family's economic well-being, he had not shouldered this burden alone. The wife had often worked as "help-meet," performing vital tasks such as keeping the accounts book or tending the shop; children ran errands or carried out odd jobs. The wife's participation in commercial life was vitally important so that in the event of the husband's death she could use her experience to keep the family and its enterprise functioning.

The growth of industrial cities accentuated the divide between domestic and economic life. With the decline of cottage production and the rise of the factory system, workers increasingly found themselves employed outside the home. In middle-class families that moved to the suburbs, husbands traveled to and from the workplace, often arriving home only in the evening, while wives and children remained in the house. Increasingly, the bourgeois domestic unit consisted of the nuclear family, along with servants, rather than the web of relatives, apprentices, and so forth, who had populated the premodern middle-class household. Consequently, wives began to withdraw from productive work, focusing their energies primarily on raising children and managing the household. This trend toward separating the home from the workplace was evident, to varying degrees, on the Continent as well, where the bourgeoisie remained mainly in the city.

The new primacy of the nuclear family, along with the ideal of an emotionally powerful "companionate marriage," stemmed in part from rising life expectancies, which increased the stability of the family unit. As Lawrence Stone has argued, the intensification of emotional bonds within marriage may also have reflected the development of merchant capitalism, because by emphasizing the importance of individual autonomy, capitalist values encouraged men and women to choose their own mates.[11] Other cultural factors came into play as well: for example, the Evangelical revivalism in England beginning in the mid-eighteenth century, which celebrated the home as a place of refuge from the corruption of public society. William Wilberforce, one of the leading figures in this movement, praised women

---

[11] Lawrence Stone, *The Family, Sex, and Marriage in England 1500–1800* (New York, 1977).

as "naturally more disposed to Religion than men," and hence as ideally suited to educating their children and providing spiritual sustenance to their husbands. By serving these roles, Wilberforce declared, women would become the "medium of our intercourse with the heavenly world." In short, by the Victorian era, British bourgeois culture vested high emotional and spiritual expectations on the institutions of marriage and the family. In the literature of the age, wives and mothers were increasingly depicted as civilizing and moralizing forces, whose mission was to counteract the anomie and immorality of industrial society.

The labor historian Deborah Valenze observes that eighteenth-century British "polite" society was "as yet more Rabelaisian than Victorian in its manners." Moralists frequently complained of luxurious and sexually revealing costumes, of women's widespread use of profanity, and of men's proclivity to urinate in the streets. In the emerging struggle for intensified social discipline, middle-class women "were named guardians not only of the domestic sphere but of morality itself."[12] One consequence of this development was the promulgation of a distinction between virtuous middle-class and "lost" lower-class women, who were said to be ignorant of proper morality. Bourgeois women increasingly engaged in philanthropic projects, such as rescuing prostitutes and educating their domestic servants in the principles of good conduct. Thus, the new gender roles were complemented by newly defined class distinctions. On the one hand, the moralizing literature of the Victorian era depicted middle-class women as agents of civilization, and working-class women as benighted victims in need of moral instruction. But on the other hand, since middle-class status was itself predicated on one's ability to employ domestic servants, bourgeois women had a vested interest in perpetuating, rather than dissolving, the class distinctions between rich and poor.

Bourgeois women's charitable work played an important role in disseminating the new ideals of family life beyond the ranks of the middle class. Yet within working-class families, the ideology of domesticity necessarily took a different form, in large part because the husband's wages alone rarely sufficed to sustain a comfortable existence for the family. In Britain and France during the mid-nineteenth century, about 30 percent of the workforce consisted of women, and children were frequently sent to work in order to supplement the family's earnings. The figures on labor-force participation varied widely, however, according to economic conditions and the life stages of various family members. In general, young women worked for wages while

[12] Deborah Valenze, *The First Industrial Woman* (New York, 1995), p. 145.

Frontispiece from *The Greatest Plague of Life: Or, the Adventures of a Lady in Search of a Good Servant,* by Henry and Augustus Mayhew. The caption reads: "Nearly 'worried to Death' by the Greatest Plagues of one's Life."

they were single; after marriage they continued to do so until they went into confinement before the birth of their first child. In less industrialized regions where wage labor could be performed at home, many married women continued to work during their childbearing years, but where the factory system predominated, this was much rarer. Overall, probably only about 10 percent of married women worked outside the home. Wage levels reflected the cultural expectation that men should be the primary economic providers for the family. For piecework and hourly work, women earned about 60 percent of men's wage rate—a figure that changed little between 1750 and 1914. The overall income differential between working men and women was substantially greater than this, because a larger proportion of women worked part time. Children working in textile mills generally earned between 5 and 25 percent as much as their fathers.

The social reform literature of the Victorian era expressed horror about the corrupting effects of industrialization on working-class families. The spread of the wage-labor economy to women and children was thought to undermine domestic bonds. One author declared: "The plague that devours society is the destruction of family feeling and paternal authority. We must

. . . attack this problem to prevent the decomposition of the family." A stock character in this literature was the girl forced to choose between a starvation wage in a factory and life as a prostitute. Writers also decried the practice of "baby-farming," under which infants were sent to paid nurses in the countryside so that their mothers could continue to work. The mortality rates of infants in these arrangements were notoriously high.

Though we must not minimize such real and tragic dimensions of nineteenth-century urban life, working-class families proved surprisingly resilient during the industrial age despite bourgeois fears about their disintegration. Unlike middle-class households, where the nuclear family increasingly became the dominant form, working families frequently expanded during this era. Children typically lived with their parents longer than in previous centuries, when they had often entered apprenticeships or agricultural service around the time of puberty. The common practice among factory owners of paying children's wages directly to the head of their household reinforced this pattern, because it extended children's economic dependence on their parents. Families also often took in relatives, such as widowed parents or orphaned nieces and nephews; and they offered guidance to kin who were moving to the city from their home village. Thus, working-class families transformed themselves in order to cushion the disruptions caused by the transition from an agrarian to an industrial social order.

Class Identities

The concept of "class" emerged in Europe as an important social category during the first decades of the nineteenth century. In an often-quoted definition, E. P. Thompson has observed:

[C]lass happens when some men, as a result of common experiences (inherited or shared), feel and articulate the identity of their interests as between themselves, and as against other men whose interests are different from (and usually opposed to) theirs. The class experience is largely determined by the productive relations into which men are born—or enter involuntarily.[13]

Thompson thus depicts class not as a thing but as a process, something that "happens" in the course of social interactions. Moreover, he portrays this process as involving the combination of objective work conditions with the subjective experiences of workers: in other words, class formation occurred only when workers became conscious of their commonalities with each other.

[13] Thompson, The Making of the English Working Class (New York, 1966), p. 9.

The decades since the publication of Thompson's study of the English working class have witnessed a vigorous debate about class formation in nineteenth-century Europe. Numerous historians have analyzed the connections between class relations and gender relations, moving beyond the fundamentally male identity of the working class presumed in Thompson's analysis. Other scholars have questioned the extent to which a unified working class took shape over the course of the nineteenth century. Should we rather speak of the "working classes," given the deep differences among occupational groups, for example, artisans versus factory workers? Thompson's approach remains of seminal importance, however, because it calls attention to how classes emerged not simply as economic entities, but as new cultural and social communities.

Until the era of the French Revolution, social identities in western Europe were defined not so much in terms of classes as in terms of "ranks," "orders," and "estates," which were envisioned as reflecting natural and hereditary inequalities. Social, political, and religious institutions were generally organized according to patriarchal principles. Within the Catholic Church, ultimate authority resided in the papal "father." Likewise, on the manor, the lord was seen as ruling over his peasants as a father over his children; and in the guilds, the masters exercised authority over the journeymen and apprentices. The word "class," by contrast, initially lacked these hierarchical connotations. In *What is the Third Estate?*, published in 1789, the Abbé Sieyès used this term to designate the four categories of useful labor: agriculture, industry, commerce, and services, none of which he saw as intrinsically "higher" than the others. As late as 1810, the Prussian reformer Karl August von Hardenberg spoke of *classes* of the population in order to substitute a neutral term for the more highly charged word *estates*.

In England, political pamphleteers began to use the term *middle class* — or *middle ranks* — in the 1790s. These authors often identified the "middle class" as a virtuous and politically progressive segment of society, consisting of merchants, entrepreneurs, and so forth, whom they contrasted with the corrupt aristocracy and the degraded poor. By the first decades of the nineteenth century, the concept of the "middle class" had become solidly entrenched in English political vocabulary. For example, in a sermon of 1809 calling for peace with Napoleon, the Reverend Charles Colton declared:

[T]he middle order must be supported, or the whole fabric will tumble in; if the higher ranks have been oratorically termed the "Corinthian capital of polished society," the middle class is the strong pillar that supports, and lifts it from the dust. It forms that arch in our constitution, which springing from the foundation supports, the superstructure.

The term *working class* came into widespread use later than *middle class*, though the awareness of a shared identity of workers developed gradually from the late eighteenth century onward. This consciousness evolved not only through the common experiences of factory life, but also through developments in a variety of other spheres. The growing physical segregation of the working poor from middle-class residents in the new industrial cities created one bond among workers of diverse occupational groups. The Methodist revival that swept Britain during the late eighteenth and early nineteenth centuries offered workers an egalitarian religious ideology that had the potential to be extended to the realm of politics as well. Participation in social clubs and in fraternal associations known as "friendly societies" also forged cultural links across occupational lines.

The first wave of workers' protests during the early nineteenth century may be seen partly as an attempt to defend traditional occupations against the advent of industrial capitalism. In the Luddite revolt of 1811–1812, English hand weavers burned textile factories and destroyed machinery in an effort to maintain their traditional livelihood; and from the 1820s through the 1840s, further episodes of machine breaking by displaced artisans occurred in Britain, France, and Germany. In Germany, one of the most serious uprisings during the first half of the nineteenth century was a revolt of hand loom weavers (*Weber*) in Silesia in 1844. Exploited by their entrepreneurs and ruined by competition from mechanized cotton manufacturing plants, several thousand weavers burned and looted the houses of their employers. The episode was dramatized at the end of the century by the German playwright Gerhard Hauptmann in a play entitled *The Weavers*.

A number of scholars have argued that a new working-class consciousness crystallized in Britain and France during the early 1830s. In the turmoil surrounding France's July Revolution and the passage of England's Reform Bill of 1832, strikes and industrial actions occurred in both countries. By this time, both "working class" and the "middle class" had become common phrases in the popular press. In the German states, various writers began to speak of the existence of a "working class" and a "labor movement" by the 1840s.

It is important to recognize, however, that workers' identities remained socially and politically fractured throughout the nineteenth century: their solidarity was sharply circumscribed by factors including gender, occupation, and ethnicity. For example, in many parts of Europe, women workers were an important presence in rural manufacturing and in service trades, as well as in factories. Nineteenth-century unions, however, frequently excluded women's participation; men went so far as to strike in order to force the firing of female workers. From the 1830s onward, skilled male workers in Britain began lodging demands that their employers pay them a "family wage," which would uphold their respectability by permitting them to support their families solely on the basis of their own labor. In such cases, the solidarity of male workers was predicated on the existence of a sharp division between men and women. As will be discussed further in Chapter 5, working-class men capitalized on the Rousseauian notion of innate sexual differences to advance their political, as well as their economic, agendas. By portraying themselves as part of a community of rational men, in contrast to irrational and instinctually driven women, working-class men pressed their claim for the right to vote.

Along with this gender-based divide, significant differences also existed between artisans, who worked in guilds and small shops, and workers in larger factories. In France, for example, worker activism during the early nineteenth century developed primarily within traditional artisan trades such as leather tanning, shoemaking, and tailoring. Artisans' associations were often called "corporations," a term that had previously been used to denote the trade guilds of the Old Regime, which had been formally abolished by the Le Chapelier Law of 1791. Unlike the old guilds, with their rigidly hierarchical structure under the leadership of the masters, the new corporations were relatively egalitarian entities consisting entirely of workers. Still, these new bodies, like the old guilds, remained restricted to individual occupational groups, which limited their horizon of political activity. Over the course of the 1830s, some worker activists began calling for an "association of workers of all trades," and, during the 1840s, French socialists such as Louis Blanc articulated more fully this theme of the unity of interests of all workers. Yet even during the Revolution of 1848, attempts to coordinate the political activities of workers' corporations met with limited success: these bodies continued to emphasize primarily their own specific concerns.

Though certain social theorists, most notably Karl Marx and Friedrich Engels, prophesied an apocalyptic struggle between the working class and the bourgeoisie, this ideology of radical struggle was slow to take root. Many workers persisted in perceiving their interests in local rather than in universalist terms; moreover, they did not always see their agenda as intrinsically opposed to that of their employers. Though their class identity was forged in large part through their efforts to organize in order to improve their conditions of life, workers rarely anticipated a global conflict between the working class and the bourgeoisie. During the Revolution of 1848, writes William Sewell, French socialists embraced "the consciousness of enlightened humanity, not the consciousness of a class": they sought not "revenge on their exploiters but a means of transcending exploitation and creating a just society."[14] They envisioned a cooperative rather a conflict-based relationship across class lines.

POLITICAL IDEOLOGIES

Two of the dominant political ideologies of the nineteenth century, liberalism and socialism, evolved in large part as responses to the experiences of industrialization. Both movements had their roots in the political theory of the Enlightenment and the French Revolution, but they interpreted this eighteenth-century legacy in divergent ways. Liberalism, which in nineteenth-century Europe was associated primarily with the bourgeoisie, emphasized the centrality of individual economic and political freedom. Socialism, though initially articulated by middle-class authors, focused primarily on the condition of the working classes. Socialists stressed the good of the collectivity over that of the individual, arguing that legal and political freedoms were meaningless as long as profound social inequalities persisted. Thus, socialists elaborated on the legacy of the French Revolution, expanding the definition of "equality" to include economic well-being along with political rights.

Liberalism

The "classical liberalism" of nineteenth-century Europe differed significantly from the liberalism of our own day. Since the early twentieth century, liberalism has come to embrace not only political rights but also various social entitlements, such as the right to a minimum standard of living, including food, housing, education, and health care. Nineteenth-century liberals, though they supported the principle of universal equality under the law, generally did not acknowledge such social rights. Placing supreme value on the rights and dignity of the individual human being, they argued that humans were best capable of attaining their full potential when given the capacity to act freely, without government restraint. "Liberty," which was central to their credo, included freedom from arbitrary arrest and imprisonment, freedom of speech, freedom of assembly, and freedom of the press. Finally, liberals also emphasized the authority of reason, rather than tradition, and they stressed the perfectibility of social and political institutions. In contrast to conservatives, who often idealized the past, liberals tended to

---

[14] William H. Sewell, Jr., *Work and Revolution in France: The Language of Labor from the Old Regime to 1848* (Cambridge, 1980), p. 284.

view history as progressive in nature: they believed that rational government would bring about a better society in the future.

Early nineteenth-century liberalism combined moral and economic arguments. German liberals, such as Wilhelm von Humboldt (1767–1835), built on the theories of Enlightenment philosophers such as Immanuel Kant (1724–1804), who had portrayed freedom as indispensable for the development of moral judgment. For Humboldt the "true end of man" was the "highest and most harmonious development of his powers to a complete and consistent whole," and the best way to attain this goal was by strictly limiting the powers of the state. In Britain and elsewhere, liberalism was also shaped by the economic theories of the Scottish political economist Adam Smith (1723–1790), who argued for laissez faire policies minimizing government control over the economy. Smith's *Wealth of Nations*, published in 1776, attacked the prevailing philosophy of mercantilism, under which the government sought to maximize its revenues by closely regulated manufacturing and trade. Smith contended that such efforts were inevitably counterproductive: for example, by erecting high tariffs against foreign goods, mercantilist policies slowed economic growth, which was the basis for national prosperity. Instead, he proposed a "system of natural liberty" in economic life. Government's primary function, according to Smith, was to maintain competitive conditions, for only within such a framework would the unrestricted self-interest of the individual be forced to operate for the general good.

The specific programs of liberal parties varied widely in different parts of Europe. Where the landed aristocracy or the clergy were still entrenched and retained unique privileges, liberals focused their attack upon these privileges. In France, most of these prerogatives had been lost during the revolution but from 1815 to 1830 liberals had to remain constantly on guard against attempts by both the nobility and the clergy to recover them. In Britain, where the Industrial Revolution was already causing significant changes in the social structure, representatives of the newer manufacturing interests sought to free themselves of restrictions inherited from a preindustrial era and to compel the older landed and merchant classes to share their control of the House of Commons.

British liberals, historians have argued, put a greater emphasis on the individual and the desirability of individual liberty than did liberals on the Continent. Of tremendous influence on British liberalism, along with Smith's free-market theory, was the argument of Jeremy Bentham (1748–1832) that the "greatest good for the greatest number" would result if each individual were allowed to pursue his or her own self-interest with a minimum of outside interference. On the Continent, wherever there were peoples who had not yet achieved political unity or who were living under a foreign ruler, "liberty" and "freedom" were likely to denote liberty from foreign control and freedom for the nation. "Freedom" for the Greeks meant freedom from Turkish control; "liberty" for the Italians meant the overthrow of Austrian domination. And many of those in the German states who thought of themselves as liberals sought above all "freedom" for the German "nation" — some form of closer union among the German people, without which personal or individual freedom appeared meaningless. For these peoples, liberalism and nationalism were closely allied; indeed, nationalist aspirations often tended to overshadow, and occasionally overwhelmed, other liberal values.

In the states of central, southern, and eastern Europe, where constitutions and representative institutions were virtually nonexistent, the goal of liberals was a written constitution which would limit the authority of the ruler and provide for an elected parliament or assembly that would share in the formulation of laws. The word *constitution* took on an almost mystical significance for liberals in some of the German and Italian states, who assumed that by its mere existence such a document would solve all their problems. But in the countries of western Europe where a constitution and an elected assembly already existed in 1815, liberals naturally had different goals. Their primary task was to see that representative institutions functioned in such a way that the government was genuinely responsible to the people — or rather to the propertied segment of the population represented, for example, in the French Chamber of Deputies. Accordingly, they tried to limit the authority of the king and make his ministers responsible to the elected chamber for their actions. Some even recommended broadening the base of the electorate to include men of lesser wealth.

Though liberals demanded that the people have a role in political decision making, they were far from being radical democrats. In most European countries, at least until 1848, liberals generally supported the preservation of monarchical government, and they strongly opposed the principle of universal male suffrage. The prominent French liberal Benjamin Constant de Rebecque (1767–1830), for example, argued that the tyranny of the mob could be just as dangerous as the tyranny of a king. "Property alone, by giving sufficient leisure, renders a man capable of exercising his political rights." Justifying the property qualification, he argued that the vote was accessible to all men: the poor man had only to acquire the requisite amount of property in order to vote.

For most of the nineteenth century, liberal theorists almost uniformly rejected the notion of woman suffrage, holding that women, like children, lacked the capacity to exercise rational judgment in political affairs. An important exception was John Stuart Mill (1800–1873), who advocated universal suffrage for both men and women. In *The Subjection of Women* (1869), Mill argued that women existed in a condition of legalized "slavery" to their husbands and fathers, and thus were inhibited from developing their natural abilities.

If early nineteenth-century liberals spoke frequently of "liberty," they referred less often to "equality." Certainly they saw nothing essentially wrong with the gross inequalities in the distribution of property and wealth that existed throughout Europe. Indeed, classical economists such as Thomas Malthus (1766–1834) and David Ricardo (1772–1823) drew on Smith's logic in order to demonstrate that natural "law" mandated the poverty of the working classes. Any efforts to raise workers' standard of living, they contended, would simply enable workers to have more children. The resulting expansion of the labor pool would ultimately depress the level of wages as a consequence of the law of supply and demand. What liberals did insist on, in theory at least, was equality before the law. This principle was already generally recognized in Britain and was now guaranteed in France by the Code Napoléon, but in many parts of Europe where it was still denied, the abolition of the special legal privileges of the nobility and clergy became a central part of the liberal program.

Utopian Socialism

Whereas liberal authors, by and large, defended the new economic order in Europe, socialism emerged as a critique of industrial capitalism. During the first decades of the nineteenth century, a group of authors known as "utopian socialists" denounced the inequities and injustices of unrestricted competition. The term is used in part because they, or their disciples, tried to establish model communities of a utopian character — many of them in the United States; it also distinguishes these socialists from the followers of Karl Marx, a little later in the century, who referred to themselves as "scientific socialists" or as "communists." In Marx's view, the socialism of the utopians exhibited excessive nostalgia for the preindustrial past, and it failed to recognize the inexorable forces of history that produced the capitalist order. Despite the differences between utopian socialism and Marxism, both currents of thought attacked capitalism as a cause of alienation and social isolation, and they sought to define new communities that would reintegrate individuals into a harmonious social order.

The utopian socialists, such as Henri de Saint-Simon, Charles Fourier, and Robert Owen, based their arguments on an ethical foundation. The existing economic system, they contended, placed far too much emphasis on the production of goods and far too little on their distribution. The result was that those who were most in need of the products of industry were frequently unable to secure them. This is the way an Owenite publication put the problem in 1821:

England possesses the means and the power of creating more Manufactured Goods than the world can consume; and her soil is capable of furnishing several times the number of her present population with food.

Notwithstanding this power, and this inalienable source of superabundant subsistence, millions of her own people are but imperfectly supplied with some, and are entirely destitute of most, of the necessaries and comforts of life, and of the numberless articles of convenience or of elegance which inventive skill has contrived for the accommodation or embellishment of society.

Socialist writers could also point to the frequent crises, attended by large-scale unemployment and suffering, that seemed to be inherent in a system of unrestricted competition. Where was the basic flaw in the system? The Utopians offered no single answer, but they generally shared the view that excessive individualism and self-seeking were characteristic of capitalism, and proposed in its place systems of social organization based on cooperation and mutual respect.

Henri de Saint-Simon (1760–1825), one of the pioneer socialists in France, maintained that industrial society should be organized on a "scientific" basis, in accordance with certain social "laws" that could be discovered through the study of history. Rejecting ideals of political and social equality, he proposed a hierarchy of classes; the dominant class was to be an intellectual and moral elite concerned with the general improvement of humanity. Below it he placed the propertied class—the captains of industry, charged also with governmental and administrative functions. Finally, at the bottom, was the "most numerous" class, the unpropertied laborers, whose welfare was to be the responsibility of those above them. The most important feature of Saint-Simon's cooperative commonwealth was its goal: the improved material condition and moral and intellectual regeneration of the lowest class.

Charles Fourier (1772–1837), another French socialist, was admired by later socialists for his systematic exposure of some of the glaring abuses and wasteful practices of the capitalism of his day. But he is perhaps better remembered for his blueprint of a cooperative community that he believed would so transform the human environment as to bring about a fundamental change in human behavior. His theory was based on the view that men's actions were governed by a set of "passions," or instincts, which under existing conditions were misused or misdirected because of the faulty environment. Accordingly, he proposed the establishment of a number of small communities or self-contained societies, called *phalanges* ("phalanxes"), in which work would be performed and social life organized so as to make the most effective use of the "passions." To make work attractive (that is, satisfying to the passions) jobs would be rotated, giving everyone an opportunity to perform "agreeable" as well as "necessary" tasks in the community. Moreover, Fourier proposed that all of the members of the community should perform those tasks to which they were naturally suited. For example, old women would serve as matchmakers; and little boys and girls — because they loved dirt — would be responsible for garbage disposal. Despite the communal nature of these enterprises, Fourier did not intend to abolish private property. Indeed, he anticipated that considerable differences in wealth might remain. Fourier, whose own means were modest, announced after the publication of his proposals that he would be at home daily at noon, ready to discuss them with anyone interested in financing a phalanx. He hoped to establish a limited number of phalanxes which would prove so successful that they would be imitated throughout the world. Reportedly, he returned home punctually at noon every day for ten years, but no patron ever appeared.

Utopian socialism was not confined to France. One leading socialist who had an opportunity to put his theories into practice was the Welshman Robert Owen (1771–1858), a self-made manufacturer who bought a cotton mill at New Lanark, in Scotland, and turned the town into a model community organized on cooperative principles. Like Fourier, Owen believed in humans' natural goodness and was convinced that they were corrupted only by an improper environment. If people could live in a society based on cooperation and mutual respect rather than self-interest and competition, their true nature would reveal itself. At New Lanark, beginning about 1800, Owen converted a miserable factory town into a clean, orderly community with educational facilities for children and a remarkably high standard of living. The extent to which this achievement resulted from the application of cooperative principles and not from Owen's own benevolent rule is a matter of dispute, but the project has been viewed as one of the first successful socialist experiments. Like Fourier, Owen tried to interest others, particularly his fellow manufacturers, in establishing cooperative communities, but he met with little response. Believing that his ideas might have greater success in the less tradition-bound atmosphere of the United States, he took over an existing community in Indiana in the 1820s and rechristened it New Harmony, but this experiment was marked by internal dissension

Cotton mills at New Lanark, Scotland, where Robert Owen established a utopian social welfare community during the early nineteenth century.

and collapsed after three years. Owen was subsequently active in the trade-union movement in Great Britain and in founding consumers' cooperatives for workers, but experienced failure and disillusionment in his later years.

The French social theorist Louis Blanc (1811–1882) has been described as a figure of transition between the utopian socialism of the first half of the century and the "proletarian socialism" of the second half. His ideas — as expressed, for example, in his essay *The Organization of Labor* (1839) — were simpler and had a more direct appeal to the working class in France than those of either Saint-Simon or Fourier. Writing in an era plagued by depressions, he charged that under the system of laissez faire, workers were often denied one of their basic rights, the right to work and earn a decent living. To the state belonged the responsibility of guaranteeing this right. Aware that the bourgeois-dominated July Monarchy would never fulfill this obligation, Blanc viewed political reform and the broadening of the franchise as essential prerequisites to social reform. Once the state was sympathetic to the cause of the laboring classes, it would subsidize the formation of "social workshops," cooperative enterprises for production which would in time dominate the most important branches of industry. The workers themselves would assume control of the workshops, repaying the government loans over a period of years. Blanc further hoped that the association of workers for economic ends would lead them into voluntary associations for the satisfaction of other needs as well. In other words, the social workshops would form the nucleus of a fully cooperative society. The simplicity of Blanc's ideas—particularly his emphasis on the right to work and the responsibility of the state to provide work—constituted their appeal. *The Organization of Labor* went through numerous editions in the 1840s and seems to have reached a fairly wide audience. During the Revolution of 1848, Blanc's propaganda was reflected in the demand of Paris laborers for recognition of the "right to work" and in the revolutionary government's establishment of "National Workshops." These turned out, however, to be little more than caricatures of Blanc's original proposal.

With the possible exception of Louis Blanc, these early socialists had relatively little influence on their contemporaries. Aside from small bands of disciples and a few attempts, almost all abortive, to establish model socialist communities, they were ignored. For this neglect there is a variety of explanations. Yet one assumption, common to all of the utopian socialists, may help to explain their failure; this was their belief, derived from certain of the philosophes of the eighteenth century, that man was naturally good, so that once his social environment and institutions were changed, all evil and suffering would automatically be eliminated. Adherence to this view clearly resulted in their underestimating the complexity of human institutions and the obstacles to social change.

Communism

During the mid-nineteenth century, a new generation of radical social critics, led by Karl Marx (1818–1883) and Friedrich Engels (1820–1895), challenged the idealist foundations of utopian socialism. Marx and Engels were both born in the Prussian Rhineland. Marx's father was a Jewish lawyer who had converted to Christianity during the anti-Semitic backlash following the Napoleonic wars. Marx himself studied law briefly in Bonn and Berlin before completing a doctorate in Greek philosophy at the University of Jena. After failing to find a teaching position, Marx became a journalist and newspaper editor in the Rhineland, where he met Engels in 1842. Banned from Prussia in 1844 for his radical views, Marx lived in Paris, then in Brussels and London. Unlike Marx, who never held a steady job, Engels ultimately became the owner of a factory in Manchester; he supported his collaborator financially during the decades that Marx was working on his great economic critique *Capital*, the first volume of which was published in 1867, and the subsequent ones only after his death.

Marx and Engels' political theory was indelibly influenced by the writings

Karl Marx, depicted as Prometheus bound in chains to his printing press, with his liver being eaten by an eagle. Allegory of the suppression of *Die Rheinische Zeitung*, the radical newspaper that Marx edited until 1843.

of Georg Wilhelm Friedrich Hegel (1770–1831), the most prominent German philosopher of his age. Hegel envisioned history as a dialectical struggle between clashing forces that led to the unfolding of the "world spirit." For Hegel, spirit (*Geist*) was a universal animating principle, simultaneously creative and destructive. Hegel observed that, in history as in nature, new entities were created only through the destruction of old ones. A butterfly came into existence by "overcoming" or "negating" its previous form as a caterpillar; an oak tree emerged only by destroying the acorn from which it stemmed. Hegel argued that the world spirit achieved its fulfillment through an analogous series of metamorphoses directed toward the realization of human freedom. According to his view of history, in the first, or oriental, stage of historical development the *monarch* alone had been free; in the Greek and Roman stages the *few* had achieved freedom; and only in the last, or Germanic, stage of history, were *all men* destined to be free. Some of Hegel's disciples interpreted him as a deeply conservative philosopher, because he appeared to glorify the Prussian state as the vessel of the world spirit. Yet Hegel also inspired a group of young radicals known as the Left Hegelians (a group to which Marx belonged briefly), who argued that only a profound political and social transformation would make possible the transition to this ultimate stage of universal freedom.

By the mid-1840s, Marx had decisively rejected the idealist foundations both of utopian socialism and of Hegelian philosophy, embracing a social theory based on "dialectical materialism." According to this perspective, economic forces rather than spirit moved history. "The history of all hitherto existing society is the history of class struggles," he and Engels proclaimed in *The Manifesto of the Communist Party*, published on the eve of the Revolution of 1848. During the medieval period, the slave economy of the classical world had been supplanted by feudalism; in the French Revolution of 1789, the capitalist bourgeoisie had triumphed over the feudal aristocracy. But the victory of the bourgeoisie, Marx and Engels contended, laid the seeds for its ultimate downfall. The capitalist economy inevitably concentrated ever greater wealth within an ever smaller group of entrepreneurs, while expanding and impoverishing the industrial working class or "proletariat." Paradoxically, the very brutality of the proletariat's exploitation enabled this class to become a revolutionary force, because it destroyed the "religious and political illusions" (such as Christian beliefs and patriotic feeling) that had disguised previous forms of class oppression. Marx and Engels predicted that the workers' suffering would enable them to achieve "true consciousness" of their class solidarity, and thus to throw off their chains by organizing a violent revolution against the bourgeoisie.

Like utopian socialism, Marxist doctrine had little immediate effect on European politics. Though Marx and Engels rushed back to the Rhineland on the outbreak of the Revolution of 1848, they were unable to garner much support for their communist program, and they were intensely disappointed by the triumph of the counterrevolution the following year. Over the longer term, the capitalist system proved far more resilient than they had anticipated. Marx and Engels predicted that the communist revolution would occur first in the most advanced industrial societies, such as Britain and Germany, because the contradictions inherent in capitalism would be most fully exposed there. In practice, however, communist revolutions ultimately occurred primarily in countries that were relatively underdeveloped economically, and that had been destabilized politically by warfare or by the legacy of colonial domination. Moreover, these communist revolutions generally were organized not by the industrial working class, but by regimented cadres of predominantly bourgeois radicals. Not only did Marx and Engels substantially underestimate the staying power of capitalism, but they woefully misjudged such phenomena as nationalism and religious faith, which they dismissed as forms of "false consciousness" destined to disappear on the advent of communism.

Whatever the shortcomings of Marxism as social science, during the twentieth century it became a political ideology of virtually unparalleled importance. By the height of the Cold War, one third of the world's population lived under Marxist regimes: among these were the Soviet Union, China, all of eastern Europe, and various newly independent states of Asia and Africa. Even after the revolutions of 1989 toppled communist governments throughout Europe, Marxist principles continued to inform the arguments of leftist political parties across the Continent. Perhaps one of the secrets of Marxism's enduring appeal was the way in which it wedded utopian and scientific elements. Like the romantics and the utopian socialists before them, Marxist activists embraced the quest for a just and harmonious community that would overcome the alienation produced by industrial capitalism. Yet this romantic ambition was clothed in the rhetoric of science, coolly demonstrating the certainty of the workers' victory even as it demanded their participation in the revolutionary struggle. For many on the left, communism appeared to offer the best hope for preserving a sense of humanity and belonging in a relentlessly modernizing industrial world.

CHAPTER 4

Restoration and Romanticism

AT THE time of Napoleon's final defeat in 1815, most of Europe still remained relatively untouched by the Industrial Revolution. Yet the twenty-six-year upheaval of the French Revolution and the Napoleonic era had irrevocably transformed the political landscape of the Continent. Napoleon had deposed ruling dynasties across Europe and obliterated hundreds of smaller states. Moreover, he had swept aside deeply rooted traditional hierarchies in regions that had come under French hegemony. The Catholic Church had lost both land and prestige, the stature of the aristocracy had been challenged, and new egalitarian principles had been enshrined in law. Moreover, in striving to resist French domination, rulers of various European countries had adopted many of the innovations of their conqueror, such as abolishing serfdom, establishing constitutions, and attempting to mobilize nationalist sentiments among their subjects.

Although the period between 1815 and 1848 is commonly termed the Restoration, a complete reversal of these profound social and political changes proved impossible. In striving to end the cycle of revolution and warfare that had engulfed the Continent, Europe's leading statesmen were forced to strike compromises between the old and the new orders. The Vienna Settlement of 1815 established an international framework for diplomacy emphasizing collaboration among the European states in order to preserve peace and maintain the balance of power. Within the various countries, governments attempted to repress nationalist and democratic movements that threatened their own authority, but they left intact many of the social reforms that had been carried out during the Napoleonic era. Moreover, industrialization and the growth of cities transformed patterns of daily life across Europe.

The first decades of the nineteenth century marked the height of the cultural movement known as romanticism. Though this movement defies any simple definition, the romantics frequently emphasized the alienation of individuals from modern society, and expressed a longing for harmony and organic community. The romantic temperament manifested itself not only in the realm of culture, but also in political movements such as conservatism and nationalism. Though conservatives and nationalists often were pitted against one another in the political struggles of this era, both movements disparaged the fragmentation of modern society, and they both aimed to restore harmonious communities in which individuals would find themselves at home.

THE SETTLEMENT OF 1815 AND THE CONCERT OF EUROPE

The Vienna Settlement of 1815 ranks with the Peace of Westphalia (1648), the Peace of Utrecht (1713), and the Peace of Paris (1919) as one of the four most significant international agreements in the history of modern Europe. The task of the statesmen at Vienna was nothing less than to dispose of all the lands that had been conquered by the French armies over two decades, and their agreements shaped the European political order throughout the following century. Some adjustments were made shortly after 1830, and more significant changes accompanied the revolutions of 1848 and the movements for German and Italian unification later. However, no war among the major European powers occurred until the Crimean War during the 1850s, and a general European conflict comparable to the Napoleonic wars was avoided until 1914. Perhaps even more interesting in retrospect is the fact that the allied statesmen created in 1815 the system of international relations which came in time to be known as the Concert of Europe. This system, which provided for periodic conferences among the so-called Great Powers (Great Britain, Russia, Austria, and Prussia) to discuss problems affecting the peace of Europe, lasted, with some alterations, until well past the middle of the century. France, after an initial probationary period, joined the ranks of the Great Powers in 1818. Ultimately, the system was replaced by a diplomacy of alliances and alignments associated with Bismarck, but the precedent of holding general international conferences for the peaceful settlement of differences had been established and would be revived in the twentieth century.

The Congress of Vienna

In March 1814, even before the war with Napoleon had ended, the four major powers — Great Britain, Russia, Austria, and Prussia — negotiated the

Treaty of Chaumont, which became the cornerstone of the Quadruple Alliance. In it the allies pledged to remain united not only until France was defeated but for twenty years after the conclusion of hostilities, in order to ensure France's observance of the forthcoming peace. After Napoleon's defeat two months later, this group organized the Congress of Vienna, which convened, with interruptions, from September 1814 until June 1815. The initial hope had been that it would last only four weeks, but sharp divisions among the delegates slowed the pace of negotiations. Though invitations had been extended to "all the Powers engaged on either side in the present war," the delegates never met in plenary session. A secret article of the Treaty of Paris stipulated that the disposition of territories and other important decisions would be left to the four Great Powers of the Quadruple Alliance. Though the delegates from the lesser states were entertained with lavish banquets and balls at the Hofburg throughout the winter of 1814–1815, they were excluded from the most significant diplomatic deliberations. Their resentment over the closed negotiations made them reluctant to ratify the decisions of the major powers.

Despite the wounded pride of the lesser princes, the peace settlement largely reflected the interaction of the chief representatives of the five major powers—France and the members of the Quadruple Alliance. The only ruler who took part personally in the negotiations was Alexander I, who was convinced that Russia's major share in the victory against Napoleon entitled him to the dominant role in drawing up the peace. Emperor Francis of Austria, though host to the congress, preferred to leave the burden of diplomatic negotiations to his chief minister, Prince Klemens von Metternich (1773–1859). In 1814 Metternich was already an experienced diplomat. He had served the Austrian foreign office since 1801, first as minister to Saxony, then as minister to Prussia, and from 1806 to 1809 as ambassador to the court of Napoleon in Paris. In 1809 he was appointed foreign minister, a position he held without interruption until 1848. Great Britain was represented in the negotiations at first by its foreign minister, Viscount Castlereagh (Robert Stewart, second marquis of Londonderry, 1769–1822), and after February 1815 by the duke of Wellington, who came as first British plenipotentiary. Prussia played a lesser part in the deliberations at Vienna, partly because the deafness of its chief representative, Prince Karl August von Hardenberg, made it difficult for him to follow the discussions closely, and partly because the Prussian king, Frederick William III, was personally subservient to the tsar. France's chief delegate, Prince Talleyrand, was initially excluded from the key deliberations, but he aquired greater influence as the congress progressed.

The leaders of the four victorious powers clashed both over their political

The Congress of Vienna, 1814–1815. Hardenberg (seated in the left foreground), Wellington (standing next to him), Metternich (standing in the left foreground), Castlereagh (seated to the left of center foreground), and Talleyrand (seated on the right at the table).

philosophies and over their territorial ambitions. Alexander I was an erratic prince who vacillated among idealism, religious mysticism, and shrewd calculations of what would best serve Russia's interests; he was the despair of those who had to deal with him. Metternich, a supreme practitioner of Realpolitik, sought above all to preserve Austria's dominance over central Europe and to prevent the resurgence of French aggression. Famous among his contemporaries for his vanity, he wrote in his memoirs in 1819, "There is a wide sweep about my mind. I am always above and beyond the preoccupation of most public men; I cover a ground much vaster than they can see. I cannot keep myself from saying about twenty times a day: 'how right I am, and how wrong they are.' " According to Metternich, all society rested ideally in a kind of equilibrium, or "repose," that was periodically upset. In his own time, the balance had shifted too far in one direction with the violence attendant on the French Revolution and the Napoleonic conquests. Now it would be the task of Europe's rulers to restore equilibrium, for which a period of peace was essential. The British negotiator Castlereagh, while equally determined to restrain France, had no desire to claim control of territory on the Continent. Because he was mainly concerned with securing Britain's maritime and commercial interests, he was able to play the role of a disinterested mediator among the continental states. His position was enhanced by the fact that Britain had restored to France almost all of its colonial possessions and could therefore call for comparable generosity on the part of the other allies.

The most important issue creating suspicion among the powers during the Vienna congress was the fate of Poland. Russian troops had occupied the former duchy of Warsaw, and Tsar Alexander hoped to establish a Polish kingdom under Russian protection. The tsar's reconstituted Poland would include not only the duchy of Warsaw but also the territories that Prussia and Austria had acquired during the partitions in the last decades of the eighteenth century. Alexander harbored this plan for some time and encouraged Polish leaders — among them Prince Adam Czartoryski (1770–1861), whom he had appointed as his own foreign minister — with promises of a liberal constitution for the revived kingdom. Frederick William III of Prussia had no objections to the tsar's project, even though Prussia would have to yield the lands it had taken during the partition, so long as compensation was provided in the form of other territory — preferably that of the kingdom of Saxony, whose ruler, Frederick Augustus I (ruled 1806–1827), had sided with France once too often during the final stages of the Napoleonic wars. Metternich, however, viewed with distrust any proposal that would involve Austria's abandonment of territory acquired during the partitions. Moreover, both Metternich and Castlereagh were skeptical about Alexander's reassurances to the Poles that they would retain their freedom, and saw the entire scheme as a plot for extending Russian influence in central Europe. With Poland in the Russian orbit, Alexander's troops would be within easy striking distance of both Berlin and Vienna. The tsar would then replace Napoleon as the principal threat to European peace and stability.

In Vienna during the fall of 1814, Castlereagh did his best to persuade Tsar Alexander to scale down his demands for Polish territory and to arrange some sort of compromise, but he failed. Metternich's attempt at direct negotiations with Alexander resulted in a scene so violent that the tsar threatened him with a duel and refused to speak to him directly for three months thereafter. Even Hardenberg entered into discussions with Alexander that were designed to bring about a compromise, but Prussia's insistence on the acquisition of the whole of the kingdom of Saxony did not predispose the tsar to moderate his own demands. By December the atmosphere between Britain and Austria, on one side, and Russia and Prussia, on the other, was so tense that there was open talk of the possibility of war. At this point Prince Talleyrand stepped in with a stratagem that appeared at first to heighten the crisis but ultimately resulted in its solution. He proposed to Metternich and Castlereagh a secret alliance to be directed against Russia and Prussia. The agreement, which was signed on January 3, 1815, provided that France, Austria, and Great Britain would support one another in the event that any of them should be attacked by Russia or Prussia and specified the number of troops each would contribute to the joint defense. Rumors of the alliance's formation were allowed to leak out, and they reached the rulers of Russia and Prussia almost immediately. The secret alliance was largely a bluff: indeed, Castlereagh acted against the orders of his government in signing the agreement. Nonetheless, the expectation that further attempts would result in a general European war was sufficient to convince the tsar and his Prussian supporters to back down, and the crisis was effectively ended. Talleyrand's intervention had a further consequence as well: by forming an alliance with two of France's conquerors, directed against the other two, he effectively ended the diplomatic isolation of France. From this time on, Talleyrand sat with the inner group at the conference.

Once the Polish-Saxon issue had been resolved, the diplomats at Vienna were able to reach agreement on other aspects of the territorial settlement without further crises. Their decisions were embodied in a document known as the Final Act, which was completed and signed in June 1815. Poland emerged as an ostensibly independent kingdom, but it was a greatly reduced version of the state Alexander had hoped for, since Prussia was allowed to retain Posen, and Austria to keep Galicia, territories they had taken during the partitions. Krakow, with the area immediately around it, was established as a free city, nominally independent but under the joint protection of Austria, Prussia, and Russia. The rest of the former duchy of Warsaw constituted the new Polish state, with Alexander as its ruler. In time, the tsar conferred on the Polish kingdom a liberal constitution that guaranteed full independence and a separate political structure to the Polish people; however, the preamble made clear that the constitution was being granted not as a right but a favor. Furthermore, the kingdom was to be a hereditary possession of the Romanov dynasty, and its foreign policy was to remain under the control of Russia.

Prussia may not have come away with all that it had hoped for, but it fared reasonably well, receiving two fifths of the territory of Saxony, with a population of eight hundred and fifty thousand; the remainder of Saxony was restored to its former ruler, who retained the title of king. Prussia also received additional territories in Germany—Swedish Pomerania, and portions of Westphalia and the Rhineland—in part as compensation for lands ceded to Hanover and Bavaria.

The primary objective of the statesmen at Vienna was to ensure that

France would not trouble the peace of Europe in the future. To this end they established around France two defensive barriers made up of neighboring states. At the northernmost end of the first of these barriers, which was formed by states touching France's borders, was the new kingdom of the Netherlands, under the rule of the ex-*stadholder* of Holland (the heir of the house of Orange), who was given the title King William I. The reunification of the two regions of the Low Countries, formally separated since the Peace of Westphalia in 1648, was one of the less durable achievements of the congress. Linguistic and religious differences contributed to the dissatisfaction of the people of the southern provinces, and in 1831 they revolted and proclaimed their independence as the new kingdom of Belgium.

Along the eastern border of France were ranged a number of German states (including Prussia, in that it was given control of the territories along the left bank of the Rhine); Switzerland, which was reestablished as an independent confederation of cantons; and the kingdom of Sardinia, which included not only the island of Sardinia but also the territory of Piedmont on the mainland. The kingdom of Sardinia (also referred to as the kingdom of Piedmont) was enlarged and strengthened with the addition of Genoa, Nice, and part of Savoy. On France's southwestern border Spain was again under Bourbon rule; Ferdinand VII had been restored to the throne by Wellington in the final stages of the Peninsular War.

Reinforcing the states along France's borders was the second defensive barrier, lying farther to the east: Prussia proper, Austria, and the remaining German states. The British intended Prussia to emerge from the settlement as a formidable power in central Europe, standing as a bulwark against both French and Russian aggression. Ultimately, Metternich agreed to support this policy even though it was strongly attacked by other Austrian statesmen as a threat to Austrian domination of the German states.

Austria received major territorial restorations in the south. These included on the Italian peninsula the provinces of Lombardy and Venetia, and on the Dalmatian coast the Illyrian provinces — all of which were directly incorporated into the Austrian empire. Austria also recovered Salzburg and the Tyrol, both lost to Bavaria during the Napoleonic wars. A Deutscher Bund ("Germanic Confederation") was established as a kind of successor to the defunct Holy Roman Empire. It was composed of thirty-nine states, including four free cities and Austria and Prussia (except for their non-German territories), bound together in a loosely organized union under the presidency of Austria.

On the Italian peninsula, beyond the second defensive barrier, a number of rulers were restored to their thrones. The Papal States were returned to the pope. In central and northern Italy, three small duchies — Tuscany, Parma, and Modena — were given to princes related to the Austrian royal family, and Austrian influence was to remain strong throughout the peninsula in the years after 1815. The kingdom of Naples and Sicily (the kingdom of the Two Sicilies) was ultimately restored under Joachim Murat, Napoleon's brother-in-law, until he made the mistake of rallying to the emperor's standard during the Hundred Days.

In other provisions of the Vienna settlement, Sweden was allowed to retain Norway, acquired from Denmark in the preceding year, but was forced to accept Russia's conquest of Finland. Great Britain voluntarily abandoned all colonial conquests with the exception of those taken from France in the first Treaty of Paris, Helgoland and the former Dutch colonies of Ceylon, the Cape Colony, and Demerara, in Guiana.

The Second Treaty of Paris and the Holy Alliance

Napoleon's escape from Elba and the episode of the Hundred Days delayed the discussion at the Congress of Vienna but did not affect the overall territorial settlement. Indeed, the Final Act of the congress was signed before the battle of Waterloo. The principal consequence of Napoleon's return for the settlement of 1815 was the change it brought about in the terms imposed upon France. The failure of the French to oppose Napoleon — indeed, the enthusiastic reception that many Frenchmen gave him — seemed to call for harsher punishment than the first Treaty of Paris had imposed.

Quick action by the British brought about a second restoration of Louis XVIII, who returned, according to the current phrase, "in the baggage of the allies." Because they had played the principal role in the final battles against Napoleon, the British and the Prussians took the lead in drafting the second Treaty of Paris, which was signed only in November 1815, after five months of wrangling among the allies. Hardenberg had to contend with the vigorous demands of the Prussian general staff for a treaty that would strip France of Alsace-Lorraine, the Saar Valley, and the rest of Savoy and impose a crushing indemnity. These demands for a vengeful peace were also resisted by Castlereagh, who hastened to Paris in July and remained there until November, patiently working for a moderate settlement. In his view the considerations that had made lenient treatment of France desirable a year earlier were still present. The resulting treaty, somewhat of a compromise, was nevertheless notable for its moderation. The first treaty had cut France back to the boundaries of 1792; this one specified the boundaries of 1790, which meant the loss of several fortresses, a few small strips of territory on the Belgian and Swiss frontiers, and an additional slice of Savoy, ceded to

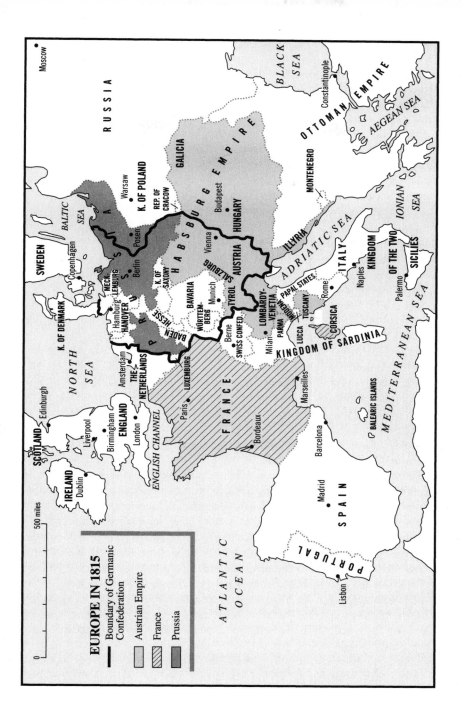

EUROPE IN 1815

Boundary of Germanic Confederation

Austrian Empire

France

Prussia

500 miles

0

Moscow

RUSSIA

BLACK SEA

OTTOMAN EMPIRE

Constantinople

AEGEAN SEA

BALTIC SEA

GALICIA

HABSBURG EMPIRE

Warsaw

K. OF POLAND

REP. OF CRACOW

Budapest

HUNGARY

Vienna

AUSTRIA

SALZBURG

MONTENEGRO

ILLYRIA

ADRIATIC SEA

IONIAN SEA

SWEDEN

Copenhagen

Posen

Berlin

K. OF SAXONY

MECK-LENBURG

TYROL

LOMBARDY-VENETIA

ITALY

KINGDOM

OF THE TWO

SICILIES

Naples

Palermo

K. OF DENMARK

Hamburg

HANOVER

HESSE

BAVARIA

Munich

WÜRTTEM-BERG

BADEN

SWISS CONFED.

Berne

Milan

MODENA

PARMA

PAPAL STATES

Rome

LUCCA

TUSCANY

CORSICA

KINGDOM OF SARDINIA

NORTH SEA

Amsterdam

THE NETHERLANDS

LUXEMBURG

SCOTLAND

Edinburgh

IRELAND

Dublin

Liverpool

Birmingham

ENGLAND

London

Paris

FRANCE

Bordeaux

Marseilles

Barcelona

Madrid

SPAIN

BALEARIC ISLANDS

MEDITERRANEAN SEA

ENGLISH CHANNEL

ATLANTIC OCEAN

PORTUGAL

Lisbon

the kingdom of Sardinia. The first treaty had imposed no indemnity; this one required France to pay 7 hundred million francs to the victors and to support an army of occupation of one hundred and fifty thousand troops for five years. (This force was reduced to thirty thousand in 1817 and removed entirely in 1818.) Finally, France was required to return the art treasures it had kept under the first treaty.

France's renewed defiance of Europe during the Hundred Days made a reaffirmation of the Quadruple Alliance appear essential. A declaration signed on the same day as the second Treaty of Paris was designed as a guarantee of that treaty. In it each of the four powers pledged to supply sixty thousand men in the event of a violation of the Treaty of Paris, particularly another attempt at the restoration of the Bonapartist dynasty. Of special interest was the article of this document calling for periodic conferences of the contracting powers for discussion of their "common interests" and for "the examination of measures which . . . will be judged most salutary for the repose and prosperity of peoples, and for the maintenance of peace in Europe." In this statement were contained the germs of the conference system, which persisted well into the nineteenth century.

The Quadruple Alliance was reaffirmed for the limited purpose of preventing violations of the Treaty of Paris, not to guarantee the broader settlement made at the Congress of Vienna or the more general goals of the contracting monarchs. But it was to become confused in the public mind with another alliance, which was proposed by Tsar Alexander and signed by the monarchs of Prussia and Austria in September 1815. In the Holy Alliance, the three contracting monarchs declared "their fixed resolution to take no other guide for their conduct . . . than those precepts of that holy religion, namely the precepts of Justice, Charity, and Peace . . . as being the only means of consolidating human institutions and remedying their imperfections." It went on to state that the three monarchs, acting as Christian brothers, would on all occasions and in all places lend each other aid and assistance to protect religion, peace, and justice. Precisely where Alexander got the idea for this Holy Alliance has never been determined, though it is clear that considerable influence was exerted on him by Baroness Barbara von Krüdener (1764–1824), a Pietist mystic. The concept of a general agreement among the European states for the renunciation of war and the establishment of international order seems to have been in Alexander's mind for at least ten years, and the religious sanction that underlay the proposal reflected his mood at the time.

Whatever the motives behind the Holy Alliance, there is no question that within a few years it was serving Metternich and the tsar as an instrument for the repression of liberal and revolutionary movements throughout Europe — a development that caused considerable tension between Britain and the three eastern powers. Thus, the conference system delineated by the Quadruple Alliance came to be viewed by many merely as a device for enforcing reactionary policies.

The Conference System and the Revolutions in Southern Europe, 1820–1823

In the years immediately following 1815, the Great Powers met regularly in a series of conferences dealing with problems of mutual concern. The last of these was held in 1822. By that date — and indeed, even earlier — Great Britain's differences with Austria, Russia, and Prussia over the nature and purpose of the alliance had reached a stage where collaboration on a permanent basis was no longer possible. Yet the collapse of the plan for regular meetings did not end the Concert of Europe. For the continental powers — joined occasionally by Britain — continued to assemble whenever crises developed, and the idea persisted that any threat to peace in Europe was automatically of concern to all. The period following 1815 was certainly not free of tensions, but the fact that no war was fought among the major powers may be attributed at least in part to this new system of European diplomacy.

For the first three years after the conclusion of peace, the primary task of the representatives of the Quadruple Alliance was to supervise the enforcement of the Treaty of Paris and the occupation of France. By 1818 France had arranged for the final payment of its indemnity and the allies decided that the time had come to evacuate the occupation troops and adjust relations between France and the other powers. This was the principal task of the Congress of Aix-la-Chapelle of 1818, which brought together leaders of the four Great Powers and France. To all appearances the congress went smoothly and achieved its stated purpose. The withdrawal of troops from France was agreed on, and as a token of complete reacceptance by the treaty nations, France was included in a newly formed Quintuple Alliance with the four other powers.

Yet the discussions at Aix-la-Chapelle also brought out sharp differences between the British and Russian views of the alliance and its purposes. Tsar Alexander had taken the opportunity to propose an Alliance Solidaire, by which the powers of Europe would guarantee not only each other's borders and possessions but also the security in each country of whatever form of government then existed. Castlereagh sharply rejected this proposal, declaring that the Quadruple Alliance had never been more than a specific commitment to prevent French military aggression, rather than to preserve established regimes or suppress revolutions. In the face of this determined stand, Tsar Alexander withdrew his proposal.

Two years later, in 1820, the unity of the Great Powers was tested more concretely when a series of revolutions broke out in Spain and on the Italian peninsula. For the first time the differences among the Great Powers were brought into the open. The first of the revolts was directed against Ferdinand VII of Spain, the Bourbon ruler who had been restored in 1814. He had been returned on condition that he would observe the liberal Constitution of 1812, which had been drawn up by an elected national assembly, the Cortes, in Cádiz, the one region of Spain that Napoleon had never subdued. Yet as soon as Ferdinand had been restored, he dissolved the Cortes, abandoned the constitution, and proceeded systematically to persecute the liberals who had been responsible for it. The general inefficiency of the government, evidence of corruption in high places, and an economic crisis provoked further antipathy to the regime. The rebellion began in the army, among regiments about to be sent to the Spanish colonies in Latin America to suppress revolts that had erupted there, but it quickly gained the support of upper-middle-class merchants whose business had dwindled in the postwar era and of a handful of liberal intellectuals sympathetic with the ideals of the French Revolution. Although the revolution had only limited popular support, the rebels were strong enough to force their will on the king, who agreed in March 1820 to respect the constitution and to summon the Cortes once again. For two years, until the French rescued him, the king remained the captive of the revolutionaries.

The response of the Great Powers to news of the revolt in Spain was far from uniform. The strongest reaction, not surprisingly, came from Tsar Alexander, who before the revolution succeeded, sent notes to the other allies suggesting some sort of joint intervention in defense of Ferdinand VII. Among the most amenable to this proposal was France, which had a particular interest in Spain because of its proximity, and saw intervention as an opportunity to counteract British influence in the Iberian peninsula. Prussia, although less directly concerned, was also willing to follow Russia's lead. Given Metternich's general horror of revolutions, it is a little surprising that he hesitated to support the tsar's proposal, but his conviction that the Iberian peninsula was Britain's particular sphere of influence led him to await the British reaction.

The British position was unequivocal. Although Castlereagh had no sympathy for the revolution, the British were determined for several reasons to prevent joint allied intervention in Spain. In the first place, intervention was contrary to Britain's view of the Quadruple Alliance, and England's Protestant rulers had little desire to rescue the monarchy of Catholic Spain. Second, the presence of the allies in Spain might threaten British commercial interests there. Finally, Britain saw that intervention by the allies in Spain might reverse the successes of the Latin American independence movements. Although several of Spain's Latin American colonies had established independence already, including Argentina (1810), Paraguay (1811), Chile (1818), and Colombia (1819), the struggles were still underway elsewhere on the Continent. Mexico would achieve independence in 1821. Brazil, Portugal's immense Latin American colony, established its independence in 1822. In Venezuela, Ecuador, Peru, and Bolivia, insurgent forces led by Simon Bolívar and his lieutenant Antonio José de Sucre waged an ongoing campaign against their colonial masters until December 1824, when Sucre overwhelmed a larger Spanish army in the battle of Ayacucho.

These independence movements offered Britain the prospect of lucrative trade with the Americas, which was too tempting to resist. Acting on motives of principle and pocket, on May 5, 1820, the British government circulated a memorandum to the other powers opposing allied intervention in Spain and reiterating the view that the alliance had originally been directed against France and that it had never been intended as "an union for the government of the world or for the superintendence of the internal affairs of other States." In the face of such categorical opposition, the Russian proposal was temporarily dropped.

When a series of revolts, apparently inspired by the Spanish example, erupted later in 1820 in other parts of Europe, Alexander's appeals met with more enthusiastic support. Indeed, Metternich, resorting to his most extravagant metaphors, referred to the revolutions as "conflagrations," "torrents," and "earthquakes." Spain's neighbor Portugal was affected in August. Here a peculiar situation existed; John VI, the king, was still in Brazil, where he had fled during the Napoleonic wars. The government of Portugal was in the hands of a regent who had the support of Marshal William Carr Beresford (1768–1854), the British general commanding troops stationed in the country. Taking advantage of the temporary absence of Beresford, a group of Portuguese army officers raised the standard of rebellion and established a provisional government that announced its support of the king, provided that he returned to his country. Meanwhile, a newly summoned assembly began to draft a constitution on the Spanish model.

More alarming to the powers, particularly to Metternich, was a concurrent revolt in Naples that threatened Austrian control of the entire Italian peninsula. Metternich spoke of this as the "greatest crisis" of his career. The rebellion was directed against Ferdinand I, the restored king of Naples and Sicily, who was an uncle of the king of Spain and resembled him in many respects. Like the Spanish king he had broken the promises he made to his people on his return in 1815 by abolishing reforms introduced during the French occupation and restoring the nobility and clergy to their privileged positions in the state. Further, since Metternich had helped place him on the throne, he was regarded as subject to Austrian influence. Opposition to Ferdinand came in large measure from the same groups that supported the rebellion in Spain: army officers and members of the business class. They had the additional support of nationalist secret societies such as the Carbonari, which had emerged during the Napoleonic occupation and now directed their attack against Austrian influence as well as the reactionary government of Ferdinand. The demands of those who revolted in Naples were primarily negative. The rebels did press for a constitution based on the Spanish Constitution of 1812, but there is some evidence that they were ignorant of its actual provisions.

The Neapolitan revolt aroused great excitement throughout the peninsula, but only in the northern Italian kingdom of Sardinia did an actual insurrection break out. Here the hopes of the revolutionaries were focused on Charles Albert (1798–1849), nephew of King Victor Emmanuel I and heir to the throne, but the irresolute behavior of the young prince when the rebels sought to make him their leader in March 1821 helped doom the revolt to failure.

Metternich was horrified by the revolt in Naples; yet he delayed taking measures to suppress it. It would have been relatively simple for an Austrian army to invade the kingdom and crush the rebels, but Metternich preferred to win the support of the Concert of Europe before adopting such a course of action. Despite Britain's refusal to condone intervention in Spain, Metternich now appealed to Castlereagh for backing in Italy. The British foreign minister's reaction is interesting. Though he fully sympathized with Metternich's concern over a revolt that might easily spread to the rest of the peninsula and affirmed that Britain would have no objection to armed Austrian intervention in Naples on behalf of Ferdinand, he opposed here — as he had in Spain — the principle of joint allied intervention. Rebuffed by the British, Metternich turned somewhat reluctantly to a quarter where he knew he could get support. He arranged for a congress of the rulers of Austria, Russia, and Prussia to be held at the Austrian village of Troppau in the autumn of 1820. Both Britain and France refused to participate officially but sent observers to the meeting. Apparently Metternich would have preferred to limit the discussion to the question of intervention in Naples, but Alexander insisted that the congress draw up a more general statement. The result was the Troppau Protocol, which in effect asserted the general right of the European powers to intervene in states that had undergone revolutions and to bring them back, by force if necessary, to the "bosom of the Alliance." This document referred throughout to the "European Alliance," never specifying whether the congress was acting in the name of the Holy Alliance or the Quadruple Alliance.

In accordance with the protocol, the eastern powers agreed to authorize intervention in Naples, but they postponed determination of the form it should take until January 1821, when the congress reconvened at Laibach, with Ferdinand of Naples invited to consult with them. There it was decided that an Austrian army, acting in the name of the allies, should be sent to Naples. Quickly dispatched, the army suppressed the revolt and restored Ferdinand to his throne. Then it moved northward to join the royalists in Sardinia, and the two forces defeated the rebels there.

Metternich had apparently achieved his goal of securing international support for the suppression of the Italian revolutions, but the victory was sealed at the cost of British friendship. For Castlereagh, incensed that the action in Italy was undertaken in the name of the allies, issued an official statement in January 1821, dissenting from the action of the other powers and proclaiming publicly the British position. Repudiating the Troppau Protocol, the declaration stated that the British government "cannot admit that this right [of interference in the internal affairs of another state] can receive a general and indiscriminate application to all revolutionary movements, without reference to their immediate bearing upon some particular State or States, or be made prospectively the basis of an Alliance." The statement was hailed by liberals throughout Europe with great enthusiasm. They looked to Britain as the champion of the liberal cause against the leaders of the Holy Alliance, whose apparent intention was to police the European continent and suppress liberal movements wherever they existed.

Those who viewed Britain as the defender of liberal aspirations throughout Europe were mistaken, for the Tory government headed by Lord Liverpool (Robert Banks Jenkinson, 1770–1828) had no such intentions. Its actions reflected instead the growing rift between Britain and the three eastern powers. Castlereagh had worked more closely with his continental colleagues than any British foreign minister before him; he had been, indeed, the prime mover behind the Quadruple Alliance and the conference system which grew out of it. But when he saw that system being perverted, being exploited for purposes for which it had never been intended, he felt that there was no alternative to withdrawing Britain's support. Castlereagh had already embarked on the policy that was later to be characterized as "splendid isolation." When he committed suicide as a result of overwork and fatigue, George Canning, his successor at the foreign office, continued with enthusiasm the policy that Castlereagh had adopted with regret.

Canning's acceptance of the post of foreign minister preceded by only a few weeks the Congress of Verona in 1822, the last in the series of regular postwar conferences among the allies, and the meeting at which the split between Britain and the other powers was formally confirmed. The congress was summoned to discuss further measures to be taken in Spain and to deal with still another revolution, the Greek war for independence from the Ottoman empire, which had begun in the preceding year. By the time the congress met, a temporary settlement of the Greco-Turkish affair had been reached, but sentiment for intervention in Spain was strong, since Ferdinand's position was steadily worsening. In the forefront of those urging action in Spain was France. France's attitude during the 1820–1821 crisis had been ambiguous. Like Britain, it had sent only an observer to the Congress of Troppau, but, although not formally adhering to the Troppau Protocol, France had made no protest against it. In the interim between Troppau and Verona, the ultraroyalist faction had gained the upper hand in Paris. It advocated a French invasion of Spain to restore the king and to extend French influence in the Iberian peninsula. At Verona, France got the support of all three eastern powers and was authorized by them to act on behalf of the concert. Before the agreement was complete, however, Canning instructed the duke of Wellington, the British delegate to the congress, to inform his colleagues that the British would not be a party to any intervention in Spanish internal affairs, "come what may."

Britain could protest, but could not prevent the action decided on by the others. When the Spanish revolutionary government refused to modify its constitution at the request of the continental powers, a French army crossed the Pyrenees (April 1823) and drove the revolutionary government from Madrid. By autumn the last resistance of the rebels had been crushed at Cádiz, and the king was restored to his throne. Ignoring the advice of the French to maintain a moderate constitutional regime, Ferdinand VII proceeded to eliminate the last vestiges of constitutionalism and to carry out mass reprisals against the liberals. Those who escaped torture and execution were imprisoned or driven into exile. Spain had been restored, in the words of the Troppau Protocol, to the "bosom of the Alliance."

Having failed to thwart intervention in Spain, Canning still hoped he could prevent the restoration of the Latin American republics to Spain. This aim was shared by President James Monroe of the United States, which in 1822 had recognized these new republics. Somewhat suspicious of British designs on Cuba, Monroe refused a British proposal for joint action and proceeded alone. In December 1823, in a statement that came to be known as the Monroe Doctrine, he proclaimed that the Americas were henceforth closed to European colonization and intervention. Great Britain subsequently recognized the independence of the Latin American republics from Spain and Portugal. Because British sea power helped guarantee this independence, Canning could boast in 1826, "I called the New World into existence to redress the balance of the Old."

The Settlement of 1815 Appraised

The Vienna settlement was notable for having imposed an enduring peace: no war broke out among the European powers until nearly forty years after Napoleon's defeat, and the first continentwide war occurred only in 1914. An important reason for the long-lasting peace was the remarkable consensus that existed among the powers despite their ideological differences. During the decades after 1815, all major European leaders accepted the principle of the balance of power and the implied assumption that no state should expand its influence without the consent of the others. Each government was therefore willing to temper its international conduct. Moreover, the powers displayed respect for treaties, as well as willingness to participate in joint efforts to maintain peace.

In part, the powers displayed restraint in their dealings with one another because they saw no compelling need for territorial expansion. For example, during the 1820s and 1830s, Russia, France, and Britain all sought to expand their influence within the Ottoman empire, but they made relatively little effort to annex new lands outright. A more fundamental reason for international stability was fear of a new continental war. Between 1792 and 1815, Europe had endured twenty-three years of nearly uninterrupted warfare and political upheaval. Following Napoleon's defeat, the leaders of the Great Powers were determined to reestablish both international and domestic stability. To this end, they treated France generously in the Vienna settlement, so that the French had no overwhelming desire for revenge or for rectification of their country's boundaries. The treatment of the defeated power under the Vienna settlement contrasted sharply with the Peace of Paris of 1919, at the conclusion of World War I, whose punitive treatment of Germany would fuel intense popular resentment and contribute to the rise of Adolf Hitler.

Not only did the leaders of the powers fear the rise of a new Napoleon; they were equally concerned about the threat of domestic subversion. They were intensely aware that the Napoleonic wars had provoked political upheavals throughout Europe, and they were determined to avoid giving an opening to potential revolutionary movements. Although members of the opposition, such as liberals in France and Britain, at times advocated military action on behalf of oppressed nationalities in Poland, Italy, and elsewhere, the governments steadfastly resisted these demands. It is no coincidence that the first major European war following 1815, the Crimean War of 1854–1856, erupted just a few years after the unsuccessful revolutions of 1848–1849. Having witnessed the suppression of political insurrections throughout Europe, the leaders of the powers had renewed confidence in their ability to engage in military adventures abroad without jeopardizing the stability of their own regimes.

ROMANTIC CULTURE AND POLITICS

In our discussion of the Industrial Revolution in Chapter 3, we have already seen how Europeans struggled to form new communities in response to the social dislocations of the early nineteenth century. For example, the bourgeois "cult of domesticity" was infused by the longing for a peaceful and harmonious private realm that would offer refuge from the perils of the industrial world. Similarly, socialist political theorists, ranging from Charles Fourier to Karl Marx, hoped that their critiques of capitalism would help lead to organic communities in which the full potential of humanity would be realized. This desire for harmony and belonging reflected the temperament of romanticism, one of the most powerful cultural currents of this age. The romantic temperament also manifested itself — in strikingly different ways — in such diverse political ideologies as conservatism and nationalism, both of which reached their full flowering in Europe during the first several decades after the French Revolution.

Romanticism

Romanticism was an amorphous movement that appeared across much of Europe from the late eighteenth through the mid-nineteenth centuries. The romantics reacted against the Enlightenment or against views that they attributed to writers of the Enlightenment. Whereas the philosophes had in general stressed the role of reason and the intellect in discovering truth, the romantics ascribed much more importance to feeling and emotion. The reality of human experience for them lay in the soul rather than the mind, in the heart rather than the head. Goethe's Faust, though created by a writer who defies classification as either classicist or romantic, was nevertheless the prototype for the romantic age: the scholar, disillusioned and discouraged by his long quest for intellectual understanding, who finally turns to sentiment, dreams, and action for the redemption of his soul.

How the romantic mood affected the visual arts can best be discovered through a brief discussion of some individual painters of the period: a German, Caspar David Friedrich (1774–1840); a Briton, Joseph Mallord William Turner (1775–1851); and a Frenchman, Eugène Delacroix (1798–

1863). None of these can be described as the prototype of the romantic artist, but together, their works reveal some of the most prominent features of painting during the romantic era. All of them reacted against existing artistic conventions and rules in their choice of subjects, the composition of their paintings, or their actual painting techniques. Like almost all painters of the romantic era, they believed that artists must express themselves—their instincts and their passions—through their work. A painting was to be not a formalized representation of some preexisting order, but rather the individual artist's vision of the cosmos, a vehicle for the imagination. A successful painting would play on the feelings and emotions of the viewers and stimulate their own imaginations.

Friedrich, who is most noted for his landscapes and seascapes, reflects the romantics' profound interest in nature. His drawings reveal his close familiarity with natural detail, but his paintings of mountains towering in the morning mists or gnarled trees silhouetted against the moonlight end by transforming nature and giving it an almost supernatural or spiritual quality. His landscapes invariably have an aura of the mysterious or sinister, a sense of foreboding. Friedrich attempts to convey his vision of the relationship of

Ruins of a Monastery and its Graveyard [Abtei im Eichwald] (1809), by Caspar David Friedrich.

the individual to the cosmos by placing in the foreground of his landscapes one or two isolated figures with their backs to the viewer, contemplating the grandeur of the natural scene. Through his composition he appears to be indicating the smallness and insignificance of human beings before the vast forces of nature, but he also seems to convey a sense of the individual's longing for the infinite, the desire to lose oneself in the cosmos.

Turner, too, is noted for his landscapes and his dramatic paintings of the sea, but a concern with the individual's relationship to nature is less obvious in his work. His subjects are varied: historical and mythological scenes, shipwrecks, dramatic episodes such as the burning of the Houses of Parliament in 1834, and above all, sunrises and sunsets over the water. Whereas Friedrich was not particularly innovative in his painting techniques, Turner developed a new freedom in his brushstrokes and became particularly skilled in the rendering of light. Using watercolors, he succeeded in capturing nuances of light and color in nature, which he later reproduced in oils. As he grew older, he tended more and more to blur the contours of the objects he painted, so that a ship, for example, seemed to melt into the surrounding sea and sky. In these techniques he anticipated devices later to be used by the impressionists, who like him were less concerned with objective detail than with the total impact of a scene on the viewer.

Delacroix, perhaps the most celebrated of French romantic painters, wrote in his journal, "If by my Romanticism people mean the free display of my personal impressions, my remoteness from the servile copies repeated *ad nauseam* in academies of art and my extreme distaste for academic formulae, then I am indeed a Romantic." In his choice of subjects, his arrangement of figures, and his daring use of color, Dèlacroix liberated himself from established conventions and gave full expression to his aesthetic imagination. He was particularly sensitive to the relationships among poetry, music, and the visual arts, and contended that the color harmonies of a painting could stimulate sensations comparable to those aroused by the combination of sounds produced by an orchestra. He drew many of his themes from Byron, Sir Walter Scott, and Shakespeare. In his choice of subjects, Delacroix, like many other romantic painters, was guided by the desire to tell a story or celebrate an event. An ardent political liberal, be commemorated the Revolution of 1830 in France with his *Liberty Leading the People*, a dramatic painting dominated by the bare-breasted figure of a woman standing on the barricades, holding aloft the tricolor in one hand and a gun in the other, as she spurs the revolutionaries on. Beneath her lie the disheveled corpses of those who have fallen; the entire scene is illuminated by the flames of buildings burning in the background. The same theatricality and sense of movement is revealed in many of the oriental scenes he was fond of painting,

Liberty Leading the People (1830), by Eugène Delacroix.

such as the famous *Massacre at Chios*, depicting the slaughter by the Turks of the Greek inhabitants of the island of Chios during the Greek revolution. Delacroix's fascination with the Orient, which was shared by many of his contemporaries, is an example of the romantic taste for the exotic and the bizarre.

In music, romanticism tended to be less revolutionary than in the visual arts. Historians of music generally identify the period of classicism with the eighteenth century and that of romanticism with the nineteenth, but they stress the continuity between the two periods and point out that the classical forms, developed or refined by Haydn, Mozart, and Beethoven — the sonata, the string quartet, and the symphony — persisted into the romantic era. And though some romantic composers took liberties with it, the classical system of harmony too remained dominant in the nineteenth century. But the early romantic composers — men such as Franz Schubert (1797–1828), Robert Schumann (1810–1856), Felix Mendelssohn (1809–1847), and Hector Berlioz (1803–1869) — infused the traditional forms with new meaning and reinterpreted the function of music. They tried to work directly on the mind and the senses of the listener so as to evoke an infinite range of impressions, emotions, and thoughts. Some, such as Berlioz, sought to do this by using much more varied and complex orchestration and by developing "program music," in which they attempted to convey, by means of imaginative suggestion, descriptive or poetic subject matter. Mendelssohn, for example, imparted a sunny and vibrant mood to his *Italian* Symphony, while the mood of his *Scottish* Symphony was gray and somber, with a suggestion of the bagpipes and the sound of heroic ballads. A more explicit attempt to achieve the fusion of poetry and music was made by the German romantics, particularly Schubert and Schumann, in the *Lied* ("song"), an art form in which words and melody are blended in perfect harmony. Hardly a mood or a nuance of feeling does not find expression in Schubert's *Lieder*, but the dominant impression is one of sadness, nostalgia, or yearning.

In literature, the revolt against the Enlightenment began as early as the mid-eighteenth century, although romanticism as a literary movement did not come to fruition in most countries until the first half of the nineteenth century. For example, in the growth of British Methodism after 1740 we find a reaction against the prevalent deism of the eighteenth century and a return to enthusiasm and emotion in religion. The writings of Jean Jacques Rousseau (1712–1778), himself a philosophe, also foreshadowed various aspects of romanticism: extreme sensitivity to nuances of feeling, concern with the individual personality, preoccupation with nature and the "natural." In Germany, the literary movement known as *Sturm und Drang* ("storm and stress"), out of which German romanticism developed, dates from the 1770s. By the early 1800s, romanticism as a literary movement was in full sway in Germany and had its representatives in Britain and France as well.

In matters of style, the romantics revolted against strict adherence to discipline and form that had characterized the classical tradition in literature. The measured Alexandrine verses of the seventeenth-century dramas of Racine and Corneille, which Racine and Corneille used a regular twelve-syllable line, were now considered stilted and "artificial." The romantics regarded their own literary creations as freer and more "natural." The attitude of most romantic writers toward the individual also differed from the point of view prevalent in the Enlightenment. Although the philosophes had expressed an interest in the individual and his rights, their main concern had been to discover what qualities humans had in common, what characteristics united them. In other words, they sought to generalize about human nature. Most romantic writers, on the other hand, were convinced of the uniqueness of the individual personality and suspicious of the kind of generalizations their predecessors had made. To them, diversity was not only natural but right and desirable. Carried to an extreme, this attitude led

Portrait of Johann Wolfgang von Goethe, painted by Tischbein in the Italian Campagna.

to a sense of isolation or alienation on the part of the individual, to self-dramatization and self-pity. Many a romantic figure, such as the hero of Goethe's novel *The Sorrows of Young Werther* (1774), suffered from this sense of isolation and self-pity, though not all resorted, like Werther, to suicide as the only way out. The emphasis on individuality also found expression, in some of the romantics, in revolt against society and its conventions.

For others romanticism meant a return to the past and a sentimental nostalgia for earlier eras of history, particularly for the Middle Ages. Where writers of the Enlightenment like Voltaire had felt nothing but contempt for the Middle Ages as an era of superstition and obscurantism, François René de Chateaubriand (1768–1848) in France, Novalis (Friedrich von Hardenberg, 1772–1801) in Germany, and Sir Walter Scott (1771–1832) in Britain all romanticized the medieval period and compared it favorably with their own. Not all of them found the same virtues in the medieval past, nor did they all object to the same things in their own age. But the vogue of the Middle Ages was in part a reaction against the ugly, materialistic, and heartless industrial civilization that seemed to be emerging. The romantics thought they had found in the Middle Ages a society in which the individual had security and a sense of belonging, an organic community in which the poor were contented with their station and deferred to their betters, and the noble lords recognized their responsibility to protect those dependent on them.

Perhaps, above all, they saw the Middle Ages as a time when faith prevailed, not the cold reason and skepticism of the Enlightenment. Romantic writers of a conservative turn were especially likely to look back nostalgically to an era when faith had provided a sense of cohesion and unity that was missing from their own society. Certainly a return to religion, and particularly to Catholicism, was an important feature of romanticism. For many, it was less the beliefs than the colorful ceremonial, or ritualistic, aspects of Christianity that exercised a particular appeal. In this period also can be found the roots of the Gothic revival in architecture, which a few decades later saw the construction of the British Houses of Parliament and other monuments in Gothic style and the restoration of long-neglected Gothic cathedrals.

The romantic mood affected writers of practically all political and ideological persuasions and cannot be identified exclusively with any one group. Clearly, political conservatives shared many of the assumptions and points of view that have been attributed to the romantics: the reaction against the Enlightenment and its undue emphasis on reason, the return to the past, and the reversion to orthodox forms of Christianity. Particularly in Germany the major writers of the romantic school were conservative in their outlook; indeed, the German conservative tradition owes a great deal to romanticism. The admiration of romantic writers such as Novalis for the organic society of the Middle Ages led them away from another romantic trait, the stress on the individual, and prepared the ground for the doctrine of the total submission of the individual to the state. Romanticism in Germany was both conservative and nationalist in tone. Yet exceptions may be found even to this generalization. The romantic writer Heinrich Heine (1797–1856), often called modern Germany's greatest lyric poet, was devoted to the cause of individual liberty and violently opposed the extreme positions taken by German nationalist writers in the first half of the nineteenth century. In Great Britain, some of the most noted romantic poets began their careers as radicals and ended as conservatives. William Wordsworth (1770–1850), an outspoken admirer of the French Revolution in its early stages, gradually turned against it, and in the end became a die-hard conservative opposed even to parliamentary reform. Samuel Taylor Coleridge (1772–1834) experienced a similar change of views. But in the second generation of English romantic poets, George Gordon, Lord Byron (1788–1824) championed the cause of oppressed nationalities everywhere and participated in the movement for Greek independence, and Percy Bysshe Shelley (1792–1822) shocked his contemporaries with views that caused him to be branded an atheist and an anarchist.

The element of nationalism in the romantic point of view was another expression of the reaction against the Enlightenment. Whereas the philosophes tended to be cosmopolitan in their outlook and to emphasize the similarities among peoples and nations, romantic writers turned with curiosity to their own national origins and traditions. As creative writers they were naturally interested in their native languages and often sought inspiration from folktales and legends. Consequently, they became increasingly aware of differences among cultures and tended to stress their national distinctiveness.

A similar pride in the nation appeared in the writing of romantic historians, though there may be disagreement as to which historians deserve this label. Few would question the term *romantic* when it is applied to the French historian Jules Michelet (1798–1874), best known for his multivolume *History of France*, a work that revealed his passionate devotion to his nation and its past. Like other romantic historians, Michelet viewed history as literature, or even art, and his histories abound in imaginative, detailed, descriptive passages full of color—though they are also careful to remain factually accurate. A man of the people himself, he intended his history of the nation to reveal the life and soul of the French people rather than to be a chronicle of its kings and queens or a history of its institutions. In England, Thomas Babington Macaulay (1800–1859), a Whig statesman as well as a historian, revealed a comparable pride in his own nation, whose moral and material progress he attributed to the British love of liberty. Characterized by its vigorous language, its sense of drama and movement, and its author's profound knowledge of his nation's past, Macaulay's *History of England* became a classic, read by generations of Britons. In Germany, where romanticism was so closely tied to the revival of a German national consciousness, historians wrote of Germany's medieval past, recounting the exploits of the Franconian and Hohenstaufen emperors as well as of the Teutonic knights who had settled Prussia. But the most noted German historian of the nineteenth century, Leopold von Ranke (1795–1886), though sharing the romantics' interest in Germany's past, went beyond them by developing a new approach to historical study. Rejecting the traditional reliance on earlier historical narratives, Ranke stressed the importance of going to the sources—contemporary documents and other records—and using them critically. In his *History of the Popes* and his *German History in the Era of the Reformation* he exploited hitherto unused materials, such as the diplomatic reports of the Venetian ambassadors, in such a way as to "get inside" the eras he was studying and deal with them on their own terms. Although his work was certainly not devoid of interpretation, his ideal was objectivity in dealing with past events, and he insisted that conclusions must arise strictly from the historical evidence. From Ranke's work stemmed the concept of professional or "scientific" history, which has had a profound influence on historians ever since.

Finally, the romantic mood influenced the cause of social reform particularly during the 1830s and 1840s. Reformers appealed to the humanitarian feelings of their contemporaries by dramatizing the plight of African slaves and the sufferings of their own poor. The sense of conspiracy and adventure associated with the activities of republican secret societies in France after 1830 was consonant with the current romantic atmosphere and contrasted strongly with the prosaic qualities of the established order. The dreams of socialists for the creation of utopian communities, perfect societies here on earth, though comparable in some ways to the visions of the philosophes, had an irrational appeal that distinguished them from the utopias of their eighteenth-century predecessors.

Romanticism was a many-faceted, pervasive phenomenon that left almost no doctrine or ideology untouched. Some have attributed to the influence of the romantic mood the soft-mindedness and fuzziness of so much of the thinking and writing of the first half of the nineteenth century. In this view the romantic era marked an interlude between the more disciplined, rationalist *Weltanschauung* (worldview) of the eighteenth century, which reflected the order and regularity of the Newtonian universe, and the positivist, science-oriented outlook that was to triumph in the second half of the nineteenth century. To be sure, this interpretation is an oversimplification. In politics, the romantic temperament continued to shape nationalist movements throughout the nineteenth century and beyond. In science, new disciplines such as geology and evolutionary biology, which emerged after 1850, were more organic than mechanical in character — a reorientation that may have been influenced partly by romanticism. But whether one was a romantic conservative yearning for the rebirth of a society that had disappeared, a romantic liberal serving the cause of freedom for oppressed peoples, or a socialist reformer dreaming of the establishment of a society free of poverty and social ills, the mid-century revolutions of 1848 would be a shattering experience. The abortive uprisings of that year seemed to prove that ideals were not enough, that in the last analysis physical force, material resources, and power were what counted in human relations.

Conservatism

Conservative political thought is often characterized largely as a response to the Enlightenment and the French Revolution. The French Revolution had barely begun when one of the most gifted and influential of all conservative philosophers, Edmund Burke, wrote his *Reflections on the Revolution in France*, which questioned the entire basis of the revolution and became a handbook of conservatism for the generations that followed. During the last decade of the eighteenth century two French authors, Joseph de Maistre (1753–1821) and the viscount of Bonald (1754–1840), both émigrés, spent their years in exile writing elaborate treatises in defense of absolute monarchy and the authority of the Catholic church. Less systematically, Metternich and his aide Friedrich von Gentz, both before and after 1815, joined in the attack on revolutionary principles and the appeal to traditional institutions. And German philosophers such as Fichte and Georg Wilhelm Friedrich Hegel (1770–1831) certainly reflected some of the assumptions of early nineteenth-century conservatives in their emphasis on the importance of the state. The philosophy of conservatism that developed between 1790 and 1820 was in many respects far more original than the liberal thought of the era.

Although individual variations existed, several common themes and arguments ran through the work of practically all the conservative intellectuals. For the most part they took the French Revolution as their springboard, presenting lengthy attacks on revolutionary principles and criticisms of the philosophy of the Enlightenment, which they held chiefly responsible for the catastrophe of 1789. In particular, the conservatives objected to what they considered the excessive reliance of the philosophes on reason, especially the kind of abstract reason that was used to justify "natural rights" and the introduction of new political and social institutions. Burke, with his great admiration for Britain's unwritten constitution, took an unmistakable stand against revolutionary programs:

The science of constructing a commonwealth, or renovating it, or reforming it, is, like every other experimental science, not to be taught *a priori*. . . . The science of government being therefore so practical in itself and intended for such practical purposes—a matter which requires experience, and even more experience than any person can gain in his whole life, however sagacious and observing he may be—it is with infinite caution that any man ought to venture upon pulling down an edifice, which has answered in any tolerable degree for ages the common purposes of society, or on building it up again, without having models and patterns of approved utility before his eyes.[1]

---

[1] Burke, *Reflections on the Revolution in France*, pp. 69–70.

Burke's appeal to "experience" as a guide in politics was echoed by other conservatives, particularly in Britain. It was part of a broader appeal to "tradition" and "history" that could be found at the very heart of conservative political thought. In this view, both society and government, because they are products of a long historical development, must be treated with respect. If changes or reforms are to be made in either, they must come gradually and only with proper consideration for historical antecedents and national traditions. This doctrine, carried to its logical extreme, could be used to justify complete adherence to the status quo on the grounds that tampering with any part of the delicately balanced institutional structure might endanger the whole. This tendency to resist any changes whatsoever to the traditional order was evident, to varying degrees, in the writings of French conservatives such as Bonald and de Maistre, and in the works of the Swiss political theorist Carl Ludwig von Haller (1768–1854). Burke, in contrast, was a supple and sophisticated thinker who insisted simply that change must occur naturally, rather than according to artificial principles. Indeed, Burke's conservatism anticipated, in certain respects, the Darwinian principle of natural selection, because he emphasized that a political system could survive over the long term only if it could meet the practical tests of experience.

A second weakness that conservatives attributed to the political philosophy of the Enlightenment was its emphasis on the individual and individual rights. The entire tradition of John Locke and his disciples came under attack both in Britain and on the Continent—the view that society and government are necessary evils or artificial constructions for the preservation of the natural rights of the individual. For conservatives, it was meaningless to talk of "individual liberty," apart from society, since freedom could be achieved only through the community. The individual was not distinct from society, an end in him- or herself, but part of a collectivity that was somehow more than the sum of its various members. Conservative political thinkers handled this theme in many different ways, but almost all shared the view that society was an organism that had evolved over the centuries and that the individuals who composed it were indissolubly bound with those who had preceded them as well as those who were to follow.

Conservatives deplored, in varying degrees, the lack of respect for established religion and ecclesiastical authority that had found expression during the revolution in the persecution of the clergy and attacks on Christian dogma. Some, notably Joseph de Maistre, held the skepticism and anticlericalism of men such as Voltaire directly responsible for the revolution. Many conservatives valued religion chiefly as a kind of cement that contributed to the preservation of social order; they regarded the Catholic church as one of the traditional institutions of society whose fortunes were linked with those of the monarchy and the aristocracy. But for de Maistre, Catholic Christianity was the very foundation of the social order. He believed that all sovereignty is derived from God and is vested in the monarch. Because of the divine origin of his authority, the king is absolute in his realm; his power can be limited in no way by his subjects. Religion provides the people with a motive for obedience and submission to the king and at the same time reconciles them to the natural inequalities that exist in society. Having provided a justification for absolute monarchy, de Maistre went on to argue that church and state must collaborate in promoting man's moral welfare and in preserving order. Should a conflict between the two arise, the authority of the church is higher than that of the monarch. Indeed, de Maistre ended by regarding the pope as the supreme political and religious authority in what amounted to a universal theocracy.

As was reflected in de Maistre's writings, support and sympathy for the Catholic church among the governing classes was unquestionably stronger in 1815 than in 1789. The revolutionary years witnessed a revival of faith and religious observance among many of the educated who had succumbed during the Old Regime to the rationalism and anticlericalism of the Enlightenment. In particular, members of the nobility who had witnessed during the revolution the simultaneous assault on the churches, the aristocracy, and the monarchy often concluded that their own fortunes were closely tied up with those of organized religion. Nor were they unmoved by the suffering and martyrdom of members of the clergy at the hands of revolutionary governments and the dignity with which Pope Pius VII withstood the harsh treatment Napoleon inflicted on him. Whatever the sources of the Catholic revival, the church was viewed in 1815 as one of the bulwarks of the social order and enjoyed a position of favor with European rulers.

Despite conservatives' emphasis on the need to reestablish traditional social and political hierarchies, they stopped well short of restoring everything that had existed before 1789. Had the principle of legitimacy been carried to its logical extreme by the statesmen at Vienna, the Holy Roman Empire would have been reestablished, along with the more than three hundred petty states into which Germany was divided before the revolutionary era. Actually, the principle of legitimacy was so haphazardly applied that Napoleon's brother-in-law Joachim Murat could have remained permanently on the throne of Naples in the place of the "legitimate" Bourbon ruler if he had not sacrificed his position by rashly supporting Napoleon during the Hundred Days. Nevertheless, the statesmen at Vienna regarded hereditary monarchy as one of the fundamental institutions to be restored, for they felt it was the only form of government capable of ensuring continuity and stability in human affairs. Metternich, who is usually viewed as the prototype of all that was conservative in the Restoration, did not subscribe to the divine-right theory of monarchy, but he was convinced that the hereditary succession of kings served as a guarantee for all other social institutions. Tsar Alexander I's Holy Alliance was a union of monarchs who pledged to lend each other assistance for the protection of religion, peace, and justice.

In almost every country in Europe, the Restoration also brought a revival in the status of the nobility. In France and the parts of Europe conquered by the French the members of the nobility had, during the revolution, suffered fates ranging from the loss of economic and legal privileges to exile or execution. But even in areas not ruled by the French the events of the 1790s had seriously frightened the aristocracy, who saw traditional prerogatives threatened by the advance of revolutionary ideas. With the advent of the Restoration, the nobles sought to recover the privileges and property they had lost, and so allied themselves with monarchs against changes that might further endanger their position in society. There was a particular irony in this drawing together of king and nobility in defense of the established order in a country such as France, where the feudal aristocracy had traditionally opposed the centralizing tendencies of the monarchy. But both monarch and aristocracy were now confronted with a strong bourgeoisie intent on preserving the gains of the revolution and consolidating its political power. In central Europe the threat was less immediate since the bourgeoisie was still weak, but Metternich nonetheless allied himself with the imperial aristocracy against the middle classes, which he found seriously infected with the "revolutionary virus." In Britain, where the aristocracy was already an amalgam of landed and commercial interests, a parallel to the conservative reaction on the Continent nonetheless can be found after 1815 in the determined resistance of the Tory leadership to attempts to widen parliamentary representation in the House of Commons to include the new class of manufacturers.

At least two of the conservatives' arguments came to exert considerable influence beyond their own camp. Their renewed emphasis on the historical conditioning of all social institutions proved to be a much-needed corrective to the antihistorical outlook associated with the Enlightenment and contributed to the nineteenth-century habit of viewing almost all problems historically. Conservatives were not alone in seeking to explain the present in terms of the past. By mid-century Karl Marx had developed a theory of social evolution whose basic premise was historical. And even "classical" liberals adjusted their thinking to include a historical dimension and a heightened awareness of the past.

In the same way, the conservative stress on the community (which had been foreshadowed by Rousseau a generation before) gradually weakened the atomistic, individualistic view of society that had prevailed in the preceding century. Socialists accepted as a basic premise the need for individual self-sacrifice to the community, and some of them moved to the position that a strong state was the only agency capable of achieving social reform. Liberals — at least British liberals — persisted in the view that government was a necessary evil and sought to maximize individual liberty and freedom from social restraints. But even John Stuart Mill, the classical defender of individual liberty, was forced to admit the inadequacy of a totally atomistic view of society and recognized that individuals in society bore a responsibility for the welfare of their fellow citizens, and that it might fall to government to see that these obligations were fulfilled.

Nationalism

Perhaps the most important of all political developments in Europe during the early nineteenth century was the rise of popular nationalism. The powerful appeal of nationalism over the past two hundred years has mystified many political theorists. Already in the 1840s, Marx prophesied that the impending workers' revolution would render national identities obsolete. More recently, many social scientists and historians have argued that the power of nationalism is on the wane in the modern world.[2] Yet the resurgence of nationalist movements since the end of the Cold War, both in eastern Europe and elsewhere, has made such obituaries appear premature. An understanding of how and why nationalism emerged in Europe during the era of the French Revolution and Napoleon can help illuminate its continuing power today.

The word *nation* was itself hardly new in the nineteenth century. The Latin term *natio*, meaning "tribe" or "race," dates from the era of the Roman Empire. In central Europe, the "Holy Roman Empire of the German Nation" had been known by that name since the fifteenth century. But these early uses of the word differed significantly from the modern concept of nationhood. In medieval and early modern Europe, the term *nation* con-

[2] For example, on the eve of the Eastern European revolutions of 1989, E. J. Hobsbawm wrote that "the owl of Minerva . . . which flies out at dusk" was now circling around nations and nationalism (*Nations and Nationalism since 1780* [New York, 1990], p. 173). See also Ernest Gellner, *Nations and Nationalism* (Ithaca, N.Y., 1983). According to both Hobsbawm and Gellner, the essential function of nationalism is to constitute a territorially bounded national economy, which requires a mobile and educated workforce sharing a common language. In an era of global interdependence, they argue, the importance of this function is diminished; hence, they claim that nationalism is losing force in contemporary industrialized societies.

noted at most an amorphous linguistic and cultural community. In the modern era, by contrast, the "nation" is seen as a political entity consisting of the entire native population living within a contiguous and bounded territory. Thus, the word carries democratic connotations, because it implies that everyone living within the same nation state has a stake in political life and is in some sense equal with his or her co–nationals.

To define the foundations of national identity, however, is a problematic task. In a famous lecture of 1882 entitled "What is a Nation?" the French philosopher and historian Ernest Renan rejected a series of conventional interpretations of nationhood, such as that it was rooted in natural bonds based on a common language, territory, culture, history, or ethnicity. He pointed out that in some regions of the world (such as Latin America), a variety of nations shared a common language, whereas in other places (for example, Switzerland) a single nation possessed multiple linguistic groups. Likewise, the notion that national boundaries were naturally inscribed in the geography of Europe was fallacious. Renan noted that the Rhine River, which French patriots sometimes identified as France's "natural" boundary, could alternatively be interpreted as uniting a single political territory, rather than as dividing two nations from one another. Having dismissed all claims that the nation could be defined as an objective, naturally existing entity, Renan proposed a subjective definition instead. The nation, he argued, was "a soul, a spiritual principle" preserved through a "daily plebiscite": in other words, the nation owed its existence to the continuing allegiance of its citizenry.[3]

Like Renan, modern scholars generally reject the notion that nations can be understood as natural and primordial communities originating in the mists of time.[4] The anthropologist Benedict Anderson has defined the nation as an "imagined political community" that is envisioned as "sovereign and bounded." The inherently limited nature of the nation distinguished it from earlier political and cultural communities such as the Roman Empire and the Catholic church, both of which were imagined to be potentially universal in their extent. Anderson notes that the rise of print capitalism in Europe from the sixteenth century onward "laid the bases for national consciousness" by creating "unified fields of exchange and communication" in vernacular languages. The invention of national identity, in other words,

---

[3] Ernest Renan, "What is a Nation?", in *Becoming National: A Reader*, edited by Geoff Eley and Ronald Grigor Suny (New York, 1996), pp. 52–53.

[4] Some sophisticated scholarship, e.g., Anthony Smith, *The Ethnic Origins of Nations* (Oxford, 1986), does emphasize the deep roots of nations in long-standing historical and cultural differences.

provided a basis for unifying diverse regions that were increasingly linked both economically and through the exchange of ideas. Moreover, Anderson observes, nationalism answered a deeply felt cultural need. He points out that nationalism possessed "a strong affinity with religious imaginings"; in the face of the "modern darkness" of "rationalist secularism," it aimed to achieve "a secular transformation of fatality into continuity, contingency into meaning."[5] During the early nineteenth century, when traditional hierarchies and communities had been disrupted throughout Europe by cataclysmic political and economic changes, nationalist movements offered their adherents a powerful new source of identity and meaning.

Scholars sometimes distinguish between "cultural" and "political" forms of nationalism. Historically, cultural nationalism has often preceded political nationalism: it helps define, in embryonic form, the national community that political activists subsequently work to mobilize. In Germany, an early contributor to the birth of cultural nationalism was Johann Gottfried Herder (1744–1803), a Protestant pastor and theologian who wrote extensively on philosophy, history, and literature. When Herder was born, Germans did speak a common language, but because they were divided into hundreds of petty states they generally lacked any conception of Germany as a national entity. On the contrary, German intellectuals tended to share in the cosmopolitan outlook of the Enlightenment and the general admiration for the French philosophes. Herder was one of the first to object to what he considered the excessive dependence of the educated classes in Germany on French thought and manners, and urged his compatriots to develop their native culture. He believed that each people — that is, the body of persons sharing a common language — possessed a unique *Geist* ("spirit," or "genius") that had to be developed in its own particular way. The national culture, to be authentic, had to arise from the life of the *Volk*, or people, and draw its inspiration from them. Herder's nationalism was exclusively cultural in character. He was not concerned with political questions and never argued that the political unification of Germany had to accompany its cultural renaissance. Moreover, Herder's theory of national development was applicable to peoples other than Germans; he did not intend to imply that German culture was superior to any other.

Many literary figures of the German romantic school, such as the Grimm brothers, took seriously Herder's injunction to explore Germany's cultural past, and through their writings brought about an awareness of German folklore, law, and religion. But among some of Herder's disciples in the

[5] Benedict Anderson, *Imagined Communities: Reflections on the Origin and Spread of Nationalism*, 2d ed. (London, 1991), pp. 6, 10, 11, 44.

generation after 1800, the character of German nationalism began to change. The writings of the philosopher Johann Gottlieb Fichte, twenty years younger than Herder, reflected the beginnings of the transition to a more aggressive political nationalism. Fichte's outlook resulted in part from his reaction to the French invasions of Germany and particularly to Prussia's humiliation by the Napoleonic armies in 1806, which occasioned his famous series of lectures, *Addresses to the German Nation*, delivered in the winter of 1807–1808. In these lectures he called for a system of national education in Germany that would ultimately result in the moral regeneration of the German people. Education was to make Germans aware of themselves as a unique people, reveal to them their national character, and teach them to love the fatherland. In describing the kind of spirit that should prevail in a time of national crisis, Fichte wrote: "[It is] not the spirit of the peaceful citizen's love for the constitution and the laws, but the devouring flame of higher patriotism, which embraces the nation as the vestures of the eternal, for which the noble-minded man joyfully sacrifices himself, and the ignoble man, who only exists for the sake of the other, must likewise sacrifice himself." In his earlier works Fichte was concerned with the problem of individual freedom, but he came to regard a strong state as the prerequisite for true freedom. He offered no simple definition of "freedom," but became convinced that the individual could only attain it by identifying with the greater personality of the nation. Moreover, Fichte, unlike Herder, attributed to the Germans an originality and a genius not possessed by other peoples. He carried none of these ideas to extremes, but his *Addresses to the German Nation* became a source of inspiration and ammunition for subsequent German nationalists.

Herder's injunction to Germans to concentrate on their own cultural heritage was taken up by writers of other nationalities, who displayed a new interest in their own history, language, literature, and art. For example, among the Slavic peoples of southeastern Europe, many of whom had been living for centuries under the domination of the Austrian or the Ottoman empire, a cultural renaissance beginning at the end of the eighteenth century was in full swing after 1815. Slavic philologists, historians, and literary figures devoted themselves to unearthing their respective national traditions by compiling collections of folk legends, poems, and chronicles, and to systematizing knowledge of their languages by writing grammars and dictionaries. Where a language had gone out of use, attempts were made to revive it in the schools and in books and newspapers.

Such nationalist movements were at first almost entirely cultural, and their leaders were largely intellectuals — scholars, clerics, and liberal nobles. But as the century proceeded they assumed an increasingly political character. Though a revolt of the Serbs against Turkish rule in 1804 did not stem directly from such a cultural revival, the Greek revolt of 1821 was certainly inspired in part by a literary and linguistic renaissance that had begun in the last years of the eighteenth century. In the Habsburg empire, the nationalist movements of the Slavic peoples remained primarily cultural, but the revival of the Magyar language and the growing Magyar literary production in Hungary stimulated the demand for greater autonomy of the Hungarian Diet. And Italians whose territories had been annexed to the empire in 1814–1815 grew increasingly restive under the impact of nationalist propaganda in the 1830s and 1840s.

During the early nineteenth century, nationalism displayed close affinities with liberalism, because the faith in popular sovereignty was fundamental to both movements. For nationalists of this era, the French revolutionaries had provided a stunning example of what a people could achieve when they were unified under a government that they themselves had created. The tremendous release of national energy and the stirring patriotism that had characterized the revolutionary armies impressed those Europeans who were still divided or living under foreign rule after 1815. They were convinced that if only they could achieve a similar national consciousness and enthusiasm, they too could overcome the obstacles that stood in the way of independence and unity. People living under a dynasty or ruling caste whose ends seemed to differ from their own could not feel quite the same stake in their country as people living under a regime that proclaimed, as did the Declaration of the Rights of Man and the Citizen, that "the source of all sovereignty resides essentially in the nation." Only when the government was closely identified with all the people could a nation be considered "free."

Furthermore, in the first half of the nineteenth century, liberals and nationalists could be closely allied because nationalism had not yet taken on the exclusive, parochial character that it assumed later. Paradoxical as it may seem, some of the leading nationalists were still influenced by the cosmopolitan heritage of the Enlightenment. Thus Giuseppe Mazzini (1805–1872), one of the most famous of all nationalist propagandists before 1850, saw no incompatibility between loyalty to one's nation and loyalty to humanity: "In laboring according to true principles for our country we are laboring for Humanity; our country is the fulcrum of the lever which we have to wield for the common good." The achievement by each people of its own "national existence" was merely the prelude to the association of all in a higher community of nations. At the same time, Mazzini shared some of the views of liberals concerning the institutions that the nation should possess. The only true country for him was a "fellowship of free and equal men bound together in a brotherly concord of labor towards a single end."

RITRATTO PSICOGRAFICO DI
G. MAZZINI

(a) Giudizio massimo della Sapienza divina.
(b) Affetto massimo - patriottismo.
(c) Carattere - liberale

"Psychographic" portrait of Giuseppe Mazzini. The letters *a, b,* and *c* indicate divine wisdom, patriotism, and liberality.

Indeed, he went beyond most contemporary liberals, advocating a republican form of government and a radical egalitarianism.

Although nationalism shared important characteristics with liberalism, a fundamental tension existed between nationalist and liberal ideals. Whereas liberal doctrine was based on universal principles that applied to all humanity, nationalists were more concerned about the particular historical characteristics of their own people. Since, as Anderson observes, the nation is imagined as an inherently "bounded" entity, nationalist authors and activists have often devoted considerable energy to defining and enforcing the boundaries of their national community. During the French Revolution, for example, the "nation" was initially mobilized in 1789 in opposition to the privileged estates of the aristocracy and the clergy, which, argued authors such as Sieyès, were not an integral part of the nation. After 1792, the revolutionary fervor was sustained through the military struggle against "counterrevolutionary" forces both at home and abroad. During the Napoleonic era, political leaders in Spain, Russia, and the German states all invoked nationalist rhetoric to mobilize the populace against French domination. We might plausibly conclude that the obsession with defining one's own political community in opposition to a foreign "other" is an inevitable consequence of national consciousness. But this potentially xenophobic, aggressive tendency of nationalism manifests itself to widely varying degrees in different political contexts and at different times.

One of the most troubling aspects of nineteenth-century nationalist movements both in Germany and, to some extent, elsewhere in Europe, was the rise of political anti-Semitism. One leading exponent of nationalist anti-Semitism in Germany was Friedrich Ludwig Jahn (1778–1852), who founded both the gymnastics movement known as the Turner and the first nationalist student organization (the Burschenschaft). Jahn's writings emphasized the need for the purity of the German nation, and he denounced both Judaism and French culture as antithetical to the German spirit. In October 1817, during a festival at the Wartburg (the fortress where Luther had translated the Bible three centuries earlier), members of the Burschenschaft burned "anti-German" books while chanting mocking anti-Jewish slogans.

The festival of the Burschenschaften at the Wartburg, October 18, 1817. The students are burning books by antinationalist writers.

The anti-Semitic rhetoric of the student fraternities was part of a larger backlash against the Jews of central Europe in the aftermath of the Napoleonic era. Many German states in the Rhineland rescinded the provisions for Jewish emancipation contained in the Code Napoléon, even though they left the remainder of this law code intact; during an economic downturn of 1819, anti-Semitic riots erupted in various parts of Germany. In 1816, Jakob Friedrich Fries, a philosophy professor at the University of Jena who was one of Germany's leading Kantians, wrote a virulent diatribe denouncing the Jews as "junk dealers and pillagers of the *Volk*." The Jews of central Europe, he argued, formed "a separate nation" that inhibited the attainment of German unity; thus, it was vital "that this caste be exterminated root and branch, as it is manifestly the most dangerous of all the secret and public political societies and states within the state."[6] Fries's anti-Semitic cant chillingly anticipated the rhetoric of Adolf Hitler over a century later.

Although by no means all nationalists were anti-Semites, either in Germany or in other countries, the preoccupation with the conditions for inclusion in the national community was a common characteristic of nationalist writings. To a great extent, nationalism may be understood as a form of political romanticism. Like other romantics, nineteenth-century nationalists argued that modern individuals had become alienated from their fellow humans, and that they were desperately in need of reintegration into a harmonious national community. This romantic appeal accounts for much of the continuing attraction of nationalist movements in our own era.

[6] Quoted in Matthew Levinger, *Enlightened Nationalism: The Transformation of Prussian Political Culture, 1806–1848* (New York, 2000), p. 118.

CHAPTER 5

Political and Social Transformations,

1815—1848

ATTEMPTS TO preserve the status quo during the Restoration era lasted longer in some parts of Europe than in others. In Great Britain, France, and the Low Countries, major changes in the political climate or alterations of the 1815 settlement took place in 1830 and 1831. In the rest of Europe, despite temporary and isolated disturbances the political arrangements of Vienna persisted at least until the revolutions of 1848. Economic and social changes did occur in central and eastern Europe during this era, but they proceeded more slowly than in western Europe, and their political consequences were not openly manifested until at least the middle of the century.

REACTION AND REFORM IN GREAT BRITAIN

Though Britain escaped any revolutionary upheavals between 1815 and 1848, it experienced successive waves of social and political protests during this era. A series of deeply conservative Tory ministries after 1815 gave way, in 1830, to a more progressive Whig government. The Whig leadership achieved the passage of the Reform Bill of 1832, which brought about sweeping electoral reforms and implemented economic policies promoting free trade.

Tory Rule, 1815–1830

The end of the Napoleonic wars found George III, who had assumed the crown in 1760, still on the throne in Great Britain. But since he was subject to recurrent fits of insanity, his son had become prince regent in 1811, and after his father's death, ruled in his own right as George IV from 1820 to 1830. During this reign the prestige of the British monarchy sank. A clever but disreputable man, George earned the enmity of a good part of the nation when he attempted to divorce his wife Caroline, from whom he had been separated for many years, and prevented her from being crowned as queen in 1820.

The irresponsibility of the ruler served to increase the importance of the Tory ministers, who had held office almost without interruption during the three decades prior to 1815. Although both Whig and Tory parties were still dominated in 1815 by members of the landed elite, the composition of this class had changed dramatically over the previous hundred years. Since the seventeenth century, the country's great estates had increasingly come into the possession of merchants and entrepreneurs who had acquired large commercial fortunes. In Parliament, membership in the House of Lords was restricted to those with noble titles (the peers of the realm) and the bishops; the House of Commons was dominated by the untitled landed gentry.

From the standpoint of political philosophy, the Tories were more inclined to sympathize with the conservative view of British society and institutions that Burke had praised in his *Reflections on the French Revolution*. Moreover, their leadership of Britain during the prolonged wars against France had made them profoundly suspicious of radicalism and movements for reform. The Whigs received support from the newer moneyed interests and from Protestant dissenters. They were therefore more amenable to the gradual reform of laws and governmental institutions and the removal of mercantilist restrictions on commerce and industry.

In the years immediately after 1815 the Tory view prevailed; indeed, the government of Lord Liverpool, which lasted from 1812 until 1827, was one of the most reactionary in modern British history. Its actions and policies between 1815 and 1820 must be seen against the background of the severe depression that attended the transition from a wartime to a peacetime economy. The sudden drop in government expenditures and the loss of wartime markets for British manufactures and grain brought a period of falling prices, unstable currency, and widespread unemployment. The government's remedy for this situation, hardly calculated to meet with general approval, was the Corn Law of 1815, a protective tariff that prohibited the importation of foreign grain until the price of English grain rose above a specified level of eighty shillings per quarter. (The Corn Law, it should be noted, applied mainly to wheat imported from Europe, not American maize.) This measure, unabashedly favoring the landowners, naturally antagonized urban laborers who were forced to pay a higher price for their bread in circumstances that were already difficult. No one in either party came forward to champion the cause of the working classes, so the task fell to radical agitators and writers and to clubs organized for reform. Some men, among them William Cobbett (1763–1835), the most famous of the radical pamphleteers, attacked all kinds of abuses, but most radicals concentrated on trying to reform the methods of selecting representatives to the House of Commons. For they were convinced that as long as control of the lower chamber remained in the hands of the landed gentry, there was no hope for legislation that would benefit the country as a whole.

Acute economic distress after 1815 led to a series of public meetings at which radical orators called for the repeal of the Corn Law of 1815 (along with earlier corn laws still on the statute books) and for parliamentary reform. Although almost no violence was associated with these demonstrations, the Tory ministry, taking alarm and seeing the danger of revolution everywhere, acted against the reform societies in 1817 by temporarily forbidding all public meetings, suppressing all societies not licensed by government, and suspending the Habeas Corpus Act. These measures brought a brief lull in

Peterloo Massacre, 1819. A contemporary caption to this print referred to the "wanton and furious attack by that brutal armed force The Manchester & Cheshire Yeomanry Cavalry." Eleven people died and six hundred were wounded.

popular agitation, but a new economic slump the following year resulted in a series of mass meetings in some of the larger cities of the north and Midlands. The most famous of these was held, despite a government ban, in St. Peter's Fields in Manchester in August 1819. Local authorities sent a squadron of cavalry into the crowd of sixty thousand to arrest the fiery radical orator Henry Hunt (1773–1835). In the resulting panic, eleven people were killed and several hundred injured. The incident was immediately branded the Battle of Peterloo, or the Peterloo Massacre. To the popular outcry that greeted this episode the government responded only with further measures of repression. In November, Parliament passed the famous Six Acts, a series of drastic restrictions intended to eliminate large public meetings, suppress or seriously weaken the radical press, and speed up conviction of offenders against the public order. As if to justify these measures, the government three months later uncovered a radical plot organized by Arthur Thistlewood (1770–1820) for the assassination of the entire cabinet, the seizure of the Bank of England, and the establishment of a provisional government. Betrayed by an agent provocateur, the conspirators were arrested in a house on Cato Street in London; as might be expected, the Tory ministry gave widespread publicity to the Cato Street Conspiracy, pointing out how narrowly the country had escaped disaster.

Perhaps because of the repressive measures, perhaps because the economy picked up, after 1820 the radical movement in Britain subsided for almost a decade. During this period the Tory ministry was broadened considerably. On the death in 1822 of the foreign minister, Viscount Castlereagh, Lord Liverpool added to his cabinet three men who were a good deal more amenable to change than their colleagues: George Canning (1770–1827) as foreign minister and leader of the House of Commons; William Huskisson (1770–1830) as head of the Board of Trade; and Sir Robert Peel (1788–1850) as secretary for home affairs, the beginning of his long career. None of these men went so far as to favor major parliamentary reform at this time, but they were ready to carry out a series of pragmatic, piecemeal changes in laws and institutions that helped bring the British government into closer touch with economic and social realities.

Peel was responsible for a long-needed revision of the criminal code, which still carried the death penalty for some two hundred offenses, among them pocket picking, sheep stealing, and forgery. Because juries refused to convict offenders for such petty crimes when the punishment was death, disregard for the law had become widespread. Peel reduced the number of capital crimes and made the penalties more nearly commensurate with the offenses. This achievement, combined with his introduction in 1829 of a regular metropolitan police force in London (called "bobbies" after him), led to a considerable reduction in the crime rate in Britain.

Huskisson was primarily responsible for the elimination of restrictions on British trade inherited from the mercantilist era. He was able to reduce the tariff on many items needed by British manufacturers as well as on some consumer goods, such as wine, coffee, and sugar. Many restrictions (including those on the importation of corn) still remained, but his policy was continued by subsequent ministries and in the 1840s culminated in complete free trade.

Although others prepared the way, Peel and Huskisson also deserve some credit for the repeal in 1824 of the Combination Acts, which had prohibited the formation of labor organizations. The impact of this repeal was reduced somewhat when, after a year of strikes and violence, Parliament in 1825 passed a law that restricted labor unions to bargaining over wages and hours and effectively prevented them from striking. But the right of labor to organize had been recognized.

Despite the gains achieved through these laws, the Tory ministry remained unpopular. Lord Liverpool's death in 1827 opened the way for the brief ministries of Canning (who died after a few months in office) and the ineffectual Lord Goderich (Frederick John Robinson, 1782–1859). The appointment in 1828 of the duke of Wellington, the celebrated national hero, as prime minister prolonged the Tories' incumbency, but Wellington's alliance with the most reactionary elements in the party alienated young Tory liberals and contributed to the growth of the Whig opposition. During Wellington's ministry one more major reform was achieved, despite his personal distaste. This was the passage in 1829 of the bill for Catholic emancipation, which permitted Catholics to sit in Parliament and to hold all public offices except those of lord chancellor of England and lord lieutenant of Ireland. This reform, proposed many times before, had been repeatedly thwarted by the opposition of the king or the House of Lords. Now the pressure from an active movement in Ireland, led by the Irish barrister Daniel O'Connell (1775–1847), forced the issue. Convinced that civil war would result if they tried to hold out, Wellington and Peel pushed the bill through the House of Lords, and Wellington's threat to resign brought the king's assent. Passage of the bill did not solve the problem of England's relationship with Ireland, particularly since the ministry immediately raised the property qualification for voting there, but it was an important step in the long process of eliminating religious discrimination.

The Catholic Emancipation Act was the last significant contribution of the Tories before they left office after almost a half century of rule. Two events in 1830 helped to topple the Wellington ministry and prepare the way for passage of the Reform Bill of 1832. One was the news of the July Revolution in France, which overthrew the restored Bourbon regime and brought to power a government supported by the middle class. The other was the death of King George IV and the accession of his brother William IV, an event that according to constitutional tradition required the holding of a general election. The election resulted in sizable gains for those favoring reform. But more significant than either of these events was the cumulative effect of the Industrial Revolution on British society; it had created social groups, forces, and problems that the old Tory leaders were incapable of handling. To the Whigs fell the task of breaching the old order and of taking into partnership new "captains of industry" along with the older aristocracy.

As we have just seen, the growing sentiment for free trade among manufacturers and workers met with some response when Huskisson secured a reduction of duties on certain imports and set a precedent for further reductions. In 1828 a change in the corn laws allowed the importation of grain according to a sliding scale of duties. Yet as long as landowners remained dominant in both houses of Parliament, the new manufacturers (the "Manchester men" as they were called) could not hope to achieve free trade. For this reason, reform of the methods for choosing representatives to the House of Commons became the overriding concern of the manufacturers.

Parliamentary Reform, Free Trade, and Chartism, 1830–1848

The Reform Bill of 1832, passed under Whig leadership, constituted the first recognition in British political life of the tremendous changes wrought in British society by the Industrial Revolution. In the years before 1832, the migration of workers from one region to another as industrialization progressed, the emergence of new cities, and the dramatic growth of some old cities accentuated the injustices of a system of representation that had remained practically unaltered since the seventeenth century. The most glaring weakness was the underrepresentation, and sometimes the lack of representation, of new centers of population in the northern and western parts of England. Old boroughs lying in the eastern and southern counties had declined markedly in population but still sent two members each to the House of Commons. Among the most celebrated of the "rotten boroughs" was Old Sarum, which was still represented although no town existed there at all. Thriving new cities such as Manchester, Birmingham, Leeds, and Sheffield, on the other hand, sent no representatives to Parliament. There were also "pocket boroughs," in which no real election took place because the seats were "in the pocket" of powerful landlords who used their influence

REDISTRIBUTION UNDER THE
REFORM BILL OF 1832

CHANGES IN REPRESENTATION IN THE HOUSE OF COMMONS

Counties gaining 6 or more county and borough members

Counties gaining 5 or less members

Counties losing representation or remaining stable

SCOTLAND

Newcastle
Gateshead
Middlesbrough

NORTH
SEA

Ouse R.

IRISH
SEA

Leeds
York Hull

Liverpool
Manchester
Wakefield
Grimsby
Northwich
Lincoln

Trent R.

Nottingham
Stoke
ENGLAND
Leicester

Ouse R.

Walsall

Norwich
Great Yarmouth

Ipswich

CARDIGAN
BAY

WALES

Avon R.

Gloucester
Oxford
Aston
Swansea
Newport
Bristol
London
Cardiff
Devizes
Reading
Thames
Bath
R.
Chatham

Southhampton
Hastings
Bournemouth
Portsmouth
Brighton

Strait of Dover

Plymouth

ENGLISH CHANNEL

to name their own candidates. As long as the Tories remained in office, the cause of reform was stalled. But in 1830 the death of King George IV and the accession of William IV made a general election necessary, and the campaign was fought at least in part on the issue of reform. The Tories lost some fifty seats in the House of Commons, most of them to Whigs or to other advocates of reform; Commons was now in the control of the Whigs. The duke of Wellington, who had remained adamant in his opposition to reform, finally left office in November 1830, and was succeeded by Charles Grey, the second Earl Grey (1764–1845), a Whig committed to the cause. But for Grey to get the Reform Bill through Parliament took another year and a half — a stormy period characterized by mounting popular violence, strenuous measures on the part of the Whig leadership, and last-ditch resistance by Tory peers in the House of Lords. Only the threat of the king, under pressure from Grey, to create enough new peers to secure passage of the bill in the House of Lords finally persuaded the intransigents to abandon their opposition.

The Reform Bill of 1832 did not immediately revolutionize British political life. Indeed, one contemporary admitted that the House of Commons named in the first general election after the act turned out "to be very much like every other parliament."[1] Certainly those who voted for the bill had no intention of creating a thoroughly democratic political system in Great Britain. Though the electorate increased by about 50 percent after 1832, only one in five British men had the privilege of voting, and the franchise still depended on possession of a minimum of property. Yet the Reform Bill of 1832 was one of the most significant measures in the evolution of modern Britain. By redistributing seats in the House of Commons to increase representation of the new towns and cities, it enabled the new class of industrialists and manufacturers to begin to challenge the political supremacy of the older landed and commercial aristocracy. Although the industrial elites did not take over the government of Britain in 1832, in succeeding decades the balance of power gradually shifted to them. In two other respects the Reform Bill of 1832 was of great importance. It opened the way for a series of reforms in other spheres of British life — municipal administration, relief of the poor, and church-state relations — and more important, it established a precedent for further extensions of the franchise. If representatives of the manufacturers were to be taken into partnership in the governing of the nation, why should not the more prosperous and reliable workers be repre-

---

[1] Charles Greville, quoted in Asa Briggs, *The Age of Improvement* (London, 1959), p. 261.

sented? This question was raised within a decade by the organizers of the Chartist movement.

The reform of Parliament made possible the eventual triumph of economic liberalism in Great Britain by giving greater legislative voice to the proponents of laissez faire. Yet the new economic doctrines did not take hold at once. The principal demand of the economic liberals — the repeal of the corn laws — was not met for a decade and a half despite vigorous action and massive propaganda campaigns by proponents of repeal. The main opposition to repeal came, of course, from the landlords, who feared that an influx of cheap foreign grain would ruin British agriculture. The proponents of repeal joined together in 1838 to form the Anti–Corn-Law League, a well-financed and highly effective pressure group. Prominent among its supporters were such manufacturers as John Bright (1811–1889) and Richard Cobden (1804–1865), who argued not only that repeal was in the national interest but that free trade would promote international understanding and the cause of peace. Yet the campaign might have failed had it not had the support of the laboring classes, who were convinced that repeal would lower the price of bread. A turning point came with the conversion of Sir Robert Peel, the leading Tory minister of the period, to this cause, once he became convinced that continued maintenance of the corn laws was not essential to British prosperity. The failure of the Irish potato crop in 1845 provided further impetus: a threat of famine hung over Britain, which could be dispelled only by supplementing British wheat with foreign grain. In 1846 the corn laws were finally repealed. That year marked the beginning of a free-trade era for Britain that lasted until the First World War. The abolition or reduction to a minimum of duties on practically all other imported goods followed the repeal of duties on grain.

If free trade was one of the principal goals of the liberals, elimination of government regulation of the domestic economy was the other. Adam Smith emphasized this aspect of laissez faire less than has been generally supposed, but it became an important principle for the group of writers in England known as the classical economists, who elaborated Smith's doctrines. These thinkers "discovered" a comprehensive system of economic "laws" that operate in a competitive economy, comparable to the laws governing the physical universe. They believed that government interference with the natural operation of these economic laws was harmful to the economy. This point of view was adopted, for example, by the economist David Ricardo. Although his ideas concerning wages were interpreted more rigidly by his followers than he intended, he did advocate a strict laissez faire position with respect to the rise and fall of the price of labor. Workmen might be doomed to an eternal cycle in which higher wages resulted in larger families and an increased supply of labor, followed by a corresponding increase in competition for jobs and an inevitable drop in wages, but it was not the function of government to try to interfere with free competition in order to maintain wages at a high level; the fluctuation of wages would be determined by the law of supply and demand operating in the labor market.

To what extent did a laissez faire attitude prevail in Britain during the first half of the nineteenth century? This view, without question, became increasingly influential during this period. Yet a closer look at the role played by government in the British economy of the mid-nineteenth century reveals that during the years of expansion of the free-enterprise system there developed also a tradition of state intervention and regulation of industry on behalf of the working class that was at odds with the laissez faire position. There was never a lack of critics to attack the excesses of a system that seemed to leave the wage earner at the mercy of economic "laws." Ironically, a year after the Reform Bill, when manufacturing interests had increased their representation in the House of Commons, Parliament passed the first effective Factory Act, curbing the hours of employment of children in the textile mills and prescribing other regulations for their treatment. The following decade saw the passage of further legislation restricting the employment of women and children in the mines and enforcing the introduction of safety devices and of better methods of sanitation in the factories. The Ten Hours Act of 1847 applied officially only to women and young persons, but had the practical effect of limiting the working day of adult males as well. Such statutes, involving interference by government with the functioning of free competition, were generally opposed by manufacturers. But the fact that they were passed and enforced suggests that the philosophy of laissez faire never held undisputed sway in Great Britain.

It would be tempting for the sake of simplicity to view the opposition to economic liberalism in purely class terms. Thus, it could be argued that although bourgeois manufacturers favored the application of laissez faire doctrines and opposed restrictions on their activity, members of the land-owning aristocracy, seeing their political and economic domination threatened, sought to retain government restrictions or impose new ones on rapidly growing industries. According to this view, the members of the working class were in an ambiguous position. They sided with their employers on the issue of free trade, in the hope that lowered tariffs would reduce the cost of living; on the other hand, they viewed the manufacturers as exploiters bent on securing maximum profits at labor's expense, and consequently sought an alliance with the land owners as a means of imposing regulations on industry.

There is just enough truth in this interpretation to make it appealing.

Land owners did stubbornly resist the repeal of the corn laws until finally forced to capitulate by growing pressures from manufacturers and workers. The Tory leaders, who defended the property holders' interests, did support legislation regulating working conditions in retaliation against the manufacturers for their opposition to the corn laws. Finally, the working-class movement was indeed divided over its goals.

But the divisions along class lines were not so clear cut as this interpretation suggests. The movement for restricting the working day of women and young persons to ten hours, for example, had the support of a variety of individuals. The two principal leaders of the movement in Parliament, Michael Sadler (1780–1835) and Lord Ashley (Anthony Ashley Cooper, later earl of Shaftesbury, 1801–1885) were Tories. Sadler had been a businessman before becoming a social reformer, and Ashley, though a landowning aristocrat, appears to have been motivated not so much by a desire for revenge against the manufacturers as by religious and humanitarian impulses linked with a traditional sense of *noblesse oblige*. The campaign for the Ten Hours Act had the active support of many who called themselves radicals, but it also was backed by some maverick manufacturers, such as John Wood of Yorkshire and John Fielden of Lancashire. Reform was not, therefore, exclusively the goal of one social class or group.

The most important single manifestation of working-class sentiment in these years, the Chartist movement, seems to have sprung not from discontent with laissez faire economic policies or from specific grievances against the new manufacturers, but rather from a generalized distress in the 1830s and 1840s for which the workers saw one principal remedy — political representation. Finding inadequate the Reform Bill of 1832, for which they had agitated along with the middle classes, they sought further parliamentary reform. Chartism drew its support from at least three different groups among the working classes. One of these consisted of the rather moderate, quite respectable artisans of the London Workingmen's Association, founded in 1836 by a cabinetmaker, William Lovett (1800–1877). They were joined by members of the more radical Birmingham Political Union, a propagandist group dating back to 1816 that was revived in the 1830s by a radical Birmingham banker, Thomas Attwood (1783–1856). The third group, led by Feargus O'Connor (1794–1855), a fiery Irish land owner and demagogue, appealed to the most distressed elements of the population of Leeds and the northern counties. All three groups threw their support behind the People's Charter, the document that gave its name to the Chartist movement. The Charter, a list of political demands to be presented to Parliament, called for universal male suffrage, equal electoral districts (that is, districts with equal numbers of inhabitants), vote by secret ballot, annual elections to Parliament, the abolition of the property qualification for members of Parliament, and the payment of stipends to those elected to the House of Commons. The last demand was important, since workers or those representing them could hardly afford to run for Parliament as long as its members were unpaid.

During 1838–1839 a massive campaign to enlist support for the Charter was organized, complete with large public meetings, inflammatory speeches, and torchlight processions. This culminated in the spring of 1839 with the assembling in London of a National Convention (the name was chosen for its associations with the French Revolution) and the presentation to Parliament of a huge petition on behalf of the Charter signed by several hundred thousand individuals. Despite this wave of agitation, which was attended by great publicity, Parliament refused even to consider the petition. The Chartists found themselves in a dilemma. Some of the more radical branches of the movement staged riots and local strikes, but the majority were not prepared to resort to violence to attain their ends. After 1839 the movement split into rival factions and temporarily collapsed. The National Chartist Association continued to uphold the principles of the Charter and presented the demands again in 1842 and in 1848, the year of revolutions on the Continent, but Chartism was never as strong in the 1840s as it had been at the outset and fell into the hands of less responsible leaders, such as Feargus O'Connor, ready to use the movement for the advancement of personal ends.

From the standpoint of gender relations, one fascinating aspect of the workers' suffrage movement was the disappearance of women from public roles after the early 1840s. Between 1815 and 1820, various female radical societies had been established in England, and many women participated actively in the Chartist cause during the late 1830s. By the 1850s and 1860s, working-class radicalism was rooted increasingly in the exclusively male preserves of political associations and trade unions. In part, this shift was a product of the economic transition in Britain to large-scale industrialism. Yet working-class men also sought to bolster their claims to full citizenship by differentiating themselves increasingly sharply from women. For example, they asserted that working men would purify the political system through their "manly virtues," which they contrasted with the "effeminacy" of the corrupt nobility. Their claim to be "rational and respectable men" implicitly differentiated them from "irrational women." Some historians have argued that this vigorous exclusion of women from working-class political activism after the mid-nineteenth century helped make the prospect of broader male suffrage less threatening to Britain's upper classes.[2]

---

[2] See the articles by Anna Clark and Keith McClelland in *Gender and Class in Modern Europe*, edited by Laura L. Frader and Sonya O. Rose (Ithaca, 1996).

Although the Chartist movement failed in its own time, the goals of the Chartists, including universal male suffrage, were realized between 1858 and 1918. Only the requirement of annual elections to Parliament has not become a part of the English electoral system. Perhaps most interesting about the Chartist agitation is the fact that although it arose from severe economic distress, British workers were convinced that they could improve their conditions not by direct action against their employer or a generalized attack on laissez faire policies, but rather by peaceful, legal means and direct representation in Parliament. Workers on the Continent, in contrast, frequently resorted to more confrontational tactics.

THE RESTORATION AND THE JULY MONARCHY IN FRANCE

France, the birthplace of the revolution, experienced far more political turmoil than Britain between 1815 and 1848. King Louis XVIII (ruled 1814–1824) succeeded in preserving political stability in France by steering a middle course between the revolution's champions and its enemies; he shied away from challenging the revolutionary legacy too directly. His younger brother Charles X (ruled 1824–1830), by contrast, rashly sought to restore many of the most hated features of the Old Regime. A new revolution in July 1830 established a more liberal constitutional monarchy under Louis Philippe, the duke of Orléans. But increasing social and political unrest during the 1830s and 1840s undermined the legitimacy of his regime, paving the way for the outbreak of revolution of 1848.

The Bourbon Restoration and the Revolution of 1830

During the decade after Napoleon's fall, French political life was marked by a bitter struggle between the ultraroyalists, who sought to wipe out all the revolution had achieved, and the liberals and their allies, who were intent on preserving the reforms secured between 1789 and 1814. Between them stood Louis XVIII (ruled 1814–1824), basically sympathetic with the ultras, but shrewd enough to realize that any attempt to wipe out the gains of the revolution would end in disaster for his dynasty. The new constitution — the Charter of 1814, Louis's "gift" to the people — recognized the major achievements of the revolutionary years. It specifically guaranteed the principle of equality before the law and the retention of the Civil Code. It confirmed the titles to their property of those who had purchased national and church land during the revolution and preserved the Napoleonic Concordat, along with the principle of religious toleration.

The Charter did not determine where the real power should lie, and this question was debated by political theorists, whose views ranged from the defense of absolute monarchy to the assertion of popular sovereignty, and fought out at a less theoretical level by politicians. Specifically at issue were the powers of the bicameral Assembly: the Chamber of Peers, whose members were appointed to hereditary tenure, and the Chamber of Deputies, whose members were elected in accordance with a highly restricted franchise based on property ownership. What was to be the relationship of the Assembly to the king? Executive power was vested in the king and his ministers, but legislative power did not clearly rest with the chambers. The king (or his ministers) had the sole power to initiate legislation; the chambers could only petition the king to do so. According to the Charter, the chambers could reject a bill proposed by the king but could not amend it without royal consent. Nor was the position of the ministers clearly defined. According to the Charter the ministers were officers of the king, appointed by him and charged with the execution of his policy. Nowhere did the Charter say that the ministers must represent the majority in the legislature. Yet, in fact, between 1815 and 1830 the leading minister did represent the majority group in the Chamber of Deputies except on two occasions, in 1815–1816 and again in 1829–1830. The principle of ministerial responsibility was thus gradually established, although it was never explicitly conceded by the king.

Some fundamental procedures of parliamentary government developed in France during the Restoration, and a generation of statesmen gained valuable political experience. But the basic issue was left unresolved, for the restored Bourbon rulers failed to establish a working compromise between the traditional claims of monarchy and the revolutionary principle of popular sovereignty. The regime foundered over this issue in 1830.

The fifteen-year era falls into three political periods. During the first, which lasted for only a year (1815–1816), the Assembly was dominated by the ultraroyalists, who won a majority in the Chamber of Deputies and embarrassed the king and the moderate-royalist ministry by announcing their intention of sweeping away a number of institutions inherited from the revolutionary and Napoleonic eras and restoring confiscated estates to their prerevolutionary owners. Actually they achieved very few of their goals, though they did set up special courts to try Bonapartists and revolutionaries whom they charged with treason. Even before the ultraroyalist Chamber of Deputies was elected, an unofficial White Terror erupted, a counterpart of the Terror of 1793–1794, carried out by royalists during the summer of 1815 in the south of France. Bands of royalist volunteers, remnants of an army organized at the time of Napoleon's escape from Elba by a nephew of the king—Louis Antoine de Bourbon, duke of Angoulême (1775–1844)—now arrested, imprisoned, or massacred hundreds of individuals suspected of Jacobin or Bonapartist sympathies. The White Terror spread from Marseilles to other parts of Provence and Languedoc. At Nîmes and in the department of the Gard the victims included many Protestants suspected by the Catholic royalists of disloyalty to the Bourbon monarchy. It appears that the White Terror was neither instigated nor directed by the restored monarchy, but government officials looked the other way as the royalist bands carried out their vigilante purges. When Louis XVIII realized that the extremism of the ultraroyalists was alienating the nation from the monarchy, he dissolved the Chamber of Deputies in September 1816 and called for new elections.

In the new chamber the majority consisted of moderate royalists who between 1816 and 1820 supported the ministries headed by the duke of Richelieu (1766–1822) and his successor, Duke Élie Decazes (1780–1860). This second period of the Restoration was one of relative calm despite frequent verbal attacks on the ministry by both ultraroyalists and liberals. New electoral laws extended the franchise somewhat, though there were still only about one hundred thousand voters out of a total population of 30 million.

This tranquility was shattered in 1820 — the year of revolutions in Spain, Portugal, and Italy — by the assassination of the duke of Berry, the son of Louis's younger brother and presumably the last of the Bourbon line. (The hope of the assassin that he was putting an end to the Bourbon dynasty was frustrated when the duke's widow was discovered to be pregnant, and in due course produced a male heir.) Although the murder was the act of an isolated fanatic, the ultras charged the king's minister, Duke Élie Decazes, with responsibility for the crime because of his alleged laxity in dealing with the opposition. So strong was the pressure put on the king that he was forced to abandon Decazes and appoint a new minister. At this point began the final period of the Restoration in France, an era of growing reaction that lasted until 1830. During this period Louis took a less active role in government, and the initiative gradually passed to his younger brother, the count of Artois, who became Charles X on Louis's death in 1824.

The assassination of the duke of Berry was used as an excuse for imposing restrictions on the press and for revising the electoral law to give increased influence to the landed aristocracy at the expense of the bourgeoisie. Between 1822 and 1828, under the ministry of the count of Villèle (1773–1854), the ultras were finally able to secure legislation favorable to their own interests. For example, the Law of Indemnity (1825) compensated nobles who had emigrated during the revolution for the loss of their landed estates. This measure was doubly offensive to the members of the bourgeois opposition because they were the principal holders of the government bonds whose interest rate was reduced to provide funds for the indemnity. Although the Law of Indemnity finally ended the controversy over the revolutionary land settlement, it was not viewed in this favorable light in 1825.

One of the principal features of Charles X's reign was the close tie established between throne and altar. The Law of Sacrilege (1825) imposed the death penalty for offenses of an allegedly sacrilegious character and for the theft of sacred objects from churches. The law was particularly odious to liberals because it appeared to put the state at the service of the church in a manner reminiscent of the Old Regime. Villèle also did his best to undermine the Université, the state educational system founded by Napoleon, by placing a bishop at its head and dismissing many of its liberal teachers. At the same time he encouraged the growth of Catholic seminaries outside the state system. Their function was ostensibly to train priests, but in fact they competed with the state secondary schools for students. Finally, although the Jesuit order was still formally banned in France, the government openly countenanced the presence of Jesuits as teachers in Catholic schools. Indeed, liberals were convinced that Jesuits had infiltrated everywhere and were secretly directing government policy.

Developments like these resulted in steadily mounting opposition to the Villèle ministry. Liberal newspapers, such as the *Constitutionnel* and the *Journal des Débats,* contributed to the struggle. A liberal political society called *Aide-toi, et le ciel t'aidera* ("Help thyself and heaven will help thee") was formed in 1827; its goals were to prevent falsification of electoral lists by government officials and to spread liberal propaganda. Formerly enthusiastic backers of the regime now began to join the opposition. So too did a number of wealthy bankers and manufacturers who resented legislation that favored the nobility and the clergy.

In 1827 Charles X made the error of dissolving the Chamber of Deputies and calling for new elections. When a majority of moderate royalists was returned, the king reluctantly yielded to the principle of ministerial responsibility by dismissing Villèle and summoning the moderate viscount of Martignac (1778–1832) to take his place. Martignac relaxed the restrictions on the press and dismissed some of the more notoriously reactionary ultraroyalists from the civil service. However, the hounding of this ministry by both the ultra and the liberal extremes made its existence difficult and ultimately provided the king with a pretext for dismissing Martignac in 1829. He then named the prince of Polignac (1780–1847), clearly flouting the will of the Assembly: Polignac, who in 1816 had refused to swear to uphold the Charter, was one of the most notorious of the ultras and could not possibly command a majority in the Chamber of Deputies.

From this time on, the alternatives for France seemed to be royal despotism and revolution. A protest against the Polignac ministry by a majority of the deputies in the spring of 1830 merely provoked the king to dissolve the chamber and call for new elections. But the result was an even larger majority for the opposition. Confronted with the prospect of a recalcitrant Assembly, Charles decided to seize the initiative; before the new body could meet, he issued the royal decrees known as the July Ordinances. The decrees dissolved the newly elected Assembly, established a new electoral system, arbitrarily deprived the wealthy bourgeoisie of the right to vote, and imposed rigid censorship on the press. Though the king could argue that the Charter gave him the right to issue such decrees, the opposition correctly interpreted the July Ordinances as an attempt to abandon the Charter. The promulgation of the decrees gave rise to an insurrection — the July Revolution of 1830.

The revolution occurred with a minimum of violence, partly because the government, not anticipating trouble, had made few preparations to resist. What fighting there was occurred in Paris and was all over in three days. It began on July 26, when spontaneous demonstrations greeted publication of the royal ordinances. The following day unemployed workers, joined by students and some republican agitators, threw up barricades in the streets of Paris to prevent the passage of government troops. On July 28 the insurrectionists captured the Hôtel de Ville and raised the tricolor flag. The king, who was hunting on his estate at Saint-Cloud, offered to withdraw the ordinances and dismiss the ministry, but it was already too late. A group of liberal leaders, who had been meeting daily since July 26, fearing a republican seizure of power, announced the formation of a provisional government. Favoring a constitutional monarchy, this group proposed giving the crown to Louis Philippe, the duke of Orléans, a cousin of Charles X. The duke was a natural rallying point for monarchists dissatisfied with Charles X. He had remained in France during the first stages of the great revolution, fought with the revolutionary armies before going into exile early in 1793, and professed liberal views. At first, he hesitated because the legitimate king had not abandoned his title to the throne, but he agreed to serve as "lieutenant general" of the realm until the succession was settled. Then the agreement of the marquis de Lafayette, the aged hero of the American and French revolutions and an unofficial leader of republican forces in Paris, was secured. In a dramatic scene on July 31, the duke of Orléans entered the capital and paraded through streets lined with silent and sullen workers until he reached the Hôtel de Ville. There he met Lafayette for an interview, and then they appeared together before the crowds with a tricolor flag draped over their shoulders. Lafayette had satisfied himself that the duke would sit on a "throne surrounded by republican institutions." To no avail did Charles X announce that he was abdicating in favor of his young grandson. Next, a majority of the old Chamber of Deputies met and formally offered the throne to the duke of Orléans. Charles had no alternative but to go into exile in England. Within a few days the new king accepted a revised version of the Charter that eliminated the preamble stating that the document was

Storming the Louvre, by Jean Louis Bezard. The massacre of the Swiss guards, July 29, 1830.

the "gift" of the king to his people. Instead, his title — "king of the French People" — clearly implied that he owed his throne to the popular will. The July Revolution had put an end to the Restoration in France.

Louis Philippe and the July Monarchy, 1830–1848

Although those who had engineered the July insurrection were under the impression that they had carried out a genuine revolution, the constitutional changes that resulted in France from the change of dynasty were relatively slight. As "king of the French People" Louis Philippe presumably recognized the principle of popular sovereignty, but in point of fact he never fully accepted this doctrine. The Charter of 1814 was retained with only slight modifications, and the right to vote was still restricted to substantial property owners. The suffrage was extended from about 100,000 to 170,000 in a nation of 30 million. Nonetheless, the July Revolution represented the final triumph of the *haute* ("upper") *bourgeoisie* over the nobility. It was, after all, representatives of the bourgeoisie who had helped bring the new king to power and who thereafter held a privileged position in his regime. The constitutional embodiment of their victory lay in the provision that appointments to the Chamber of Peers, the upper house, would henceforth be held for life only, instead of being hereditary. A few liberal members of the noble class continued to play a role in politics, but most nobles viewed the new regime with contempt and retired to their homes in the exclusive Faubourg Saint-Germain of Paris or to their country estates.

Louis Philippe's regime is often termed "the bourgeois monarchy." It drew its principal support and its allegedly drab, materialistic character from the middle class, and the monarch himself appeared to embody many of the virtues exalted by this class—thrift, sobriety, a propensity for hard work. A devastating, if somewhat exaggerated, portrait of the vices of bourgeois society under the July Monarchy can be found in the novels of Honoré de Balzac (1799–1850). In works such as *Eugènie Grandet, Le Père Goriot,* and *Cousine Bette* (all part of his vast *Comédie Humaine*), Balzac exposed a society obsessed with the acquisition of money and the power it could bring. At all social levels, but especially among the bourgeoisie, the class from which he himself came, Balzac found ambition, greed, and corruption poisoning the relationships among human beings. The policies of the government favored the interests of the wealthier manufacturers and tradesmen, and after an initial wave of enthusiasm for the new regime, disillusionment began to set in among the *petite* ("lesser") *bourgeoisie*, who were still excluded from political participation, and among the Parisian working class, whose contribution to the Revolution of 1830 had apparently counted for nothing. The history of the July Monarchy is, in large part, the history of the mounting dissatisfaction of these social groups with the government and the consolidation of opposition to it, which culminated in the Revolution of 1848.

Even among the upper bourgeoisie who were represented in the Chamber of Deputies there were different opinions about the direction the regime should take. Led by François Guizot (1787–1874), a group designated as the right-center—later known as the Party of Resistance—supported the view that France had now arrived at the perfect and final form of government, a balanced system in which the monarch, the peers, and the elected representatives of the propertied classes each played their allotted role. Anyone excluded from political participation had only to "get rich" (in a phrase often attributed to Guizot) in order to secure the privilege of voting. Now that France had achieved this state of perfection, further changes in its institutions were unnecessary. The other group, the left-center, or Party of Movement, was represented by Adolphe Thiers (1797–1877), a statesman whose political career spanned the better part of the nineteenth century; its members argued that the Revolution of 1830 was merely a stage in the political evolution of France and that the electoral base should be gradually broadened. At first these two factions were evenly matched, but by 1840 the right-center (with which the king was in sympathy) had won the day. As premier during the last eight years of the king's reign, Guizot effectively suppressed opposition to the regime in the Chamber of Deputies.

Outside the chamber the opposition was vigorous, particularly in the early years of the regime. It came from a number of sources. The Legitimists remained loyal to the dynasty that had been overthrown and hoped for a restoration of its heir. Then there were the Bonapartists, and in these years the Napoleonic legend won increasing popularity among Frenchmen. A new, young generation tended to contrast their own prosaic, money-grubbing society and the cautious foreign policy of Louis Philippe with the dramatic exploits of the Napoleonic regime when life had been exciting and opportunities for heroism and glory were available to the young. The fascination that Napoleon had for the post-Napoleonic generation can be seen in the novels of Stendhal (pseudonym for Henri Beyle, 1783–1842). Of his major works, only *Lucien Leuwen* was set in the era of the July Monarchy, but the heroes of *The Red and the Black* and *The Charterhouse of Parma* embody the energy, the intelligence, and the will that Stendhal found in Bonaparte.

The death without heirs of the duke of Reichstadt, Napoleon's son, in 1832, temporarily weakened the Bonapartist cause, and at first nobody took very seriously the claims of the emperor's nephew, Louis Napoleon, as his successor. Two ill-planned and rather ridiculous attempts by the young pretender to seize power, one in 1836 and another in 1840, were quickly thwarted by the government. Arrested and tried after the second of these, he was condemned to life imprisonment, but he escaped to England in 1846 and remained there until 1848.

The only group that appeared potentially dangerous to the July Monarchy consisted of those who favored the establishment of a republic. In 1830 they were still few, mainly students and young radicals drawn from the lesser bourgeoisie. Having initially accepted the new regime, they quickly became disillusioned with it and began to renew their republican propaganda, multiply their secret societies, and attract new recruits from the discontented. Except for the aim of eliminating the monarchy, their program was not particularly extreme; they advocated extension of the suffrage, salaries for members of the Chamber of Deputies, and free public education.

Since censorship was one of the issues over which the Revolution of 1830 was fought, the July Monarchy began by allowing considerable freedom of expression in the press. The result was an outburst of political commentary and criticism. In this age political and social satire was a powerful weapon, and the caricaturist Honoré Daumier (1808–1879) was only one of the more successful social satirists. Daumier's caricatures of Louis Philippe shaped

LES POIRES,

Faites à la cour d'assises de Paris par le Directeur de la CARICATURE.

Vendues pour payer les 6,000 fr. d'amende du journal le *Charivari.*

" Si, pour reconnaître le monarque dans une caricature, vous n'attendez pas qu'il soit désigné autrement que par la ressemblance, vous tomberez dans l'absurde. Voyez ces croquis informes, auxquels j'aurais peut-être dû borner ma défense :

Ce croquis ressemble à Louis-Philippe, vous condamnerez donc ?

Alors il faudra condamner celui-ci, qui ressemble au premier.

Charles Philippon's famous caricature of Louis Philippe in which the king's head is gradually transformed into a pear. Other satirical papers took over the representation, and even street urchins began to chalk "la Poire" on the walls of Paris.

Puis condamner cet autre, qui ressemble au second.

Et enfin, si vous êtes conséquens, vous ne sauriez absoudre e tte poire, qui ressemble aux croquis précédens.

Ainsi, pour une poire, pour une brioche, et pour toutes les têtes grotesques dans lesquelles le hasard ou la malice aura placé cette triste ressemblance, vous pourrez infliger à l'auteur cinq ans de prison et cinq mille francs d'amende!! Avouer, Messieurs, que c'est là une singulière liberté de la presse?!

like a pear were so popular that opposition newspapers could be sure of being understood when they spoke simply of *La Poire.* Before long the tolerance of the government (and of the king) began to wear thin and steps were taken to curb the excesses of the opposition press. As we shall see, in defense of its restrictions the government pointed to public demonstrations and riots allegedly inspired by press attacks on the regime and to a series of attempts on the life of the king that more than once came dangerously close to success.[3]

---

[3] The fact that the king was the target of attempted assassinations on ten different occasions during the first decade of his reign led him to remark, "[T]here seems to be a closed season on all kinds of game except me." Quoted in Gordon Wright, *France in Modern Times,* 5th ed. (New York, 1995), p. 112.

In a country where the Industrial Revolution was still in its infant stages, no sizable urban proletariat existed in 1830. But the rapid expansion of French industry in the 1830s and 1840s, and its concentration in a few regions, led to the development of an urban working class. Conditions in industrial areas were as bad, and in some cases worse, than in the corresponding parts of Britain. In the textile mills of the north, women and children commonly worked fifteen-hour days. Epidemics were frequent, particularly among children, because of poor hygienic conditions in homes and factories. Periodic economic crises led to temporary unemployment and consequent suffering for laborers living at a bare subsistence level. In contrast with Great Britain, France made practically no effort to regulate conditions in the factories and mines. With the bourgeoisie firmly in control, the government's laissez faire policy went largely unchallenged. The few reforms that reached the statute books, such as a child-labor law passed in 1841, were unenforced. Under these circumstances, the working class in France behaved with remarkable restraint.

The only significant working-class disturbances under the July Monarchy took place in 1831 and 1834 at Lyons, the center of the silk industry and the second largest city in France, but their repercussions were felt elsewhere. Because the silk industry was well established, the workers were relatively

Rue Transnonain, April 15, 1845, by Honoré Daumier.

class conscious and receptive to programs of political and social reform. The first insurrection seems to have been a largely spontaneous affair resulting from discontent over low wages, but there is evidence of collaboration between the workers and republican secret societies in a more generalized protest during the uprising in 1834. Both outbreaks were suppressed by government troops. In the second one the workers held Lyons for five days. The government had to bombard sections of the city before the rebellion could be quelled. The Lyons insurrections, the most important social uprisings in France since the French Revolution, marked the beginning of an alliance between republicans and the working class against the July Monarchy. One month after the insurrection of 1834, an attempted republican uprising in Paris led to brutal reprisals by government forces. This was the occasion memorialized by Daumier in his famous print *Rue Transnonain, April 15, 1834*, showing victims of a government raid; the father, clad in his nightshirt and cap, stretched out at the foot of his bed and covered with bayonet wounds.

These insurrections were followed by the mass arrest and trial of republican and radical leaders, and the republican opposition was driven completely underground. The government used the uprisings and the attempts on the life of the king as pretexts for the September Laws of 1835. These brought the press under strict censorship and simplified and speeded up judicial proceedings against those accused of provoking insurrection against the state. The September Laws marked a turning point in the history of the July Monarchy: they did not end criticism, but they drastically curbed the opportunities for its expression. With the safety valve of a free press no longer available, pressure built up steadily in the final years of the regime, until it finally exploded in the Revolution of 1848.

Perhaps the most serious charge that can be brought against the leaders of the July Monarchy is that they made no real effort to understand the underlying causes of the insurrections and demonstrations against the regime. Refusing to recognize the legitimacy of republican demands for broader political representation and of working-class demands for an amelioration of social conditions, they simply chose to ignore popular unrest. As premier from 1840 to 1848, François Guizot bears much of the responsibility for the failure of the July Monarchy. Though a brilliant historian and one of the instigators of the Revolution of 1830, he seems to have been incapable of understanding the forces active in his own time. In an era when important economic changes were taking place in French society, he adopted a policy of almost total immobility and resistance to change. In the realm of foreign affairs, his do-nothing policy could be justified on the ground that peace was in France's self-interest, but the absence of adventure and the drabness of

France's role on the international scene contributed to the unpopularity of the government. In economic matters he retained the laissez faire policy pursued by the July Monarchy from the outset, though the government did take the initiative in establishing a plan for a national network of railroads in 1842, offering subsidies to private firms that undertook their construction. No serious attempts were made to regulate or improve working conditions even though abuses were widespread. Where Guizot particularly excelled was in the manipulation of elections and the corruption of elected representatives, activities that were essential if he was to maintain a majority in the Chamber of Deputies. By carefully selecting the time at which elections were to be held, choosing the towns where the voters were to meet, and promising patronage where it would do the most good, he could secure the return of a favorable majority. And to ensure the continuing support of those elected, he offered them lucrative government posts, which they could hold while serving as deputies. Political devices like these are employed to some extent in all parliamentary regimes, but Guizot so abused them that the representative system became a farce. One of the most serious consequences of Guizot's method was that the king and the government were prevented from discovering the true sentiments of the French people. Repeated proposals from a minority of deputies for a reform of the electoral system or the elimination of office holding by deputies were overridden or disregarded by Guizot's majority. With a growing sense of frustration, liberal reformers in the Assembly finally decided they must turn to extraparliamentary means for achieving their ends. From this resolve were to originate the electoral banquets held in the winter of 1847–1848 throughout the country, in the propaganda campaign for electoral reform which helped precipitate the Revolution of 1848.

INTERNATIONAL REVERBERATIONS OF THE REVOLUTION OF 1830

In the aftermath of the July Revolution of 1830 in France, nationalist revolts erupted in Belgium and Poland, as well as in several Italian and German states. These uprisings heightened diplomatic tensions among the Great Powers, testing the resilience of the Congress of Europe. The Belgian rebellion against Dutch rule was the first successful challenge to the European territorial settlement imposed at Vienna in 1815. The other political upheavals of 1830, such as the Polish revolt, proved unable to overturn the established order.

Belgian Independence

The Belgian provinces had been annexed to the Netherlands in 1815 as a barrier against French aggression, but the Belgians had never been enthusiastic about the union. The Belgian population outnumbered the Dutch by 3.5 million to 2 million. Differences in traditions, language, religion, and economic interests aggravated tensions between the two population groups. The Dutch, proud of their two centuries of independence, were contemptuous of the Belgians, who had been subjected to Spanish, then Austrian rule. The policies of King William of Orange further aggravated tensions between them. The predominantly Catholic population of the Belgian provinces resented the Protestant king's policy of equality for all religious denominations. The establishment of Dutch as the official language of the realm except in the French-speaking Walloon districts of Belgium annoyed the Flemings, whose dialect was very different from Dutch. And although the economic activities of the two parts of the kingdom actually complemented each other rather well — the industry and agriculture of the southern provinces finding outlets through the commercial centers of the northern — Belgian manufacturers felt that the Dutch tariff system did not sufficiently protect their industries.

Opposition to the Dutch was concentrated mainly in two political groups, the Clericals and the Liberals, themselves often at odds. The Liberals were resentful of the constitutional structure of the state because it gave an equal number of representatives in the elected States-General to the Dutch and the Belgians, even though the Belgian population was nearly twice as large as the Dutch. They were critical of the high-handed way in which the king dealt with the States-General and often dispensed with the advice of his ministers; they protested government persecution of the opposition press. The Clericals resented the creation of state secondary schools and the extension of state control over independent (that is, ecclesiastical) schools through a system of government inspection. In 1828, Liberals and Clericals managed to bury their differences and formed a "union of parties" that drew up a common program demanding freedom of the press, freedom of teaching, and ministerial responsibility in government. Neither group contemplated the overthrow of the dynasty; rather, they hoped to achieve their demands within the framework of the existing regime.

The success of the July Revolution in France quickened the spread of discontent in Belgium. Moreover, a temporary economic decline brought particular hardships to the working classes in Belgium's larger cities. But the Belgian revolt was actually touched off by the performance of an opera. After a stirring rendition in Brussels of *La Muette de Portici*, an opera by Eugène

Scribe and Daniel Auber about a revolt in Naples, students left the theater shouting "Down with the Dutch!" and "Down with the Ministry!" The student riot turned into revolt, and the revolt spread. The king sent troops to Brussels, but after three days of bitter fighting they were forced to withdraw, leaving the city in the hands of the rebels. By October a provisional government had been established and a national congress summoned to draw up a constitution for the new Belgian state.

The independence of Belgium clearly violated the settlement of 1815, and on this basis King William of Holland appealed to the Great Powers for their help in reestablishing his authority in the Belgian provinces. Tsar Nicholas of Russia was eager for intervention, and he appeared to have the support of Metternich and King Frederick William III of Prussia. Yet the French, having just emerged from their own revolution, were sympathetic to the cause of Belgian independence and hoped it would result in greater French influence in the region. In Britain, the new Whig foreign minister, Lord Palmerston, was hardly enthusiastic about the revolt in Belgium but concluded that it could not be reversed. Moreover he was not eager to see troops of the eastern powers move into an area where Britain traditionally had interests.

In November 1830, representatives of the Great Powers convened in London to discuss the Belgian crisis. By this time, the revolt of the Poles against their Russian overlords in November had distracted Tsar Nicholas from Belgian affairs; he was now far more concerned with suppressing the revolution in his own territory than in intervention in the Netherlands. Both Austria and Prussia were concerned about the possible spread of the Polish revolt to subject Poles living within their own borders. By early 1831, Metternich was also preoccupied with revolts in Italy. In the end, Russia, Prussia, and Austria played only a small role in the settlement of Belgium's status. By stipulating that Belgium would remain a neutral state under the permanent guarantee of the Great Powers, Britain and France succeeded in persuading them to accept a protocol that virtually recognized Belgium's independence.

The handling of the Belgian revolt suggested that the Great Powers could act together in reaching a solution to a thorny diplomatic crisis despite the sharply opposing views of the several governments. The Russian and Austrian governments may have been more willing to accept Lord Palmerston's solution for Belgium because of the restraint shown by both the British and French governments toward the revolts in Poland and the Italian states. Despite impassioned pleas from liberals in both the House of Commons and the French Chamber of Deputies for intervention on behalf of the Poles and the Italians, neither government had seriously considered going to the support of the rebels against Russia and Austria. Each of the major powers appeared determined in 1830–1831 to avoid any action that might precipitate a general European war—a war they feared would destabilize their regimes and bolster the power of revolutionary elements in their societies.

The Polish Uprising of 1830–1831

Under the Vienna Settlement of 1815, Poland had been reconstituted as a semi-autonomous state under Russian hegemony. In a gesture of good will toward the new client state, in 1818 Tsar Alexander I granted Poland one of the most liberal constitutions in Europe. This constitution guaranteed individual liberties, including free speech and a free press, and provided for a diet to be elected on a broad franchise. Poland was permitted to maintain its own army and administrative personnel and to use Polish as the official language.

Yet over the decade following the Vienna Congress, as Alexander's political attitudes became increasingly illiberal, he frequently clashed with his Polish subjects. In practice, the autonomy of the Poles was restricted and the will of the diet thwarted by Alexander's brother, Constantine (1779–1831), who commanded the Polish army and interfered frequently in the administration of the country. Compared with the Russians or with those Poles living in territory directly annexed by Russia, the inhabitants of "Congress Poland" were well off; but the violation of their constitution by the tsar, combined with a revival of Polish national sentiment after 1815, made them restive even during Alexander's reign. With the accession of Nicholas in 1825, tension between the Poles and their Russian masters increased. In November 1830, when a rumor circulated that the tsar was about to march a joint Russian-Polish army into France and Belgium to suppress the revolutions there, a group of army cadets supported by university students revolted in Warsaw.

Only a handful of rebels was involved at first, but the departure of Grand Duke Constantine opened the way for the establishment of a provisional government dominated by Polish landed aristocrats. Had the Poles been unified, their revolution might well have succeeded, for they controlled a well-disciplined military force. But after the initial victory the revolutionaries divided into the Whites, feudal aristocrats who tried to negotiate with the tsar for moderate reforms, and the Reds, a more radical element drawn from the gentry, who opposed any sort of compromise. The peasants who constituted the mass of the population saw no reason to support the revolt, since they had been exploited by both land-owning groups. The Polish rebels had counted strongly on intervention on their behalf by France or Britain, since liberals in these states were clamoring loudly for support of the Polish cause, but neither government was willing to commit itself to such action.

Blindfolded Polish rebels are interrogated by Russian officers during the uprising of 1830–1831.

The Poles did win some initial victories, but in September 1831, the Russians captured Warsaw and ended the revolt. Nicholas took ruthless reprisals. The constitution granted by Alexander was withdrawn, thousands of Poles were executed or banished to western Europe, and Poland was governed thenceforth by what amounted to a military dictatorship.

REPRESSION IN CENTRAL EUROPE

During the Restoration era the various peoples inhabiting the central part of the European continent, from the Baltic Sea in the north to the island of Sicily in the south, fell under the domination of the Habsburg dynasty, or rather of its chief agent, Prince Klemens von Metternich. The Austrian chancellor had his emissaries or his spies everywhere, sending back reports to Vienna, constantly on the alert for evidence of liberalism or subversion that might threaten the status quo. In point of fact, in the years immediately after 1815, active opposition was confined to a small minority of students, army officers, liberal nobles, and merchants. The peasants who constituted the great mass of the population were little concerned with political questions. Such grievances as they had were directed primarily against their landlords, not the government. Since industrialization did not get under way until the

1830s and 1840s, and then only in the Rhineland and northern Italy, there existed no numerically significant middle class to assume the leadership of a liberal opposition.

The opposition that did exist in central Europe was as often nationalist as liberal, though no clear-cut distinction between the two was made by Metternich or, indeed, by those who agitated against the status quo. In Austria, nationalist sentiment normally took the form of demands by representatives of non-German groups for greater use of their language in schools and administrative offices. In Italy and the German states, nationalism meant the desire for freedom from Austrian domination and a greater measure of unity for the respective peoples. To all these aspirations, Metternich's answer was the same. They were ruthlessly suppressed as threats to the delicate equilibrium of existing institutions. He was convinced that—particularly within the Austrian empire proper—any attempt to tamper with the elaborate structure might bring the entire edifice tumbling down. If the chancellor's goal was the maintenance of order and a reasonable degree of calm, his policy worked remarkably well during the better part of the period between 1815 and 1848. But by refusing to face up to the real and complex problems existing in the Habsburg realms, and by stifling the growing nationalist desires of Germans and Italians, he merely postponed the explosion that finally erupted in 1848.

The German Confederation, 1815–1832

The German Confederation, created by the Congress of Vienna, initially consisted of thirty-nine states, several of which subsequently merged together. Austria and Prussia were the largest and most powerful member states, though their non-German territory was not included. The institutional embodiment of this loose federation was a federal diet, or assembly, consisting of delegates appointed by the rulers of each of the member states, which met in the free city of Frankfurt am Main. The function of the diet was ill defined, especially since the Confederation had no executive to implement its decisions. Metternich soon came to manipulate the Confederation to exercise influence throughout the German states. Though Metternich seems to have viewed the Confederation initially as a kind of defensive alliance against encroachment on German territory by France or Russia, in fact it came to be used primarily for the repression of liberal movements throughout Germany.

Not all of the thirty-nine states had governments quite as reactionary as Austria's. Although Metternich had discouraged them from doing so, rulers in most of the states granted constitutions to their subjects to fulfill promises made during the final years of the Napoleonic era; among them were the medium-sized states of southern Germany—Bavaria, Württemberg, and Baden, along with many smaller principalities. These constitutions, like the French Charter, did not acknowledge the principle of popular sovereignty; indeed, suffrage was heavily weighted to the landed aristocracy and the administrative bureaucracy. Where elected assemblies existed, their primary function was merely to ratify legislation proposed by the sovereign.

At first, liberals throughout Germany looked hopefully to Prussia for inspiration. King Frederick William III not only had promised a constitution to his people, on the eve of Waterloo, but had also agreed between 1807 and 1814 to a series of reforms that made Prussia appear to be one of the more progressive states in Germany. Leadership in initiating these reforms came from Baron Heinrich Friedrich Karl vom und zum Stein (1757–1831), who was chief minister in 1807–1808. Although he was dismissed from office in 1808 because of pressure from Napoleon on the king, Stein's program of reforms was carried on by his successors. Among these, the most important was Baron (later Prince) Karl August von Hardenberg (1750–1822), who served as chancellor from 1810 until his death. Stein and Hardenberg were convinced that Prussia's recovery from the defeat inflicted by Napoleon could occur only as the result of a series of political and institutional reforms comparable, in some respects, to those undertaken by the French during the revolution. After the humiliating defeat of Prussia at Jena in 1806, Hardenberg is alleged to have told the king, "Your Majesty! We must do from above what the French have done from below." By giving its citizens greater opportunity for participation in the affairs of state, Prussia could develop a new patriotic spirit.

Among the reforms were the abolition of serfdom, though landlords retained manorial jurisdiction over the peasants. Some of the more rigid class distinctions were abolished by decrees making it possible for nonnobles to buy land formerly restricted to noble ownership and permitting members of the noble class to go into trade. Stein's Municipal Ordinance of 1808 introduced a system of municipal self-government that permitted towns to control their own affairs through town councils and salaried magistrates. Opportunities in primary and secondary education were broadened by Wilhelm von Humboldt (1767–1835), the Prussian minister of education in 1809–1810. Humboldt was also responsible for founding the University of Berlin in 1810. Inspired by a new humanistic educational philosophy, the university became the rallying point of intellectuals seeking Prussia's regeneration and liberation from foreign control. Finally, an important series of reforms in the army was undertaken by Gerhard von Scharnhorst (1755–1813) and Neithardt von Gneisenau (1760–1831), who eliminated some of the barbarous punishments hitherto inflicted on enlisted men, encouraged promotion by merit in the officer corps, and introduced universal military conscription to create a truly national army. A new emphasis on infantry and artillery tended to weaken the traditional, feudal character of the Prussian army.

Both Stein and Hardenberg had looked forward to the creation of a legislative assembly as the culmination of this program of reforms, and the king's promise of a constitution establishing some sort of representative government appeared to confirm their hopes. But no constitution was forthcoming. In 1817, the king established a council of state composed of the royal princes, ministers, heads of departments, and army commanders. In 1823, Frederick William III created eight separate provincial assemblies, which he consulted periodically concerning legislative proposals, but he refused to establish a general assembly for the entire realm. Although Hardenberg continued to lobby the king vigorously for the establishment of a constitution until the end of his life, he was outflanked by a group of conservatives at the court who feared the potentially revolutionary effects of parliamentary institutions. Moreover, after 1819, when the Carlsbad Decrees imposed strict press censorship throughout the German states, liberals found it more difficult to argue for a representative assembly and a constitution. The Prussian government became more efficient than that of any other German state, but it remained absolutist.

Ultimately, no central representative assembly met in Prussia until 1847, when King Frederick William IV convened a United Diet in order to seek funding to build a new Berlin–Königsberg railroad. The failure of this assembly presented an object lesson in the difficulties of uniting parliamentary and monarchical forms of government. The delegates to the United Diet, demanding a broader legislative role than Frederick William was willing to allow them, denied the king's request for a bond to finance the railroad. The highly publicized deadlock between the monarch and the assembly raised the temperature of political debate in Prussia, contributing to the outbreak of the Revolution of 1848.

Those who had hoped for a greater measure of unity among Germans after the Napoleonic wars were far from satisfied with the Austrian-sponsored German Confederation and resented the particularism of the rulers of the individual states. To spread the ideal of unity and "freedom" for Germans, students organized Burschenschaften, or student societies, in a number of German universities. These drew their inspiration from such men as Joseph von Görres (1776–1848), an ardent nationalist who edited *Der Rheinische Merkur*; Ernst Moritz Arndt (1769–1860), a poet and Prussian patriot; and Friedrich Ludwig Jahn, who had become famous during the Napoleonic wars when he organized an association of *Turngemeinden* or gymnastic societies, whose aim was to bring about the physical and moral regeneration of German youth. "Turnvater Jahn" was perhaps the noisiest and most aggressive of the German nationalists of his time. Preaching hatred of foreign influence and even of foreign dress, he urged young Germans to return to their Teutonic heritage. By engaging Germany's youth in gymnastic exercises, Jahn intended that the *Volk* would become "manly and patriotic"; and he required the *Turner* to dress in identical gray linen uniforms in order to break down the social differences among them. He also encouraged such unruly behavior as the disruption of lectures by professors who were insufficiently nationalist in their outlook. Jahn was responsible, along with others, for injecting anti-Semitism into the doctrines of the Burschenschaften, though some members of the societies resisted this tendency.

During their early years the Burschenschaften staged a number of popular demonstrations. An assembly in 1817 brought young people from all over Germany to the Wartburg Castle, near Eisenach, where Luther had taken refuge from his persecutors. Timed to coincide with the three-hundredth anniversary of Luther's posting of his Ninety-five Theses and the fourth anniversary of the German victory at the battle of Leipzig, the assembly opened with speeches exhorting the students to dedicate their lives to the "holy cause of union and freedom." The group then marched in a torchlight parade to a nearby hilltop to witness the burning of books by conservative and antinationalist writers. Eighteen months later, Karl Sand, a mentally unbalanced theological student who was a Burschenschaft member, assassinated the dramatist August von Kotzebue, known for his reactionary views. Sand was condemned to death. Metternich decided the time had come to proceed against the Burschenschaften. Acting with representatives of the nine most important German states, Metternich drew up the draconian Carlsbad Decrees (1819) and submitted them to the diet of the German Confederation for ratification. These decrees dissolved the Burschenschaften, set up rigid censorship and press control throughout the Confederation, and created an elaborate system for rooting out subversive individuals in schools and universities.

The enforcement of the Carlsbad Decrees was a serious blow to the liberal and nationalist movements, which had never been very strong, and political opposition to the Metternichian system was practically nonexistent for several years after 1819. With the collaboration of Frederick William III of Prussia, Metternich actively intervened in those states of the Confederation where legislative bodies still existed in order to restrict their influence and stifle potential opposition. Only in the latter part of the 1820s did nationalist student societies reappear, meeting clandestinely to avoid the secret police.

In 1830 news of the July Revolution in France touched off a flurry of excitement in Germany and inspired minor revolutions in Brunswick, Saxony, and Hesse-Cassel, where the rulers were forced to abdicate in favor of sons or brothers who then granted constitutions to the people. Metternich was convinced that these revolts were part of an international radical conspiracy. In 1832, at an all-German festival at Hambach, twenty-five thousand people drank to Lafayette and denounced the principles of the Holy Alliance; and once again Metternich seized the occasion of a demonstration as the pretext for issuing series of decrees that strengthened the princes in dealing with their parliaments, brought the universities under renewed surveillance, and prohibited all public meetings. Within a year or two, all open opposition had ceased.

Economic Developments in the German States During the Vormärz Era, 1830–1848

Because the revolutions that were to disrupt the German states in 1848 occurred in March, the decades in Germany preceding these mid-century upheavals are often referred to as the *Vormärz* ("pre-March") era. The 1830s and 1840s were a period of relative political stagnation. The German princes, with Metternich's encouragement, clung stubbornly to established institutions and rigorously suppressed dissent. However, the years between 1815 and 1848 were of great economic importance for Germany's subsequent progress. Although the development of German industry at this time can hardly be compared with that of Great Britain, France, and Belgium, the groundwork was laid for the major advance that occurred in the second half of the century. Even during these early years, industrial progress was great enough to disturb the existing equilibrium of social forces in certain regions of Germany, thereby creating significant sources of unrest. In addition, the steps taken to break down the economic barriers between the various states of Germany were to have important political as well as economic consequences.

German economic development in the first half of the nineteenth century varied greatly from one region to another. What industrialization there was tended to be concentrated in certain regions, such as the Rhineland and Saxony, while other areas were almost entirely unaffected. Even in Prussia there were vast differences between the Rhine provinces of the west, which enjoyed an industrial development comparable to that of France, and the provinces of the east, where an almost feudal agrarian society persisted well into the nineteenth century. Obstacles to industrialization were many. Although events of the French revolutionary and Napoleonic eras had shattered traditional economic patterns and modes of organization, the period after 1815 brought a revival of the authority of the guilds in many regions, and the handicraft system persisted in most industries. Governments were still dominated by the landed interests, and manufacturers found it difficult to secure the removal of restrictions on business enterprises and trade. Many conservative Germans associated economic liberalism with political liberalism and therefore viewed it with suspicion.

Despite these difficulties significant advances in German industrial development occurred after 1830, particularly in the coal-mining and metallurgical industries. Deep mine shafts were sunk in the Ruhr Valley and coal production increased substantially. By the early 1840s the Krupp works at Essen was producing high-grade steel. Developments in the textile industry were slower, since Germany produced mainly linen and woolen cloth, both less adaptable to manufacture by machinery than cotton and silk. But there were advances here as well. Industrial growth was supported by new transportation systems; by 1850 the German states could boast of three thousand miles of railroad track, although the first line had been laid only in 1835.

To the German manufacturer or merchant seeking customers beyond his local market, the most serious obstacle was the vast network of tariff barriers that separated the German states and hampered trade even within some of the larger states, such as Prussia. During the early nineteenth century goods, shipped from Hamburg, on the North Sea, to Austria had to cross ten different states with ten different customs systems, all exacting transit duties. No wonder German manufacturers, unlike their French counterparts, were reluctant to produce for national consumption. For this reason the most important single economic development in this era was the establishment of a *Zollverein* ("customs union"), which by 1844 included most of the states of Germany. Prussia took the lead in 1818 by abolishing all tariff barriers among the provinces within its own borders and establishing a uniform tariff rate on imports. Within the next few years Prussia concluded tariff treaties with a number of neighboring states and provoked the negotiation of similar treaties among some of its rivals. In 1834, seventeen states with a population of 26 million came together in the Zollverein, a union that established free trade among them and provided for annual meetings of their delegates.

By 1844 all German states except Austria, Hanover, Oldenburg, and the Hanse cities (Hamburg, Bremen, and Lübeck) adhered to the union; the result was a remarkable expansion of the volume of trade among them. Gradually the political implications of this economic collaboration became clear: Prussia's leadership of the Zollverein was undermining the hitherto dominant position of the Habsburg monarchy. The Zollverein turned out to be of decisive importance in preparing Germany for unification under Prussian leadership.

For the nineteenth-century political economist Friedrich List, the railway and the Zollverein were indivisible "Siamese twins" contributing to Germany's economic betterment. But his rapture over the railroad went far beyond its economic benefits: he believed that it would stimulate Germany's political and spiritual renewal, as well as strengthen its military power. The railroad, he wrote, was a Hercules "who will deliver nations from the plague of war, inflation, famine, national hatreds, unemployment, and ignorance." Germany, he lamented, had been "robbed of almost all attributes of nationality by earlier divisiveness" and thus "so desperately needs internal unification of its limbs." Railroad building, List declared, would unify the country by drawing "a tight belt around the loins of the German nation."[4]

In estimating the effects of these economic changes on German society we must remember that as late as 1848 at least two out of three Germans still made their living from the land. Yet even in rural areas the years from 1815 to 1848 were characterized by change and unrest, for in many regions the peasants were trying to adjust to legislation, introduced during the revolutionary and Napoleonic eras, that radically altered their status. Serfdom had been abolished in the parts of Germany under French control and even in some areas, such as Prussia, not annexed by the French. But freedom from personal servitude did not necessarily mean improvement of the peasants' material status, for many were still saddled with manorial dues or other obligations, and only in certain regions and under certain circumstances did they receive clear title to the land they farmed. Indeed, in Prussia the legislation abolishing serfdom strengthened many of the great landholding *Junker* aristocrats. Freed from the feudal obligation to protect the serfs and to provide them with lodging and other necessities of life, the Junker took possession of his land and exploited it for his own profit, employing his former serfs, now landless, as agricultural laborers. The condition of the "free" peasants of East Prussia was far worse after their so-called emancipation than before. When the peasants did secure title to a piece of land, it was often so small that they could not farm it productively. Whether peasants were freeholders, tenant farmers, or landless laborers, they had grievances. And they could hardly hope to secure redress of them from a government dominated by the large land owners.

Among the workers living in the towns and cities, those employed in factories were still in a minority as late as 1848. The majority were artisans working under the traditional handicraft system, and it was among this group that there was the greatest unrest. Suffering from the competition of new industries in Germany and abroad, the old craft guilds went into a decline,

---

[4] Quoted in James J. Sheehan, *German History, 1770–1866* (Oxford, 1989), p. 468.

and the artisans found themselves either unemployed or earning starvation-level wages. Their discontent found occasional expression in riots and blind onslaughts on the machinery that they held responsible for their situation. For example, Silesian linen weavers rioted in 1844, attacking factories and destroying the homes of the owners. By comparison, factory workers in Germany enjoyed steady employment and relatively high wages.

As elsewhere, the impact of industrialism brought a rapid expansion of the middle class during the *Vormärz* era. Neither as large nor as concentrated as the bourgeoisie of England and France, this class assumed in Germany an economic influence far out of proportion to its size. German manufacturers and merchants, denied the right to participate actively in the governing of their respective states, managed to win concessions as their rulers began to be aware of their potential strength. The Zollverein, for example, was established largely in response to their pressure. The cause of national unification had no stronger supporters than German businessmen anxious to promote greater efficiency of government and smoother economic operations. A comment in the *Düsseldorfer Zeitung* in 1843 gives an indication of their outlook: "Thus we have instead of one Germany thirty-eight German states, an equal number of governments, almost the same number of courts, as many representative bodies, thirty-eight distinct legal codes and administrations, embassies and consulates. What an enormous saving it would be, if all of that were taken care of by one central government. . . ."[5]

The decentralization, if not fragmentation, of Germany on the eve of 1848 contrasts markedly with the relatively high degree of centralization in France, where a development in Paris might carry the entire country with it. During the *Vormärz* era Germans were still seeking the unity that the French monarchy had achieved long before 1789. The lack of centralized political institutions in Germany, along with conflicts over which territories should be included in a united German nation, would prove a major obstacle to the success of the revolutions of 1848 in German-speaking Europe.

Metternich and the Austrian Empire, 1815–1848

Within the Austrian empire proper, Metternich's main problem, which haunted him throughout the three decades leading up to the Revolution of 1848, was the emergence of a growing national consciousness among the various peoples under Habsburg rule. This was to remain the central problem for the empire throughout the nineteenth century and was resolved only with the breaking up of the empire at the end of the First World War. For

---

[5] Quoted in T. S. Hamerow, *Restoration, Revolution, Reaction* (Princeton, 1958), p. 17.

Austria in 1815 was not a national state like France or Britain, but a collection of peoples and territories united only by their common allegiance to the Habsburg ruler. The broad territorial outlines of the Habsburg empire had been set since the sixteenth century, but only at the beginning of the nineteenth century was it given a name. Until Francis adopted the title emperor of Austria in 1804, anticipating Napoleon's dissolution of the Holy Roman Empire two years later, the territories of Austria were simply referred to as the "lands of the House of Habsburg" or the "lands of the Holy Roman emperor." Most of the peoples in the empire thought of themselves not as Austrians, but as subjects of the Habsburg emperor. Although Francis ruled as emperor over Austria, Bohemia, and other dependencies, the Hungarians refused to accept the imperial role as applying to them: thus, his title was emperor of Austria and king of Hungary.

It is difficult to find agreement on the precise national identities of the peoples that composed the Habsburg empire. However, three major national groups can be specified. The first of these consisted of the Germans; forming no more than a quarter of the population, they were concentrated primarily in the western part of the empire in the old Habsburg lands around Vienna. Large groups of Germans also lived on the fringes of Bohemia, the territory to the north which had once been a separate kingdom, and in all the major cities of the empire. To the extent that there was a middle class in Austria, it was made up of Germans. The growth of German nationalism in the first half of the nineteenth century caused division among the Germans in Austria. The strong nationalists were prepared to sacrifice the Austrian empire, if necessary, in order to join a unified German nation. The moderates hoped to see other states of Germany merge with Austria under the continued rule of the Habsburgs.

The national group second in importance — in influence if not in numbers — consisted of the Magyars, who lived in the crown lands of Saint Stephen, in the eastern half of the empire, which included Hungary, Transylvania, and Croatia. The Magyars were proud of their origins, which could be traced to the Middle Ages: their first crowned ruler, Stephen ascended the throne in the year 1001. Traditionally the most independent people in the empire, they maintained their own diet and their own local administration. Every emperor was still required, by tradition, to go to Budapest to be invested separately with the crown of Saint Stephen. Even before 1815, the cultural revival had begun among the Magyars that was to grow into a movement for greater autonomy within the Austrian empire. At the same time, the Magyars constituted a minority in their own lands and were faced with nationalist movements among the Slavic peoples and the other groups subject to them.

The third major group consisted of the Slavs. Including almost half the population of the Austrian empire, the Slavs formed its largest single national group. But they were divided into a number of subgroups and before the nineteenth century had little national consciousness. Of the greatest potential political importance among the Slavs were the Poles, who had been attached to the empire only at the end of the eighteenth century and therefore retained a strong sense of national identity, and the Czechs, who had earlier ruled the independent kingdom of Bohemia. Because the great majority of the Slavs were peasants working the estates of German or Magyar masters, their nationalist aspirations were often mingled with social grievances.

To these three major groups should be added the Italians of the provinces of Lombardy and Venetia, which had been annexed to the Habsburg lands by the settlement of 1815, and the Romanians, a sizable minority concentrated in the eastern part of the Hungarian kingdom.

What policies did Metternich adopt in governing this congery of peoples under Habsburg control? In general, he tried to avoid the problems posed by the emerging nationalism, and in the early part of the century, such an attitude served reasonably well. By the 1830s, however, it had become increasingly difficult for the government to ignore the demands of nationalist groups for greater autonomy. Still Metternich did not propose a broad solution; rather he resorted to a number of temporary expedients for neutralizing nationalist sentiment and tried to play off one national group against another. Certainly he did little to forestall the explosion of 1848, which resulted from a combination of nationalism and social discontent. In his defense it may be said that Metternich had the misfortune of serving under two emperors — Francis I and his successor, Ferdinand I — who had neither the will nor the capacity to support any program of constructive reform. Ferdinand, in fact, was an imbecile and an epileptic who was allowed to inherit the throne in 1835 because of his father's wish that the direct line of succession not be interrupted. During his reign, which lasted until December 1848, he was authorized to sign documents presented to him and reacted, on occasion, to events that occurred; but Austria was, in fact, ruled by a body of councillors (of whom Metternich was the most important) acting in the emperor's name. But Metternich did not take full advantage of the opportunities this situation offered for exercising his personal control. Indeed, there was much truth in his own admission, "I have governed Europe on occasion; Austria, never."

ITALY: THE RISORGIMENTO, 1815–1848

Events in Italy between 1815 and 1848 were similar in many ways to those in the German states. For the mass of Italians, the change from French to Austrian domination made very little difference. But for the small, educated middle class in the cities of northern Italy and for other groups that had benefited from the introduction of French institutions, the restoration of petty despotic governments under Austrian domination proved a disappointment. Those who had hoped during the Napoleonic era for a closer union among Italian-speaking peoples were reluctant to accept Metternich's view of Italy as a mere "geographical expression." The peninsula was once again divided into a number of lesser states: the kingdom of Naples and Sicily (the Two Sicilies) under the restored Bourbon Ferdinand I; the Papal States, to which Pope Pius VII returned after several years of exile; the smaller principalities of Parma, Modena, and Tuscany, all ruled by relatives of the Austrian emperor who took their directions from Metternich; the provinces of Lombardy and Venetia, directly incorporated into the Austrian empire and administered from Vienna; and the kingdom of Sardinia, ruled until 1821 by Victor Emmanuel I, of the house of Savoy. None of these states possessed constitutions or representative assemblies in 1815. The restored rulers retained only those French institutions which tended to strengthen their despotic regimes. Then, as now, the northern half of the peninsula was better off economically than the southern. Only in Sardinia, Lombardy, and Venetia was there significant industrialization before 1850, and only in these areas were attempts made to increase agricultural production through experimentation with new techniques.

The failure of the revolutions of 1820–1821 in Naples and Sardinia (discussed in Chapter 4) and the reprisals taken against the rebels tended to weaken and discourage nationalist and liberal opposition. As in Germany, the decade 1820–1830 saw little overt resistance to established authority, although secret societies such as the Carbonari continued to operate underground. Again as in Germany, the July Revolution in France was the signal for a series of minor revolts; these occurred in Modena, Parma, and the Papal States, beginning in December 1830. But unlike their German counterparts, the Italian revolutionaries of 1830–1831 counted on the active support of the new government of Louis Philippe in France, hoping it would oppose any Austrian attempt at intervention. However, Louis Philippe was not willing to risk his international position, and the French Assembly was not prepared to risk a war with Austria. Metternich therefore had a free hand; he sent troops to Modena, Parma, and the Papal States, put down the revolts, and restored their legitimate rulers.

The activities of the revolutionary societies discussed so far constituted the faint beginnings of what came to be known as the *Risorgimento* ("Resurgence"), the movement for Italian national unification. But the failure of the revolutionary movements in 1830–1831, following the suppression of revolts in Naples and Sardinia ten years earlier, tended to discredit the methods of secret societies like the Carbonari. The Risorgimento entered a new phase in the 1830s, with new leaders and different methods.

Among the leaders of the Risorgimento before 1848, Giuseppe Mazzini (1805–1872) is unquestionably the most renowned, though recently historians have suggested that classic accounts of the movement for national unification exaggerate his role. With his idealistic, semireligious faith in Italian nationalism, he was undoubtedly the chief inspiration for radical students and intellectuals who hoped to see Italy emerge as a unified republic. Mazzini was born in Genoa, in the kingdom of Sardinia. During his youth he was active in secret societies. In 1821, when he saw refugees streaming northward from Naples after the suppression of the revolt there, he put on a black suit to signify his mourning for the condition of Italy, and he affected this costume for the rest of his life. He participated in the revolts of 1830–1831 and was imprisoned for six months, being released on the condition that he remain outside of Genoa. Instead, he chose exile from all of Italy, and spent most of the remaining forty years of his life in Switzerland, France, and Great Britain. There he wrote inspirational tracts and pamphlets that were circulated in his homeland and founded Young Italy, the organization particularly associated with his name. The goal of this movement, whose membership was restricted to men under forty living either in Italy or in exile, was the expulsion of foreign tyrants from the Italian peninsula and the establishment of a united republic. However, Mazzini's skills at organization and administration fell short of his ability as a propagandist, and his few attempts to foment uprisings in his native land failed.

Schooled in the writings of the French revolutionaries, Mazzini believed strongly in the principle of popular sovereignty. At the same time, he felt that during the French Revolution the *rights* of man had been emphasized too much and the *duties* too little. Drawing on the heritage of Rousseau and to some extent on the German idealist tradition, he was convinced that people could be happy only while devoting themselves to a collective enterprise. In the work which he appropriately called *The Duties of Man* (published in two parts, 1844 and 1858), Mazzini argued that the highest collective enterprise to which the individual could dedicate one's life was the nation. In a lyrical passage typical of his prose, he wrote, "O my Brothers! love your Country. Our Country is our home, the home which God has given us, placing therein a numerous family which we love and are loved by, and with which we have a more intimate and quicker communion of feeling and thought than with others; a family which by its concentration upon a given spot, and by the homogeneous nature of its elements, is destined for a special kind of activity."

Yet important as love for the nation was to Mazzini, he regarded national loyalty as part of a higher duty toward "Humanity," to whom men owed primary allegiance. "You are men before you are either citizens or fathers." The nation was for him the vehicle through which men fulfilled their obligations toward humanity as a whole. His concern for other nationalities led him to found in 1834 a movement known as Young Europe, which was to establish national committees for patriotic agitation in Germany, Poland, and Switzerland. Mazzini was convinced that by encouraging nationalist movements among the peoples still divided or living under foreign domination, he was working toward the day when all nations, having realized their national aspirations, would work for humanity at large. For this reason, Mazzini is often viewed as the prophet of the ideals that President Woodrow Wilson (1856–1924) tried to embody in the peace settlement of 1919: national self-determination and the association of all peoples in the League of Nations.

Many Italians who desired the unification of the peninsula viewed Mazzini as a dangerous radical whose ideal of a democratic republic implied social revolution and a threat to property. Some of these rallied to the Neo-Guelph movement, which took its name from the papal faction in the medieval struggle between popes and emperors. The principal impetus to the Neo-Guelph cause came from the publication in 1843 of *The Civil and Moral Primacy of the Italians,* by Vincenzo Gioberti (1801–1852), which called for the establishment of a federation of Italian states under the leadership of the papacy, with executive authority vested in a college of princes. To those who were skeptical about the willingness of the pope to lead a crusade for Italian unity, the election of a new pope in 1846 seemed to offer hope, for the man who took the name Pius IX had a reputation as a liberal. His initial measures in the Papal States — granting an amnesty to political offenders and relaxing the restrictions on freedom of speech and of the press — suggested that he might indeed become the rallying point for a liberal Italian federation.

A third faction working for the cause of unification consisted of the so-called Moderates, most active in the kingdom of Sardinia, with supporters in Lombardy and Venetia. Principally liberal nobles and members of the bourgeoisie, the Moderates looked to Sardinia for leadership in unification and foresaw the establishment of a constitutional monarchy. They believed that economic unification had to precede political unity. Accordingly, they strove for the elimination of tariff barriers and the stimulation of commerce among the Italian states. While urging industrial development, they nevertheless realized that they must concentrate on improving and modernizing agricultural methods since farming was still Italy's principal industry. Young aristocrats such as Count Camillo Benso di Cavour (1810–1861), later prime minister of Sardinia, set up model farms and established agricultural societies to disseminate knowledge of new techniques. Some historians argue that the efforts of northern Italian liberals and Moderates for economic reform contributed more than all the propaganda of Mazzini toward the unification of the peninsula. An elite of educated, influential individuals in a number of Italian states became accustomed to exchanging ideas and collaborating in the attainment of certain limited goals. Their efforts were partially rewarded when Charles Albert, the king of Sardinia, lowered tariffs, reformed the finances of his country, and officially encouraged agricultural improvements, but his liberalism did not extend to political matters until the eve of the revolutions of 1848.

Thus, at least three different movements had been organized in the peninsula before 1848, each working in its own way for greater unity among the Italian peoples. Yet it should be emphasized that the strength of the Neo-Guelphs and the Moderates was concentrated almost exclusively in the northern regions of Italy and that even Mazzini's Young Italy won the support of only a small minority of the population. As yet most Italians were untouched by the Risorgimento.

THE GREEK REVOLT AND THE DECLINE
OF THE OTTOMAN EMPIRE

The revolt of the Greeks against Turkish domination and the reaction of the European powers to this uprising were aspects of a larger problem that was to plague European diplomats throughout the nineteenth century. This was the "Eastern Question," which had its origin in the continuing decline of the Ottoman empire and the weakening of its authority over its outlying territories. Each European government had to decide whether to stem the disintegration by bolstering the sultans, or to hasten it and exploit the decay to its own advantage. No power pursued a perfectly consistent course with respect to the government of Sultan Mahmud II (ruled 1808–1839). The Russians hoped to profit from their proximity to the Turkish empire and from the religious tie between Russians and Greek Orthodox Christians living within the empire to acquire special privileges from Turkey. The British, suspicious of Russian ambitions in the Near East, more than once defended the sultan against his enemies; their support of the Greek revolt was an exception to this general policy.

The Greek Independence Movement, 1821–1832

The Greeks had been incorporated into the Ottoman empire since the mid-fifteenth century, and to most Europeans, Greece was merely a province of the empire. Actually, Greece had enjoyed a privileged position within the empire from the seventeenth century onward, for the sultans used educated Greeks from Istanbul (the so-called Phanariot Greeks) in their administrations and permitted Greek merchants (along with Armenians and Jews) a near monopoly of trade in the eastern Mediterranean. Moreover, within Greece the Turks permitted the teaching of the Greek language and the exercise of the Greek Orthodox faith. The Greeks, then, had never entirely lost sight of their past and their identity.

Greek nationalist sentiment began to emerge during the era of the French Revolution and Napoleon, and with this came a growing desire for independence from Turkish rule. The immediate impetus for revolt came in 1821 from a secret society known as the Hetaíria Philiké ("Society of Friends"); the society had been organized in 1814 and consisted primarily of Greeks living outside of Greece who hoped for a revival of the Greek empire of the early Middle Ages. The leader of the society was Prince Alexander Ypsilanti (1792–1831), son of a Greek provincial administrator and himself a former general in the Russian army. Having been given the impression by the tsar's Greek-born foreign minister, Count Johannes Antonius Capodistrias (1776–1831), that he would get Russian support for a Greek uprising, Ypsilanti led a band of volunteers into the Turkish province of Moldavia, where he summoned the native Romanians as well as his fellow Greeks to revolt against their Turkish masters. Ypsilanti's attempt failed because the Romanians refused to respond to his call and because the tsar disavowed him. Two weeks later a more spontaneous revolt erupted in the Morea and spread to some of the Aegean Islands and to central and northern Greece. The avowed goal of the revolutionaries was complete independence from the Ottoman empire and the creation of a new Greek state.

The European powers initially reacted unsympathetically to the Greek revolt, considering it one more threat to established authority that had to be suppressed. Chiefly at Metternich's urging, the tsar denounced the rebels and dismissed Capodistrias. Not even Britain, on whom some liberals had counted for support, showed any inclination to aid the Greeks. Indeed, the principal goal of Castlereagh and the British government was to see order restored in the Ottoman empire and to forestall the possibility of Russian intervention.

But a new force became involved in the Greek revolt, a force that did not come into play in the revolutions in Spain and Italy and that gradually compelled the governments of Britain, Russia, and France to repudiate their initial stand and throw their support to the rebels. This was the movement known as Philhellenism, a groundswell of popular backing for the rebels that included admirers of Greece all over Europe and America. To generations brought up on the classics, the Greek revolt had a romantic appeal unlike that of any other. Moreover, the fact that the Greeks were Christians struggling to free themselves from Muslim domination gave the entire movement the flavor of a crusade. Unable to express opposition to their own regimes, liberals throughout Europe rallied to the cause of Greek independence and organized committees to provide the rebels with money, supplies, and even volunteers. And the success of the Philhellenic cause was in no small part due to the fervent support of some of the leading romantic writers of the era, Byron and Shelley foremost among them. Byron had gone to Greece in 1810 and subsequently expressed his hope "that Greece might still be free." To this cause he devoted his last years, and he died in Greece in 1824.

Sympathetic to Greek independence though they were, the Philhellenes were thoroughly horrified by the brutality of the Greeks in the Morea revolt. But they were quickly stirred to renew their sympathy by the vicious retaliatory measures taken by the Turks, who on Easter Sunday, 1821, hanged the Greek patriarch in his sacred vestments at Constantinople, and in 1822 massacred most of the hundred thousand Greeks living on the island of Chios, an event commemorated by Delacroix in a famous painting.

Despite popular sympathy for the Greek cause, several years of public

The Massacre at Chios, by Eugène Delacroix.

pressure and protracted negotiations were required before any European government actively intervened. Finally, in 1827, France joined Russia and Britain in signing the Treaty of London, which stated that if Turkey refused to accept an armistice, the three powers might support the Greeks with their naval forces. When Turkey did indeed reject an armistice, in October 1827 a joint force of French, British, and Russian ships bottled up the fleet belonging to the sultan's vassal Mehemet Ali (1769–1849), pasha of Egypt, in the bay of Navarino on the west coast of the Morea. Unable to force either Greeks or Muslims to stop fighting, the allied naval commanders met the Egyptian fleet in a close artillery engagement and almost completely destroyed it. Philhellenes cheered the news of the victory at Navarino. But the conservative governments of Great Britain, France, and Russia were somewhat embarrassed by it, and the duke of Wellington, who had succeeded Canning as prime minister of Great Britain and was much less sympathetic to the Greek cause, apologized to Mahmud II for the action of the allied naval commanders.

A few months later, in April 1828, Tsar Nicholas I, who had come to the throne in 1825, used a hostile statement by the sultan as a pretext for declaring war on Turkey. The tsar was interested not so much in achieving Greek independence as in capitalizing on the weakness of the Ottoman empire to expand Russia's sphere of influence. Confronted by strong Turkish resistance and by objections from the other Great Powers, however, the Russian forces stopped short of Istanbul. In September 1829, Russia imposed on the Ottoman empire the Treaty of Adrianople, which made the provinces of Moldavia and Walachia (present-day Romania) virtually Russian protectorates. The treaty also stipulated that the Ottoman empire must abide by decisions that Russia, France, and Britain reached concerning Greece. The three powers met in London in 1830 to settle the Greek situation. They declared Greece an independent kingdom under their protection, but two years of negotiations were necessary before the boundaries of the new state were definitively settled and a ruler named. The crown of the new kingdom was refused by two German princes before it was finally accepted by Otto, the son of King Ludwig of Bavaria, in February 1832, eleven years after the outbreak of the revolt.

The revolt of the Greeks and their ultimate achievement of independence made a great impression on contemporary Europeans. For this was the first successful breach of the status quo after 1815 and seemed to mark a significant victory for the idea of nationality as well as for the cause of liberalism. That these were not necessarily the motivating concerns of the British, French, and Russian governments is indicated by their decision to name a German-born ruler for the new Greek state, but factionalism among the

Otho of Bavaria arriving in Athens in 1832 to become king of the newly independent Greece.

Greeks would have made it difficult for the guaranteeing powers to find a Greek ruler whom all could support. In any event, European liberals, temporarily disillusioned by the defeat of the revolutions of 1820–1821, derived new hope from the success of the Greeks and the support given their cause by Britain, France, and Russia. Thus the Greek revolt helped keep alive the revolutionary sentiment that would manifest itself again in the popular upheavals of 1830 and 1848.

The "Eastern Question," 1832–1841

The revival of the Eastern Question after the Greek settlement of 1830 illustrates the tenuous character of Anglo-French relations and the degree of flexibility still present in the European Concert. This time the trouble arose out of the conflict between the sultan of Turkey and his vassal Mehemet Ali, viceroy of Egypt, whose aid he had secured during the Greek revolt. As a reward for his support, Mehemet Ali now demanded the cession of Syria, and when the sultan refused, he proceeded in 1832 to send an army, led by his son Ibrahim, into this territory. After a number of victories by Mehemet Ali's forces seemed to threaten the sultan's regime, Russia decided to intervene on behalf of the Ottoman empire and early in 1833 sent a squadron to Istanbul. Alarmed by the threat of Russian domination over Turkey, the French and the British marshaled their fleets in the eastern

Mediterranean and joined Russia in imposing a settlement on the sultan and his vassal. Turkey was saved from collapse, but the sultan was forced to cede Syria to Mehemet Ali. Soon afterward, in July 1833, Russia and Turkey concluded the Treaty of Unkiar-Skelessi for mutual assistance in the event of attack. In a secret clause, Turkey was excused from fulfilling its obligation in return for closing the Dardanelles — the straits that linked the Black Sea to the Mediterranean to all non-Russian vessels of war. When Britain and France discovered the existence of this clause a short time later, they protested the treaty because it gave a favored position to Russian warships in the straits and seemed to leave Turkey at the mercy of Russia. But for the time being, they did nothing.

A second crisis developed when, in 1839–1840, the growing power of Mehemet Ali once again appeared to endanger not only the sultan but also other powers with interests in the eastern Mediterranean. Lord Palmerston, now convinced of the seriousness of the threat from Mehemet Ali and suspicious of Russia's designs on Turkey, decided that Britain should support the sultan more effectively. But France, whose interest in Egypt dated back to the Directory, was sympathetic to Mehemet Ali and encouraged him in his ambitions for an empire in the Near East. The issue came to a head in 1839 when the sultan renewed hostilities by invading Syria. His forces proved no match for those of his enemy; his army was defeated by Ibrahim, and his leading admiral shortly afterward deserted with the fleet to Mehemet Ali. At this crucial point the sultan died, leaving the Ottoman empire in the hands of a young boy, Abdul-Medjid I, who was prepared to yield to his more powerful vassals, Mehemet Ali and Ibrahim.

The crisis brought renewed attempts to revive the Concert. Even before the outbreak of hostilities Palmerston had tried to secure a general guarantee of Turkish integrity from the Great Powers. But he encountered French hostility to the sultan and could get no support from Russia, which was still adhering to the unilateral promise of aid to Turkey made in the Treaty of Unkiar-Skelessi. In September 1839, after the defeat of the sultan's forces, Tsar Nicholas had his representative in London approach Lord Palmerston with a proposal for settlement of the crisis. Palmerston was initially wary of the Russian plan since he suspected that the tsar would attempt to drive a wedge between Britain and France by insisting that France's protégé, Mehemet Ali, back down despite his victories and return his conquests to the Ottoman empire. But he welcomed the tsar's simultaneous offer to abandon the Treaty of Unkiar-Skelessi and substitute a general guarantee of Turkey's integrity.

Accordingly, Palmerston invited the other Great Powers to London to join in a general settlement. Austria and Prussia quickly agreed. But France, now under the premiership of Adolphe Thiers (1797–1877), demurred. Public opinion in France was running strongly in favor of the Egyptian viceroy, and Thiers was convinced that Britain would not act independently of France in the Near East. He was soon proven wrong, for Palmerston was convinced that "for the interests of England, the preservation of the balance of power and the maintenance of peace in Europe" a settlement of the sort proposed had to be reached. Overcoming opposition within his own cabinet by threatening to resign, he forced acceptance of his position, and the four-power Treaty of London was signed in July 1840. Mehemet Ali was offered Egypt as a hereditary possession along with control over southern Syria for the remainder of his life, but he was to relinquish everything else he had conquered from the sultan and return the Turkish fleet. Counting on French support, the Egyptian pasha refused to accept the terms of the treaty and announced that he would stand firm. The result was renewed conflict in the Near East. The British bombarded the Syrian coast and landed troops. But France, despite repeated threats of war with Britain, which kept international tension at a fever pitch for three months, never did join the conflict. Realizing that war with Britain would not be in France's interest, Louis Philippe dismissed Thiers from office in October 1840, and entered into negotiations with the other powers. No longer supported in his intransigent position by France, Mehemet Ali was persuaded to conclude an agreement with the sultan which embodied the provisions of the Treaty of London, except that it did not give him control even over southern Syria. In July 1841, the five Great Powers signed the Straits Convention, which stipulated that the straits, both the Bosporus and the Dardanelles, were to be closed to all foreign warships when Turkey was at peace. France's participation in this agreement signified its return to the Concert of European Powers and the end of the diplomatic crisis.

What was perhaps most interesting about the crisis of 1839–1840 was the diplomatic alignment of powers that were at ideological extremes. The principal antagonists in the crisis were Britain and France, whose political systems were more alike than those of any other two powers. Britain's principal collaborator was Russia, whose absolutist government was anathema to liberals throughout Europe. At the height of the crisis Metternich seems to have suspected Britain and Russia of planning war against France and even considered seceding from the London agreement, drawing Prussia with him and concluding a separate agreement with France. Moreover, it was Metternich who was instrumental in bringing France back into the Concert of Europe by mediating between it and the other powers. Ideological considerations seem, then, to have played a relatively minor role in the relationship among the Great Powers in this crisis, as in others before 1850.

THE PERSISTENCE OF ABSOLUTISM IN RUSSIA

Like Prussia and the Habsburg empire, Russia experienced a sharp turn to the right politically after the conclusion of the Napoleonic wars. Tsar Alexander I, who had begun his reign in 1801 as a proponent of enlightened political reforms, became increasingly fearful of revolutionary movements after 1815. During the final decade of his life, he worked vigilantly to stamp out political dissent not only in Russia but around Europe. Following Alexander's death in 1825, liberal opponents of the regime staged the abortive Decembrist revolt, demanding the establishment of a constitutional monarchy. The rebellion was easily put down, and Alexander's successor Nicholas I brutally suppressed opposition to tsarist control for the next thirty years.

Alexander I and the Decembrist Revolt of 1825

Despite her reputation as an "enlightened" monarch, Catherine the Great (ruler of Russia from 1762 to 1796) never relaxed her control over her subjects. At the beginning of the nineteenth century, Russia was the most autocratic of the European states. Catherine's son Paul I (ruled 1796–1801) recognized no limits on his authority and possessed a strong sense of his position as a divine-right monarch. To a foreign envoy he is supposed to have remarked, "Know that no one in Russia is important except the person who is speaking with me; and that, only while he is speaking." In practice, however, the authority of the tsar had certain limits. One of them resulted simply from the size of the vast empire under his rule; it extended from the Baltic Sea to the Caucasus, from the borders of Poland to the Pacific. With the modes of transportation and communication then in existence, it was impossible for the central government to extend its control into every corner of the realm.

Recognizing the danger to absolutism posed by Western ideas and influences, Paul did his best to isolate Russia, restricting foreign travel by his subjects and forbidding the importation of European, and particularly French, books. He rightly estimated that the greatest threat to his autocratic control came not from the masses — peasants and serfs — but rather from the educated aristocracy, which had been exposed to French culture during the reign of Catherine. And indeed, it was this group that brought his brief, tyrannical reign to an end. In 1801 he was assassinated by a cabal of aristocrats seeking to bring to the throne his twenty-four-year-old son Alexander, whose outlook was known to be much more liberal than his father's.

As we have seen, Tsar Alexander I, who ruled from 1801 to 1825, was an unstable personality, characterized by changing moods and inconsistent actions. Viewed by some as a hypocrite and a traitor to the ideals of his youth, he seems rather to have been genuinely torn between the liberal, humanitarian impulses acquired during his progressive schooling and the more traditional authoritarian policies of his father. His struggle against the armies of Napoleon undoubtedly contributed to his abandonment of liberal projects after 1812. But in 1801 his accession was welcomed by those who hoped for a liberalization of the regime, and they took heart from his immediate relaxation of many of the restrictions Paul had imposed. At the outset, Alexander surrounded himself with an "unofficial committee" of advisers, men of known liberal views such as Frédéric César de La Harpe (his former tutor) and Prince Adam Czartoryski, the Polish patriot who served for a time as foreign minister. The task of this committee was no less than to bring about the regeneration of Russia, and Alexander made it clear to his intimates that the granting of a constitution and the abolition of the institution of serfdom were important parts of his overall program. Despite these laudable intentions, the reforms he did in fact achieve were very limited, partly because be and his advisers failed to appreciate the complexities and practical difficulties involved. The reforms actually carried through were made during two periods of the first half of Alexander's reign, each brought to an end by the renewal of the war against Napoleon.

The most significant reforms of the first period (1801–1805) included changes in the governmental structure, among them the establishment of Western-style ministries, each headed by a minister responsible to the tsar; the founding of six new universities; and an increase in the number of secondary schools. As for Russia's principal social problem, serfdom, no substantial steps toward abolition were undertaken, probably because the tsar and his advisers were reluctant to mount a full-scale attack on the privileges of the landed aristocracy. However, a government decree of 1803 encouraged the voluntary liberation of serfs by their masters under government supervision. Although fewer than fifty thousand male serfs (about 1 percent of the total serf population) were freed during Alexander's reign, this was the first step toward the emancipation in 1861.

The second period of reforms (1807–1812) was dominated by Count Mikhail Speranski (1772–1839), who served as a kind of unofficial prime minister to the tsar during these years. The results were again disappointing to those who expected any significant change in the character of the regime. Instructed to draft a constitution, Speranski prepared a moderate scheme that would have introduced self-government in stages, beginning with electoral assemblies at the local level and culminating with a state assembly at the top. However, his plan did not envisage giving real legislative initiative to the state assembly; the law-making powers were to rest rather with a council of state composed of high dignitaries and presided over by the tsar. The establishment of the council of state was, in fact, the only part of the proposal that was realized. Whatever additional reforms Speranski undertook resulted from his thorough familiarity with Russia's bureaucracy, and tended toward improving the efficiency of its operation.

Even if Napoleon had not invaded Russia in 1812, it is doubtful whether Speranski would have remained in office much longer. For in an effort to meet the serious financial crisis from which the Russian government was suffering, he proposed financial reforms and new taxes that aroused the bitter antagonism of the landed nobility. Branded a "Russian Jacobin" by his opponents, he was suddenly dismissed by Alexander in 1812 and sent into exile. He was later recalled to government service and became a member of the council of state in 1821.

Speranski's dismissal did not result in a sudden reversal of imperial policy. The transition from liberalism to reaction was rather gradual and uneven, reflecting the tsar's erratic and inconsistent behavior. In general, Alexander appeared more liberal abroad and in the outlying parts of his empire than he was at home. The Polish constitution of 1818, for example, was modeled in part on Speranski's proposal, which had been rejected for Russia. In St. Petersburg, however, the nobility of an older generation — some of whom had been associated with Tsar Paul's government — recovered influence, particularly after 1815, and the regime became increasingly repressive. The changed policy was felt especially in the educational system, which served as a kind of barometer of reaction in nineteenth-century Russia. Universities and schools were put under the control of religious bigots who established an elaborate system of surveillance, expelled professors on the slightest pretext, and prohibited study at foreign universities. Censorship regulations were complex, arbitrary, and absurd. The government not only forbade writing on political and constitutional questions but also sought to pass judgment on the alleged morality or immorality of artistic productions. The measure that aroused the most widespread resentment, however, was the establishment in 1816 of military colonies. Their original purpose was to reduce the cost of keeping an army by setting up self-supporting units of soldiers and their families to cultivate the land. But in many areas peasants were put into uniform and subjected, along with their families, to strict military discipline under the command of troops from the regular army. Bitterly resented by the peasants, the military colonies provoked movements of protest and became one of the principal grievances of opponents of the regime.

The mounting reaction of the last decade of Alexander's reign could hardly fail to arouse opposition among members of the educated classes who had placed such high hopes in the young monarch. Numerous influences helped to create this liberal opposition. To the influx of Western ideas during Catherine's reign was added the stimulation of French revolutionary doctrines. During the wars against Napoleon, Russian officers and soldiers, exposed to other European cultures, could not help contrasting the relative freedom of the average western European with the absence of liberty at home. Disappointed by Alexander's failure to provide Russia with a constitution or representative institutions, they were frustrated by their inability to express their criticisms openly. Almost inevitably the opposition was forced to act after 1815 through the secret societies that eventually engineered what has come to be known as the Decembrist Revolt.

From the outset two general tendencies were present in the movement for reform. The more moderate aims eventually found expression in the Northern Union, a group composed primarily of young aristocrats and literary men who sought to establish a constitutional monarchy on the British model. More radical measures were favored by the Southern Union, consisting mainly of impoverished army officers and led by Colonel Paul Pestel, who advocated the assassination of the tsar and the establishment of a highly centralized republican regime patterned after the Jacobin dictatorship of 1793. In some respects Pestel anticipated the Soviet regime. He favored draconian powers for the revolutionary government to prevent counterrevolution. His program of agrarian reform included the abolition of serfdom and state confiscation of all land. Thereafter, the land would be divided into a public and a private sector; every citizen would be guaranteed an allotment within the public sector.

The two societies were not tightly organized or disciplined, and little was done to coordinate their activities. The sudden death of Tsar Alexander I late in 1825 found them ill prepared for the revolt which followed, triggered by the confusion that arose over the succession. Constantine, the brother nearest in age to Alexander, was serving as governor general of Poland and had secretly renounced his claim to the throne in 1823 in favor of the youngest brother, Nicholas. When Alexander died, each proclaimed the other tsar, and a period of uncertainty ensued. Since Nicholas was known to be much more conservative than his older brother, the insurgent leaders of the Northern Union decided to press for the accession of Constantine and in December persuaded two thousand troops of the St. Petersburg garrison to refuse their allegiance to Nicholas. The soldiers marched to the Senate Square shouting "Constantine and Constitution," with many of them apparently under the impression that Constitution was Constantine's wife. Once on the square they were given no further orders, and remained there in the cold all day. It was Nicholas who finally took action, bringing in loyal troops who fired on the mutinous soldiers and killed many of them. Another uprising, by the Southern Union, also failed.

Not only was the Decembrist Revolt of 1825 badly prepared and badly led; it also lacked real popular support. Its only immediate consequence was to intensify the new tsar's antiliberal sentiments. Hundreds of those involved were arrested, and five of the leaders, including Pestel, were summarily tried and executed. Nevertheless it was a significant episode in Russian history, for it marked the first open challenge to Russian autocracy and this challenge came from some of the best-educated men in Russia — young army officers, including some of the elite Grenadier Guard, and representatives of the liberal nobility. Most important of all, it provided a revolutionary legend and a host of martyrs for later groups that sought the overthrow of the tsarist regime.

Russia Under Nicholas I, 1825–1855

Tsar Nicholas I, who assumed the throne during the Decembrist Revolt and ruled Russia until 1855, is traditionally viewed as the most reactionary of Russia's nineteenth-century autocrats. Strongly impressed by the events at the outset of his reign, he was determined to prevent their recurrence. Personally meticulous and conscientious in the performance of his duties, he carried out a prolonged investigation of the origins of the revolt, interrogating prisoners himself in some instances in order to get an idea of the true nature of the opposition. But this activity, which might have led to reform or the elimination of abuses, resulted instead in an intensification of the repressive policies pursued in the later years of Alexander's reign. Indeed, Nicholas developed an almost pathological fear of revolution at home and abroad, leading contemporary liberals to call him the Gendarme of Europe.

Under Nicholas an attempt was made to freeze the social structure of Russia by discouraging or actively preventing members of any but the upper classes from securing an education. The educational system itself was put under even closer surveillance and suffered a further decline in standards. S. S. Uvarov, Nicholas's minister of education for the better part of his reign, formulated the principles to be inculcated by the schools: autocracy (a belief in the unlimited powers of the tsar), orthodoxy (adherence to the official church and the morality for which it stood), and nationalism (devotion to the traditions of "Russian national life").

Nicholas's particular innovation was the concentration of power in His Majesty's Own Chancery, a bureau that had originally been organized to deal with matters requiring the sovereign's personal participation. He expanded the functions of this body and divided it into several sections. One of these, the notorious Third Section, or political police, was given almost unlimited powers of surveillance over every aspect of Russian life, with the duty of arresting and exiling any "suspicious or dangerous persons," of reporting on the state of public opinion, and of keeping a close watch on all foreigners living or traveling in Russia. The tsar particularly distrusted the intelligentsia—largely writers, teachers, and liberal nobles—since many of them had been involved in the secret societies. The system of preliminary censorship (which required approval by the government censor of all written material before publication) was particularly intense after the revolutions of 1830–1831 and the revolutions of 1848, and effectively stifled the discussion of all political or potentially dangerous social questions.

It is tempting to compare the police state of Nicholas I with the totalitarian regimes of the twentieth century, but such a parallel is false and misleading. In the first place, tsarist control was limited by its own inefficiency. When Nicholas broadened his chancery and established the Third Section, he left numerous existing bureaus and administrative units intact; consequently there was extensive overlapping of functions and confusion of jurisdiction. Second, though the elaborate censorship made clear what subjects were forbidden, it did not attempt to prescribe the subjects writers should discuss. The atmosphere of Russia under Nicholas was unquestionably stifling, yet this era paradoxically saw the beginning of Russia's golden age of literature, counting among its luminaries the poets Alexander Pushkin (1799–1837) and Mikhail Lermontov (1814–1841), the novelist and dramatist Nikolai Gogol (1809–1852), and finally the novelists Ivan Turgenev (1818–1883) and Fyodor Dostoevski (1821–1881), some of whose earlier works were published during Nicholas's reign. True, both Turgenev and Dostoevski were arrested in the reaction following the revolutions of 1848, but until then they had been left relatively undisturbed. As long as writers avoided discussion of proscribed subjects and direct criticism of the autocratic regime, they were allowed to publish their works.

Despite these compensating features, which made Nicholas's reign less oppressive than has sometimes been thought, the refusal of the tsar to deal with such basic problems as the discontent of the serfs, the low productivity of the farms, and the backwardness of technology and communications meant that Russia lagged seriously behind the western European nations in economic and social development. Its weaknesses in this respect were illustrated dramatically at the end of Nicholas's reign, when Russia suffered defeat by France and Great Britain in the Crimean War (1854–1856).

CONCLUSION

Despite two successive waves of revolution, in the early 1820s and in 1830–1831, the Restoration was still intact after 1830 and the old order persisted in most of Europe up to 1848. Only in France, Belgium, and Greece had successful revolutions occurred, and in the latter two, the revolutionaries had succeeded because they were supported by certain of the Great Powers. Great Britain, of course, underwent important changes in its institutions, particularly after 1830. Elsewhere in Europe—in Spain and Portugal, in some of the German states, on the Italian peninsula, in Russia and Poland—revolutions had collapsed or been suppressed. Despite the rallying power of liberal ideals and goals, the revolutionaries had proved no match for the regimes they challenged. Against the secret societies composed of disaffected soldiers, liberal nobles, artisans, students, teachers, writers, and adventurers the rulers could usually muster loyal troops, and they could count on the backing of nobility and clergy in the suppression of the revolts. Often a lack of unity among the revolutionaries, along with poor organization and leadership, turned initial victory into defeat.

But the strength of the dissatisfied groups continued to mount after 1830 under the impact of the two most powerful forces of the age: the Industrial Revolution, which was significantly changing Europe's economic and social structure by bringing new classes into existence and weakening old ones; and the legacy of the French Revolution, which continued to inspire opponents of the old regimes with the ideals of liberty, equality, and fraternity.

CHAPTER 6

The Revolutions of 1848

ON JANUARY 12, 1848, the people of Palermo revolted against their ruler, Ferdinand II, since 1830 king of Naples and Sicily. At the moment the uprising attracted little attention; yet it was the first of almost fifty revolutions that occurred within the first four months of 1848, disturbances that rocked France, Austria, Prussia, and almost all of the lesser German and Italian states. By April, 1848, no European ruler appeared to be safe on his or her throne, and Tsar Nicholas I, horrified at the spread of revolution, could write to the English queen, Victoria: "What remains standing in Europe? Great Britain and Russia."[1] Despite differences in language and nationality, in political and economic development, the countries of Europe showed remarkable uniformity in their response to the revolutionary impulse.

Tensions had been mounting throughout the 1830s and 1840s. In France there had been growing resentment of Guizot's manipulation of the electoral machinery, his corruption of the deputies, and his almost total disregard of the distress of the working class. In the German states, bourgeois political activists had long been dissatisfied by continued political division, and the artisans and peasants had been suffering economic deprivation. Within the Habsburg empire and Italy, nationalist aspirations had been continually thwarted. With all this combustible material, only a spark was needed to set off the conflagration. A particularly acute economic crisis helped to precipitate the revolutions. The crisis had its origins in low grain production in Britain and Europe in 1845 and 1846 and in the failure of the potato crop in Ireland in 1845. Harvests in the British Isles improved somewhat in 1847, but in France and Germany they were again bad. Food prices, particularly the price of bread, the staple of the lower classes' diet, rose markedly during

---

[1] Quoted in L. B. Namier, *1848: The Revolution of the Intellectuals* (London, 1946), p. 3.

1847. The crisis in agriculture had repercussions in the world of finance, with bankruptcies and bank closings. In France, where industrial expansion had not been accompanied by a corresponding development of new markets, overproduction in a number of industries led to falling prices for manufactured goods, business failures, and widespread unemployment.

The revolutions of 1848, however, were born of hope as much as of despair. Behind them was a whole range of ideals and aspirations for a better world. So pervasive was the idealism of the revolts that it has been argued that they had a common denominator in a uniform ideological outlook developed during the first half of the nineteenth century. A classic work by Sir Lewis Namier refers to the events of 1848 as "the Revolution of the Intellectuals." Although this characterization effectively captures the striking parallels among the various uprisings of that year, it is important to recognize that these revolutions emerged in diverse social and political contexts and were directed toward widely differing objectives. There was no single revolutionary organization or movement encompassing all of Europe, and although revolutionaries everywhere adopted similar phrases and slogans, the words meant quite different things to different peoples. Moreover, although bourgeois intellectuals indeed played an important role in a number of the revolutions, these events could not have occurred without widespread support from the working classes. Any explanation of the upheavals of 1848 must take into account how new "languages of labor" and new forms of political activism by European workers shaped the various revolutionary movements.[2]

In general, all of the revolutions took much the same course. Though France's February Revolution followed the revolt in Palermo by more than a month, it was this outbreak in Paris that sparked revolts elsewhere in Europe, and the subsequent fate of the revolution in France seemed to foreshadow developments in central Europe. The overthrow of Louis Philippe in February triggered successful revolts during March, first in the Austrian empire, then in many of the lesser German states, and finally in Prussia. During the same period revolts spread northward in the Italian peninsula from Naples and Sicily into Sardinia, Tuscany, the Papal States, and finally the regions directly under Austrian control. In this initial stage the frightened rulers capitulated with practically no resistance to the revolutionary demands, promising their subjects constitutions and representative assemblies and hastily granting the freedoms that had been denied their peoples.

---

[2] See for example William H. Sewell, *Work and Revolution in France: The Language of Labor from the Old Regime to 1848* (Cambridge, 1980); Jonathan Sperber, *Rhineland Radicals: The Democratic Movement and the Revolution of 1848* (Princeton, 1991).

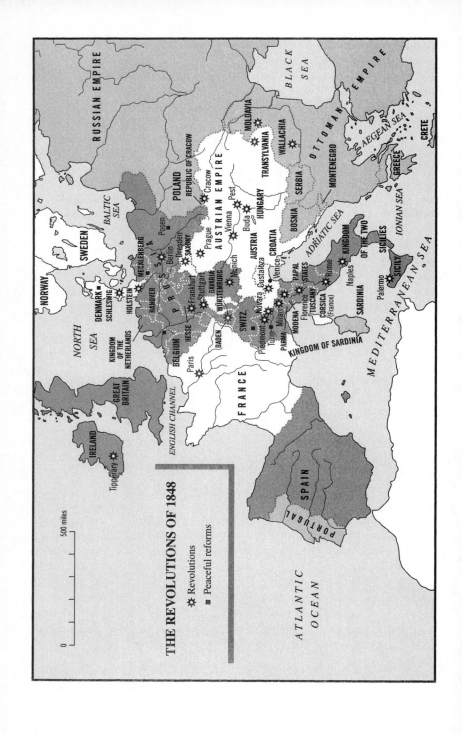

THE REVOLUTIONS OF 1848

✦ Revolutions
■ Peaceful reforms

0 ⊢─────┤ 500 miles

Unlike Louis Philippe, the central European rulers managed to retain their thrones while their more unpopular ministers were dismissed or, like Metternich, forced to flee. For the moment the revolutionaries appeared triumphant.

The turning point in the course of the revolts came during the summer of 1848. In France, an insurrection of disillusioned workers against the new government in June was decisively defeated. The victory of "forces of order" in France encouraged counterrevolutionary forces elsewhere in Europe. In most instances the armies of the central European states had remained loyal to their respective rulers during the revolts, and now they were ordered to attack the revolutionaries, whose ranks were weakened by the divisions that inevitably appeared after their initial successes. In this counterrevolutionary assault the rulers were supported by the land-owning aristocracy and in some states also by elements of the bourgeoisie who, though they had participated on the side of the revolutionaries at the outset, were now alarmed at the possibility of thoroughgoing social revolution.

By December 1848, the revolutionaries had been defeated or were fighting rearguard actions almost everywhere in Europe. The overthrown dynasty was not restored in France, but in December the first presidential election under the new republican constitution resulted in an overwhelming victory for Louis Napoleon Bonaparte, who emerged as a savior and symbol of order for many Frenchmen frightened by the bloodshed and social upheaval that had occurred earlier in the year. Another eight months passed before the Habsburg monarchy, with the aid of Russian troops, suppressed the revolt in Hungary. In the early months of 1849 the Sardinians renewed their struggle against Austria for the liberation of Italian territory, and elsewhere in the peninsula the Roman Republic was proclaimed. But these were short-lived episodes that merely prolonged the revolutionary agony but could not reverse the general trend. By the end of 1849 the counterrevolution was everywhere triumphant. To the bitterly disillusioned revolutionaries it seemed that nothing had been gained. In fact, the situation in many countries appeared worse than it had been before the revolts. Where constitutions had been granted, they were either suspended or rendered ineffectual. Revolutionary leaders were imprisoned or exiled and the freedoms for which they had fought were systematically denied.

Such were the general outlines of this period of upheaval. But a closer look at the separate revolutions is needed, for 1848 proved to be a watershed in the history of nineteenth-century Europe; in the writings and speeches of the 1850s a new atmosphere can be detected, setting this decade off from those that preceded it.

THE FEBRUARY REVOLUTION IN FRANCE

On January 29, 1848, a little more than three weeks before revolution erupted in France, Alexis de Tocqueville, who was a member of the parliamentary opposition, addressed his colleagues in the Chamber of Deputies:

I am told that there is no danger because there are no riots; I am told that, because there is no visible disorder on the surface of society, there is no revolution at hand. Gentlemen, permit me to say that I believe you are mistaken. True, there is no actual disorder; but it has entered deeply into men's minds. See what is preparing itself amongst the working classes, who, I grant, are at present quiet. No doubt they are not disturbed by political passions, properly so called, to the same extent that they have been—but can you not see that their passions, instead of political, have become social? Do you not see that they are gradually forming opinions and ideas which are destined not only to upset this or that law, ministry, or even form of government, but society itself, until it totters upon the foundations on which it rests today? . . . This, gentlemen, is my profound conviction: I believe that we are at this moment sleeping on a volcano. I am profoundly convinced of it. . . . [3]

Tocqueville's speech was greeted with ironical cheers from the majority; no one took seriously his prophecy of catastrophe.

Yet signs of the forthcoming troubles were certainly not lacking. The combination of food shortages, a rising cost of living, and widespread unemployment had led to an increasing number of working-class demonstrations during the winter of 1847–1848. Sometimes sheer hunger was to blame. Yet because the workers were not effectively organized, their demonstrations attracted relatively little attention. The most obvious expressions of opposition to the July Monarchy were banquets to popularize the cause of electoral reform. Political leaders, frustrated in their attempt to effect changes through normal legislative channels and forbidden by law from organizing political rallies, used the device of the dinner meeting to focus opposition to the regime. Participating in these dinners were not only members of the so-called parliamentary opposition, such as Adolphe Thiers, but also men of known republican views. Some seventy banquets were held all over France during the winter, and this campaign was to culminate in a large banquet scheduled for February 22, 1848, in Paris. On the very day of the banquet, Guizot's government banned both the dinner and the procession that was to precede it. This was the episode that precipitated the revolution.

[3] Alexis de Tocqueville, *The Recollections of Alexis de Tocqueville*, translated by Alexander Teixeira de Mattos (London, 1948), pp. 12–13.

February Days in Paris (1848). Revolutionaries, ill equipped with arms.

The revolt lasted only four days. At first the crowds that gathered on the Paris boulevards were dispersed without difficulty. Gradually the movement gathered momentum, as regiments of the bourgeois National Guard joined the opposition. Inhabitants of working-class districts began to tear up the paving stones in the streets in order to erect barricades.

Louis Philippe, now seventy-five, refused to take the first demonstrations seriously. But by February 23 the situation had become so acute that he dismissed the unpopular Guizot and replaced him with an old friend, Count Louis Molé (1781–1855). Guizot's dismissal might have placated the middle-class opposition; it did not satisfy the Parisian working class, which became ever more radical in its demands. By February 24 the situation in the capital was so serious that the king decided to abdicate in favor of his ten-year-old grandson, the count of Paris. But his decision came too late, for the popular forces now controlled most of the city and were approaching the Tuileries, the royal residence. The king escaped through the garden to a waiting carriage, which started him toward exile in England.

A crucial point in the revolution had been reached. The symbol of authority was gone, and the new form of the French government had to be determined. The Chamber of Deputies was still in session, and the king's daughter-in-law, the duchess of Orléans, decided to attempt to have herself proclaimed regent for the count of Paris. When the duchess appeared on the rostrum with the young count and her brother-in-law, the duke of Nemours, the poet-turned-politician Alphonse de Lamartine (1790–1869) was speaking. Some members of a mob had forced their way into the assembly hall and stood menacingly at the rear, behind the deputies. The fate of the royal family rested with Lamartine, who at this point abandoned the dynasty and declared his support of a republic. The crowd responded by swarming over the hall; deputies retreated hastily, and the duchess fled with her son. In this chaos a provisional government was chosen. As Lamartine read aloud the names that had been proposed for the new government, the crowd shouted its acceptance or rejection of each in a kind of impromptu election. When the list was complete the crowd adjourned to the Hôtel de Ville, where revolutionary ritual demanded that the republic be proclaimed.

Those who had been named to the provisional government at the Chamber of Deputies were moderate republicans, men generally sympathetic to the program advocated by the republican newspaper, *Le National*, which had called for electoral reform in the last years of the July Monarchy. When they arrived at the Hôtel de Ville, however, they found a delegation from a more radical republican newspaper, *La Réforme*, which was far more concerned than *Le National* with social issues. Since the radical republican group had named its own provisional government, the two lists had to be combined. To the original moderate republicans, therefore, were added three men supported by the radical faction: the socialist Louis Blanc, a mechanic named Albert, and the astronomer François Arago.

In the moment of victory the moderate and radical republicans had closed ranks and agreed on the provisional government for the Second French Republic. But in the months that followed, the cleavage between the two factions broadened. The moderates were concerned primarily with political questions, such as the nature of representation, qualifications for suffrage, and the working of the electoral system. The radicals, though they did not neglect political issues, talked largely of social reform. They had no well-formulated program — indeed, their proposals were vague and amorphous — but their basic concern was improvement of the condition of the working classes. The history of the first four months of the republic is the history of a growing divergence between the moderate republicans, who had the confidence of the majority of the French, and the radical republicans, who had the support of the Paris working class.

One question that confronted the provisional government immediately, and about which moderates and radicals disagreed, was what to do with the vast numbers of unemployed who were concentrated in Paris and who had contributed to the success of the revolution. One of the few coherent demands of the members of the Paris crowd in the February Revolution had been for recognition of the "right to work"; they expected the new government to provide employment for all who wanted it. Pressed by the Paris crowd for an immediate solution, the provisional government announced the establishment of "National Workshops," on the pattern outlined by the socialist Louis Blanc in his *Organization of Labor*. It would have seemed natural to confide direction of this project to Blanc himself, especially since he was already a member of the new government. But the task of establishing the National Workshops was given to Alexandre Marie, the minister of public works, while Louis Blanc was sidetracked in a newly created "Worker's Commission." Instead of being autonomous cooperative enterprises operated by the workers, as envisioned by Blanc, the National Workshops became in fact vast relief projects in which the unemployed were put to work on hastily contrived road-construction jobs. To complicate matters, the number of unemployed far exceeded the number of jobs the government was able to provide and the surplus laborers were put on what amounted to a dole. Although the moderate republicans in the government may have been sincere in their desire to provide jobs, their decision to entrust the program to Marie, an avowed antisocialist, proved that they had no intention of making the National Workshops the nucleus of a social transformation. Instead, one of their motives was to immobilize the Paris crowd and thus avert the threat of further social revolution. Ironically, this is precisely what they failed to do. The enrollment in the National Workshops jumped from an initial ten thousand in March, to seventy thousand in April, one hundred thousand in May, and an estimated one hundred and twenty thousand in June. Unable to provide employment for such vast numbers, the government discovered it had created a huge army of idle proletarians in Paris ready to support radical leaders and demagogues in further demands on the republic.

The split between moderates and radicals was further widened in a national election held on April 23, to name the National Assembly, which was to draw up a constitution for the republic. In the general state of euphoria immediately following the February Revolution, the provisional government had proclaimed universal male suffrage. By a stroke of a pen the electorate was increased from the two hundred thousand qualified to vote by the end of the July Monarchy to 9 million. How would this vastly expanded electorate vote? The results of the election showed the essentially moderate and even conservative character of the country as a whole, as opposed to the radical complexion of the capital. Out of nine hundred seats, approximately five hundred went to moderate republicans and only one hundred to radicals. Most surprisingly, the remaining three hundred seats were won by avowed monarchists, supporters of either the Legitimist Bourbon dynasty or the recently overthrown Orléanist succession. The elections

La République (1848), by Honoré Daumier. Marianne, the symbol of French liberty, suckles her astonishingly muscular infant boys.

had proved conclusively that the provinces of France were far more conservative than the capital; the French peasantry, alarmed by radical statements that implied a threat to property, had united with the bourgeoisie against the radical republicans and the Paris proletariat. The new five-man executive committee chosen by the National Assembly to replace the provisional government included no representative of the working class. Indeed, Lamartine, the committee's head, was an outspoken opponent of Blanc.

In the face of direct defeat in the elections, the workers of Paris staged a demonstration on May 15 that looked at first like a repetition of the February Revolution. Again the workers overpowered guards and invaded the hall where the assembly was meeting. After listening to harangues by Armand Barbès and Auguste Blanqui, leaders of two revolutionary clubs, they moved to the Hôtel de Ville, where a provisional government was proclaimed. But the established government was better prepared than its predecessor had been in February and used the National Guard and a newly formed mobile guard to clear the assembly hall and reoccupy the Hôtel de Ville. Barbès, Blanqui, and a number of other leaders were imprisoned, and their radical clubs were dissolved. The abortive uprising increased the government's fear of the left and precipitated a decision to dissolve the National Workshops. Anticipating a violent reaction, the government delayed announcing the liquidation of the workshops until reinforcements had been mobilized. On June 22, just four months after the outbreak of the February Revolution, the termination of the National Workshops was proclaimed. The reaction of the Paris workers was immediate and spontaneous. Disillusioned by the government's failure to fulfill its promise of work for all, many workers disobeyed the order to disband and took up arms instead. So began the bloody June Days.

In February workers and members of the lesser bourgeoisie had fought side by side. Now the class lines between them were rigidly drawn. For three days Europe witnessed some of the bloodiest street fighting of the nineteenth century, as the Paris proletariat battled the government forces. A state of martial law was declared in the capital; General Louis Cavaignac (1802–1857), former governor of the French Colony of Algeria, became virtual dictator of Paris. Benefiting from the experiences of 1830 and of February 1848, Cavaignac allowed the fighting to spread before moving in with guns trained on the barricades. At the end of three days, the toll of dead and injured was estimated at ten thousand. And this was not all. Cavaignac used his emergency powers to carry out vigorous reprisals against those suspected of leading the insurrection. Most of the eleven thousand prisoners taken were deported to Algeria. Cavaignac could boast that order had been restored.

The June Days constituted a clear-cut victory for the moderate republicans over the radicals. But it was an expensive victory, for it left great bitterness among the working classes and opened up wounds that took many years to heal. The propertied classes were convinced that they had barely escaped the overthrow of the entire social order; thus, the June Days strengthened what came to be known vaguely as the Red Fear. In the months that followed, conservatives capitalized on this fear by introducing legislation to curb freedom of the press, limit the right of political association, and outlaw secret societies. The reaction to the June Days was also reflected in the constitution of the Second Republic, which was finally completed in November. In providing that the president should be elected by universal male suffrage and that the executive and legislative powers should be separated, the framers of the constitution intended to create a strong executive who could deal effectively with any future proletarian uprisings.

A final effect of the June Days was to strengthen the appeal of one of the candidates for the presidency in the first election, held under the new constitution on December 10, 1848. Charles Louis Napoleon Bonaparte (1808–

1873), the nephew of Napoleon I, had returned from exile in England and entered the lists against candidates whose names were associated with the early months of the Second Republic. These included, in addition to Lamartine and General Cavaignac, Alexandre Auguste Ledru-Rollin (1807–1874), who had been minister of the interior in the provisional government, and François Raspail (1794–1878), who had been active as a republican as early as the Revolution of 1830. Posing as the defender of order, Napoleon's nephew won a landslide victory: 5,500,000 votes compared with the 1,500,000 of his nearest opponent, Cavaignac.

Louis Napoleon had not been taken very seriously by his opponents. In his two personal appearances before the National Assembly his awkward bearing, his German accent, and his halting speech had made him a subject of ridicule. Apparently some monarchists voted for him, as a harmless stopgap who could serve as president until France was ripe for a royalist restoration. Although he had written vaguely socialist tracts during his years of imprisonment and exile, it is doubtful that these views won him many working-class votes. His great appeal unquestionably lay in the magic of his name. In the more than three decades that had elapsed since the defeat of the first Napoleon, the French people had had an opportunity to forget the unpleasant aspects of the Napoleonic regime. The Napoleonic legend had grown particularly during the drab years of the July Monarchy, when Louis Philippe's foreign policy had appeared timorous and inglorious. In contrast, the name Napoleon symbolized an era when France's power had been second to none. But the three years following his election revealed that Louis Napoleon had been greatly underestimated by those who hoped to use him. Like his uncle before him, Louis Napoleon saw himself as the instrument of destiny, and he was determined to make himself the master of France.

THE REVOLUTIONS OF 1848 IN CENTRAL AND EASTERN EUROPE

When news of France's successful February Revolution crossed the Rhine, a wave of popular discontent spread through the states of Germany, beginning in the south and west, then extending into the central areas, and reaching Prussia and the north by the middle of March. Most of the German rulers, frightened by the fate of the French king, capitulated even before the opposition had a chance to organize, and replaced their conservative ministers with men of known liberal views. Many promised constitutions and other reforms, and offered to give their subjects a share in government. These concessions did not eliminate the threat of violence, however, for the causes of the revolutions in Germany were social as well as political. The smoldering bitterness of handicraft workers against the industrialization that had deprived them of a livelihood burst forth in attacks upon machinery and factories. In rural areas the peasants' pent-up resentment of manorial dues and obligations, the hunting and forest privileges of the nobility, and inadequate land allotments found expression in orgies of looting and burning. The first task faced by the new liberal ministers in many states was the suppression of popular disturbances and the restoration of order.

Prussia

Prussia was most seriously affected at the outset, in part because of the irresolute behavior of King Frederick William IV (ruled 1840–1861). The king's accession to the throne had given rise to hopes for constitutional changes and for Prussia's leadership in a movement for national unification, but these hopes proved groundless.

Although the king talked of national unity for the Germans, his nationalism was imbued by a romantic feeling for a common German past, and his conception of political representation had little in common with that of the liberals. Rather, he clung to an idealized medieval view of the state as a structure in which the various estates of the realm were to be grouped under a king whose position derived from divine right. In 1847 Prussian liberals were temporarily encouraged when the king summoned the *Landtag*, or United Diet, which brought together representatives of provincial diets named by the long-established estates. But in his first speech to the diet he showed that he had no intention of relinquishing any real control over legislation or the budget, and the diet was terminated shortly afterward, to the disillusionment of the liberals.

When popular demonstrations broke out in Berlin in the middle of March 1848, the king refused to believe that they were directed against him and ordered his troops not to fire on his "beloved Berliners." Nevertheless he decided that concessions were in order; on March 18 he announced his readiness to participate in the drawing up of an all-German constitution, indicating also that the United Diet would be reconvened. Serious trouble for the government might have been averted had it not been for an episode that occurred later the same day. An apparently good-natured crowd that had gathered outside the royal palace was being dispersed by the cavalry when two shots rang out from an unknown quarter. Within minutes, the crowd had been transformed into an angry mob that engaged the troops in eight hours of bitter street fighting. So disturbed was the king over the violence and loss of life that he yielded to popular demands and ordered the

Barricade and street battle in Berlin, March 18–19, 1848.

departure of the troops from the city. Without armed protection, he was left in Berlin a captive of the aroused citizenry and was subjected to a series of humiliating experiences that he was never to forget. On one occasion he was summoned to the palace balcony with the queen to view the mutilated corpses of those who had died in the street fighting. As each body was thrust toward the monarch, the name of the victim and the manner of his death were intoned.

During this crisis the king issued a proclamation declaring his willingness to assume leadership among the German princes and added that Prussia would "merge itself" into a new German empire. For the moment he was not called on to fulfill this promise. But he did agree to the election by universal male suffrage of an assembly, which met in May to draw up a constitution for Prussia. This constituent assembly, which included a generous representation of liberals and democrats, became increasingly radical in its deliberations during the summer and fall. Meanwhile the king, encouraged by the mounting counterrevolutionary trend elsewhere in Europe, regained his nerve and consolidated the conservative groups around him. In November he was strong enough to order troops back into the capital and to banish the constituent assembly to a nearby town, where it was finally dissolved on December 5.

Curiously enough, the efforts of this body were not entirely without results. In December 1848, Frederick William promulgated a constitution of his own that was quite similar in many respects to the one drafted by the assembly. It included safeguards for the liberties of Prussian subjects and provided for a bicameral legislature whose lower house would be chosen by universal male suffrage though through a system of indirect election. However, in the following year modifications of the electoral system made the provision for universal suffrage almost meaningless. (It should be noted that most liberals in the Prussian revolutionary assembly had opposed the principle of universal suffrage, calling for property qualifications for the franchise. Thus, this provision of the revised constitution was not entirely at odds with the will of many revolutionaries.) The voters were divided into three categories, or classes, according to the amount of taxes they paid, and the votes of the wealthy counted far more heavily than those of the poor. Indeed, two thirds of the delegates to the lower house were chosen by about 15 per cent of the population. In this way the authority of the king and the privileged orders was preserved in the lower as well as in the upper house, whose

Caricature of Frederick William IV firing a cannonball at his "beloved Berliners." In March 1848, the Prussian king expressed a sympathy for the goals of the revolution, but by November of that year he reversed course, ordering the army to banish the constituent assembly from Berlin.

Das Mifsverständnifs

Druck v Verlag v Ed Gus May in Frankfurt *M

members inherited their seats or were appointed to them by the king. Prussia retained this constitution until 1918.

The Frankfurt Parliament

The revolution in Prussia had its counterpart in virtually every one of the thirty-eight German states, including Austria. During 1848 liberals from all over Germany made a concerted attempt to establish a unified nation under liberal auspices. The vehicle for unification was to be the Frankfurt Parliament (sometimes called the Frankfurt Assembly). The failure of this body to unify Germany in 1848 marked a significant defeat for German liberalism and a major turning point in the development of modern Germany.

The origins of the Frankfurt Parliament help, in part, to explain its weakness. It emerged not from any official action by the governments of the German states but from a spontaneous gathering of about fifty German liberals inspired by the March revolts, who met in Heidelberg. They issued invitations to a preliminary parliament (*Vorparlament*); this group, in turn, arranged for elections to be held in each of the German states for delegates to an all-German national parliament. Voting was to be by universal male suffrage, and each delegate was to represent fifty thousand Germans. The elections were duly held, though the electoral laws and methods varied considerably from state to state. When the delegates came together for the first time on May 18, 1848, in the free city of Frankfurt am Main, the event attracted great excitement. The galleries of the old Saint Paul's Church, where the assembly met, were crowded with journalists from all over Europe; the altar was draped with a huge portrait representing "Germania." The spectators and delegates believed that they were witnessing the birth of a new nation.

The professions and social origins of the 830 delegates are of particular interest. The overwhelming majority were university-educated members of the upper bourgeoisie. Among those elected were more than a hundred professors and teachers and numerous lawyers, doctors, ministers, bankers, merchants, and manufacturers. Some of Germany's leading scholars, writers, and publicists were present. Particularly noteworthy was the paucity of statesmen and of men with experience in practical politics, a shortcoming that handicapped the assembly throughout its brief history: far too much time was spent in arguments over theoretical or doctrinaire issues, while practical problems tended to be neglected.

The assembly was also hampered from the start by the conflicting aims of its members. With no established political parties to marshal a consensus on particular issues, it was extremely difficult for the assembly to take any concerted action. The delegates did all agree that their goal was a unified German nation. But they disagreed on the form of government—whether

German National Assembly, Frankfurt am Main, 1848. Contemporary wood engraving. The procession moves into Paulskirche (St. Paul's Church) for the opening of the Frankfurt Parliament on May 18, 1848.

it should be a federation or a unitary state, a monarchy, an empire, or a republic — and on who, if a monarchical or imperial regime was selected, would be the German ruler. They disagreed, furthermore, on what the boundaries of the new state should be; indeed, this proved to be a particularly divisive issue.

Perhaps the most serious weakness of the Frankfurt Parliament was its anomalous position in regard to existing German governments and their princes. For the assembly did not conceive of its purpose as merely the drafting of a constitution for a united Germany but claimed to be a government speaking and acting for the German people as a whole. Yet its relationship to the rulers and governments of the German states was undefined, and these did not accept its leadership. The diet of the old German Confederation, for example, continued to meet for several weeks after the formation of the Frankfurt Parliament. At the root of this general question of sovereignty was the fact that the Frankfurt Parliament had no armed forces at its disposal. The armies of the individual states were left intact. When it became necessary for the assembly to use force — as, for example, when it declared war on Denmark in response to the appeal of German-speaking inhabitants of the territories of Schleswig and Holstein for protection against the Danes — Frankfurt had to call on Prussia to supply the necessary troops. The lack of a consolidated armed force under its control also hampered the new German government's dealings with foreign powers. Nevertheless the assembly did attempt to pursue an independent foreign policy, to the annoyance of the Prussian and Austrian governments, which maintained their own foreign offices and diplomatic relations.

There were other fundamental weaknesses. In their excitement and enthusiasm over the prospect of founding a new nation, the delegates to the Frankfurt Parliament failed to take into account the power relationships in Germany. With Austria and Prussia the strongest states, no enduring nation could be founded without the approval and support of at least one of these. Misled by the temporary weakness of the Prussian and Austrian governments after the March revolts, the delegates assumed that the two rulers would follow Frankfurt's lead and permit their states to be absorbed into a new German nation. They were wrong. In the end, neither government was willing to merge with the new nation, and neither ruler was willing to accept its leadership.

The delegates considered the drafting of a constitution for the new Germany their principal task, and because so many of them were scholars, professors, and lawyers, they threw themselves into this project with great enthusiasm. Members of the committee writing the constitution spent six months constructing a statement of the "Fundamental Rights of the German People." Drawing on the French Declaration of the Rights of Man and the Citizen, the American Declaration of Independence, and other similar documents, they incorporated into their statement the major principles of mid-nineteenth-century liberal philosophy. The result became a part of the constitution completed in March 1849, which guaranteed the basic liberties of speech, assembly, and the press; it was particularly advanced in its provisions for public education and religious toleration. But by the time the deliberations were over and the draft was completed, circumstances in Germany had changed so significantly that there was little chance for its acceptance.

One issue divided the members of the assembly and prevented them from concluding their task sooner—the question of the boundaries of the new state. One group of delegates favored what came to be known as the *Kleindeutsch* ("Little German") solution: the inclusion in the new Germany only of Prussia and the lesser German states. Another group of delegates favored the *Grossdeutsch* ("Big German") solution: the incorporation into the new state, in addition to the territories just named, of the German provinces of Austria (including Bohemia, with its large Slavic population). A compromise was reached in October 1848: all German territory would be joined in the new nation, but any state with non-German possessions (that is, Austria) would be accepted as part of the new Germany only by abandoning its non-German possessions or by holding them exclusively through a personal union in the crown. This condition meant that Austria could not join the German nation unless the emperor abandoned his Hungarian territories as an integral part of his empire. Such a possibility was remote, and Francis Joseph I (ruled 1848–1916) indicated his opposition to this solution early in March 1849 by promulgating a new constitution that reaffirmed the unity and integrity of the Habsburg empire and thus precluded any possibility of the inclusion of Austrian territory in the new Germany. The *Kleindeutsch* faction appeared to have won out, and the Frankfurt Parliament voted not long afterward to offer the crown of the "emperor of the Germans" to the king of Prussia. At first Frederick William IV refused to give a direct reply to the offer, on the grounds that he needed the consent of the princes of the lesser German states. But when twenty-eight princes indicated their willingness to accept the constitution, the king rejected the offer outright and ordered the Prussian delegates to quit the Frankfurt Parliament. He refused to accept what he had earlier termed a "crown picked up from the gutter," like that worn by Louis Philippe.

Austria, too, withdrew its delegates, and a number of lesser states followed. There remained only a "rump" parliament of radicals; these subsequently moved to Stuttgart, in Württemberg, whence they issued appeals to the German people and tried to foment new uprisings. Revolts did occur in a few of the lesser states of Germany in May 1849, but they were quickly suppressed — in some instances with the support of Prussian troops. The remaining members of the Frankfurt Parliament finally dispersed ignominiously in June 1849.

Thus ended the attempt of the liberals to establish a united Germany. Had the nation been unified under liberal auspices in 1848 rather than under Prussian leadership, by Bismarck, in the 1860s, the subsequent history of Germany might have been different. It is often argued that instead of becoming an aggressively nationalistic and militaristic state, Germany would then have joined the company of peace-loving nations. But how peace loving were German liberals? An examination of the deliberations and actions of the Frankfurt Parliament with respect to other nationalities and national groups shows that these liberals were far from tolerant and peace-loving; on the contrary, their speeches reveal exactly the strain of aggressiveness and contempt for other nationalities that recurred in the declarations of succeeding German statesmen.

A case in point involves the attitude of the assembly members toward the Polish minority in the eastern provinces of Prussia. Though no full-scale revolution occurred in Polish-speaking Europe in 1848, this region did experience the so-called Springtime of Nations, which involved the formation of Polish National committees and limited popular uprisings against local Prussian and Austrian bureaucrats. This popular activism was centered first in the Prussian province of Posen, during the spring and early summer of 1848; and subsequently in the Austrian province of Galicia. In neither province did these movements meet with success.

Before 1848 German liberals, like other European liberals, were sympathetic to Polish aspirations for an independent state. As late as April 1848, in the *Vorparlament*, they talked of a restored Poland with the boundaries of 1772. But when put to the test, these German liberals reversed their stand. The Poles living in the Prussian province of Posen (where they outnumbered Germans eight to five) became restive after the king made some vague promises. They began to demand the autonomy or independence of Posen as a preliminary to the restoration of an independent Poland. A Polish National Committee was set up, but Polish peasants became impatient and rose up against Prussian officials administering the region. When the Prussian government responded by sending in troops, the Poles appealed to the Frankfurt Parliament for support. In the ensuing full-scale debate during July 1848, one speaker after another denounced the Polish pretensions and supported Prussian suppression of the revolt. The overwhelming majority of the assembly renounced their earlier sympathy for Polish nationalism because it now appeared to conflict with German national aims. If the eastern provinces of Prussia (such as Posen) were abandoned to the Poles, they would be lost forever to the new German nation. Some of those most emphatic in their speeches were precisely the liberals who had a few months earlier spoken in favor of Polish independence. To justify their position some argued that the Poles had shown themselves unable to maintain their existence as an independent nation and therefore deserved to be subjected to the rule of another people. One delegate declared that Germany's right to dominate the Poles was "the right of the stronger, the right of conquest." Only a small minority of extreme left-wing deputies held out; the Frankfurt Parliament voted 342 to 31 to support Prussian suppression of the Polish bid for independence.

This was not an isolated episode. Another test of German liberalism developed with respect to the Austrian empire. Because of the large German-speaking population in Bohemia, the Frankfurt Parliament considered its inclusion in the new German state. But the even larger Czech population in Bohemia not unnaturally objected to this proposal and talked of a closer union with other Slavic peoples. Where Czech nationalism conflicted with German nationalist goals, most Frankfurt delegates were willing to sacrifice Czech aspirations.

It is impossible to say what kind of Germany the liberals might have established had the Frankfurt Parliament succeeded. But evidence suggests that in 1848 German liberals were no less nationalistic than other Germans. The fact that many liberals rallied to Bismarck during the 1860s, when it became clear that he was achieving the unification of Germany, seems to confirm this judgment.

The Habsburg Empire

Metternich's attempt to stem the tide of change by insulating Austria from the rest of Europe became increasingly difficult during the 1840s. Though the Habsburg empire lagged behind Prussia and some of the other German states in economic development, its chief cities — Vienna, Prague, and Budapest — did not remain immune to industrialization, with its consequent pattern of social change. In the large cities a growing bourgeois class became restive under the backward economic policies of Metternich's government and impatient with the intrusion of the bureaucracy into its business affairs. The small urban proletariat was subject to the same hardships and uncertainties that plagued the working classes elsewhere. Handicraft workers, resentful of the introduction of machines that deprived them of employment, were particularly discontented. The peasants, the overwhelming mass of the population, showed increasing annoyance with the *robota*, a provision which obligated them to perform a stipulated number of days of forced labor for their landlords. When a revolt broke out in Galicia in 1846, the imperial government had to promise to abolish the *robota* in this region, thereby provoking demands during the revolutions of 1848 for its abolition in other parts of the empire.

Subversive political ideas managed to seep into the Austrian empire despite Metternich's strict censorship. Books and pamphlets, smuggled into Bohemia, found their way to universities throughout the empire, which became centers of opposition to the regime. Students exposed to the egalitarian ideas of Rousseau and to the constitutional studies of the German writer Friedrich Dahlmann (1785–1860) envisaged a greater measure of political freedom for Austrians.

Perhaps the greatest threat to the regime, however, lay in the growing nationalist aspirations of the various peoples of the empire. More than one movement which at the outset had been purely cultural, emphasizing the revival of a national language or literature, had by the 1840s become political, its aim being greater autonomy for a particular national group within the empire. The most noteworthy was the Magyar, or Hungarian, national revival. During the 1840s, under the leadership of Louis Kossuth (1802–1894), a dynamic journalist and orator, Hungarian nationalists demanded the complete autonomy of Hungary and the establishment of a Hungarian national parliament. In 1844 the Hungarian Diet, consisting of representatives of the semifeudal Magyar nobility, abolished Latin as its official language and decreed that Magyar would henceforth be used in all government transactions and in the schools. Similar nationalist revivals occurred among the Czechs of Bohemia, the Croatians on the Adriatic, and the Romanians of Transylvania, in the eastern region of the empire.

News of the February Revolution in France was the spark dropped into this combustible mass of grievances — social, political, and nationalist. Revolts broke out in the major cities of the empire. In Budapest, Kossuth addressed the Hungarian Diet, denouncing the Metternichian system and calling for a constitution for the empire granting responsible government to Hungary. In Vienna, students drew up a petition to the emperor requesting freedom of speech and the abolition of censorship. When news of Kossuth's speech arrived from Budapest they added, as an afterthought, the demand for a constitution. Despite the relative mildness of their demands the students feared the government's reaction to their petition and therefore enlisted the support of Viennese workers for their demonstrations. On March 13 a clash between the crowd and troops resulted in bloodshed. Fearing further loss of life, Emperor Ferdinand I, like Frederick William IV of Prus-

Caricature of a frightened Metternich fleeing Vienna in March 1848. Above the crowd of citizens at the left is a banner that reads, "Long live the Constitution!"

sia, called off the troops and announced his consent to the demands, including the demand for the convocation of a constituent assembly. On the same day the aged Metternich resigned, after more than half a century of service to the Habsburgs; he left Vienna by common cab and made his way into exile in London. His departure symbolized the end of an era.

From this point on it is difficult to follow events in detail. In Italy, as we shall see, outbreaks in the Austrian territories of Lombardy and Venetia led to an attempt at a war of liberation from the empire. The revolts occurred in several parts of the empire, pursuing a more or less independent course in each. In Budapest the Hungarian Diet moved boldly; it adopted the March Laws, which left Hungary almost independent, joined to the rest of the empire only through allegiance to the emperor. Hungary was to have a regular parliament in place of the Diet, and its own army, budget, and foreign policy. In deference to the peasantry, the forced labor obligations of the *robota* were abolished. Though asserting their own autonomy, the Magyars were unwilling to grant it to their subject nationalities. Both Transylvania and Croatia were absorbed into the Hungarian kingdom and their diets were abolished. Ferdinand I, on the defensive throughout the empire, had no alternative for the moment but to accept the new status of his Hungarian possessions.

Prague, the capital of Bohemia and the center of Czech national aspirations, was also the seat of a revolt in March. The initial demands of the revolutionaries were relatively modest; only after the Magyar Diet had passed its March Laws did the Czechs decide to demand their own constitution and virtual autonomy. The imperial government responded with a promise to convoke a constituent assembly and granted the equality of the Czech and German languages in Bohemia. In June the first Pan-Slav Congress assembled in Prague. This body was dominated by Czechs who hoped to demonstrate their solidarity against a proposal of the Frankfurt Parliament to incorporate Bohemia into the new German national state. Though they clearly opposed union with Germany, the Czechs had few specific proposals. They appeared to favor the transformation of the Austrian empire into a federation of nationalities in which the Slavs would have an honorable place along with other national groups. Yet neither the preferences of the Pan-Slav Congress nor the demands of the Czechs for a responsible government of their own received further consideration from the imperial government. A new radical demonstration during June gave General Alfred Windischgrätz (1787–1862), at that time military commander in Prague, a pretext for bringing in reinforcements and ruthlessly suppressing the Czech revolutionary movement. The Pan-Slav Congress was dissolved and Prague was put under a military dictatorship. The seizure of Prague was, in fact, the first victory of the counterrevolutionary forces in the Austrian empire and strengthened the determination of the imperial government to proceed against the revolution elsewhere.

Despite the revolt in March, in Vienna there was at first no radical change in the character of the regime. Though the emperor had permitted the establishment there of a national guard composed of civilians and an Academic Legion representing university students, the government remained in the hands of conservative statesmen. Ignoring the emperor's promise to call a constituent assembly, the imperial government in April simply promulgated a new constitution. But this document was not liberal enough to satisfy the radical elements in the capital. When, in addition, the government attempted to disband the national guard and dissolve the Academic Legion, there was a second uprising, in May, by students, workers, and the national guard. The emperor and his family were forced to flee the capital and took refuge at Innsbruck. The government now agreed to convoke a constituent assembly. This body met in Vienna in July and set to work on a constitution, which turned out to be far more democratic than the one issued in April. One lasting accomplishment of the assembly, achieved in September, was the abolition of the *robota* in all parts of the empire where this reform had not previously been undertaken. On the surface the revolution seemed to have triumphed in Austria.

But the actual situation was not so clear cut. From May to October, Vienna remained in the hands of the revolutionaries, and the assembly worked at giving constitutional embodiment to the gains of the revolution. But the dynasty had not been overthrown and the army remained loyal to it. While pretending to play along with the constituent assembly, the emperor — or rather the court party, composed of conservative statesmen and military leaders — encouraged General Windischgrätz to drill his troops in preparation for the recapture of the capital and the suppression of the revolution. In October he had the opportunity to strike. The Viennese radicals, learning that the court party was moving against the Hungarian revolutionary movement, staged a third insurrection, in the course of which they seized the unpopular minister of war and beat him to death in the streets. Windischgrätz used this act of violence as a pretext for treating Vienna as he had treated Prague. He bombarded the city with artillery and by the end of the month had occupied it. Many of the radical leaders were executed on the spot. The constituent assembly was exiled to the Moravian town of Kremsier. To all intents and purposes the revolution in Vienna had been defeated by October 1848.

Among the adherents to the counterrevolutionary cause in Austria the conviction had grown during 1848 that it was essential to secure the abdication of the feebleminded Emperor Ferdinand I if the power of the Habsburgs was to be restored. After the October revolt, Prince Felix zu Schwarzenberg (1800–1852), the new principal leader of the government, succeeded in convincing the emperor to yield the throne to his eighteen-year-old nephew. Assuming the crown in December, 1848, Francis Joseph I ruled Austria for sixty-eight years until his death during the First World War. The young emperor was unhampered by the promises Ferdinand had made to the revolutionaries. With Schwarzenberg, who remained as the chief minister, he was determined to restore the power of the imperial house. They did not immediately feel strong enough to dismiss the constituent assembly meeting at Kremsier, but allowed it to complete its deliberations before dissolving it in March 1849. However, Schwarzenberg rejected the constitution drawn up by this body, which would have established a decentralized, federal government, and instead issued his own. Like Frederick William's constitution in Prussia, this document contained liberal features, such as a diet of elected representatives and a responsible ministry, but having issued it, Schwarzenberg announced that it would come into operation only when the "provisional emergency" confronting Austria had ended. Meanwhile he governed the country autocratically. Schwarzenberg also put an end for the time being to the aspirations of non-German nationalities for greater autonomy by establishing a highly centralized administrative system.

Of the outbreaks in the Habsburg empire one last still smoldered — the Hungarian revolt. Efforts to suppress this revolt had begun before Francis Joseph came to the throne in December. The way in which the counter-revolutionary court party handled this problem is particularly complex. At first they merely gave unofficial encouragement to the Croatians, a dissident south Slavic people living under Magyar rule, when they revolted against the new Hungarian regime and sought autonomy from it. But by the end of 1848, the government at Vienna had decided on an all-out effort to suppress the Hungarian revolutionary movement and ordered an invasion of Hungary by imperial troops. The invaders were no match for the Hungarian defenders, who under Kossuth's leadership drove them out of the country. Had the suppression of the Magyar revolt been left exclusively to the Austrian armies, Hungary might have emerged an independent state in 1849. In April, the Hungarian parliament proclaimed a Hungarian republic, ending the tie with the Habsburgs, and made Kossuth president. At this juncture, however, Tsar Nicholas I of Russia, always the enemy of revolutionary movements and fearful that the success of the Hungarian movement might set off a revolt in Poland, offered military assistance to the Austrian emperor. A joint invasion of Hungary by Austrian troops from the west and one hundred forty thousand Russian troops from the north took place in June 1849. The Hungarians, commanded by General Arthur von Görgey (1818–1916), resisted fiercely, but weakened by further revolts of national minorities at home, they surrendered in August. Despite promises by the Austrian general, Baron Julius von Haynau (1786–1853), of clemency for the defenders, the victors wreaked a bloody vengeance, flogging, hanging, and shooting their victims. Kossuth managed to escape to Turkey and eventually reached the United States, where he made a prolonged speaking tour in an effort to raise money for Hungary's liberation.

The defeat of the Hungarians marked the end of the revolutions of 1848–1849 in the Austrian empire. Hungary, along with the rest of the empire, lost all semblance of autonomy and was thenceforth controlled absolutely from Vienna. Despite the provisions for a responsible ministry and a representative diet in the constitution promulgated by Schwarzenberg in 1849, Austria was thereafter ruled just as autocratically and a good deal more efficiently than under Metternich. In the end, the revolutions of 1848–1849 brought no improvement in the situation of the various nationalities within the empire, and in fact, sharpened the tensions among them. One of the few lasting results of the revolutions was the abolition of the *robota*; this benefited the peasantry, but it may also be one explanation for the failure of the uprisings. For once the peasants had secured this concession they were no longer interested in the fate of the revolutions, which faltered without the support of the masses and could ultimately be suppressed by the emperor.

THE REVOLUTIONS OF 1848 IN ITALY

The events of 1848–1849 in Italy fell into three phases: first, the separate revolts that took place in many of the states and in the territories under Austrian rule; second, the war for Italian independence from Austrian domination, led by King Charles Albert of Sardinia; and third, the short-lived attempt by Mazzini and others to establish the Roman Republic. As elsewhere in Europe, all the revolutions in Italy apparently ended in failure; yet in fact they marked a significant step forward in the process of Italian unification, for through them the revolutionaries learned certain important lessons.

The series of revolts began with the January uprising in Sicily. Ferdinand II, king of Naples and Sicily, the first ruler in Europe affected by a revolution in 1848, granted a constitution to his people much like the French Charter of 1830. From the southernmost state in Italy the revolts spread northward. Grand Duke Leopold of Tuscany (1797–1870) was the next to yield to the demands of his people for a constitution. In Sardinia, the moderates, including Count Cavour, prevailed on Charles Albert to promulgate the constitution known as the *Statuto*, which a decade later became the basis for the constitution of the unified kingdom of Italy. Pope Pius IX, who had already given some evidence of liberal tendencies, followed suit by granting a constitution to the Papal States, though he took care to reserve to the pope and the College of Cardinals the power to veto the acts of an elective council of deputies. Finally, the revolts spread into Lombardy and Venetia, the regions directly under Austrian rule. In January, the chief city of Lombardy, Milan, had experienced riots directed against an unpopular tax on tobacco. In March, the news of the revolt in Vienna and the flight of Metternich precipitated in Milan what came to be known as the Five Glorious Days (March 18–22), an outbreak of fierce street fighting that forced the Austrian general, Joseph Radetzky (1766–1858), to abandon Lombardy. At about the same time a republic was declared in Venice after a short uprising; its first president was Daniele Manin (1804–1857), a political prisoner released by Austrian authorities on the outbreak of the revolt there. By the latter part of March, then, each of the major Italian states had experienced a significant political crisis, though only in Milan had serious fighting occurred.

The spirit and courage shown by the Milanese inspired the liberals and moderates of Sardinia to call for an Italian war of liberation from Austrian domination. King Charles Albert, far from enthusiastic about allying himself with the revolutionary cause, was nevertheless persuaded by his advisers to assume leadership and accordingly invaded Lombardy on March 22. At the same time, he appealed for the support of all the other Italian rulers in ridding the peninsula of the hated Austrians. So great was the enthusiasm for the national cause at the outset that even Ferdinand of Naples felt obligated to supply a contingent of troops to the Sardinians, and what was more surprising, a force from the Papal States joined briefly in the war for independence, although it was withdrawn almost immediately in the face of Austrian protests. Despite his enthusiasm for the cause of Italian unity, Pius IX, as spiritual leader of Catholics throughout the world, could hardly undertake a war against Catholic Austria. The Italian forces led by Sardinia fought against heavy odds. Although enthusiastic and patriotic, they suffered from a lack of discipline, and before long dissension developed between the moderate Sardinians, whose goal was a constitutional monarchy under Charles Albert, and the republican forces that had joined them. The newly established Venetian republic had no intention of dissolving itself in order to submit to the rule of Sardinia. By May, the contingent from Naples had been withdrawn; a counterrevolution had restored absolute control there to Ferdinand. Though Charles Albert's armies won some important victories, in the last analysis they were no match for the better-disciplined armies of General Radetzky. By July 1848, Radetzky had consolidated his forces, and he inflicted an overwhelming defeat on the Sardinians at Custoza. Within ten days he had driven them from Austrian territory and imposed an armistice by which Charles Albert agreed to abandon any claim to Lombardy. A brief epilogue occurred the following spring when Charles Albert, charging the Austrians with having violated the terms of the armistice, once again attacked, but he suffered a decisive defeat at the battle of Novara in March 1849. The Austrian government was now free to complete the counterrevolution in territories under its control. Last to succumb was the Venetian republic, which yielded in August 1849, after heroically resisting a five-week siege.

The most radical event during the Italian revolutions was unquestionably the establishment of the Roman Republic in February 1849. Despite Pope Pius IX's initial concessions, radical elements in Rome became increasingly dissatisfied with his regime and particularly with the prime minister, Count Pellegrino Rossi, appointed in September 1848. In November a fanatical democrat assassinated Rossi and Pius fled Rome, taking refuge in Naples. With the pope gone, the Romans elected a constituent assembly that met in February 1849, proclaimed the overthrow of the pope as temporal ruler, and established the Roman Republic. Although the revolutionaries controlled only Rome and its immediate environs, the Roman Republic was to be the nucleus of a unified Italian state. Giuseppe Mazzini was summoned to head a triumvirate which would rule the new republic. This was the fulfillment of his lifelong dream; Mazzini issued decrees calling for the confiscation of church lands for distribution to the peasantry, public housing for the poor, and other humanitarian measures. But from the first the government was beset by serious inflation and appeared unable to solve its economic difficulties. Even if foreign intervention had not ended the Roman Republic, it would probably have collapsed in a matter of months.

Intervention on behalf of the pope came, surprisingly enough, not from a conservative central European state, but from the Second French Republic of Louis Napoleon. Leading the French assembly to believe that the move was being undertaken to forestall Austrian ambitions in Italy, Louis Napoleon secured approval for an expeditionary force. His real motive seems to have been a desire to win the support of French Catholics for his regime. In any case, he underestimated the difficulties of the enterprise and the strength of feeling in Rome for the republic; French forces attacking Rome met fierce resistance. Defenders of the city had been hastily organized by Giuseppe Garibaldi (1807–1882), whose exploits at this time won him a reputation throughout Europe. Unquestionably the most colorful figure of the Risorgimento, Garibaldi had been forced into exile in 1834 for his role in a plot against the government of Sardinia. With a price on his head he had fled to South America, where he fought for revolutionary movements in Brazil and Uruguay. Garibaldi, the son of a sailor, consciously identified himself throughout his life with the cause of oppressed peoples everywhere, but his highest dream remained the establishment of a unified Italian republic. When he returned to Italy during the revolutions of 1848, his countrymen found him a striking figure with his long blond hair, somewhat rough manner, and the distinctive red shirt that he and his followers adopted as part of their uniform. After leading a volunteer legion in Charles Albert's unsuccessful war against Austria, Garibaldi rallied to the Roman Republic.

Despite their initial successes, Garibaldi's ill-equipped and ill-trained forces were in the long run no match for the more numerous and better-disciplined French armies. In July 1849, after an existence of only five months, the Roman Republic capitulated. Garibaldi led his band in a heroic retreat across the Italian peninsula. Most of his followers died or were captured, but he ultimately escaped to the United States, where he remained until he could return to Italy in the 1850s to help complete Italian unification. After the collapse of the Roman Republic the pope returned to Rome under the protection of a French garrison, which Louis Napoleon maintained there until 1870.

By the end of the summer of 1849 the revolutionary movement appeared to have been defeated everywhere in the Italian peninsula. Only in Sardinia a moderate regime remained. There Charles Albert, after his second defeat by the Austrians at Novara in March 1849, had abdicated in favor of his son Victor Emmanuel II and retired to a Portuguese monastery. The new young monarch succeeded in winning less harsh terms than had been expected from the Austrian empire, including permission to retain the constitution granted by his father the year before.

Despite the apparent failure of the revolutionaries in most of Italy, the events of 1848–1849 provided at least three valuable lessons for patriots striving for Italian unification. First, this unification could not be accomplished under papal leadership, as those in the Neo-Guelph movement had hoped before 1848. The pope's withdrawal of his troops from the Italian army of liberation just after the initial attack on the Austrian forces discredited him as a potential leader of a unified Italy, though his defenders might argue that he had had no alternative because of his position as spiritual leader of the Catholic world. If the Neo-Guelph cause suffered in 1848, the chances of Sardinian leadership in the unification of Italy certainly improved. Here was the second important lesson of the events of 1848–1849. The Sardinians had resisted Austria, and the new king, Victor Emamanuel II, in refusing to renounce the liberal constitution of 1848 as Radetzky demanded, further enhanced the prestige of Sardinia among liberals everywhere in Italy. But the final, and perhaps most important, lesson learned in 1848 was this: Italians alone could not eject the Austrians from Italy. Though the Austrian armies had retreated initially in 1848 and the Austrians had made certain concessions, their power in Italy had never been destroyed. Among those who recognized that foreign help would be necessary was Count Cavour, who in 1851 became the prime minister of Sardinia. Convinced that Sardinia alone was not up to the task, he made his principal diplomatic goal in the 1850s the acquisition of allies for the war against Austria that he considered essential for the unification of Italy under Sardinia's rule.

CONSEQUENCES OF THE REVOLUTIONS OF 1848

Not long after the failure of the revolutions of 1848, the French anarchist Pierre Joseph Proudhon (1809–1865) wrote, "[W]e have been beaten and humiliated . . . scattered, imprisoned, disarmed and gagged. The fate of European democracy has slipped from our hands." Most of the revolutionaries throughout Europe must have reacted in this way. Begun with such high hopes, the uprisings produced results that were indeed disappointing. Almost without exception the rulers who were challenged in 1848 managed to reassert their authority by 1849. Where constitutions had been granted, they were withdrawn or replaced by documents which denied the very principles for which the revolutionaries had struggled. The revolutions appeared to have been fought in vain; yet they were certainly not without their consequences, both immediate and long range. In the judgment of one historian, the revolutions "crystallized ideas and projected the pattern of things to come."[4]

The long-term impact of the revolutions was to be felt for at least the next fifty years. The experience of 1848–1849 certainly crystallized and focused the urge toward national unity that was already present during the first half of the nineteenth century. Whether the revolutions provided a comparable impetus to the ultimate achievement of liberal goals is more debatable. The dissolution of elected assemblies, as in Prussia and Austria, the rejection by the monarchs of the constitutions drafted by these bodies, and the suppression of individual freedoms that characterized the postrevolutionary era suggest that the defeat of liberalism was nearly total. But the revolutionaries set precedents for subsequent generations of European liberals and democrats. And certain institutions managed to survive the conservative reaction of

[4] Lewis B. Namier, *Avenues of History* (London, 1952), p. 55.

1849—for example, universal male suffrage in France. Louis Napoleon came to power in France by means of universal suffrage, and no subsequent regime there has attempted to dispense with it. The principle, once established in France, became the goal of democrats and radicals throughout Europe. Indeed, the trust put in universal suffrage after the mid-century revolutions corresponds to the faith put in constitutions during the first half of the nineteenth century.

Perhaps the most unequivocal consequence of the failure of the revolutions of 1848 was the destruction of working-class hopes and illusions. With their leaders dead, in hiding, or in exile, the workers did indeed appear "beaten and humiliated . . . scattered, imprisoned, disarmed and gagged." But even here the revolts served an important function: they foreshadowed a significant change in the character of European socialism and the working-class movement by creating a strong sense of class consciousness among the proletariat. Karl Marx, writing of the revolt in France, declared, "The February republic finally brought the rule of the bourgeoisie clearly into prominence, since it struck off the crown behind which Capital kept itself concealed."[5] Perhaps Marx exaggerated, but events such as the June Days in France and the brutal suppression of the Vienna insurrection in October could not help sharpening the class consciousness of European workers. Up to 1848 they had more often than not been allied with the middle class against the old order, and they fought on the same side of the barricades in many places during the initial phases of the uprisings. But as the revolts progressed, the bourgeoisie, increasingly concerned over the extremism of the mob and the alleged threat to private property, tended to line up with the old order or at least with those intent on suppressing the threat of a thoroughgoing social revolution. In time, the bitterness and class antagonisms created by the events of 1848 declined, but the possibilities for genuine collaboration between capitalist and proletarian, employer and employee, were never quite the same. It is significant that the First International Workingmen's Association, dedicated to the overthrow of the bourgeoisie, came into being in 1864, a mere decade and a half after 1848.

Finally, a less tangible but no less important consequence of the revolts was the change in the climate of opinion in Europe, which manifested itself not only in politics but also in the realm of culture. This new climate may be characterized by the word *realism*. The shattering of the romantic hopes of the revolutionaries and the discrediting of pre-1848 utopian illusions resulted in a more sober evaluation by contemporaries of the world in which

---

[5] Karl Marx, *The Class Struggles in France (1848–1850)* (New York, 1934), p. 41.

they found themselves. The goals of Europeans did not change radically after the experiences of 1848–1849, but individuals and groups came to view their goals from a different perspective. Instead of envisioning their ends idealistically, they now tended to judge more realistically the concrete means for achieving them. And they very often reached the conclusion that abstract ideals and principles were less important in securing their goals then were power and force. A new tough-mindedness characterized the generation of the 1850s and 1860s, and this mood resulted largely from the disillusionment of 1848–1849.

Though the failure of the revolutions of 1848 was a setback for the utopian ideals of the revolutionary era, the economic and political developments of the previous six decades had profoundly transformed Europe. By the mid-nineteenth century, manufacturing rather than agriculture dominated the European economy; populations had gravitated from villages to vast new cities; and railroads crisscrossed the continent, exponentially accelerating the pace of travel and trade. In politics, the French Revolution had unleashed on the world what Alexis de Tocqueville characterized so darkly as a *"virus* of a new and unknown kind" — a variety of new ideologies that destabilized age-old hierarchies. Though the old ruling dynasties remained intact across much of the continent, governments everywhere confronted the challenge of democratic, nationalist, and socialist movements. The period between 1789 and 1850 witnessed the emergence of both material and ideological forces of immense creative and destructive power. The revolutions of these years represented only the beginning of a much longer worldwide revolutionary epoch, which has not yet reached its end.

Suggestions for Further Reading

(Books marked *are available in paperback.)

GENERAL

Two particularly stimulating overviews of European history during the revolutionary era are *Jonathan Sperber, *Revolutionary Europe, 1780–1850* (London, 2000) and *Franklin L. Ford, *Europe 1780–1830*, 2d ed. (London, 1989). See also *Robert Gildea, *Barricades and Borders: Europe 1800–1914*, 2d ed. (Oxford, 1996); *Owen Connelly, *The French Revolution and the Napoleonic Era*, 2d ed. (Fort Worth, 1991); *George Rudé, *Revolutionary Europe, 1783–1815*, 2d ed. (Oxford, 2000); and *John Merriman, *A History of Modern Europe*, vol. 2: *From the French Revolution to the Present* (New York, 1996). Several older, but still valuable, survey works are *E. J. Hobsbawm, *The Age of Revolution, 1789–1848* (New York, 1962); *Gordon A. Craig, *Europe, 1815–1914*, 3rd ed. (Fort Worth, 1971, repr. 1997); and *J. L. Talmon, *Romanticism and Revolt: Europe, 1815–1848* (New York, 1979).

NATIONAL HISTORIES

On Great Britain during the era 1789–1850, standard works are *Eric J. Evans, *The Forging of the Modern State: Early Industrial Britain, 1783–1870*, 2d ed. (London, 1996); *William B. Willcox and Walter L. Arnstein, *The Age of Aristocracy, 1688 to 1830*, 7th ed. (Lexington, Mass., 1996); *Walter L. Arnstein, *Britain Yesterday and Today, 1830 to the Present*, 7th ed. (Lexington, Mass., 1996); and Andrew Porter, ed., *The Oxford History of the British Empire*, vol 3: *The Nineteenth Century* (Oxford, 1999). Older classics include *Asa Briggs, *The Age of Improvement, 1763–1867*, (London, 1959; 2d ed. Harlow, England, 2000); and Elie Halévy, *History of the English People in the Nineteenth Century*, trans. by E. I. Watkin, 2d rev. ed., 6 vols. (London, 1949–1952). The first volume of Halévy's work, *England in 1815*, is particularly brilliant.

Surveys of French history from the Revolution through the mid-nineteenth century include *Gordon Wright, France in Modern Times: From the Enlightenment to the Present, 5th ed. (New York, 1995); *François Furet, Revolutionary France 1770–1880, translated by Antonia Nevill (Oxford, 1992); Donald Sutherland, France 1789–1815: Revolution and Counterrevolution (New York, 1986); and Roger Price, A Social History of Nineteenth-Century France (London: Hutchinson, 1987). Two distinguished older works, written during the nineteenth century by strongly republican historians, are François V. A. Aulard, The French Revolution, a Political History, 1789–1804, 4 vols. (New York, 1910); and Jules Michelet, Histoire de la révolution française, 10 vols. (Paris, 1922–1924), several volumes of which have been translated by Charles Cooks (Chicago, 1967) and Keith Botsford (Wynnewood, Pa., 1972–) under the title History of the French Revolution.

On the German states, see *James J. Sheehan, German History 1770–1866 (Oxford, 1989); *David Blackbourn, The Long Nineteenth Century: A History of Germany, 1780–1918 (Oxford, 1998); *Eric Dorn Brose, German History 1789–1871: From the Holy Roman Empire to the Bismarckian Reich (Providence, 1997); *Brendan Simms, The Struggle for Mastery in Germany, 1779–1850 (New York, 1998); Thomas Nipperdey, Germany from Napoleon to Bismarck, 1800–1866 (Princeton, 1996); and *Matthew Levinger, Enlightened Nationalism: The Transformation of Prussian Political Culture, 1806–1848 (New York, 2000). Heinrich von Treitschke's History of Germany in the Nineteenth Century, 7 vols. (New York, 1915–1919) is a strongly nationalistic older work; and Franz Schnabel, Deutsche Geschichte im neunzehnten Jahrhundert, 4 vols. (Freiburg, 1927–1936), narrates general developments to the 1820s. Other influential older studies are *Hajo Holborn, History of Modern Germany (New York, 1959–1968), vols. 2 and 3; Veit Valentin, The German People, their History and Civilization from the Holy Roman Empire to the Third Reich (New York, 1946); and Jacques Droz, L'Allemagne et la Révolution française (Paris, 1949). On Swiss history, two useful overviews are Frederick W. Dame, History of Switzerland, 2 vols. (Lewiston, N.Y., 2001); and Edgar Bonjour, H. S. Offler, and G. R. Potter, A Short History of Switzerland (Oxford, 1952; repr. Westport, Conn., 1985); see also Gordon Craig, The Triumph of Liberalism: Zurich in the Golden Age, 1830–1869 (New York, 1988).

Concerning the Habsburg empire, including its possessions in central and eastern Europe, see *Jean Bérenger, The Habsburg Empire 1700–1918 (London, 1997); C. A. Macartney, The Habsburg Empire, 1790–1918 (1968); *Peter Sugar, ed., A History of Hungary (1990); *Charles and Barbara Jelavich, The Establishment of the Balkan National States, 1804–1920 (Seattle, 1987); and *Barbara Jelavich, History of the Balkans, 2 vols. (Cambridge, 1983). On Polish history from the eighteenth-century partitions onward, see *Norman Davies, God's Playground: A History of Poland, 2 vols. (New York, 1982); and Piotr S. Wandycz, The Lands of Partitioned Poland, 1759–1918 (Seattle, 1974).

The history of the Ottoman empire during the nineteenth century is discussed in *Donald Quataert, The Ottoman Empire, 1700–1922 (New York, 2000); Alan Palmer, The Decline and Fall of the Ottoman Empire (London, 1992); and William W. Haddad and William Ochsenwald, eds., Nationalism in a Non-national State: The Dissolution of the Ottoman Empire (Columbus, 1977). On the Greek independence movement, see *C. M. Woodhouse, Modern Greece: a Short History, 5th ed. (London, 2000); Thomas W. Gallant, *Modern Greece* (New York, 2001); Richard Clogg, *A Short History of Modern Greece*, 2d ed. (Cambridge, 1986); as well as Douglas Dakin's works *The Unification of Greece, 1770–1923* (London, 1972) and *The Greek Struggle for Independence, 1821–1833* (London, 1973).

On Spain and Portugal, see John Lynch, *Bourbon Spain, 1700–1808* (Oxford, 1989); Raymond Carr, *Spain, 1808–1975*, 2d ed. (Oxford, 1982); Stanley G. Payne, *A History of Spain and Portugal*, 2 vols. (Madison, 1973); and *David Birmingham, *A Concise History of Portugal* (Cambridge, 1993).

Italian history during the early nineteenth century is outlined in *Denis Mack Smith, *The Making of Italy, 1796–1866* (New York, 1988); as well as in Harry Hearder, *Italy in the Age of the Risorgimento 1790–1870* (London, 1983). *Denis Mack Smith, *Mazzini* (New Haven, 1994) is a vivid account of the life of this pivotal figure in the Italian unification movement.

A fascinating analysis of the revolutionary events in Holland is provided by *Simon Schama, *Patriots and Liberators: Revolution in the Netherlands, 1780–1813* (New York, 1977). More generally, concerning the history of the Netherlands and Belgium, see Mark T. Hooker, *The History of Holland* (1999); and E. H. Kossmann, *The Low Countries, 1780–1940* (Oxford, 1978). On Scandinavian history, two useful works are H. Arnold Barton, *Scandinavia in the Revolutionary Era 1760–1815* (Minneapolis, 1986); and Byron J. Nordstrom, *Scandinavia since 1500* (Minneapolis, 2000).

For the history of Russia, see David Saunders, *Russia in the Age of Reaction and Reform, 1801–1881* (London, 1992), *Nicholas V. Riasanovsky, *A History of Russia*, 6th ed. (New York, 2000); and Hugh Seton-Watson, *The Russian Empire, 1801–1917* (1967). Dominic Lieven's *Empire: The Russian Empire and Its Rivals* (New Haven, 2001) presents an intriguing comparison among the historical experiences of Russia and those of the Ottoman, Habsburg, and British empires.

THE FRENCH REVOLUTION

General narratives of the French Revolution include *William Doyle, *Oxford History of the French Revolution* (Oxford, 1989); *Simon Schama, *Citizens: A Chronicle of the French Revolution* (New York, 1989); *Jeremy D. Popkin, *A Short History of the French Revolution*, 2d ed. (Upper Saddle River, N.J., 1995); *J. M. Roberts, *The French Revolution*, 2d ed. (Oxford, 1997); and Norman Hampson, *A Social History of the French Revolution* (London, 1963, reprinted 1995). R. R. Palmer presents an intriguing comparative analysis of eighteenth-century revolutionary movements in *The Age of the Democratic Revolution: A Political History of Europe and America, 1760–1800*, 2 vols. (Princeton, 1959–1964). Two works that contain useful bibliographies, as well as summaries of historiographical controversies surrounding the revolution, are *D. G. Wright, *Revolution and Terror in France 1789–1795*, 2d ed. (London, 1991), and *Gary Kates, ed., *The French Revolution: Recent Debates and New Controversies* (London, 1998).

The most succinct summary of the Marxist interpretation of the French Revolution is found in *Georges Lefebvre, *The Coming of the French Revolution, 1789*, translated by R. R. Palmer (Princeton, 1947, repr. 1967). See also the various works of Albert Soboul, most notably *A Short History of the French Revolution, 1789–1799, translated by Geoffrey Symcox (Berkeley, 1977) and *The Sans-Culottes: The Popular Movement and Revolutionary Government, 1793–1794, translated by Rémy Inglis Hall (Princeton, 1980). Alfred Cobban presented an early challenge to the Marxist view in *The Social Interpretation of the French Revolution (Cambridge, 1964; 2d ed., 1999).

The "revisionist" interpretation of the revolution, emphasizing political rather than socioeconomic causes, is presented most forcefully in *François Furet's ground-breaking work Interpreting the French Revolution, translated by Elborg Forster (Cambridge, 1981). Subsequent works that develop further the revisionist view include *Lynn Hunt, Politics, Culture, and Class in the French Revolution (Berkeley, 1984) and Colin Lucas, ed., Rewriting the French Revolution (Oxford, 1991). Concerning the intellectual and political roots of the revolution, see *Keith Michael Baker, Inventing the French Revolution: Essays on French Political Culture in the Eighteenth Century (Cambridge, 1990).

A classic nineteenth-century interpretation of the causes of the revolution is *Alexis de Tocqueville, The Old Regime and the Revolution, edited by François Furet and François Mélonio, translated by Alan S. Kahan (Chicago, 1998). More recent work on the origins of the French Revolution include *William Doyle, Origins of the French Revolution, 3rd ed. (Oxford, 1999); Keith Michael Baker, ed., The French Revolution and the Creation of Modern Political Culture, vol. 1, The Political Culture of the Old Regime (Oxford, 1987); *Daniel Roche, France in the Enlightenment, translated by Arthur Goldhammer (Cambridge, Mass., 1998); and *P. M. Jones, Reform and Revolution in France: The Politics of Transition, 1774–1791 (Cambridge, 1995). C. B. A. Behrens, Society, Government, and the Enlightenment: the Experiences of Eighteenth-Century France and Prussia (London, 1985) offers a useful comparative perspective. François Furet and Mona Ozouf, eds., A Critical Dictionary of the French Revolution, translated by Arthur Goldhammer (1989), is also a good resource.

Concerning the cultural origins of the revolution, see particularly the "debate" between *Roger Chartier, The Cultural Origins of the French Revolution, translated by Lydia G. Cochrane (Durham, 1991) and *Robert Darnton, The Forbidden Best-Sellers of Pre-Revolutionary France (New York, 1995) and *The Literary Underground of the Old Regime (Cambridge, Mass., 1982). For two perspectives on public political culture in the old regime, see *Sarah Maza, Private Lives and Public Affairs: The Causes Célèbres of Prerevolutionary France (Berkeley, 1993) and *Arlette Farge, Subversive Words: Public Opinion in Eighteenth-Century France, translated by Rosemary Morris (University Park, Pa., 1995). On the more high-cultural Enlightenment origins of the revolution, and on the role of salons and women, see *Dena Goodman, The Republic of Letters: A Cultural History of the French Enlightenment (1994), as well as Daniel Gordon, Citizens without Sovereignty: Equality and Sociability in French Thought, 1670–1789 (Princeton, 1994). Emmet Kennedy, A Cultural History of the French Revolution (New Haven, 1989) provides an informative overview of revolutionary culture; while *Mona Ozouf's Festivals and the French Revolution, translated by Alan Sheridan (Cambridge, Mass., 1988) provides a fascinating analysis of these revolutionary spectacles. Concerning the role of the press in revolutionary France, see Robert Darnton and Daniel Roche, eds., Revolution in Print: The Press in *France, 1775–1800* (Berkeley, 1989); and Jeremy D. Popkin, *The Right-Wing Press in France, 1792–1800* (Chapel Hill, 1980) and *Revolutionary News: The Press in France, 1789–1799* (Durham, 1990). *Dale K. Van Kley, *The Religious Origins of the French Revolution: From Calvin to the Civil Constitution, 1560–1791* (New Haven, 1996) examines the impact of Jansenism on revolutionary political culture.

The impact of the revolution on rural France is explored in Georges Lefebvre's classic work *The Great Fear of 1789: Rural Panic in Prerevolutionary France*, translated by Joan White (Princeton, 1982); as well as in *P. M. Jones, *The Peasantry in the French Revolution* (Cambridge, 1988). The authoritative work on the Vendée uprising remains Charles Tilly, *The Vendée: A Sociological Analysis of the Counterrevolution of 1793* (Cambridge, Mass., 1964). On the radicalization of urban revolutionaries, see Timothy Tackett, *Becoming a Revolutionary: The Deputies of the French National Assembly and the Emergence of a Revolutionary Culture (1789–1790)* (Princeton, 1996); *George Rudé, *The Crowd in the French Revolution* (Oxford: Clarendon, 1960); *Albert Soboul, *The Sans-Culottes*; and Michael L. Kennedy, *The Jacobin Clubs in the French Revolution*, 3 vols. (Princeton, 1982–2000). *R. R. Palmer, *Twelve Who Ruled: the Year of the Terror in the French Revolution* (Princeton, 1941, repr. 1958) is a revealing study of the personalities and politics of the members of the Committee of Public Safety. Two recent biographies of leading Jacobins are *David P. Jordan, *The Revolutionary Career of Maximilien Robespierre* (New York, 1985); and Norman Hampson, *Danton* (New York, 1985).

On the revolutionary wars, see *T. C. W. Blanning, *The French Revolutionary Wars* (London: Longman, 1996); and *Geoffrey Best, *War and Society in Revolutionary Europe 1770–1870* (Montreal, 1998). Concerning the militarization of the revolution, see Richard Cobb, *The People's Armies*, translated by Marianne Elliott (New Haven, 1987); J. P. Bertaud, *The Army of the French Revolution: From Citizen Soldiers to Instrument of Power*, translated by R. R. Palmer (Princeton, 1988); and *Alan Forrest, *Soldiers of the French Revolution* (Durham, 1990).

The revolution's international reverberations are explored in Otto Dann and John Dinwiddy, eds., *Nationalism in the Age of the French Revolution* (London, 1988); Joseph Klaits and Michael H. Haltzel, eds., *The Global Ramifications of the French Revolution* (Cambridge, 1994); and T. C. W. Blanning, *The French Revolution in Germany: Occupation and Resistance in the Rhineland 1792–1802* (Oxford, 1983). Two classic works on the impact of the revolution on Europe are Jacques Godechot, *La Grande Nation: l'expansion révolutionnaire de la France dans le monde de 1789 à 1799*, 2 vols. (Paris, 1956); and Albert Sorel, *L'Europe et la Révolution française*, 9 vols., the first chapter of which is available in English as *Europe under the Old Regime*, translated by Francis H. Herrick (New York, 1964).

The revolution's effects on gender roles and family life has been the subject of a great deal of stimulating work published in recent years. Among the most notable of these publications are Joan Landes, *Women and the Public Sphere in the Age of the French Revolution* (Ithaca, N.Y., 1988); *Olwen H. Hufton, *Women and the Limits of Citizenship in the French Revolution* (Toronto, 1992); Linda Kelly, *Women of the French Revolution* (London, 1987); and *Sara Melzer and Leslie Rabine, eds., *Rebel Daughters: Women and the French Revolution* (1992). Studies that focus specifically on changing ideals of family life during the revolutionary era include Crane Brinton, *French Revolutionary Legislation on Illegitimacy 1789–1804* (Cambridge, Mass.,

1936); Margaret Darrow, *Revolution in the House: Family, Class, and Inheritance in Southern France 1775–1825* (Princeton, 1989); *Lynn Hunt, *The Family Romance of the French Revolution* (Berkeley, 1992), which analyzes the revolution from a Freudian perspective; and Barbara Corrado Pope, "The Influence of Rousseau's Ideology of Domesticity," in *Connecting Spheres: Women in the Western World, 1500 to the Present,* edited by Marilyn J. Boxer and Jean H. Quataert (New York, 1987), pp. 136–45. *Isabel V. Hull's *Sexuality, State, and Civil Society in Germany 1700–1815* (Ithaca, N.Y., 1996) presents a fascinating perspective on developments in the German states, offering a useful basis for a historical comparison with France.

A number of compilations of primary sources, which are helpful in illuminating the evolution of revolutionary ideology, are available in English translation. See particularly *Keith Michael Baker, ed., *The Old Regime and the French Revolution,* vol. 7 of *The University of Chicago Readings in Western Civilization* (Chicago, 1987); John Hall Stewart, ed., *A Documentary Survey of the French Revolution* (New York, 1951); Richard Cobb and Colin Jones, eds., *Voices of the French Revolution* (Topsfield, Mass., 1988); Paul Beik, ed., *The French Revolution* (Evanston, 1970); *Darline Gay Levy and Harriet Applewhite, *Women in Revolutionary Paris, 1789–1795* (Urbana, 1979); Mary Wollstonecraft, *The Vindications: The Rights of Men, The Rights of Women,* edited by D. L. Macdonald and Kathleen Scherf (Peterborough, Ontario, 1997); and *Lynn Hunt, ed. and trans., *The French Revolution and Human Rights: A Brief Documentary History* (Boston, 1996). *Michael Walzer, ed., *Regicide and Revolution* (New York, 1992) contains a collection of speeches from the trial of Louis XVI.

THE NAPOLEONIC ERA

On Napoleon and the Napoleonic era as a whole, see Stuart Woolf, *Napoleon's Integration of Europe* (London, 1991); *Michael Broers, *Europe under Napoleon 1799–1815* (London, 1996); *Martyn Lyons, *Napoleon Bonaparte and the Legacy of the French Revolution* (New York, 1994); *D. G. Wright, *Napoleon and Europe* (London, 1984); and Jean Tulard, *Napoleon: The Myth of the Saviour,* translated by Teresa Waugh (London, 1984). *Geoffrey Ellis, *The Napoleonic Empire* (London, 1991) contains a useful bibliography and summary of historiographical controversies. Several notable older works are Geoffrey Bruun, *Europe and the French Imperium, 1799–1814* (New York, 1938);* Felix M. H. Markham, *Napoleon* (New York, 1963; repr. 1988); Georges Lefebvre's biography of Napoleon (published in a two-volume English translation in 1969); and F. M. Kircheisen's nine-volume study, *Napoleon I: Sein Leben und seine Zeit* (Munich, 1911–1934), abridged and translated into English by Henry St. Lawrence as *Napoleon* (New York, 1932). Peter Geyl's *Napoleon: For and Against,* translated by Olive Renier (New Haven, 1949), provides an interesting synopsis of the evolution of the historical interpretation of Napoleon through the mid-nineteenth century.

Concerning Napoleon's domestic policies, an excellent starting point is *Louis Bergeron, *France Under Napoleon,* translated by R. R. Palmer (Princeton, 1981). The history of the Napoleonic wars is ably summarized in *Owen Connelly, *Blun-

dering to Glory: Napoleon's Military Campaigns, rev. ed. (Wilmington, Del., 1999); and in *David Gates, *The Napoleonic Wars, 1803–1815* (London, 1997). On the emergence of national resistance movements against Napoleonic domination, see Brendan Simms, *The Impact of Napoleon: Prussian High Politics, Foreign Policy, and the Crisis of the Executive, 1797–1806* (Cambridge, 1997); Friedrich Meinecke, *The Age of German Liberation, 1795–1815*, edited by Peter Paret (Berkeley, 1977); Walter Simon, *The Failure of the Prussian Reform Movement, 1807–1819* (Ithaca, N.Y., 1955); Charles J. Esdaile, *The Spanish Army and the Peninsular War* (Manchester, 1988); Richard Herr, "The Constitution of 1812 and the Spanish Road to Parliamentary Monarchy," in *Revolution and the Meanings of Freedom in the Nineteenth Century*, edited by Isser Woloch (Stanford, 1996), pp. 65–102; Wayne S. Vucinich, ed., *The First Serbian Uprising 1804–1813* (New York, 1982); and Eugène Tarlé, *Napoleon's Invasion of Russia, 1812* (London, 1942; repr. New York, 1970). A classic account of the Haitian independence movement is *C. L. R. James, *The Black Jacobins: Toussaint L'Ouverture and the San Domingo Revolution*, 2d ed. (New York, 1963). More broadly, on the issue of slavery, see *David Brion Davis, *The Problem of Slavery in the Age of Revolution, 1770–1823* (Ithaca, 1975).

For primary source material, two vivid accounts of soldiers' lives in Napoleon's army are provided by *Jakob Walter, *The Diary of a Napoleonic Foot Soldier*, edited by Marc Raeff (New York, 1991); and Heinrich von Brandt, *In the Legions of Napoleon: The Memoirs of a Polish Officer in Spain and Russia, 1808–1813*, translated by Jonathan North (London, 1999). *Carl von Clausewitz's classic treatise on military strategy, *On War*, edited and translated by Michael Howard and Peter Paret (London, 1993), distills the lessons derived from Clausewitz's service as an officer in the Prussian army during the Napoleonic wars. Brilliant evocations of European society during the Napoleonic period are offered by novels such as *Stendhal, *The Charterhouse of Parma* (1839); Theodor Fontane, *Before the Storm* (1878); *Leo Tolstoy, *War and Peace* (1869); *William Makepeace Thackeray, *Vanity Fair* (1847–1848); and *Jane Austen, *Pride and Prejudice* (1813).

THE INDUSTRIAL REVOLUTION

General studies of the Industrial Revolution in Europe include Carlo Cipolla, ed., *The Fontana Economic History of Europe*, vols. 3 and 4 (London, 1973); *Richard Sylla and Gianni Toniolo, eds., *Patterns of European Industrialization* (London, 1991); Norman J. G. Pounds, *An Historical Geography of Europe* (Cambridge, 1985 and 1990); Alan S. Milward and S. B. Saul, *The Economic Development of Continental Europe, 1780–1870*, 2d ed. (London, 1979); *Jordan Goodman and Katrina Honeymann, *Gainful Pursuits: The Making of Industrial Europe, 1600–1914*; and Derek H. Aldcroft and Simon P. Ville, eds., *The European Economy, 1750–1914: A Thematic Approach* (Manchester, 1994). A classic interpretative work is *David S. Landes, *The Unbound Prometheus: Technological Change and Industrial Development in Western Europe from 1750 to the Present* (Cambridge, Mass., 1969). The most authoritative statistics on economic growth during the nineteenth century are found in *Angus Maddison, *Monitoring the World Economy 1820–1992* (Paris, 1995).

On the industrialization of Britain, see *M. J. Daunton, *Progress and Poverty: An Economic and Social History of Britain, 1700–1850* (Oxford, 1995); *Charles More, *The Industrial Age: Economy and Society in Britain, 1750–1995*, 2d ed. (London, 1997); D. C. Coleman, *Myth, History, and the Industrial Revolution* (London, 1992); and *Patrick K. O'Brien and Roland Quinault, eds., *The Industrial Revolution and British Society* (Cambridge, 1993). Other useful regional and national histories include *Cormac Ó Gráda, *Ireland: A New Economic History, 1780–1939* (Oxford, 1994); Eric Dorn Brose, *The Politics of Technological Change in Prussia: Out of the Shadow of Antiquity, 1809–1848*. (Princeton, 1993); David F. Good, *The Economic Rise of the Habsburg Empire, 1750–1914* (Cambridge, 1982); Iván T. Behrend and György Ránki, *The European Periphery and Industrialization, 1780–1914*, translated by Eva Pálmai (Cambridge, 1982); and William Blackwell, *The Beginnings of Russian Industrialization, 1800–1860* (Princeton, 1968). On railroad building, see Patrick O'Brien, *The New Economic History of the Railways* (New York, 1977); and James M. Brophy, *Capitalism, Politics, and Railroads in Prussia, 1830–1870* (Columbus, 1998).

The "consumer revolution" in eighteenth-century Europe is discussed in Neil McKendrick, John Brewer, and J. H. Plumb, *The Birth of a Consumer Society: The Commercialization of Eighteenth-Century England* (Bloomington, 1982); Colin Campbell, *The Romantic Ethic and the Spirit of Modern Consumerism* (Oxford, 1987); and *Sidney Mintz, *Sweetness and Power: The Place of Sugar in Modern History* (New York, 1985). A useful analysis of the social impact of agricultural innovation is Jerome Blum, *The End of the Old Order in Rural Europe* (Princeton, 1978).

*E. P. Thompson's classic *The Making of the English Working Class* (New York, 1963) remains a foundational work on class formation in nineteenth-century Britain. More recent studies on this topic include *David Cannadine, *The Rise and Fall of Class in Britain* (New York, 1999); *Dror Wahrman, *Imagining the Middle Class: The Political Representation of Class in Britain, c. 1780–1840* (Cambridge, 1995); *Gareth Stedman Jones, *Languages of Class: Studies in English Working-Class History, 1832–1982* (Cambridge, 1983); and *Leonore Davidoff and Catherine Hall, *Family Fortunes: Men and Women of the English Middle Class, 1780–1850* (Chicago, 1987). On the formation of the French working class, see *William H. Sewell's highly stimulating study, *Work and Revolution in France: the Language of Labor from the Old Regime to 1848* (Cambridge, 1980); John Merriman, *The Red City: Limoges and the French Nineteenth Century* (New York, 1985); and *Louis Chevalier, *Laboring Classes and Dangerous Classes in Paris during the First Half of the Nineteenth Century*, translated by Frank Jellinek (London, 1973). Two useful works of urban history are *Asa Briggs, *Victorian Cities*, 2d ed. (New York, 1965); and *Robert Fishman, *Bourgeois Utopias: The Rise and Fall of Suburbia* (New York, 1987).

The impact of industrialization on gender roles and family life is explored in *Louise Tilly and Joan Wallach Scott, *Women, Work, and Family* (New York, 1987); *Michelle Perrot, ed., *The History of Private Life*, vol. 4, *From the Fires of Revolution to the Great War* (Cambridge, Mass., 1990); *Deborah Valenze, *The First Industrial Woman* (New York, 1995); *Wally Seccombe, *Weathering the Storm: Working-Class Families from the Industrial Revolution to the Fertility Decline* (London, 1993); *Bonnie Smith, *Ladies of the Leisure Class: The Bourgeoises of Northern France in the

Nineteenth Century (Princeton, 1981); John Tosh, *A Man's Place: Masculinity and the Middle-Class Home in Victorian England* (New Haven, 1999); and J. A. Mangan and James Walvin, eds., *Manliness and Morality: Middle-Class Masculinity in Britain and America, 1800–1940* (Manchester, 1987). On the changing nature of marriage, see John Gillis, *For Better, For Worse: British Marriages, 1600 to the Present* (New York, 1985); as well as the works of Lawrence Stone, including *The Family, Sex, and Marriage in England, 1500–1800* (New York, 1977) and *Uncertain Unions and Broken Lives: Marriage and Divorce in England, 1660–1857* (Oxford, 1995). *Phyllis Rose's *Parallel Lives: Five Victorian Marriages* (New York, 1983) is a sensitive and evocative account of the marriages of five prominent literary figures in nineteenth-century Britain.

Environmental history is a nascent field of research which is likely to attract growing attention in coming years. Three works that analyze the ecological impact of industrialization are Peter Brimblecombe, *The Big Smoke: A History of Air Pollution in London Since Medieval Times* (London, 1987); *B. L. Turner, et al., *The Earth as Transformed by Human Action: Global and Regional Changes in the Biosphere over the Past 300 Years* (Cambridge, 1990); and *Clive Ponting, *A Green History of the World: The Environment and the Collapse of Great Civilizations* (New York, 1993).

Useful primary sources for understanding intellectual currents during the age of industrialization include *Thomas Malthus, *Essay on the Principle of Population* (1797); and *Friedrich List, *The National System of Political Economy* (1841). *Friedrich Engels's 1844 exposé *The Condition of the Working Class in England*, translated and edited by W. O. Henderson and W. H. Chaloner (Stanford, 1968), presents harrowing images of workers' lives in mid-nineteenth century Manchester. Works of fiction that vividly portray the social effects of industrialization include *Charles Dickens, *Hard Times* (1854); *Elizabeth Gaskell, *North and South* (1855); and *Emile Zola, *Germinal* (1885).

POLITICS, SOCIETY, AND CULTURE IN THE RESTORATION ERA

On the diplomatic history of the post-Napoleonic era, the most comprehensive recent studies are *Paul W. Schroeder, *The Transformation of European Politics, 1763–1848* (Oxford, 1994); and Alan Sked, ed., *Europe's Balance of Power, 1815–1848* (London, 1979). Concerning relations with the Ottoman empire, see *A. L. Macfie, *The Eastern Question 1774–1923*, 2d ed. (London, 1996). Older works, which remain useful, include Guillaume de Bertier de Sauvigny, *Metternich and His Times*, translated by Peter Ryde (London, 1962); Henry Kissinger, *A World Restored: Metternich, Castlereagh, and the Problems of the Peace, 1812–1822* (London, 1957); Harold Nicolson, *The Congress of Vienna, A Study in Allied Unity, 1812–1822* (New York, 1946); Heinrich, Ritter von Srbik, *Metternich: Der Staatsman und der Mensch*, 3 vols. (Munich, 1925–1954); and the various books of Sir Charles K. Webster, among them *The Congress of Vienna, 1814–1815*, 2d ed. (London, 1934) and *The Foreign Policy of Palmerston*, 2 vols. (London, 1951).

General works on European social and political history between 1815 and 1848 include André Jardin and André-Jean Tudesq, *Restoration and Reaction, 1815–1848*, translated by Elborg Forster (Cambridge, 1983); Paul Johnson, *The Birth of the Modern: World Society, 1815–1830* (New York, 1991); and William L. Langer, *Political and Social Upheaval, 1832–1852* (New York, 1969).

Some notable studies on more specialized topics are *David Cannadine, *Aspects of Aristocracy: Grandeur and Decline in Modern Britain* (New Haven, 1994); *James Vernon, ed., *Re-reading the Constitution: New Narratives in the Political History of England's Long Nineteenth Century* (Cambridge, 1996); Peter Mandler, *Aristocratic Government in the Age of Reform: Whigs and Liberals, 1830–1852* (Oxford, 1990); Dorothy Thompson, *The Chartists: Popular Politics in the Industrial Revolution* (New York, 1984); Guillaume de Bertier de Sauvigny, *The Bourbon Restoration*, translated by Lynn Case (Philadelphia, 1967); David Higgs, *Nobles in Nineteenth-Century France: the Practice of Inegalitarianism* (Baltimore, 1987); David Pinkney, *The French Revolution of 1830* (Princeton, 1972); H. A. C. Collingham and R. S. Alexander, *The July Monarchy: A Political History of France, 1830–1848* (London, 1988); David Barclay, *Frederick William IV and the Prussian Monarchy, 1840–1861* (Oxford, 1995); and Clara Lovett, *The Democratic Movement in Italy 1830–1876* (Cambridge, Mass., 1982).

In recent years, many British historians have focused on connections between domestic developments and the building of the British empire. See for example P. J. Cain and A. G. Hopkins, *British Imperialism: Innovation and Expansion, 1688–1914* (London, 1993); *C. A. Bayly, *Imperial Meridian: The British Empire and the World, 1780–1830* (London, 1989); J. A. Mangan, ed., *Making Imperial Mentalities: Socialisation and British Imperialism* (Manchester, 1990); and *John M. Mackenzie, *Imperialism and Popular Culture* (Manchester, 1986).

On the evolution of conservativism in nineteenth-century Europe, see Klaus Epstein, *The Genesis of German Conservatism* (Princeton, 1966), which focuses on the period from 1770 to 1806; as well as Robert Berdahl, *The Politics of the Prussian Nobility: The Development of a Conservative Ideology, 1770–1848* (Princeton, 1988); *Hermann Beck, *The Origins of the Authoritarian Welfare State in Prussia: Conservatives, Bureaucracy, and the Social Question, 1815–1870* (Ann Arbor, 1995); René Remond, *The Right Wing in France*, translated by James M. Laux (Philadelphia, 1969); and Mack Walker, ed., *Metternich's Europe, 1813–1848* (New York, 1968). *Janet M. Hartley's biography, *Alexander I* (London, 1994), sheds light on conservatism in Russia.

On liberalism, good books include *Pierre Manent, *An Intellectual History of Liberalism*, translated by Rebecca Balinski (Princeton, 1996); *James J. Sheehan, *German Liberalism in the Nineteenth Century* (Chicago, 1978); *Alan Kahan, *Aristocratic Liberalism: the Social and Political Thought of Jacob Burckhardt, John Stuart Mill, and Alexis de Tocqueville* (New York, 1992); William O. Henderson, *Friedrich List, Economist and Visionary, 1789–1846* (London, 1983); and Leonard Krieger's classic *The German Idea of Freedom* (Boston, 1957). An influential theoretical work concerning the emergence of liberal civil society in Europe is *Jürgen Habermas, *The Structural Transformation of the Public Sphere: an Inquiry into a Category of Bourgeois Society*, translated by Thomas Burger and Frederick Lawrence (Cambridge, Mass., 1989). Ernest Gellner, *Conditions of Liberty: Civil*

Society and its Rivals (New York, 1994) presents a critical reflection on Habermas's claims.

Works on utopian socialism include Frank Manuel, *The Prophets of Paris* (Cambridge, Mass., 1962); George Lichtheim, *The Origins of Socialism* (New York, 1969); as well as sections of Edmund Wilson's *To the Finland Station: A Study in the Writing and Acting of History* (New York, 1940). Barbara Taylor, *Eve and the New Jerusalem: Socialism and Feminism in the Nineteenth Century* (New York, 1983) reflects on the implications of socialism for gender relations. On Marxism, see David McLellan, *Marx before Marxism*, 2d ed. (London, 1980); and Leszek Kolakowski, *Main Currents of Marxism*, 3 vols. (Oxford, 1978), especially volume 1, *The Founders*. Those interested in the philosophical antecedents of Marxist theory may wish to consult Laurence Dickey, *Hegel: Religion, Economics, and the Politics of Spirit, 1770–1807* (New York, 1987); John Edward Toews, *Hegelianism: The Path toward Dialectical Humanism, 1805–1841* (Cambridge, 1980); and *Terry Pinkard, *Hegel: A Biography* (Cambridge, 2000).

The topic of nationalism has attracted a tremendous amount of scholarly attention in recent years. Two contrasting interpretations of this phenomenon, which have been among the most influential, are presented by *Benedict Anderson, *Imagined Communities: Reflections on the Origin and Spread of Nationalism*, revised ed. (London, 1991); and *Ernest Gellner, *Nations and Nationalism* (Ithaca, 1983). The articles in *John A. Hall, ed., *The State of the Nation: Ernest Gellner and the Theory of Nationalism* (New York, 1998) put forth perceptive critiques of Gellner's claims. Other theoretical works include *E. J. Hobsbawm, *Nations and Nationalism since 1780: Programme, Myth, Reality*, 2d ed. (Cambridge, 1992); *Miroslav Hroch, *Social Preconditions of National Revival in Europe*, translated by Ben Bowkes (Cambridge, 1985), which focuses on the Habsburg empire; *Craig Calhoun, *Nationalism* (Minneapolis, 1997); *Elie Kedourie, *Nationalism*, 4th ed. (Oxford, 1993); *Anthony D. Smith, *The Ethnic Origins of Nations* (Oxford, 1986); *Liah Greenfeld, *Nationalism: Five Roads to Modernity* (Cambridge, Mass, 1992); *E. J. Hobsbawm and Terence O. Ranger, *The Invention of Tradition* (Cambridge, 1983); and Matthew Levinger and Paula Franklin Lytle, "Myth and Mobilization: The Triadic Structure of Nationalist Rhetoric," *Nations and Nationalism* 7 (2001), pp. 175–94.

Useful case studies include *Rogers Brubaker, *Citizenship and Nationhood in France and Germany* (Cambridge, Mass, 1992); *Linda Colley, *Britons: Forging the Nation, 1707–1837* (New Haven, 1992); *George L. Mosse, *The Nationalization of the Masses* (New York, 1975); and *Matthew Levinger, *Enlightened Nationalism: The Transformation of Prussian Political Culture, 1806–1848* (New York, 2000). Friedrich Meinecke's classic work *Cosmopolitanism and the National State*, translated by Robert B. Kimber (Princeton, 1970) examines the transition from the cosmopolitan ideals of the Enlightenment to the nationalist ideology of the nineteenth century in Germany.

On the culture of Romanticism, insightful surveys include *Maurice Cranston, *The Romantic Movement* (Oxford, 1994); *John Sweetman, *The Enlightenment and the Age of Revolution, 1700–1850* (London, 1998); Iain McCalman, general editor, *An Oxford Companion to the Romantic Age: British Culture 1776–1832* (Oxford, 2001); *Hugh Honour, *Romanticism* (New York, 1979); Lilian B. Furst, *The Contours of European Romanticism* (London, 1979); Rupert Christiansen, *Romantic*

Affinities: Portraits from an Age 1780–1830 (London, 1988); Marcel Brion, *Art of the Romantic Era: Romanticism, Classicism, Realism* (New York, 1966); *M. H. Abrams, *Natural Supernaturalism: Tradition and Revolution in Romantic Literature* (New York, 1973); and Jacques Barzun, *Romanticism and the Modern Ego* (Boston, 1943), reissued as *Classic, Romantic, and Modern* (Boston, 1961).

On religion in the Romantic era, see Rogert Aubert, Johannes Beckman, Patrick J. Corish, and Rudolf Lill, *The Church Between Revolution and Restoration*, translated by Peter Becker (London, 1981); Jonathan Sperber, *Popular Catholicism in Nineteenth-Century Germany* (Princeton, 1984); *Nicholas Hope, *German and Scandinavian Protestantism, 1700–1918* (Oxford, 1995); W. R. Ward, *Religion and Society in England, 1790–1850* (New York, 1973); and Christopher Clark, *The Politics of Conversion: Missionary Protestantism and the Jews in Prussia 1728–1941* (Oxford, 1995). The philosophical currents of the age are summarized in Frederick Copleston, *A History of Philosophy*, vol. 7: *Fichte to Nietzsche* (Westminster, Md., 1985); and the evolution of new conceptions of history is outlined in Friedrich Meinecke, *Historism: The Rise of a New Historical Outlook*, translated by J. E. Anderson (New York, 1972). On literature and the arts, a standard older work is Georg M. C. Brandes, *Main Currents in Nineteenth-Century Literature*, 6 vols. (New York, 1901–1905). On music, two excellent studies are Alfred Einstein, *Music in the Romantic Era* (New York, 1947); and Paul H. Lang, *Music in Western Civilization* (New York, 1941). Wilfred Mellers, *Beethoven and the Voice of God* (New York, 1983) illuminates the grandeur of Beethoven's artistic ambitions.

A multitude of primary source materials in English translation are available for this period, including the works of major political philosophers such as Fichte, Mazzini, Hegel, and Marx; and those of numerous leading literary figures. Several noteworthy novels that vividly illustrate the temperament of the post-Napoleonic era are *Mary Shelley, *Frankenstein* (1818); *Stendhal, *The Red and the Black* (1830); and the various works in Honoré de Balzac's *Human Comedy*, including *Père Goriot* (1834) and *Cousin Bette* (1846).

THE REVOLUTIONS OF 1848

General overviews of the 1848 revolutions are provided by *Jonathan Sperber, *The European Revolutions, 1848–1851* (Cambridge, 1994); Dieter Dowe, Heinz-Gerhard Haupt, Dieter Langewiesche, and Jonathan Sperber, eds., *Europe in 1848: Revolution and Reform*, translated by David Higgins (New York, 2000); and Priscilla S. Robertson, *Revolutions of 1848: A Social History* (Princeton, 1952). *Sir Lewis B. Namier's classic *1848: The Revolution of the Intellectuals* (London, 1946; repr. 1971) concentrates primarily on the nationalism of German intellectual leaders in the revolts.

The revolutionary events in France are examined in *Maurice Agulhon, *The Republican Experiment: 1848–1852*, translated by Janet Lloyd (Cambridge, 1983); John Merriman, *The Agony of the Republic: The Repression of the Left in Revolutionary France, 1848–1851* (New Haven, 1978); Roger Price, ed., *Revolution and Reaction: 1848 and the Second French Republic* (London, 1975); and *William H. Sewell, *Work and Revolution in France*, cited above.

On the German states, see *Jonathan Sperber, *Rhineland Radicals: The Democratic Movement and the Revolution of 1848* (Princeton, 1991); and Rudolf Stadelmann, *Social and Political History of the German 1848 Revolution*, translated by James G. Chastain (Athens, Ohio, 1975). The 1847 upheaval in Switzerland is discussed in Joachim Remak, *A Very Civil War: The Swiss Sonderbund War of 1847* (Boulder, 1993). The various revolutions in the Habsburg empire are analyzed in Alan Sked, *The Survival of the Habsburg empire: Radetzky, the Imperial Army and the Class War, 1848* (London, 1979); *Josef Polisensky, *Aristocrats in the Crowd in the Revolutionary Year 1848: A Contribution to the History of Revolution and Counter-Revolution in Austria*, translated by Frederick Snider (Albany, 1980); John Rath, *The Viennese Revolution of 1848* (Austin, 1957); *Istvan Deák, *Lawful Revolution: Louis Kossuth and the Hungarians, 1848–1849* (New York, 1979); Stanley V. Pech, *The Czech Revolution of 1848* (Chapel Hill, 1969); and Jan Kozik, *The Ukrainian National Movement in Galicia, 1815–1849*, translated by Andrew Gorski and Lawrence D. Orton (Edmonton, 1986).

Useful primary sources on France in 1848 are reprinted in Roger Price, ed., *Documents on the French Revolution of 1848* (New York, 1996). Two brilliant contemporary accounts of the revolutionary events in France, which offer a stark contrast in perspectives, are *Alexis de Tocqueville, *Recollections: The French Revolution of 1848*, edited by J. P. Mayer and A. P. Kerr (New Brunswick, 1970; new edition 1987); and *Karl Marx, *The Eighteenth Brumaire of Louis Bonaparte* (New York, 1963).

Photograph Credits

Index